ADRIAN ADDISON

MAIL MEN

The Unauthorized Story of the

Daily Mail

The Paper that Divided and Conquered Britain

Atlantic Books
London

Published in hardback in Great Britain in 2017 by Atlantic Books,
an imprint of Atlantic Books Ltd.

10 9 8 7 6 5 4 3 2 1

A CIP catalogue record for this book is available from the British Library.

Hardback ISBN: 978 1 78239 970 4
E-book ISBN: 978 1 78239 971 1

Printed in Great Britain by CPI Group (UK) Ltd, Croydon CR0 4YY

Atlantic Books
An Imprint of Atlantic Books Ltd
Ormond House
26–27 Boswell Street
London
WC1N 3JZ

www.atlantic-books.co.uk

MAIL
MEN

CONTENTS

For Anna & Santi

INTRODUCTION
The Voice of Middle England?

It's only a newspaper.

Yet some believe the *Daily Mail* is imbued with almost super-natural powers – it can handpick government policy and almost single-handedly scared over half the electorate into taking Britain out of the European Union. For its fans, it has been a welcome guest at breakfast tables for over 120 years; it is simply a cracking good read and the voice of good old-fashioned common sense. Its voice, however, does carry far beyond its loyal readers; it howls through Westminster corridors befuddling politicians and infuriating metro-politan liberals before whistling on through the nation's newsrooms to help define the media agenda for the day. And for many, the *Daily Mail* is the jackbooted stomp of a bully who makes scapegoats of the weak and the vulnerable. Indeed, to them, even the very sound of its editor's name is akin to Darth Vader's tin lungs on a darkened cinema screen.

Paul Dacre, the clumsy and shy middle-class son of a well-known *Sunday Express* showbiz writer, has been in the top chair for a quarter of a century and, unlike so many of his peers, has never sought personal 'fame', yet he has still managed to become one of the most hated men in Britain. Ever more people now know his name. He even became the butt of an ad-lib joke during a live and televised Monty Python gig in London in July 2014, as John Cleese later explained to fellow Python Eric Idle.[1]

'One night, the last night of all,' Cleese said, 'when there were millions of people watching around the world, Michael [Palin] went off and I said: "I heard on the radio this morning that the editor of the *Daily Mail*" – which I hate – "Mr Paul Dacre, has had an arsehole transplant." And Michael came back on and said, "I've just been listening to the television and apparently the arsehole has rejected him."'

The joke[2] probably got the biggest laugh of the night.

'Is he still alive?' Idle asked.

'Oh yes, he's still alive. But he's quite crazy now. And, of course, nobody is allowed to write about an editor of a major British newspaper being crazy because they censor it. This is a new concept, press censorship in the sense of censorship of the Press by the Press. So, they criticize everyone else, they criticize politicians and businessmen and the church and doctors and sportsmen and, you know, actors and everyone – but they never actually get criticized themselves and I think that's why they get so power mad.'

Cleese isn't alone in reviling the Dacre name. During the media firestorm in 2013 when the Mail accused Labour Leader Ed Miliband's late father of hating Britain, *Match of the Day* presenter and former footballer Gary Lineker tweeted: '[It's] Only a matter of time before [Paul] Dacre resigns. It's what he would demand of another in this situation. Unless of course he's a hypocrite.'[3] More recently, fifty thousand people signed a petition demanding Dacre be sacked over his paper's coverage of migration and the EU referendum in the summer of 2016, claiming it spread 'misinformation and fear'.[4]

Paul Dacre and the *Daily Mail*'s millions of readers, of course, disagree with this mockery and distaste. Dacre and countless Mailmen and Femails over the years have dedicated their lives to giving their readers a newspaper in which many of its staff (but not all) do, truly, believe.

'Mailmen (not the *Express*'s reporters) had to be the first on the story, and the last to leave,' Dacre once wrote, in an obituary for the modern-day *Mail*'s founding editor, Sir David English.[5]

A *Mail* salary helped pay staff mortgages and the paper gave them the best resources in the business to do their jobs, but at the cost for many of being bullied daily at its swanky west London offices, once lampooned in a media column as 'The Death Star',[6] in which, for some – including Dacre himself – fifteen-hour working days were the norm.

'Everyone will have told you how culty it was and probably still is,' a former Mailman told the author, 'but that's a definite part of the theme.'[7]

The Mail machine, the product of this 'cult', is feared and courted by politicians in equal measure and the tension between the two has frequently caused a political punch-up. 'What you've got to understand about the *Daily Mail*,' former Downing Street spin doctor Alastair Campbell told the BBC's *Newsnight* programme, is that 'it is the worst of British values posing as the best . . . If you do not conform to Paul Dacre's narrow, twisted view of the world – you get done in.

'All I say, to all the politicians in Britain, [is that] once you accept you are dealing with a bully and a coward you have absolutely nothing to fear from them.'[8]

Dacre and Campbell, of course, loathe each other, and Paul Dacre does not share Campbell's low opinion of his *Daily Mail* nor does he agree that he wields real political power.

'My own view,' Dacre told the BBC's *Desert Island Discs* in 2004, 'is that the politicians' kind of estimation of papers being great, great political forces is a reflection of their weakness rather than newspapers' strength. I don't feel powerful, no. I feel rather humble.

'Every paper has to have a soul. And the *Mail*'s is based on family values, on the two words "self-reliance" and "aspiration". My job is to represent millions of people who don't have a voice . . . especially in countering that liberal, politically correct consensus that dominates so much of British public life.

'It says Britain is a shameful nation with a shameful history and a culture and a people who are inherently racist, sexist and anti-European. It says the nuclear family is outmoded and that injustice in education and liberal progressive values must prevail.

'Well, the fact is that most Britons don't believe this. They simply don't.'[9]

'There is an unpleasant intellectual snobbery about the *Mail* in leftish circles, for whom the word "suburban" is an obscenity,' Dacre wrote in the *Guardian* in 2013.'They simply cannot comprehend how a paper that opposes the mindset they hold dear can be so successful and so loved by its millions of readers.'[10]

Whichever viewpoint you hold, the *Daily Mail* is as British as the Royal Mail and the pound sterling. It's consumed in quaint village cafés with cream tea and scones and at breakfast tables across England's green and pleasant land.

It is a product aimed at these readers, not a political party. It's not funded by a television tax like the BBC nor controlled by a trust like the *Guardian* nor kept from the abyss by a billionaire like *The Times*. The people who make the *Daily Mail* are in the business of selling newspapers and have been, aside from a bleak period when it was almost crushed by the faster and hungrier *Daily Express*, rather good at it.

Or they used to be. The printed *Daily Mail*, like almost all news-papers, is dying. The numbers say it all: in May 2016, the *Daily Mail* newspaper sold 1,551,430[11] copies a day. Now that's a very healthy figure, a figure that other newspaper editors would kill for, but at its Dacre-era peak at the end of 2003 the paper shifted around two and a half million copies. The *Daily Mail* circulation graph, like that of almost every newspaper, is pointing inexorably to the grave. The *Mail* sheds at least 4 per cent of its readers every year: over 60,000 fewer copies a day. All things being equal the *Mail* could, even by conservative statistical estimates, be at a circulation of less than a million, within less than a decade of the time of writing.[12]

The *Independent* went online-only at the end of March 2016[13] because its 55,000 daily circulation[14] was not enough to sustain it – a figure that was less than what a decent weekly newspaper in a small town would have sold not so long ago.

Will the *Daily Mail* follow the *Independent* into a paperless newspaper world? 'One's looking way into the future there,' Vyvyan Harmsworth, whose great uncles founded the paper, told the author. 'It's rather like hanging up your rugby boots; you know when it's time to do so but you don't look forward to it at all. We will continue to publish until a time when nobody wants newspapers. But I think that may be thirty years in advance, it may be a hundred – who knows.'[15]

Those who despise the *Daily Mail*'s often shrill voice shouldn't get their hopes up. The *Mail* now reaches far more readers, far more *young* readers, than ever before, all over the planet. *MailOnline*, its celebrity-fuelled website, is the biggest English-language news website in the world and its revenues have started to offset those lost to declining print sales. The website has a different staff to that of the newspaper but its inner voice is very much that of the *Daily Mail*.

Its voice is, ultimately, that of just one man. And it's not Paul Dacre. It's that of a man who has been dead for almost a century: the paper's founding master, Alfred C. Harmsworth, a boy from the suburbs of Victorian London who would go on to become Lord Northcliffe, whose voice was once thought so powerful that the Germans shelled his seaside home during the First World War. Young 'Sunny' Harmsworth had a hobby: he liked to press words in ink on to paper and soon discovered, with impeccable timing, that he also had the knack of knowing exactly what millions of people wanted to read. Lord Northcliffe wasn't just the father of the *Daily Mail*, he was the founder of the popular press as we know it.

PART I

Schemo Magnifico

1

Magazine Boy

Sunny Harmsworth began in the middle.

The Harmsworth family weren't wealthy. They were just members of a growing class within Victorian society that sat somewhere between the gentry perusing the land on horseback and the urban poor scratching out an existence down on their manure-strewn streets. The Harmsworths had not even been 'middle class' all that long. Sunny's grandparents were actually Hampshire peasants sucked in from the shires by the ever-expanding city of London. They set themselves up as grocers on the edge of London, in what is now known as St John's Wood.

Alfred Charles William Harmsworth was actually born in Dublin on 15 July 1865, at a house on the River Liffey called Sunnybank Cottage, and was given the pet name 'Sunny' by his father, Alfred senior, the only son of those Hampshire peasants. Alfred senior had sailed to Ireland to take up a post as a teacher at a school for the sons of dead British soldiers in the days when restless Éire was still part of the United Kingdom.

Sunny's mother was a Maffett, from a wealthy family who were pillars of the Irish Protestant ascendancy, the minority that held the Catholic majority in their yoke. She could even trace her lineage back to a colonel in Cromwell's invading army. Harmie, as Alfred senior was known to his countless friends, had charmed Geraldine Mary off a park bench and they had married. But the Harmsworths didn't stay long in Ireland. Geraldine had grown up with servants and governesses, and a mere schoolteacher couldn't hope to provide her with the life to which she was accustomed, so she persuaded her husband to study law and the family moved to London.

Alfred senior was duly called to the bar and became a barrister, at which he was to prove no great success. His true calling was to an altogether different kind of bar – pubs like the King of Bohemia in Hampstead, where he'd flourish his hat, bow from the waist to the barmaids and greet them with a warm silky voice. Folk were forever buying Harmie a drink but he rarely had the cash to pay for a round himself. He was a man in a tall hat telling tall tales, his favourite yarn being how his real father was in fact the 'grand old' Duke of York. He'd stumble up from his pew like a man born a peer of the realm, lift a hand in the air and solemnly declare: 'I am descended from kings.'

There is no evidence of royal blood in the Harmsworth line, and drink would kill Harmie long before his eldest two boys became the next best thing: viscounts. The future Press Lord's father, in fact, firmly disapproved of the trade that would lift the Harmsworth name into the higher echelons of British society, where he felt it belonged. A newspaper office was not the place for a gentleman; he wanted Sunny to follow him into the law. But the addictive nature of ink seeped into Sunny's skin early.

He was only about twelve when he first sat down in front of an amateur printing press at a small London schoolhouse and began to press words on to paper. He spent hours, days, forming letters into words, sentences, paragraphs. He scribbled out the title of The Henley House . . .

SCHOOL MAGAZINE[1]

. . . giving those two words their own space and lifting them out in tall, bold type. His inky little fingers then lined up EDITED BY ALFRED C. HARMSWORTH under that mouthy masthead.

'He made a very poor impression on his teachers,' wrote *War of the Worlds* author H. G. Wells, who later taught at the school and also wrote for Harmsworth's publications. 'And [he] became one of those unsatisfactory, rather heavy, good-tempered boys who in the usual course of things drift ineffectively through school to some second-rate employment. It was J. V.'s ability that saved him from that.'[2]

It had been John Vine (J. V.) Milne, the school's kindly headmaster, who had spotted an opportunity to stimulate the boy, despite his unexceptional nature. Milne, a shy and lisping Scotsman – and father of *Winnie-the-Pooh* author A. A. Milne – gently encouraged the future Press Lord as he splattered himself with violet ink.

The first issue, in March 1881, showed a gift for hyperbole that would stay with the boy and his publications for his whole life. 'I have it on the best authority,' wrote Sunny, that the magazine 'is to be a marked success'.[3] A story about bad weather stopping the boys playing football, a subject he was keen on as captain of the school team, followed the boast. But the real scent of his future lay hidden on the back page. Here he printed questions sent in by other kids to which they hoped for an answer. It was innocuous enough, and not even original, yet this page would be the template upon which his entire empire was later built.

Another of Sunny's passions was newfangled things called 'bicycles', huge beasts with a front wheel that reached the armpit. He loved the freedom of cycling down the open dusty roads, often covering great distances with his cycling club pals who wore uniforms and followed a bugler. Sunny was a leader among the boys of Hampstead but the girls liked him too – he was an unusually good-looking boy. Around this time, a friend of Harmie's remembered seeing father and son dining together at the Middle Temple, where Harmie worked; 'a dear old Bohemian gentleman' and a teenage boy who had 'the face and figure of a Greek god'.[4]

Two key formative features of Sunny Harmsworth's early years were his perpetually pregnant mother – she'd give birth to eleven surviving children, none of them twins – and his frequent house moves, due to his alcoholic father's inability to pay the rent and the need for ever more space to house the Harmsworth brood.

One day, around the time Sunny left school, Mrs Harmsworth hired a fifteen-year-old nurse called Louisa Jane to help care for all those kids. The younger boys remembered Essex girl Louisa for having a face like a pastry, dusted with way too much powder. Handsome Sunny Harmsworth was around the house a lot, as he wasn't in school and didn't have a job. The teenagers became intimate, grabbing fumbled moments together in dark corners of the family home, somehow dodging all those wide eyes and tiny ears.

Periods of high stress would have a direct physical impact on Sunny his whole life, and the Harmsworths claimed it was a bout of pneumonia that had left their boy bedridden after a mammoth bike ride shortly after he left school. But it was not strictly true; a scandal had laid him low.

Sixteen-year-old Sunny had made Louisa Jane pregnant and she had run back to her Essex village to give birth to a boy named Alfred Benjamin 'Smith' on Bonfire Night, 1882. The box on the birth certificate for the father's name was left blank, and the first teenage mum to grace the *Daily Mail* story had been impregnated under the stairs by the newspaper's founder.

It was a nightmare for Mr and Mrs Harmsworth, who were advanced snobs even for Victorian London; the truth hardly mattered a damn and keeping up appearances was everything. So Sunny was hustled away safely out of town on a European tour after answering an advert in *The Times*. Father and son would never quite be the same again but, far worse for Sunny, his strict and deeply moral mother – whose affection he craved his entire life – felt he had disgraced the family. When he returned from his trip, Geraldine, who was pregnant herself as ever, refused to have him back in the house.

Sunny found digs with a friend nearby, put on a light suit his family had bought him for his European trip and set out on foot in the only direction he had ever really been heading: Fleet Street. All he had to do was follow the same route as the river that rises in the high ground of Hampstead and spills down over the clay upon which London rests. For over 1,000 years thirsty travellers would pause to sip the Fleet's fresh waters and bathe in her healing ponds but, as humanity took root on her banks, she ran ever shallower and slower. The settling horde sucked her dry and she became a stream, an open sewer, a ditch and finally a drain. The Fleet still oozes on down in the dark under Farringdon Road to Ludgate Circus and crosses under the street that took her name before spilling out into the Thames by Blackfriars Bridge.

The printed word first came to the City in 1500 along with the wonderfully named Wynkyn de Worde – an apprentice to William Caxton – to print the materials for the legal trade that had already settled in the area. Britain's first newspaper, a single sheet of paper called the *Daily Courant*, began publication on Fleet Street two centuries later, and dozens of other newspapers soon followed.

As Sunny covered the four miles or so from Hampstead in the early 1880s, London was expanding all around him; omnibuses pulled commuters towards town while rickety carts pulled labourers and building materials in the opposite direction, shaking dust and horsehair plaster into the air as they went, to erect the houses that were spreading out from the centre like a bruise. They were building the suburbs, places where people could live while still working in town. Six million new houses were built in London during Queen Victoria's reign alone. The people moving into these houses were *his* readers, *his* future.

Sunny stepped into the City as a boy with no need for a razor arriving in a land of beards, his Napoleonic blond forelock falling across his forehead as he peered through the window of a restaurant called Spiers and Pond at Ludgate Circus. He knew this was where many newspaper editors had their lunch and he surveyed the kings of Fleet Street for the first time: they were mostly grey and heavy old men, just like their newspapers.

It took a few years for Sunny Harmsworth to make any kind of mark, however; though he was an enthusiastic boy bristling with self-confidence, his writing had little style and no soul. It was mostly harmless pap, such as a piece about a famous ventriloquist or the origin of the bicycle. He would wander around the British Museum in a black cape and glossy silk hat, and read up on photography and write an article on 'how to take a photograph'; he would watch people enjoying the snow on Hampstead Heath and produce a story about 'forgotten frosts'. Things that interested him, he figured, would interest an editor and the readers. He'd admit later that his own material was 'poor stuff'.[5]

It didn't matter. Sunny Harmsworth's timing, like his dress sense, was impeccable. Seismic events from the previous decade had generated a human wave that he'd ride ever higher, a newly literate middle class. Yet he wasn't the first to catch this wave. The original pioneer of the popular press didn't start in London and he wasn't even a journalist. George Newnes was the owner of a vegetarian restaurant in provincial Manchester who had, quite by accident, discovered a new market. Newnes liked to collect bits and pieces of information in a scrapbook for his own amusement – his tit-bits – that he'd often read out to his wife in the evening. Mrs Newnes, presumably to deflect her beloved's tedious babbling, suggested he compile and publish them for the pleasure of others. So he did, founding a weekly magazine in 1881 called 'Tit-Bits from all the interesting Books, Periodicals, and Newspapers of the World', or *Tit-Bits* for short.

It was a soaraway success. *Tit-Bits* was bought by this new class of reader desperate for something – anything – interesting to read. *Tit-Bits'* readers had been created by the 'Forster Act' of 1870, a law that demanded the basic compulsory education of the masses from the ages of five to thirteen. Prior to the Act, only about one in seven people could read and write, but by the 1880s there were thousands of new young readers. Yet few were inclined to pick up the dense, artless, dead, self-important prose on offer in most of the newspapers and periodicals of the day.

Newnes found himself running his booming publication from a new London headquarters in 1885 when Sunny Harmsworth and a cycling pal named Max Pemberton walked through his door. The pair approached an 'amiable-looking gentleman'[6] with a beard like a badger's pelt as he ate his lunch at a table strewn with proofs of his magazine. It was Newnes, who asked the pair what they wanted. Pemberton was stumped for a second, then looked around at 'the crazy nature of the building' in which they stood and offered to write a piece on 'jerry builders'. Newnes commissioned the story and sent them on their way, and Pemberton duly wrote up a story about shoddily constructed 'jerry-built' buildings and received a healthy fee.

From that day on, Sunny Harmsworth was in the *Tit-Bits* office almost daily and soon sold Newnes a story about 'Some Curious Butterflies', then others, such as a visit to newspaper wholesaler W. H. Smith, one with a nod to his father's legal profession called 'Q. C.s and How They Are Made' and another one about 'Organ Grinders and Their Earnings'.

Sunny soon realized there was a bigger opportunity here than just selling stories to Newnes. He pushed open his flatmate's bedroom door one morning, wrote Pemberton,[7] and told him how provincial hobbyist Newnes had discovered 'a bigger thing than he imagines. He is only at the very beginning of a development which is going to change the whole face of journalism.'

Harmsworth decided to create his own magazine and, around this time, the future Press Lord began to carry a brown folder around with him that had the words 'SCHEMO MAGNIFICO' scrawled on a sticker pasted to the front. It was his master plan for the future. He would consult it and scribble down a fresh idea before flipping it closed. The battered old folder would be the fount of all his future publications and he kept it locked in an office safe almost to the day he died, four decades later. Nobody else ever saw inside.

His mind skipped back to his school magazine's questions and answers section. It was a staple of many periodicals – even *Tit-Bits* had one – but there was something more to this common format that nobody else had spotted. It could be a useful device, an excuse, really, to publish interesting little yarns and factoids for no other reason than that they were interesting little yarns and factoids. They were easy on the eye and gentle on the brain.

It took a couple of years and minor editorships of a small publication called *Youth* and a bicycle magazine in Coventry before somebody was found to back Harmsworth with the cash to launch his own magazine.

He was a big-hearted Irishman named William Dargaville Carr, who, it turned out, wasn't especially wealthy and knew absolutely nothing about publishing. He'd married the best friend of Sunny's mother back in Dublin and was using his wife's dowry to try to carve out a future in London. They moved into lodgings and Carr soon annoyed Sunny by hiring the landlady's son as the company's office boy; Harmsworth had wanted the job for one of his brothers. Carr & Co. began in a shabby little office around the corner from Fleet Street at 26 Paternoster Square, editorial divided from the trade counter by a screen knocked up by a carpenter – who told Carr he had sixteen children, and some were ill. Carr organised a whip round and handed him four shillings . . . money was never going to be under much control in Carr's hands. Harmsworth continued freelancing but Carr didn't do much of anything at all, and hated being cooped up in an office. The new office boy noted that the pair seemed to spend the whole day chatting. The boy's toughest job was waking his young boss Sunny Harmsworth every morning: 'he never liked getting up'.

By then Sunny's plan had grown flesh and a face inside his Schemo Magnifico. He'd taken a copy of *Tit-Bits* and doodled out a similar title block, a thin rectangular box – his version slashed from the bottom left corner up to the top right corner like a flag.

ANSWERS TO
CORRESPONDENTS

Underneath, a black finger on either side pointed to

ON EVERY SUBJECT UNDER THE SUN

It was a bold statement – Sunny liked bold statements – and it looked fresh and different, if a little amateurish. It was the work of an exuberant youth, the very demographic he hoped to reach. Three words would sit left to right at the top above the masthead: 'INTERESTING. EXTRAORDINARY. AMUSING.'

A friend of Sunny's father, a *Daily Telegraph* leader writer named Edward Markwick, joined the venture, and soon found more cash in the pockets of Captain Alexander Spink Beaumont, a retired soldier Sunny nicknamed 'the Admiral', who some thought[8] may have had an unrequited homosexual motive in getting behind the pretty young journalist. But Sunny wasn't at all interested in men – he was smitten by a friend's sister, a petite brown-eyed girl called Mary Milner, whose family were a peg or two up from the Harmsworths thanks to her father's success in the sugar trade from the West Indies. Molly, as she was known, was a very pretty and graceful, vivacious girl who first spotted the future Press Lord at a children's party where, she recalled eighty years later, her mother had admonished her by saying, 'Now, Molly, don't dance all the time with the best-looking boy in the room.' Sunny began to spend more time at the Milners' place than he did at home, and the young couple married the same year he founded *Answers*, the groom leading his new bride across the dance floor with a dummy copy of his embryonic magazine hanging out of his jacket pocket.[9] Molly's new husband might have been broke at the time but that magazine would lead her to a lifestyle worthy of an empress.

The first *Answers to Correspondents on Every Subject under the Sun* was printed on sixteen pages of cream-coloured, almost A4-sized paper and dated 16 June 1888,[10] but was actually marked as issue No.3. It was a minor sleight of hand, for how could there have been any letters to answer if it had yet to have any readers? The first ever answer was about 'The Queen's Private Letters' – a correspondent wanted to know if a letter he owned was from Queen Victoria. Probably, was the reply; the Queen wrote in an 'Italian hand' which was 'very thin, very slanting', and signed her letters 'Victoria R' or 'to very intimate friends simply V. or V. R.'

Another correspondent wrote about a German stealing his seat on a train. 'I felt very much inclined to take the gentleman by the neck and put him out of the carriage,' wrote 'Nimrod', 'but was advised by the others to let him alone.' A quarter-century before the Great War, Sunny was already keen to see Germans booted off trains, a subject that would perennially interest him. Page five had thousands of commuters rattling across London on trains and buses with one hand covering an eye while they read ever-shrinking letters, as Sunny had published an illustration of an opticians' eye test. *Answers to Correspondents* was information as entertainment, and it was fun.

Answers was sold by street hawkers leaping aboard these horse-drawn buses in and around Fleet Street and it was bought by many of the area's countless journalists – and one, Frank Boyd, wasn't impressed. It was, he recalled later, 'a mean, wretched-looking little production with "amateur" written all over it . . . It looked as if it had not a million to one chance of succeeding.'[11]

As the weeks passed, themes began to solidify inside *Answers*: it published anything about Queen Victoria, Charles Dickens and what people earned, from street hawkers to Fleet Street editors. And all any reader needed to do if they wanted to see their name in print was ask a question about hats – Harmsworth was hooked on hats. Sunny had been born with an oversized head and was convinced that it contained a bigger than average brain and therefore superior intelligence. For one story, a couple of hatters were consulted who explained how men who worked with horses – coachmen, jockeys, livery servants and the like – had smaller heads. The skulls of several clever chaps at London University were measured by these hatters and, reported Sunny's magazine: 'The general conclusion to be drawn from the hatters' figures is therefore favourable to the opinion that large head-dress and mental capacity go together.'

Grim little tales of death and torture got grimmer and darker, perhaps to compete with the 'penny dreadful' publications that Sunny claimed to abhor. Penny dreadfuls were simply written, cheaply printed tales aimed at adolescent boys that cost a penny and were dreadful, hence the name. Over several weeks, wide-eyed youths would be gripped by stories about criminals and vampires, made-up tales about the real-life highwayman Dick Turpin, Sweeney Todd 'the demon barber of Fleet Street', and suchlike.

Or maybe Sunny's macabre streak was simply because the *Answers* office in Paternoster Square was just a head's roll from Newgate prison, where criminals had not so long ago been hung out in the street. In issue number five, an unnamed reporter – almost certainly Sunny himself – took a two-minute walk from the office to the 'solemn and threatening old building' on the corner of Old Bailey and Newgate Street. The reporter stepped through the spiked gate and was shown into a room filled with the casts of murderers' heads taken after execution, finding 'very ordinary-looking people, with nothing particularly repulsive in their features'.

> A turnkey who was present pointed out to me their
> throats, which were all marked with deep indentations
> from the rope which had cut short their career. It is a
> popular delusion, he explained, to suppose that the fall
> from the scaffold breaks the neck. In every case death is
> the result of strangulation.[12]

Another early obsession was insanity, and one illustration for 'How Madmen Write' on the front of issue eight looked like a seismometer scratching out news of an earthquake. It was as if Sunny somehow foresaw his own fate. Harmsworth himself would die insane on a London rooftop thirty-four years later.

Answers sold an average of 8,000 copies a week in its first few months, which wasn't a great figure, and Sunny blamed a persistent heavy fog and the fear of serial killer Jack the Ripper keeping people indoors. However, he remembered these days as the happiest of his life. Proofs would be draped over chairs in the brand-new terraced house that he and his wife Mary rented in Pandora Road, West Hampstead, as his brothers and sisters sprawled around the floor finding stories or answering the handful of questions from readers who actually wrote in. Sunny soon realized that the vast majority had no questions in need of an answer but just wanted to read the thing on the bus. So stories were commissioned from writers and questions created to fit. His friend Max Pemberton became 'Mr *Answers*', heading off on adventures up a steeple or under the ocean in a diver's bell.

'Somehow I knew from the first just what people wanted to read,' Sunny said in an interview a few years later.[13]

Circulation soon settled at around 30,000, but *Answers* wasn't turning a profit and there was a real danger that it would follow most of the 200 other publications launched in 1888 into the abyss. Sunny Harmsworth was worried and took to stomping around proclaiming, 'I cannot make it pay!'[14] He was a young man with entrepreneurial flair who was great at setting things in motion, but he was no accountant. He needed the help of a man with a more stolid and calculating mind who did actually care about the price of ink and paper and, luckily for Alfred, he found one close to home.

One evening his younger brother Harold popped in to help his brother and, unable to get the *Answers* books to balance, Harold, family folklore has it, took a look at the numbers and openly wept at the damage that useless co-owner Dargaville Carr had inflicted upon those poor defenceless numbers.[15] Sunny realized he had found exactly the man he needed.

Harold Sidney Harmsworth was very different to his elder brother. For a start, while Alfred could barely count his fingers and toes without falling over, Harold was awfully good at sums. Harold adored neat little rows of figures. He trusted numbers far more than he ever trusted people. The contrasting natures of the two brothers was perhaps best summed up by the pet names their father had chosen for his two eldest boys: while Alfred was 'Sunny', the first-born and the family's shining light, Harold was called 'Bunny' on account of his timid and retiring nature.

Sunny asked Bunny to join the firm but Bunny wasn't sure, as he had a solid civil service clerk's job keeping the records of ships' crew and signing sailors on for duty. The most exciting thing ever to happen to Bunny at work was when a rat darted up his trouser leg at his pest-infested basement office.[16] It was to be the future Lord Rothermere's destiny to be but a shadow next to Sunny, the glowing Adonis of Hampstead and future Lord Northcliffe. Sunny was fair, fine-featured and arrogant. Bunny was dark and brooding, with a black moustache above a fat bottom lip. Whereas Sunny would stroll along turning heads, making friends and influencing people, Bunny would hover outside a house to which he'd already been invited, working up the courage to ring the bell. As Sunny heard a golden future calling him forth, Bunny heard only the voice of impending doom.

Bunny spent a week pondering his big brother's offer, the rats around his desk squeaking out their advice: he could stay in the civil service for life and be comfortable, or follow Sunny's brighter star on its far riskier trajectory. The rest of the family urged Harold to join his brother, and Bunny's letter of resignation was 'the most important single document in the history of the family'[17], wrote another sibling, Cecil ('Buffles' in the family's silly name stakes on account of his shaggy 'buffalo' hair).

A little while after his twenty-first birthday, Bunny chaired the company's annual meeting from a small deal table in a boxroom used for storing *Answers* back numbers, with the board members all sitting on stacked copies of the magazine. Bunny had wrestled sense into the books and the company was finally showing a gross profit of over £1,000. He also soon found a way to force out Dargaville Carr, 'the Admiral' and the other early investors. But it would take a beggar to truly set Sunny on his way to becoming the first, and only, Viscount Northcliffe and see Bunny rise to become the first in a long line of Viscount Rothermeres.

A man in dire need of soap and water rose up from the banks of the River Thames in the fading autumn light, his eyes locked on to two young gentlemen headed his way.

Sunny Harmsworth wore a light suit, a blond forelock falling into an eye, and talked away softly to Bunny, a darker boy with a thick moustache and hair swept over to his right ear, who scanned the Embankment while listening to his brother as if expecting someone to pull him into the mire. The tramp could hear what the handsome young chap was saying: he had an enemy called '*Tit-Bits*' and was fretting over 'puzzles' and 'prizes'.

Giveaways and competitions were a vital ingredient in the *Answers* formula. Readers won prizes for the best Scottish joke or for guessing how many people walked across London Bridge, and *Answers* had scored a huge success with a glass box of tiny balls that spelled out the word 'Answers' if lined up correctly. The boss of a London bank even wrote in to complain that 'whenever my back is turned, my clerks neglect their work to try shaking the little balls into the right order'.[18] The game lifted circulation permanently to 45,000. But the Harmsworth boys needed something bigger and bolder. They needed the most gigantic competition the world had ever seen, no less; something that would capture the fleeting attention of the great British public.

Tit-Bits had been around longer, and had sold more copies, and hobbyist Newnes was proving to be no fool in the face of competition: he would hide buried gold and print clues in a serialized story. A *Tit-Bits* reader won a house and one young lad even won a job as a junior clerk in the *Tit-Bits* office; the boy, Arthur Pearson, would later found his own magazine and then the *Daily Express* newspaper.

Sunny already had an idea for a new competition, but that was the easy part: he'd read a paragraph in *The Times* about the exact amount of coinage inside the Bank of England, and the winner would simply need to guess the amount on any given day – the number was posted outside the Bank anyway. But what could be the prize? The game itself didn't matter very much; it was the prize that counted.

The tattered old tramp stopped them and asked for money. Bunny recoiled from a man who probably smelled of stale urine and the cheap gin that was the alcoholic's preferred poison of the day, but Sunny stopped to chat and gave what was going on inside his head a good airing.

'Oh!' said the tramp. 'There's only one prize I want.'

'Yes?'

'A pound a week for life!'

The tramp's words hit Sunny Harmsworth like a flurry of punches. The brothers each tossed him a coin and dashed back to the office, Sunny working out how to present it and Bunny worrying about how to finance it; if the winner lived a long life it could add up to a substantial sum. The bum just slipped back under his bridge – he may even have seen the sandwich-board men passing through the throngs of people a few weeks later carrying bright orange signs but he probably couldn't read the words printed across in huge black type:

A POUND A WEEK FOR LIFE! 'The Most Gigantic Competition The World Has Ever Seen!'

It was another game-changer for Sunny Harmsworth. The competition lifted the collective imagination and sparked debate in lower-middle-class homes everywhere. Entries had to be on a postcard and include the signatures and addresses of five witnesses who weren't relatives or living in the same house in order to qualify. It was a genius plan. Bunny understood the power of numbers; five more people would get to know the magazine, and these new readers would then need their own five witnesses in order to enter.

One delivery of 255,000 postcards to the *Answers* office was such a phenomenon it got a mention in the Postmaster-General's annual report, and the police had to control the crowd in Threadneedle Street when the figure was posted up outside the Bank of England on 4 December 1889. The Christmas edition of *Answers* that published the name of the winner sold over 200,000 copies. The winner guessed to within two pounds of the correct figure and he proved to be an excellent investment; he died only eight years later from tuberculosis.

Yet a pound a week for life was always a poor man's dream. There was never any chance Sunny's ambitions could ever be so easily contained. In 1890, at twenty-four, Sunny was a handsome and successful young man behind a big desk in his own 'extremely luxurious chamber'[19] at the new *Answers* premises on Fleet Street, looking out on to the spire of St Bride's, the journalists' church. But he wanted more.

Inside the *Answers* office, the editorial room fizzed with youthful energy. His staff were all youngsters serving up interesting things to a hungry public, and most of his brothers were involved too, now

Sunny had given jobs in the firm to those of employable age, sending them off in all directions with wheelbarrows full of the magazine or having them write and edit copy. Sunny was, after all, now the head of a very large Harmsworth household. Harmie was dead. He hadn't lived to see his eldest boys fulfil his every fantasy, and then some. He didn't see them raise the Harmsworth name all the way up forever into the upper ranks of Britain's titled aristocracy. If he'd survived just a few years he could have sat, as Mrs Harmsworth was to do, in the manicured garden of a country estate as a white-gloved butler brought out his breakfast and his son's *Daily Mail* newspaper on a solid silver tray, unfolding it and tut-tutting gently at its more vulgar yarns. A few years more and he could have taken his son's *Times,* an organ much more suited to his standing. Harmie never did become the literary figure he'd dreamed of when he'd first set sail for Dublin, nor did he become the dream his perpetually pregnant wife had sold him – the solid and solvent lawyer. Harmie became a broken drunk with a blistered liver, the bills and bitter claws of defeat pulling him under. One Saturday afternoon when *Answers* was a year old, Mr and Mrs Harmsworth went to a garden party where Harmie was jolly and genial, good company as ever, but when they got home he felt ill and went to bed early. He was soon screaming for his wife and vomiting blood.

Their fourth son, Leicester – 'Puggy' – dashed for the family doctor. The physician took one look at Harmie and ruled that there was no hope. Harmie died a few days later, the day after his eldest boy's twenty-fourth birthday. Sunny knew nothing. He was at the Harmsworth family's favourite holiday destination, down by the seaside at Broadstairs. Alcoholism may or may not have a genetic link, but drink killed both Harmie and his father Charles at the age of fifty-two; they had matching death certificates that read 'cirrhosis of the liver'. There'd be evidence of this on Bunny's corpse too, half a century later.

Outside the *Answers* office, the old men of Fleet Street were predicting the imminent demise of Sunny's 'penny phenomenon', but they underestimated Harmie's boy. His Schemo Magnifico folder on his desk had plans percolating inside that reached far beyond one mere magazine and, from May 1890, a new publication began to appear every six months or so. 'I foresaw that our policy was to rain paper after paper upon the public,' Sunny would later say, 'and thus raise our prestige and block competition.'[20]

First came a magazine targeting the humour market. A thrusting young *Answers* staffer named Houghton Townley was pulled aside and given four days to set *Comic Cuts* up from scratch; poor Townley found the task so stressful he was up most nights vomiting, but he pulled it off. Though given the tagline 'amusing without being vulgar', *Comic Cuts* was considered by many of the self-appointed upholders of Victorian values to be as vulgar as any of the lurid fiction inside the 'penny dreadfuls'.

Sunny Harmsworth was a genius at turning what was, at its root, a hypocrisy into a commercial advantage – even a crusade: *Comic Cuts* and a whole host of subsequent publications were sold as 'pure healthy tales' for young minds, even an antidote to juvenile delinquency, yet were not so different from those which they attacked. *Comic Cuts* only cost a halfpenny and within a few weeks it was outselling *Answers*. So Sunny created a competitor – before someone else did – called *Illustrated Chips*, soon shortened to *Chips*. The magazine published crude cartoons and was a forerunner of the comic strip; it was another huge success. When a later Harmsworth publication called 'Marvel' was at the planning stage, a note from Harold to Alfred suggesting the boring 'Boys' Weekly Reader' as a title gave the game away. 'It sounds respectable,' Bunny wrote in a memo to Sunny, 'and would act as a cloak for one or two fiery stories.'[21]

Any policeman or magistrate who blamed a penny dreadful for corrupting a youngster's mind could be assured of a glowing write-up in the Harmsworths' publications, and authors of penny dreadfuls were 'miserable beer-swilling wretches'. A. A. Milne, *Winnie-the-Pooh* author and son of Alfred's kindly schoolmaster at Henley House, wasn't impressed. 'Harmsworth killed the penny dreadful,' he said, 'by the simple process of producing the ha'penny dreadfuller.'[22]

Young women were another overlooked market. The newsagents sold magazines such as *The Lady* for upper-class females but there was nothing at all for the shop girls, so Sunny created 'a pictorial journal for ladies' wrapped in a light blue cover, the colour of the forget-me-not flower after which the magazine was named.

Each magazine in the empire publicized the others, in a process of cross-pollination that would often include a serial story beginning in one paper and then continuing in another, much to the annoyance of the newsagents, who were slapped down in the pages of all these papers if they objected.

The family firm was gathering unstoppable momentum and Sunny was also gathering the ingredients, though he surely as yet didn't know it, for his *Daily Mail* newspaper.

Bunny, meanwhile, would bounce up the stairs to the office two at a time before pacing around the room with his hands jammed in his pockets, trying to find ways to cut costs and pay as little as possible for ink and paper. He kept costs so low that the actual physical quality of the products was often appalling. Harold's two favourite words were 'grab' and 'knife'. They needed to grab the profits quickly and knife any magazine that didn't do well on the newsstand. He grabbed the chance to push out the investors who'd helped bring *Answers* to life, Bunny's brutal instincts putting the Harmsworth boys in absolute control where they needed to be. He also invented the 'net sales certificate' – a device whereby external accountants verified how many copies were being sold, a cornerstone of how much they could charge advertisers. While Sunny genuinely adored his magazines and would give them time to grow, to Bunny they were just 'rags'.

Soon enough, Sunny and Bunny Harmsworth found they had built the biggest magazine empire in the world; by *Answers*' fifth birthday in 1893, the firm's seven major publications sold almost 1.5 million a week and the brothers Harmsworth were pretty much millionaires in today's money. Yet even with all this success, Sunny was bored with his plush office and worked mostly from home. His fuse would burn bright but then his energy would flicker and wane, his health as fickle as the English weather. Sickness, real or imagined, was never far away. He became an enigmatic figure who caused all these creations to arise in the world but then stepped away before he got ink on his clothes.

He hired a secretary called George Augustus Sutton, a man born to be at Sunny's side. Sutton was discreet, deferential, quiet and reliable, just like his coachman father, from the class of people Sunny had decided were a bit thick because they 'all' wore small hats. Sutton was a tall, skinny, uncomfortable man who spoke with a slight stammer and had the irritating habit of pulling his necktie sharply to the left before straightening it again when he couldn't make up his mind – which was all the time. The rest of Sunny's staff loathed Sutton. They thought there was a diabolical air to the man, and his eyebrows did have a distinctly Mephistophelian slant; his name was soon corrupted to Satan.

Sutton would join his master in the attic at home in West Hampstead shortly after breakfast and stay until late, taking down his thoughts and relaying instructions back to base. Some days they'd take Sunny's fox terrier Bob for a walk on Hampstead Heath, Alfred speaking more to the dog than to 'Sutkins', the stammering coachman's boy.

London too began to frustrate Sunny, so in the autumn of 1890 he bought a house near Broadstairs in Kent, called Elmwood. Doctors always prescribed Sunny fresh air for his endless ailments, and Elmwood's fresh salty air came straight in from the sea. As these sweet early years of rapid success fell by, writers and editors, family and friends would flow down to the court of the boy editor at Elmwood, where they were greeted in the hall by a stuffed polar bear from a North Pole expedition *Answers* had sponsored and would then wander out on to the lawn to eat cucumber sandwiches in a white lifeboat sunk in the ground. Sunny would lead expeditions down to the beach for a stroll or organize shooting matches with toy pistols.

It wasn't the most convenient place for a man in the communications business to live, but the telephone allowed Elmwood to become his command centre as well as his refuge. It would remain his favourite home even when he owned grand estates. Page proofs and manuscripts, printers, make-ups and memos, ideas for articles and new serials poured in and out of a Canadian-style wooden homestead he'd had erected in the garden, where he'd sit behind the cheap desk he'd had at the first *Answers* office. Secretary Sutton sat behind a curtain like a stagehand and even took his summer holidays in Broadstairs just in case 'Mr Alfred' might need him.

The biggest politicians in the land were starting to take notice too; Liberal leader William Gladstone did more than most men to bring the printed word to the masses – he'd introduced the Education Act and, earlier in his long career, abolished the tax on paper. 'I consider the gigantic circulation of *Answers* an undeniable proof of the growth of sound public taste for healthy and instructive reading,' he told the magazine. 'The journal must have vast influence.'[23]

Yet all Sunny had done was print things he found interesting and jokes he thought funny; the office boys and the shop girls laughed along with him on trains and buses, pubs and parlours, sitting on park benches or deckchairs at the seaside. Sunny nailed the popular taste like no other publisher before or since, aside, perhaps, from Rupert Murdoch.

To those who knew him he had a sharply defined, overpowering personality and could be arrogant and self-opinionated but also charming and humorous; he was easy to be attracted to yet very difficult to get to know. Sometimes he bit his nails until his fingers bled, and he was a secretive, slippery man who revealed nothing about his inner feelings, not even in his private diaries. But he clearly had an unbalanced, unquiet mind.

Inside Elmwood he would go to bed early and get up late; he ordered servants to wear shoes that didn't squeak and to make sure soft blue and black pencils were kept sharpened on his bedside table at all times, in case an idea hit him in the night. He had a morbid fear of fire, so he had an oversized fish pond sunk in the garden to create a large body of water just in case it was required. Just like any self-respecting boss of a modern-day drug cartel, out beyond the manicured lawns and rose gardens was a hot-house where Florida alligators wallowed in mud.

Sunny also kept an aquarium with two compartments in his bathroom at Elmwood; on one side of a glass partition was a pike, on the other a goldfish. The pike is an aggressive fish and has been known to turn cannibal. Sunny's magnified face would watch the gentle show for a while, his hand rising to the lid of the tank; the dark green, military-looking pike could see the goldfish on the other side gently meandering by. Harmsworth watched the pike, the pike watched the goldfish and the goldfish probably tried to look at neither. Sunny would whip away the partition between the two tanks and 'study the results'.[24]

Sunny Harmsworth had 'arrived'; he had even got there early – he was not yet even thirty – and he yearned for more.

A man named William Kennedy Jones was to prove a crucial figure in turning magazine boy Sunny Harmsworth into Alfred C. Harmsworth the newspaper man, and K. J., as he was known, was possibly the last journalist Harmsworth ever really viewed as an equal.

One summer's afternoon in 1894, K. J. was sitting at his desk in a newspaper office slashing sense into clumps of miserable text, his lungs pulling their way through one rank cigarette after another, and cursing the writer of the story he was editing. The reporter's words were chronological and deferential, focusing on the judge's lineage far more than the criminal or the crime. But there was a story in there, somewhere.

So K. J. ripped the blood and guts from the prosecution barrister's opening statement and splattered them all over the top of the story. He began to carve a lively read fit to fill two columns of the news pages of a London evening paper called the *Sun* (long defunct and not the current Murdoch paper), where he worked as its chief sub-editor. He was the last man between editorial and the printers; the chief sub is the man through whom every word of a newspaper must flow before metal is set and ink spilled.

K. J. was a leading exponent of a new kind of newspaper journalism that put real craft into the telling of a tale as well as how it was laid out on a page. Whereas in the old newspapers stories were pretty much just sent to the head printer to decide what went where and the editor slipped on his coat and hat and headed for his gentleman's club, this 'new journalism' was different. Screeds of text were broken up into wonderful things called 'paragraphs', and the most interesting elements were lifted to the top. Headlines were crisp and readable. Maps and diagrams were used to illustrate the story, and further sub-deck headlines within the body of the story were used so the eye of the jostled passenger on the bus could return more easily to the same spot.

Kennedy Jones lit another cigarette and looked out on the street and its endless flow of coaches and marching gentlemen in silk hats. K. J. had risen from rocky ground: he'd sold newspapers as a boy on the streets of Glasgow and become a sub-editor on the *Glasgow News* at the age of nineteen. He could have been any one of those nice young gentlemen out there in the street, except, with his tar-black hair and unexplained scars across his forehead, K. J. looked like a man who carried a knife. And he did, in a way. He'd slash the face of any journalist who came within reach of his razor-edged tongue. K. J. had many enemies and few friends and he even took it as a compliment to be called 'the most hated man in Fleet Street'.

'Boy!' K. J. barked, and a youngster ran and grabbed the story from his raised fist and sped off to hand it to the men who made the metal pages in the composing room.

As K. J. sat in the low, choking fug of the sub-editors' room, the office across the street looked especially charming, with its pretty flower boxes on the window-sills holding radiant red geraniums and yellow calceolarias. It could have been a whitewashed hotel in a pretty little Home Counties village instead of an editorial office on drab Tudor Street, the next street down towards the putrid River Thames from Fleet Street. Its shiny gilt sign spelled out just the one golden word: *Answers*.

An expensive, shiny carriage pulled by a pair of well-groomed horses arrived under the sign and Sunny Harmsworth, in a light-coloured coat and top hat, sprang from the carriage and helped his expensive-looking wife down to the pavement.

Kennedy Jones was a foul-tempered man at the best of times but had been especially angry lately; K. J. and Louis Tracy, a colleague on the *Sun* newspaper, had an option to buy a London evening newspaper called the *Evening News and Post*. But they had not been able to raise the funds and their option to buy it expired in a couple of days.

'They tell me young Harmsworth has got more money than there is in the Bank of England,' K. J. shouted over to Tracy. 'Go right over and talk to him.'[25]

Not long after, on 30 August 1894, Sunny became a newspaper proprietor for the first time after agreeing to back K. J. and Tracy, even though the *Evening News and Post* had been bleeding blue Tory Party money all over Fleet Street for years. Sunny admitted laterthat the 'white elephant of the press that proved the ruin of so many . . . looked like being an unpleasant handful for us'.[26]

The paper's ramshackle building and tired old presses had come with the deal, and Sunny and Bunny Harmsworth and K. J. and Tracy would meet every night under a broken skylight to work out what to do with the damn thing. They ripped it up and started again, grabbing the 'new journalism' and ringing it for all it was worth. Bunny slashed the costs of paper and ink using the stone-faced negotiating tactics he'd honed in the magazine trade; staff would often joke that when Bunny had five minutes spare he'd call in the paper merchant to shave a few pence off the price the ever-expanding firm paid for paper. The quality of the paper too never seemed to matter much to Harold Harmsworth (it would be Bunny's lack of care for the quality of their 'rags' that later pushed the brothers apart). He went out on the streets with his pocket watch and examined the busiest spots across the city. He worked out at what time the crowds peaked, worked backwards and organized deadlines and distribution to put the fresh paper in the right place at exactly the right time.

K. J.'s new journalism and Sunny's popular journalism blended well inside the pages of his *Evening News*; a sensational murder more than doubled the paper's circulation to almost 400,000 during the trial. Sunny decided to take a break in Paris; he liked France and he had a fascination with Napoleon his entire life. On one trip to Paris with his mother he even tried on the little Emperor's hat, and it fitted. Sunny's mind was fizzing with ideas as he enjoyed the sites of the city, especially after he met the owner of a morning daily paper called *Le Petit Journal*, that sold more than all the London morning and evening papers put together.[27] It was making a fortune despite selling for half the price of its competitors.

Sunny began to doodle inside his Schemo Magnifico folder, drawing up plans for a new morning newspaper of his own along the same lines as his *Evening News*.

2

Newspaper Man

It's hard now, 120 years later, to see what all the fuss was about.

The first *Daily Mail*[1] on that bright sunny morning of 4 May 1896 was not – at first glance – hugely different from the penny London dailies. It was a broadsheet with small ads and notices on the front page. It was printed on high-quality white paper, exactly the same, if not better, than the penny papers. Its masthead was the same as the *Daily Mail* of today except that the curly 'ye olde English' style serif font was a little more ornate. The lion and the unicorn of the royal coat of arms of the United Kingdom – emblazoned in gold on the front of every British passport – stood then, as now, between 'Daily' and 'Mail'.

It was eight pages thick, with content printed in long thin columns on each side, seven columns a page, the same as every penny newspaper. And it had 'ears' on either side of the title, the box on the right containing the words:

**THE BUSY MAN'S
DAILY JOURNAL.**

On the other side it read:

**A PENNY NEWSPAPER
FOR
ONE HALFPENNY.**

This was precisely the point. It looked like a penny paper, it felt like a penny paper. It *was* a penny paper. But it only cost a halfpenny. Yet it was so much easier to read, and its selection and placing of stories was all about the reading experience. The reader, from day one, issue one, was always kept in mind.

Like the penny papers, it had plenty of City news, sport and racing, and lots of snippets from the courts, such as a story about a man divorcing his wife for her adultery with a curate. Its reports from overseas were first class: natives were rebelling in Bulawayo, the British cavalry had routed Dervishes on camels in the Sudan, Hungary was celebrating its thousandth birthday and there was an update from Tehran on the Shah's assassination.

However, the *Daily Mail* was, crucially, so much easier to read than the long screeds of text in *The Times* of the same day. Whereas the *Times* editorial staff seemed happy to send their text to the head printer for him to decide what went where, infinite care was taken on every single page of the *Daily Mail*. The difference between the two approaches was most marked from day one, in a crime story that was shocking the nation. While all the papers covered the Amelia Dyer case, that of a murderer believed to have killed up to 400 babies, the *Mail* used a much more immediate and narrative style.

'Mrs. Dyer's entry had not been in the least degree sensational. Unexpectedly the door had been opened and she walked in, and without looking round simply plumped down at the end of the seat adjacent to the door,' wrote the Mailman in court. 'It was in vain that I endeavoured to realize that this woman was the author of those almost incredible crimes, crimes which have already made her name notorious throughout the civilized world, and will raise her to an evil eminence in the history of human wickedness.'

It was not until page seven that the *Mail* truly took an entirely different course in terms of the choice of content from the other morning papers, under an amateurishly scrawled masthead:

THE DAILY MAGAZINE. No 1 – AN ENTIRELY NEW IDEA IN MORNING JOURNALISM.

It looked like the Henley House school magazine and the first edition of *Answers*. They were fruit fallen, for sure, from the same mind. This was where Sunny Harmsworth could let his love of useless information spew forth; it was *Answers* in daily form.

The first ever daily magazine page started with a note from Sunny himself: 'The object of the "*Daily Mail*" is to give every item of important news . . . The object of the "Daily Magazine" is to amuse, interest, and instruct during the leisure moments of the day.

'The "Magazine" is designed to appeal to both sexes. Movements in woman's world – that is to say changes in dress, toilet matters, cookery, and home matters generally – are as much entitled to receive attention as nine out of ten of the matters which are treated of in the ordinary daily paper. Therefore two columns are set aside exclusively for ladies.'

Across the page under 'Woman's Realm' were dinner tips, an illustration of a make-it-at-home school frock and a drawing of a lady in a pretty bonnet. Stories on how Boers courted each other and the earnings of the Australian cricket team got the Sunny touch. At the foot of the page there was a serialized story.

A woman had been appointed to run the department; she'd visit the best shops in London, Paris and Brussels to report on fashion and she'd attend society weddings. The other newspapers seemed to be solely for men, they were written and run by men and covered a world in which women barely existed at all. The brothers knew this would work – their female-focused magazines sold well. Experts would be commissioned to write about children and home management. A note followed, aimed at people like K. J. – who thought all this fluff for women was madness and wanted more racing but later admitted Alfred was right: 'Perhaps the best thing about the "Daily Magazine" is that it occupies its own corner, and yet crowds-out nothing that is expected in a newspaper. The man who has not time for this class of reading can leave it severely alone and lose nothing.'

The magazine page became the most expensive on which to advertise, as a woman's hand was invariably on the purse strings at home. Bunny, of course, upped the rates for this page.

Leader pages, which would take up huge swathes of dead trees in
The Times and the *Morning Post*, were stripped back. There had even
been arguments in the *Mail*'s office for dropping them altogether, but
they were only kept, said K. J., to act as a platform 'to explain the drift
of events'. But long screeds of political speeches and Parliamentary
reports never appeared.

'It is essentially the busy man's paper. The mere halfpenny saved
each day is of no consequence to most of us,' wrote Alfred. 'The
economy of the reader's time effected by the absence of the usual
puzzling maze of advertisements is, however, of the most importance.'

Sunny hated adverts and he thought they spoilt his publications,
and as he aged, he'd grow to hate the adman ever more. However,
with his plan to reach ever greater numbers of the aspirational middle
class, he did more to facilitate the rise of the adman than anyone else,
except perhaps his brother Bunny. Harold adored the adman and
all the lovely money he generated but Bunny wasn't seen much
around the *Daily Mail* office in the early days.

Alfred had kept his kid brother away from his most precious
project from the start and Harold was never put in charge of
the management; he was, effectively, relegated to be the buyer of
high-quality ink and paper, signing the kind of cheques he loathed.
If Harold had been in financial control, younger brother Leicester
quipped, they'd have ended up with a farthing paper (a quarter
penny) for a halfpenny.

'The chief reason for Alfred's monopoly of decision regarding the
new paper was his fear of Harold's ideas of economy,' said Leicester.
'Alfred planned great expenditure on foreign telegrams and the
getting of news in general. Harold, he had no doubt, would work
against such a policy.'[2]

Harold had argued for it to be printed on tinted paper instead of
white because it was cheaper, but Alfred pulled rank and insisted it be
printed on the best white paper to allow for better illustrations. Yet
it would still be sold at the cheapest price. Between February 1896
and the paper's first day on the streets, at least sixty-five experimental
'dummies' were produced with no expense spared. For eleven weeks,

stories were covered by reporters, costly cables were received 'for real' from overseas. Offices were opened in New York and Paris. Everything was carefully sub-edited and put in the mock newspaper, which had a fake, roman-style masthead. The presses would be stopped and the results analysed. Then binned. These were endless dress rehearsals for the opening night.

Sunny also bought the best, state-of-the-art machinery.

'When we were digging the pits for the great rotary presses,' he wrote later, 'a waggish enemy spy, who came over "to see what those *Evening News* people were doing", was good enough to remark that they had an ominously big look and were large enough to swallow up all our arduous work in the establishment of many periodicals and the *Evening News* itself. "Better be satisfied with what you have done," he said.'[3]

Bunny agreed – he thought Alfred's grandiose *Mail* scheme was nuts and those pits must indeed have looked like a vast grave for the family fortune, which had, after all, been built on the cheap. Yet Alfred had studied the costs of the penny papers and, even using his fingers and toes, he knew the maths could work. 'It became clear that most of the existing dailies were really halfpennyworths sold at a penny,' he wrote. 'The proprietors had simply pocketed the difference instead of sharing the advantage with the public.'[4]

It was financially feasible to produce a classy paper for a halfpenny, and still make money. From those first scratched notes in his Schemo Magnifico – he'd actually first planned to call it the 'Daily Arrow' – Sunny's plan for his morning paper was always for something different from the family's other publications.

Sunny's vast army of readers from his other publications were key to the *Mail*'s rapid initial success. A news vendor at King's Cross station told a trade magazine that he'd sold the paper to commuters to whom he'd never before sold a morning newspaper, adding that 'There is no doubt that the *Daily Mail* has discovered a new reading public.'

But they weren't new at all. It was the same folk who bought *Answers* and the rest of the Harmsworths' publications. They'd known the *Mail* was coming, as it had been promoted in all these organs and in the *Evening News* for weeks. The clerks hadn't bought a daily paper before because there wasn't one written for them. Previously, the morning papers had been for clever people such as the Westminster elite, City types and the clergy. They were for people who could somehow keep their focus on the dense text of *The Times*; words that just left them staring at the page as if they'd never learned to read.

K. J., ever the cynic, speculated that these new newspaper readers were 'the children, the grandchildren and the great-grandchildren of a people accustomed to public hangings, public whippings, pillories, ducking stools and stocks . . . Was the taste engendered by such sights during the centuries to be outbred by the cheap schooling of a single generation?'[5]

The *Daily Mail* was born on K. J.'s thirty-first birthday and it was a fantastic birthday present to watch people give newspaper sellers a penny and be surprised to be given a halfpenny change – they'd thought it was *worth* a penny. Seven and a half per cent of this baby was his. K. J. liked a bet most days but, instead of backing some three-legged nag, he'd soon buy a stable of his own. And he did, with his horses running in the blue and yellow colours of early *Daily Mail* posters.

K. J. pushed his way through the crowd of news vendors queuing for more copies outside the *Mail*'s offices down by the river. Alfred C. Harmsworth – the paper's founder, father, editor – was already there. He'd hoped to sell 150,000 copies, but four editions had to be printed and the presses of three other newspapers were standing by to meet the demand.

'Well,' K. J. asked, 'how goes it?'

'Orders pouring in,' Alfred replied. 'We've struck a gold mine!'

The final count for the first ever edition of the *Daily Mail* was 397,215 copies, another massive success for Sunny Harmsworth.

Lord Salisbury, the Prime Minister, dismissed the new paper as 'run by office boys for office boys', in a tone only to be expected from the offspring of a long line of aristocrats and royal courtiers. Whatever he said, the *Mail*'s 'office boys' were actually the brightest of British journalism's bright young things. Many were Oxford graduates attracted to a new way of doing things and had previously joined her elder sister, the vibrant and revitalized *Evening News*.

Most of the top Mailmen had known each other for years, arriving at the Harmsworths' well-paid door via the 'new journalism' school of London evening newspapers and, though they were often older and tougher newspaper hands, the magazine boy Sunny Harmsworth was most certainly in charge.

His second-in-command, Kennedy Jones, cracked his tongue like a whip around the ears of his sub-editors as they toiled inside a smog of cigarette smoke, translating all the staff and agency copy into readable stories. The glory days of the 'sub' had arrived. A writer was free to find his own voice but the subs were the ones who forged the paper.

'Before the *Daily Mail* was published, journalism dealt with only a few aspects of life,' Sunny said. 'What we did was to extend its view of life as a whole. This was difficult. It involved the training of a new type of journalist. The old type was convinced that anything which would be a subject of conversation ought to be kept out of the papers. The only thing that will sell a newspaper in large numbers is news, and news is anything out of the ordinary.'[6]

Sometimes it was precisely the 'ordinary' that became news, as early Mailman George Warrington Steevens understood instinctively. As boisterous folk crowded into stations and squeezed into stifling carriages headed to the seaside for the bank holiday in the summer of 1896, for instance, Steevens – a small and shy intellectual who wore a fine moustache that curled away to the tips – walked the empty City streets alone and somehow saw a story through his pince-nez spectacles.

> The first Monday in August is the holiday of the London
> streets – the only one they ever get. At Easter and
> Whitsun tide and Christmas, even more than on ordinary
> days, they are hammered with iron horse-shoes, and
> chafed with rubber tyres, and ground under leather shoes.
> But on the first Monday in August, everybody goes away,

and leaves them a little rest for their aching bones. As they
stretched themselves out yesterday in the warm sunlight,
they looked wider and flatter than usual. Monday is a
poor day of the week at the best: it is something once or
twice in the year to put it off until Tuesday.[7]

Steevens somehow personified this new breed of journalist. He
wasn't just some office boy: he was a bank clerk's son but he had
excelled at school and had gone on to become a brilliant scholar
at Oxford University, where he had been known as 'the Balliol
prodigy'. Steevens, who married a woman thirty years his senior in
his mid-twenties, planned to become a historian before deciding to
become a journalist instead. Sunny hired him from the *Pall Mall
Gazette* to pen leading articles but, when he realized he was no good
at it, Steevens asked if he could write more general pieces.

He became the best of a bunch of writers that could turn bland
little tales about people traipsing to the seaside or a horse race into
vivid pictures in the days before photographs could be reproduced
effectively on newsprint. His words were impressionistic and often
short on fact but Sunny adored him; he was, in a way, exactly what
he wanted the *Daily Mail* to be. 'He showed genius in this extraordinary power of observation,' Sunny wrote, 'and his entirely new way
of recording what he had seen.'[8]

The *Daily Mail* covered far more than just events. These new
Mailmen were corralling and organizing the news. Mailmen would
drum up 'talking points' which would be the most important thing
in the world for a day or two, stories such as 'Will Men Fly?' or about
'Dancing Curates'.

Readers' letters were invented right there in the office, just like
on *Answers*. Fake notices were even placed on the personal column
that read like micro-novellas: these were Tweets almost, a full century
before Twitter.

'Uncle Jim – Come home at once. All is forgiven. Bring the pawn
tickets with you. Niece.' The next day Uncle Jim replied – 'Am
sending the tickets, but cannot come home just yet for reasons of my

own.' In another, 'Oak' told 'Ivy' that he was off to Africa, leaving her for ever. Ivy replied, 'If you go to Africa, I shall follow.'

Besotted young men placed ads for women they'd seen in 'grass green hats' or holding a red parasol, and asked them to write in with their name and address. The reader felt they'd stumbled upon a secret. Everywhere, on every single page, time and thought and effort was spent keeping the reader engaged.

George Steevens soon became the paper's star foreign correspondent, first writing a series of dispatches from the 1896 US Presidential election before becoming a war correspondent. 'The strange thing about war is that it is so wonderfully like peace,' he wrote in 'What War Feels Like', his first experience of armed conflict, the Thirty Days' War between Greece and the Ottoman Empire.

> Going to war is like coming of age. You expect to wake up one morning and find everything changed – a new self in a new world. You do wake up, and you are very much the same sort of boy at twenty-one as at twenty. So with war. You are rather disappointed to find yourself doing exactly the same things in war as you did in peace. You wear very much the same clothes; you eat very much the same amount of breakfast; your disposition is no harder nor bloodthirstier than before. The horrors of war, of which you expected so much, leave you quite unmoved – just because you did expect so much. [9]

There was an altogether different kind of struggle being fought out back home that would go down in Fleet Street legend as the 'Battle of the Bladders', a comedy played out to the amusement of Sunny and K. J. and all the other Mailmen in the office. A journalist called S. J. Pryor believed he'd been offered the editor's chair on the *Daily Mail*, answering directly to the proprietor, circumventing part-owner Kennedy Jones – who took an instant dislike to the man. So when trouble flared up into a full-blown crisis in faraway South Africa, it was decided to open a bureau in Cape Town. Pryor had worked for a press agency in New York and had once even been a telegraph operator. The best man, surely, for the task; he was shooed, reluctantly, out of the door by Sunny's right-hand man K. J. and caught a slow boat to Cape Town, only to return a few months later to find someone else in the editor's chair.

Mailman Thomas Marlowe had developed a reputation as a bit of a bar-room brawler in the pubs in and around Fleet Street as a young hack and had once even tried to take on a famous boxer until a friend pulled him clear. Born to Anglo-Irish parents, Marlowe grew up in Portsmouth and had initially set out to be a doctor before giving up medicine for ink. He'd been the news editor on the *Evening News* before moving over to the *Mail* when it launched.

A daily battle ensued, with each man hurrying into the office ever earlier to be first to plant his buttocks in the editor's chair. Marlowe carried himself like a diplomat, Pryor shuffled around like a busy little clerk, and a trip to the toilet could be career suicide. Pryor had brought a bayonet back from South Africa as a souvenir and he'd lay it on each desk at which he ended up sitting, elbowing away some lesser *Mail* mortal when he lost that day's dash for the seat. Marlowe won; he had a cast-iron bladder and, despite lacking a bayonet, he was better armed for battle: his wife Alice made him sandwiches. Mailman Pryor quit and later became Buckingham Palace's first ever press officer.

Marlowe might have won the 'editor' title but there was only one man who was ever really in charge: Alfred C. Harmsworth. Sunny would stride through his newsroom on busy nights with a big box of cigarettes, scattering them by the handful in front of toiling subs, issuing his three commandments for his editorial staff: 'Explain, simplify, clarify!'

The Mailmen with the weaker knees were dazzled by Sunny Harmsworth to the point of hero-worship; some copied the way he dressed and the more shameless sycophants even wore their hair patted down with a gentle curling lock falling on to their foreheads. 'It is difficult to convey the almost adoring respect in which Alfred Harmsworth was held by some of the younger members of staff,' wrote a junior reporter. 'There was a little chap called Mildred who said to me in an awe-stricken tone: "Do you know, I think Mr Alfred is such a great man that when I hear him coming up the stairs, I tremble all over!"'[10]

After a few years, almost everybody in the office simply called Sunny 'the Chief', after the habit in the US of the actual boss being called 'chief editor' to differentiate him from the countless minions with the word 'editor' in their job title. Even the printers and linotype operators were used to seeing the Chief around, standing in the basement in his shirtsleeves with his waistcoat pocket full of pencils, quick to take a dislike to a page when the damp yellow proof was handed to him. He'd scribble out changes and ask for another to be made.

The Chief's Midas touch had carried over from his magazines and even the *Manchester Guardian* – which later became simply the *Guardian* – liked the *Mail* in these early days, saying it 'made life more pleasant, more exciting, for the average man . . . Even those journals which decided not to try to compete with the *Daily Mail* by imitating it had to improve their news services, their make-up, their typography, their commercial arrangements; those that would not or could not improve usually perished.'[11]

By September of the first year, the *Daily Mail*'s circulation was steady at around 222,000 and within a couple of years it was selling well over 500,000 copies a day. But it would take war to push it up to a million.

War tends to be good for newspapers. And the second Boer War at the very death of the nineteenth century nailed the three-year-old *Daily Mail*'s reputation as a player truly equal to any other newspaper on the newsstand.

Sunny Harmsworth had spent much of the *Mail*'s profits on constructing probably the most effective foreign newsgathering operation in Fleet Street – he even drew £19,000 (over £2 million today) in personal cheques shortly after the paper's launch to pay the bills and he was happy to keep funding the fight in his own war: against every one of those other newspapers. It was money well spent. He also knew his readers would enjoy a good war. 'The British people relish a good hero,' he'd often say, 'and a good hate.'[12]

Farmers in faraway South Africa were daring to try to wrestle themselves free of the British yoke, and absolute faith in the British Empire was a pillar upon which the *Daily Mail* stood: an Anglo-Saxon people from a rainy little island off mainland Europe was absolutely born to rule the world absolutely. As far as Sunny was concerned, it was simply the natural order of things. And Sunny's new newspaper proprietor status was attracting people who wouldn't have wasted their time on the owner of a few silly magazines.

One new friend was the megalomaniac miner Cecil Rhodes, the empire-builder who wasn't content to have a street named after him – it had to be a whole country: Rhodesia (now Zimbabwe). Sunny was smitten by strong men like Rhodes who shared his binary view of the world; grey intricacies and subtle political currents could never hold Sunny's focus. 'We are the first race in the world,' said Rhodes. 'And the more of the world we inhabit, the better it is for the human race.'[13]

Britain at the time 'owned' half of Africa, thanks largely not to the might of the British Army but to people like Rhodes and murderous mercenaries paid for by Nathan 'Natty' Rothschild of the Rothschild banking clan. Their thumbprints were all over the Maxim guns Natty bought to shoot fat holes in semi-naked black Africans, mostly for the mineral wealth under their soil.

The Boers were different from the black natives. For a start, these farmers were crack shots who learned to hunt just about the same day they learned to crawl. Also, the Germans were playing power games in the veldt, a prelude to the monstrous conflicts to come, meaning the Boers also had been supplied with their Maxims and the latest Mauser rifles. The Boers were of the soil, same as the black Africans had been for millennia. There had already been a tepid Boer War, but then the biggest gold deposit in the world was discovered on Boer land at the white water ridge – Witwatersrand, in Afrikaans – making the want-away Boers a real threat to British supremacy in the region.

George W. Steevens was, by now, the *Mail*'s best foreign correspondent and was dispatched to cover the conflict.

> They [the Boers] are big, bearded men, loose of limb,
> shabbily dressed in broad-brimmed hats, corduroy
> trousers, and brown shoes; they sit their ponies at a
> rocking-chair canter erect and easy; unkempt, rough,
> half-savage, their tanned faces and blue eyes express lazy
> good-nature, sluggish stubbornness, dormant fierceness.
> They ask the news in soft, lisping Dutch that might be
> a woman's; but the lazy imperiousness of their bearing
> stamps them as free men. A people hard to rouse, you say
> – and as hard, when roused, to subdue.'[14]

As the war progressed, star Mailman Steevens found himself under siege in a town called Ladysmith, after a humiliating British defeat. He was trapped for weeks and was frustrated and bored, scribbling his reports in tiny handwriting and handing them to a native runner, who would dash through the enemy lines to the British positions. It was a slow process. He penned articles in November 1899 that would not appear in the *Mail* until the next century, January 1900. But by then he'd paid the price demanded of so many war correspondents then as now.

He was dead.

Yet it wasn't a Boer shell or a sniper that killed George W. Steevens on 15 January 1900. It was typhoid. Sunny Harmsworth was crestfallen. He dashed round to his friend's widow when he heard and broke down in tears, saying he couldn't forgive himself for sending her husband to Ladysmith. Steevens had already asked to get off the road and be based at *Mail* headquarters.

The war continued and the biggest number of British troops that had ever been sent on an overseas campaign amassed on South African soil to counter the defeats of previous months. Around 180,000 pairs of British boots were on the march, all to subdue a population about the same size as Brighton. The Boer farmers kept on doing what they did best: they would hit and run and then dissolve away into the veldt. The Boers knew they could never face down such superior numbers, so they stopped trying. But they didn't surrender.

Hounded by the *Daily Mail* and other newspapers at what was starting to smell like defeat, the powers that be decided to change tactics and took a decision that would forever stain Britain's reputation for fair play and decency. The British military began a scorched-earth policy, driving women and children off the land and burning down their homes, poisoning wells and destroying crops and slaughtering livestock. Then Commander-in-Chief Horatio Kitchener decided in December 1900 to 'concentrate' Boer and native African families in camps to stop them supplying the guerrillas. It would also weaken the will of husbands, sons, brothers and fathers to keep fighting. So women and children were pushed into cattle trucks and taken away.

Kitchener's decision added a new phrase to the English lexicon: the concentration camp. It was an administrative, managerial, manpower-sapping nightmare for the British soldiers on the ground. It was, as the coming man in Westminster David Lloyd George said, 'a war not against men, but against women and children'.[15]

Yet it would lead to the end of the conflict when public support for the war evaporated, thanks, largely, to the work of just one woman that the 'female-friendly' *Daily Mail* treated like a traitor. Emily Hobhouse, a vicar's daughter from Cornwall, was the first to highlight what would result in the deaths of almost 28,000 Boer women and children. Through disease, exposure and starvation, half the entire Boer population of children perished.

Hobhouse returned to England in the summer of 1901 and her report put the Government on the defensive, and galvanized the Stop the War campaign. The *Daily Mail* thought she was a troublemaker who was 'not impartial, has no balance in her judgements and does not know anything of war or its history'.[16] But a 'ladies commission' – because it was all female – set up by the Government to look into the conditions in the camps largely confirmed everything Hobhouse had reported, and when the running of the camps was taken away from the military and put under civilian control conditions rapidly improved.

Sunny Harmsworth, however, seemed to see the war rather like an entertaining drama played out in the pages of his newspaper almost like a serial story. In a story headlined 'Pandering to Sentiment' in the *Mail* in July 1901, the paper attacked the creation of the Ladies' Commission, quoting doctors who said the mortality in the camps was actually lower than the Boers had suffered when they'd lived in their own homesteads, and he implied that Boer mothers were simply neglecting their children.[17]

It was a photograph of a dying child in one of the camps, an emaciated little girl named Lizzie Vanzyle, that proved to be the tipping point in Hobhouse's campaign when she showed it to people who attended her 'drawing-room meetings' opposing the war. Yet the *Mail*'s stance didn't change. Sunny Harmsworth was always one for staying the course – he was a man absolutely sure of himself even when he was surely wrong. To the *Daily Mail*, the tent cities on the scorched South African plains sounded almost like holiday camps.

'The unscrupulous nature of pro-Boer methods is illustrated by the facts with regard to a Boer child named Lizzie Vanzyle which appear in our columns today,' the paper said in January 1902, in a voice that may well be familiar to *Mail* readers today.

> A photograph was taken of this child upon her admis-
> sion to hospital to show the condition to which she had
> been reduced by the criminal neglect of her mother. The
> mother, it seems, left her seven children to look after
> themselves . . . The woman had food in plenty in her tent;
> she had only to apply to the medical officers to obtain
> every delicacy that generosity could supply. Yet she did
> absolutely nothing. It will scarcely be believed that this
> case has been paraded by the pro-Boers as an instance in
> which Boer children were starved to death of the delib-
> erate inhumanity of our army. Miss Hobhouse, whose
> peregrinations in South Africa have tended to blacken

the reputation of this country, has used this photograph
at her drawing-room meetings, with telling effect upon
those who were not in a position to expose her methods.
Miss Hobhouse and her pro-Boer friends may explain this
as they please, they cannot remove the impression that
they were willing to make use of any weapon that could
be turned against their country.[18]

Nevertheless, by now, the British Government wanted out of the
war and an honourable peace for the Boers was a political necessity.
A treaty was signed, leaving the Boers effectively in control of their
republics and providing financial relief. The war had taken three
years, involved almost 450,000 British and Empire troops, 22,000
of whom died (16,000 from disease). And all for no result. It did
immense damage to Britain's reputation abroad, and made her look
weak and far from invincible. It was, arguably, the tipping point that
sent the British Empire into its steep decline.

However, the Boer War had been good for Sunny's now
five-year-old *Daily Mail*. The paper had regularly broken through
the million circulation barrier but, perhaps more importantly, it had
cemented its reputation as a formidable newspaper. It had become a
presence on the newsstand.

The Boer War had been a prelude of what was to come in the
Great War a little over a decade later, as the *Mail* prophesied on its
leader page at the turn of the century: 'It is not for South Africa that
we go on. Great powers look with greedy eyes on our prosperous
dominions, our world-wide dependencies. A sudden change of a
Continental Ministry, or the death of a great ruler, may force on us
a conflict compared with which our present campaign would appear
trifling . . . This is our hour of preparation; tomorrow may be the
day of world-wide conflict.'[19]

It was the clerks that had driven up the circulation, not so much
their wives. The *Mail* was far more surefooted with war than with
women, and that would remain the case until the tabloid-era of the
1970s. Women in the *Daily Mail*'s world (to be fair, in Victorian

society at large) were not quite members of the human race. Inside the *Daily Mail* office, the women's editor, Mary Howarth, was – in the beginning – the only female member of the editorial staff. She'd been with Sunny since his *Answers* days, writing serial stories, Sunny pacing up and down and insisting her villains had sinister names and her heroes noble ones. Her 'Women's Realm' section in the *Mail* was daintiness in folded paper form. Even the font for the title would be wrapped with sketches of birds or cherubs or flowers. It was tame stuff, but at least the *Mail* was aware the wives of shopkeepers, clerks and civil servants actually existed. Most papers ignored them completely.

While the *Mail* viewed women as simple, sexless creatures, the reality was a lot more earthy for Sunny Harmsworth. He had sexual relations with countless women other than his wife and would sire at least four illegitimate children. His secretary George Sutton had been making discreet payments for years to help raise Alfred Benjamin, his illegitimate son from his teenage liaison with the nurse, Louisa. He even paid for him to live in Hampstead with a private tutor. It was top secret, as scandal was a real risk. Sunny would occasionally turn up at the door in dark glasses and walk the streets at night with the tutor, whispering plans for the boy's future.

Votes for women, in particular, was to prove tricky ground for the 'female-friendly' paper to negotiate. A month after the paper's birth, a Mailman was sent to a women's suffrage meeting at Westminster Town Hall, where 'The Hall was fairly filled, and the proceedings began with quite unfeminine punctuality.'[20] It was a calm and quiet affair. Ten years later, things got a lot louder. In October 1906, the paper carried a story headlined 'Suffragettes in Parliament – Riotous Scenes in the Lobby – Police Carry Out Shrieking Women'. It was a report of a protest led by campaigner Emmeline Pankhurst and her daughters. The word 'suffragette' – from the word 'suffrage' – had, incidentally, been coined by Mailman Charlie Hands in January of that year as a mocking term to distinguish the new militant wing of the votes-for-women movement, as distinct from the 'constitutional' suffragists. The Pankhursts defiantly accepted the label as their own.[21]

As the Mailman on the spot reported: 'Ordinary visitors to the central lobby of the House of Commons yesterday afternoon were persuaded that they had been suddenly transported to the parrot house at the "Zoo".' 'Shrieks, inarticulate calls, and a shrill phrase monotonously repeated caused the illusion. It was the Suffragettes engaged in their task of persuading the Legislature that they are fit to be given the franchise.'[22]

It must have made a welcome break from the usual plodding Parliamentary proceedings for the *Mail*'s lobby correspondent, who wrote: 'That they knew they were doing something seriously against order could be seen from their pale and rather frightened faces.' Twenty or so protestors were bodily removed, ten were arrested.

> One of the women, as the burly, handsome inspector picked her off the seat, threw her arms round his neck and clung to him with seeming fondness. 'It is not every day she gets a chance of hugging a good-looking police inspector,' said a Cabinet Minister to the *Daily Mail* representative as they witnessed the scene together. Spectators after the first astonished moment were convulsed with laughter. The women themselves made it very hard for the police to remove them. They struggled violently and threw themselves about so that the policemen had to clutch their dresses as if they were so many drabs being put out of a public-house. One of the Suffragettes passing one of the mildest-mannered journalists in the House shook her fist fiercely in his face and said: 'You coward!' It was a favourite phrase. 'Call yourself a man and treat women like this!' remarked one grey-ringleted old lady to the *Daily Mail* representative.

In February 1907, Lady Charlotte from the *Mail*'s women's pages wrote a feature under the headline 'When Women Vote – What Will Happen?' that caused quite a stir among *Mail* readers, who bombarded the paper with letters. The piece was illustrated with a drawing of an indecisive lady sitting with her head spinning back and forth between two politicians. 'Nothing, I do truly believe, very terrible will happen when we obtain the vote . . . Why are men so jealous of their exclusive position as voters? Why should they strive to keep us from the polling booths almost at the point of a bayonet?'[23]

The paper was filled with letters for days after. Many were, of course, from women who had no desire to be given the vote. Readers also mused about what would happen if females were indeed enfranchised – would war be abolished, would divorce courts close and would men be left to care for babies? Alfred C. Harmsworth himself, in 1912, made it clear that his papers were not in favour of women's suffrage in a letter to his friend Lord Curzon. 'I am one of those people who believe that the whole suffrage movement is a bluff', adding he had 'strong reasons . . . for believing that there are very few people who are sincerely anxious about the securing of suffrage for women. If it were not for the support of one or two wealthy women of my acquaintance we should hear very little of the matter.'[24]

It would not be until after the Great War that women were given the right to vote, but women readers were surely a conundrum for Sunny Harmsworth; if the *Daily Mail* had truly captured the female market, he wouldn't have created a newspaper written exclusively by and for women in 1903. The *Daily Mirror* was a paper for women who were passionate about making their husband's dinner and frilly bonnets. It bombed.

'There was consternation at Carmelite House,' said Sunny's brother Cecil. 'Alfred had for once completely misinterpreted the popular mind.'[25] The *Mirror* was only saved when its all-female staff were fired and it was turned into a picture paper – a process its new editor, Hamilton Fyfe, said was 'like drowning kittens'. Its editor, Mary Howarth, the *Mail*'s women's page editor whom Alfred liked to take on fast drives in his cars, was spared. Photographs in the *Mirror* were crude at first but it stabilized and its circulation began to rise. Sunny had, said Fyfe, 'dramatically disappointed all who believed that his career was broken. He had snatched victory from the jaws of defeat.'[26]

Harmsworth himself even turned defeat into a boast: 'How I dropped £100,000 on the *Mirror*,' he wrote in the *Mail*, confessing to 'flat, rank and unmitigated failure.'[27] But Sunny never loved his *Mirror* like he loved his *Mail* – perhaps because it was a reminder of when his touch had failed him. He later sold it to Bunny. A generation later, under their nephew Cecil Harmsworth King, the paper would dominate the working-class market in the same way the *Mail* had captivated the middle classes.

3

Mr Leonard Brown

By the turn of the century Sunny Harmsworth was a millionaire many times over in today's money,[1] yet he was still only plain old Mr Harmsworth . . . and it rankled.

Even his *Tit-Bits* rival had become Sir George Newnes in 1895, and Sunny's publishing successes had long since eclipsed those of Newnes. Never shy, Sunny pestered government members for years arguing that Newnes's elevation somehow gave his rival a competitive edge. And in July 1904, sure enough, Harmsworth was made a baronet; the new King had decided to apply the golden grease that kept the wheels of the Establishment rubbing smoothly against each other and raised up the self-made men from the end of his mother's reign. But Sunny was Sir Alfred C. Harmsworth, Bart, for less than eighteen months; soon after, he was made a baron at the age of forty, the lowest rank in the peerage with a seat in the House of Lords, a body with real political power at the time – Lord Salisbury had even governed as Prime Minister from the Lords. Incidentally, Sunny had actually tried to enter Parliament through the other door the year before the *Mail*'s birth when he had failed to get elected as Tory MP for Portsmouth; his attempt had even delayed the paper's birth for six months or so. The experience, he once told a private secretary, was 'like wading through a sea of filth';[2] simply being handed a seat must have felt so much cleaner.

Alfred struggled with what name to give this new lord. Elevated men tend to be lords of an actual physical place on a map and he wanted a link to the seaside he adored. Baron Elmwood was rejected as it was the wood from which coffins were made. Baron Broadstairs was suggested, which would have made Alfred lord of the seaside, but that didn't appeal either. So he invented a place: Northcliffe – after the north cliff near Elmwood where he would take long strolls with his dogs. He could now even sign himself with a Napoleonic 'N'.

Sunny Harmsworth – Lord Northcliffe, the brand new peer of the realm – ruled over his folded-paper empire from Room One, a massive office on the first floor of his imperial headquarters in Carmelite House, a brand-new purpose-built building on the Embankment that held most of his printed organs. 'Big rooms,' Sunny the Press Lord liked to say, 'big ideas.'[3]

Room One reflected his lack of coherent taste: it was a boudoir with a mismatch of furniture from across the empire planted in luscious thick carpet. A bust of Napoleon stared in from a window-sill as Sunny, Lord Northcliffe, sat behind a leather-lined barge of a desk with his back to the window, facing leather-bound volumes of his publications. Editors and executives would file in and find him reclining in an armchair or lying down on a dark green couch with his back to the light.

Sunny could be a sweet and charming, kindly boss and promoter of talent who would remember an employee's birthday and send around flowers to a sick reporter. But he was a hard taskmaster and when he became angry, his lip would draw back on his lower teeth as if about to deliver a bite and his bland, accent-free voice would drop to a whisper. The *Mail* had a reputation as a tough, brutal place to work; it was relatively easy to get a job there but damn hard to keep it.

Mostly, though, Northcliffe simply wasn't in Room One. He wasn't even in London. He was away travelling or down at Elmwood. His family and senior employees would dutifully stay with him there and watch the beam from the North Foreland lighthouse scan across the ceiling of the guest rooms before it spun out over the north cliff and away from England's shores. The sabre of light would then cut across the German Ocean, the name of the North Sea on some older maps, and return again to Elmwood; reporting all was well – for now.

Northcliffe constantly worried for the future of the British Empire and, ever since his first edition of *Answers*, he'd nursed a dislike of those Germans. Sunny Harmsworth was a man pursued by personal demons but never self-doubt; he had felt the conditions for the coming war building like a human barometer. He visited Germany in 1902, arriving in the fatherland by train from Strasbourg to Stuttgart, and told a friend he thought the country 'new, masterful, alive, brutal, and horribly nouveau riche . . . I shall never forget the first sight of Germany,' he wrote in his diary, 'as we approached it from the other side of the Vosges mountains.'[4]

'I have German relatives,' he wrote to a colleague in 1908. 'I know them, they will bide their time, but Der Tag will come. Remember what I say.' Harmsworth liked to think he was an expert on Germany partly because of these relatives; two of his mother's sisters were married to Germans and had emigrated there. One of the men told him: 'We are a nation of land crabs. If you advance, we retreat. If you retreat, we advance.' Harmsworth claimed that even the Kaiser himself had tried more than once to get in 'personal touch', but 'I prefer to keep away from him.'[5]

Harmsworth was fascinated by Germany. Many people were; its strict discipline and militaristic culture – its cleanliness, its efficiency – were both appalling and appealing. The *Daily Mail* was not the only newspaper keeping tabs on the rise of Germany but its tone stood out; whereas other papers worried, the *Mail* raged. From the beginning, for instance, the *Mail* had been formulating its argument for compulsory military service to match that of the Germans, and began calling for it openly from 1904. Many liberals of the day accused Harmsworth of doing more, through his newspapers, to create the conditions for war than any other man. He was regularly called a warmonger and even an 'enemy of the human race'. But to his friends and his supporters – maybe even his readers – he was up there in the crow's nest of the flagship *Daily Mail* pointing his telescope at the horizon. And he had visions of the British fleet – so glorious under Nelson only a hundred years before – finally being defeated out there in those cold waters near his seaside home.

So in early 1909 his paper harried the Government to build more Dreadnoughts, a symbol of national power and at the core of the escalating arms race with Germany.[6] The Royal Navy's first ship of this brand-new class, HMS *Dreadnought*, was the fastest, deadliest battleship in the world when she entered service in 1906. The heavily armed, steel-armoured sea monster made all other warships look like hapless wooden tugs in her wake. In 1908 the Liberal Government was trying to decide how many Dreadnoughts to lay down, four, six, or eight – 'We Want Eight, We Won't Wait' was a popular slogan at the time for those who wanted more of these vessels. Sunny had no doubt – he drew up a bill to sit outside newsagents and newsstands selling his *Daily Mail* which had just one numeral on it: 8.

Sunny was, of course, heavily armed himself. He owned the *Evening News*, the *Daily Mail*, the *Daily Mirror*, the *Observer* and the *Weekly Dispatch* as well as dozens of magazines. Then, in 1908, he bought the rustiest old cannon of them all: *The Times*, a newspaper imbued with the deep, resonating voice of British authority, founded in 1785 by John Walter as the *Daily Universal Register*. The Monks of Blackfriars, as Northcliffe called the *Times* staff, felt themselves to be of a higher calling than mere mortal journalists. But the paper then, as now, could never pay its own way for long without a generous proprietor covering the bills with the cash skimmed off more profitable titles. And the Monks of Blackfriars never did warm to their new abbot. Its acquisition was, arguably, Sunny's biggest mistake, draining his already fickle energies and taking his hands away from the tiller of his beloved *Daily Mail*. Even his mother thought it a bad idea, telling him when he dashed in to tell her about his new toy: 'I'm sorry, Alfred. You have lost your horizon.'[7]

At the *Mail*'s launch in 1896, to the man on the Clapham omnibus the British and the Germans were family not foes – Germany's Kaiser was Queen Victoria's grandson. The Kaiser himself said that one of the most significant events of that year was the birth of the *Daily Mail*. And George Steevens, the *Mail*'s biggest gun in those first years, was aimed squarely at the German leader when he travelled to

Germany to write a series titled 'Under the Iron Heel' and watched the Kaiser on parade.[8]

> He looked like a man without joy, without love, without
> pity, without hope. He looked like a man who never
> laughed, like a man who could never sleep. A man might
> wear such a face who felt himself turning slowly into
> ice . . . He may boast, but his boasts are no way empty
> ones. As near as any man can be absolute, he is absolute
> lord over fifty million souls.

The series concluded with 'Hostility to England is the mission of young Germany . . . for the next ten years, fix your eyes very hard on Germany.' Steevens hadn't been far wrong in 1897; it only took a few extra years for war to come.

By 1914 Sunny Harmsworth, the handsome Hampstead schoolboy with a love of ink and paper, had truly morphed into Lord Northcliffe – a man with a loud voice heard by millions of people every day through his newspapers and periodicals. And Northcliffe used this voice to warn his country of impending danger. He was ready for war.

A Mailman named Lovat Fraser was Sunny's big pen now. Fraser was a living, breathing 'John Bull' character, a caricature of an Englishman similar to America's 'Uncle Sam'. Rotund, with a thick black moustache, he peered out at the world through round glasses wondering what the hell was going on. Northcliffe thought him 'the brightest exponent of English journalism in the British Empire'.[9] They were bound to get on, as their views were in perfect harmony. Fraser warned from the start that Britain would soon have to face her enemies. 'Great Powers are drifting towards a collision like ships whose anchoring cables have parted in a tideway,' he wrote at the end of 1912. Apathetic Britain faced her greatest threat since Napoleon. The Triple Entente between Britain, France and Russia would lead to war with the opposing Triple Alliance bloc of Germany, Austria–Hungary and Italy, he argued, over an issue that was not even a

British problem; these blood pacts would have to be honoured. And he was, of course, right. 'The real answer rests, or ought to rest, with the man in the train. Does he want to join in Armageddon? It is time that he began to think about it for his answer may soon be sought.'[10]

Fraser had a vision that foretold of a conflict in which the obliteration of cities and slaughter of innocent civilians became the object – terror the goal; over and above the destruction of mere armies. His story 'A Dream of War in the Air – A True Record' appeared in June 1914, six weeks before war was declared.

> 'Aerial warfare,' I thought, 'means the end of our civilisa-
> tion . . . Victory must be won through terror. Why smash
> an army or a fleet when they can smash a capital. No laws
> can overcome the temptation, and humane constraints
> will not do it, for war is bound essentially to be inhuman.
> They will smash and smash each other's cities until our
> civilisation is smashed too.'[11]

Yet the news of the assassination of Archduke Ferdinand crossed the *Daily Mail*'s deck with no impact. The archduke was just one man, and not even a very popular man among his own people at that. Few Mailmen, the *Mail*'s news editor Tom Clarke wrote later, spotted it as the spark that ignited a trail of gunpowder that would explode into the Great War a few weeks later.[12] 'Great Britain at midnight declared war upon Germany,' said the *Mail* on Wednesday, 5 August 1914.

> Thus in the short space of three days Germany has
> attacked or driven into war no fewer than four Powers,
> three of them of the first class. She declared war upon
> Russia on Saturday evening, upon France on Monday
> night, upon Belgium yesterday afternoon, and last
> night her invasion of Belgium compelled the British
> Government to take action. Nothing like this has ever
> been seen since Napoleon's time. But not even Napoleon
> quarrelled with his neighbours at such a mad rate.[13]

The *Daily Mail* came of age; the paper had only just turned eighteen when the war with Germany arrived, and soon Earl Kitchener, his moustachioed face and finger pointing out from Army recruitment posters, was firmly in the *Mail*'s cross-hairs. There was a shortage of high explosive shells at the front and the *Mail* said it was simply the Secretary of State for War's fault. The paper accused Kitchener of still fighting the Boer War (and it wasn't an unfair accusation, as he was secretly sceptical, for instance, of a new armoured vehicle called 'the tank' which was being developed away from his deadening hands by Winston Churchill's Admiralty). Northcliffe penned the attack himself in May 1915, under the headline 'The Tragedy of the Shells – Lord Kitchener's Grave Error'. Fiery and strident, he wrote that the country was now facing the threat of actual foreign feet marching upon British soil for the first time since the Norman Conquest of 1066.

> The admitted fact is that Kitchener ordered the wrong
> kind of shell – the same kind of shell which he used
> largely against the Boers in 1900. He persisted in sending
> shrapnel – a useless weapon in trench warfare. He was
> warned repeatedly that the kind of shell required was a
> violently explosive bomb which would dynamite its way
> through the German trenches and entanglements and
> enable our brave men to advance in safety. The kind of
> shell our poor soldiers have had has caused the death of
> thousands of them.[14]

Britain also required more fighting men and the *Daily Mail* had published an advertisement the day before, with Kitchener urging married men of forty to enlist, but Northcliffe vowed not to publish the ad again, as he sought the compulsory conscription of all able-bodied men, not husbands and fathers.

> We invite him [Kitchener] on Sunday to take a stroll
> down Oxford Street to the City and return by the
> Strand. He will meet some thousands of capable young

'slackers' who are staying at home, and, as one of our
correspondents said yesterday, 'stealing the businesses of
married men who have gone to the front'.

There was outrage at the *Daily Mail*'s sedition, and 3,000 members
of the Stock Exchange assembled after lunch to give three cheers for
Kitchener and burn a copy of the paper. Police guarded Carmelite
House in case Northcliffe was attacked and circulation even fell,
briefly, by 100,000.

Northcliffe caused more trouble a few months later with the help
of a young reporter called Keith Murdoch, who had been sent to
Turkey from London by an agency that covered the war for newspapers back in his native Australia, to investigate if the post was
getting through to the men. Murdoch would return to London with
an explosive letter of his own. Winston Churchill's plan to bring the
war to a swift end by opening a new front against Germany's allies
the Turks in the Dardanelles had turned into a bloody catastrophe at
a place called Gallipoli. The only solution was a massive evacuation,
but military censors would not let this unpalatable truth out and a
letter Murdoch was carrying back to London from a *Daily Telegraph*
correspondent addressed to the Prime Minister, Herbert Asquith,
was confiscated by a British officer. So Murdoch sent a letter of his
own to the Australian Prime Minister, Andrew Fisher, as fighting
men from Australia and New Zealand – ANZACS – had, after all,
been slaughtered in their thousands.

The offices of the press agency Murdoch worked for were in the
Times building and Northcliffe heard of the letter through the paper's
editor. 'I should not be able to rest until the true story of this lament-
able adventure was so well known as to force immediate steps to be
taken to remedy the state of affairs,' Northcliffe told Murdoch. 'The
matter has haunted me ever since I learned about it.'[15]

Murdoch's letter was published as a secret state paper and the
troops were evacuated and, as an aside that still resonates a century
later, Northcliffe became Keith Murdoch's benefactor. Murdoch –
nicknamed 'Lord Southcliffe' – was one of the few men who could

stroll into Northcliffe's office without knocking. Keith Murdoch's son, of course, is Rupert Murdoch, a boy of intergalactic ambition who'd put newspapers on shelves, films on cinema screens and satellites into space to beam down football matches and twenty-four-hour news.

The *Mail* continued to harry and hassle the Government but newsprint rationing meant his newspapers were shrinking in size. 'It will mean going back to the cult of brevity which we started twenty years ago,' he said in an internal message to *Daily Mail* staff, adding later, 'What with the price of paper and the calling up of married men, it looks as if we shall have nothing to print, and no one to print it.'[16] His *Daily Mail* also asked its readers to report suspected draft dodgers to the authorities. But Lord Northcliffe wasn't about to be accused of being a slacker – he made frequent trips to the Western Front himself. In February 1916 he headed for the French town of Verdun, which had become the focal point for the German attack, and boarded a small boat to cross the Channel with *Times* chief foreign correspondent and its future editor Wickham Steed. 'I had never travelled with Northcliffe before, and his cheerfulness and patience under discomfort won my admiration and that of our companions,' wrote Steed in his autobiography. 'There were but three berths left. He insisted on tossing for them, and, having lost the toss, curled himself up in a macintosh on a seat.' It was a struggle to reach Verdun; they headed in the direction of the mortar fire in a taxi that had to frequently be cooled down with snow and then 'thumbed a lift' the last part of the way to General Pétain's headquarters in a French military truck. When Northcliffe climbed up into the cab, typical of Sunny Harmsworth, he recognized the driver as a garage owner he'd met during happier times in Biarritz.[17]

'Though not an exceptionally strong man,' wrote Steed, 'he had borne exceptional strain and fatigue, with little sleep and less food from the Thursday afternoon until 2.30 a.m. on Sunday, his mind constantly on the alert and his pencil continually jotting down impressions in his notebook.' Steed was fascinated by the man, whose mind, he said, 'worked curiously' – they both saw exactly the same things but whereas Steed would see them in a mundane way, Northcliffe naturally saw and recorded them 'in a form which the public would understand . . . which might be called the public eye in miniature'.

Northcliffe wrote a 5,000-word piece, with the help of Steed, but collapsed before he could finish it. Steed finished it for him. It appeared in the *Mail* under the puff 'Lord Northcliffe on the Battlefield of Verdun' on 6 March and was syndicated to newspapers around the world. 'That the sufferings of the wounded lying out through the long nights of icy wind in No-man's Land between the lines would be great probably did not disturb the [German] Crown Prince,' he wrote. 'Yet it is a gruesome fact in the history of the war that the French, peering through the moonlight at what they thought to be stealthily crawling Germans, found them to be wounded men frozen to death.'[18]

These trips were not, however, without their moments of comedy: a visit to British HQ was a reminder that the ennobled Sunny Harmsworth, at fifty-one, was no longer the 'Adonis of Hampstead' when he was taken to see 'the newest form of arm', the tank. 'Northcliffe tried to enter one of them through the manhole on the top,' wrote Steed, 'but as his girth was some inches larger than the hole, he stuck midway and had to be hauled down to the inside by the feet while I sat on his shoulders above. Getting him out again was an even harder matter.'[19]

On his return from the front, his family were concerned for his state of mind. Lady Northcliffe was moved to write to the ever-loyal George Sutton, who was now running the Amalgamated Press – the new name for Sunny's massive magazine empire. 'The Chief strikes me as being far from what he should be,' she told him, 'much too excitable and beginning his old habit of abusing his friends at his own table if they venture to disagree with him. It is most painful – and he looks puffy and generally wrong and is not very wise about his diet.' And after he abused the *Daily Mail* editor Thomas Marlowe in an editorial conference in front of his senior editors, the other Mailmen dispersed muttering, 'Something's wrong with the Chief.'

Yet outside the office, some were pushing him on towards real political power. The Bishop of Birmingham wrote that he hoped that 'before long we may see you directly responsible for the policy of this country'. Even H. G. Wells, weirdly, seemed to suggest in a letter that Sunny should become some kind of dictator.[20]

Around this time, the *Daily Mail*'s news editor, Tom Clarke, had a friendly face-to-face relationship with his proprietor that few mere heads of an editorial department today enjoy, and it showed just how hands-on Northcliffe still was at the *Mail* after twenty years and despite owning countless other organs – including Britain's most respected newspaper, *The Times*. Clarke would frequently be summoned to Northcliffe's house in St James's Place, where he'd discuss attacks on what he saw as the ineffective war Government of Herbert Asquith. As he entered the room on 2 December 1916, Northcliffe looked over his spectacles at Clarke 'like a somewhat benevolent mandarin'.

'I thought you were dead,' Northcliffe told Clarke.

'Dead?' Clarke replied.

'Killed. I thought there were no young men left.'

They then discussed the next day's leader page and Northcliffe ordered that the word Government be put in quotes and a contents bill that screamed 'Asquith a National Danger'. Northcliffe then added: 'That will shake them up. It will make things lively for you tomorrow. The police will be after you all.'[21]

The rival *Daily News* responded with an attack of its own on 'the colossal vanity of this neurotic child Northcliffe . . . If the present Government falls, it will fall because Lord Northcliffe decreed that it should fall, and the Government that takes its place, no matter who compose it, will enter on its task as the tributary of Lord Northcliffe.' The Asquith Government, of course, fell a week later and David Lloyd George – Northcliffe's favoured man, whom he called 'the little wizard from Wales'[22] – became Prime Minister. Lloyd George had already, with the support of Northcliffe's papers, taken over from the hated Kitchener at the War Office after Kitchener's ship was torpedoed as he made his way to Russia in June that year.

Sunny had stormed into his mother's drawing room at a family event and declared, 'The British Empire has had the greatest stroke of luck in its history – Kitchener is dead, drowned at sea!'[23]

'Fashioning the New England' was a long portrait around a big photograph of the new premier 'By Lord Northcliffe' for his *Weekly Dispatch*. 'He is constantly referred to as "the little Welshman", but he is not at all little. You probably have his portrait before you as you read these lines. The head is not that of a little man, mentally or physically. It is the head of a man with the sparkle of genius, combined with Celtic energy and intense industry.'[24] Sunny Harmsworth, still measuring a man by the size of his skull. But the alliance between Prime Minister and newspaper proprietor wouldn't hold.

On the other side of the North Sea, the German high command were taking the *Daily Mail* seriously – even, perhaps, personally.

In 1916, an undercover Mailman managed to sneak into a banquet with the Kaiser at the German headquarters in the Balkans, and the paper even printed the menu to prove their man had, for sure, been there. The Mailman found the Kaiser 'a tired and broken man. The hair is white, though the moustache is still suspiciously dark.'

> . . . had I been recognised by one of the secret service officers who are around the Kaiser, or by any other person who had happened to see me before (for this was not my first journey to the Near East), there would have been a short and simple ceremony against the wall of the town hall in which I should have played the principal part . . . Lord Northcliffe and *The Daily Mail* are as much disliked by the Germans in Germany as by the pro-Germans in England.[25]

The *Mail*'s Berlin Correspondent reported that the establishment German newspaper *Vossische Zeitung* credited the part Lord Northcliffe and 'his powerful press' had played in Britain's war efforts, especially during the Battle of the Somme.[26] German archives containing notes of conversations between German officers and hundreds of captured British soldiers revealed that some were irritated during the latter stages of the battle by 'Letters from the Front' from serving soldiers published regularly in the *Daily Mail*. At the end of 1916 when, as one captured soldier put it, 'the so called walk over has turned into a steeplechase with an infinite number of obstacles', many soldiers had had enough and some were even glad to have been captured as the battle slithered on through the mud and rotting corpses towards winter. 'Every single man expresses his disgust at the unconscionable machinations of the British press and the lies that it constantly publishes in the guise of "news",' wrote one German intelligence officer in his report at the end of 1916, after interrogating British prisoners. 'And in particular the so-called "Letters from the Front" that appear in the *Daily Mail* which are evidently written by someone who has never set foot in France.'[27]

Yet, still – three months after the Somme slaughter ended in a bloody draw – it must have seemed an odd mission for the commander of the German destroyer as he aimed his guns at a specific little scratch of Kent countryside, the beam of the North Foreland lighthouse gently scanning the black night over the North Sea before returning to cross the north cliff. The patch of coastline near Broadstairs was of zero military significance; it wasn't fortified nor were its waters well patrolled. It was just a strip of crusty shore of an island with 12,000 miles of crusty shore. Silencing the press baron must have been the mission, and shells began to burst around Elmwood on 26 February 1917. 'Incidentally, the paper was nearly deprived of its chief Proprietor last night, a source of mingled feelings among the staff,' Northcliffe wrote in his daily staff communique.

> At 11.30 my house was lit up by 20 star shells from the
> sea, so that the place was illuminated as if by lightning.
> Shrapnel burst all over the place, some of it hitting the
> Library in which these notes are prepared every day, and
> killing a poor woman and baby within 50 yards of my

home and badly wounding two others. The bombardment lasted from 6 to 10 minutes according to various
estimates, and was the result of a Destroyer raid. The
Authorities have no doubt that my house was aimed at
and the shooting was by no means bad. I understand that
the Destroyer was three miles out.[28]

During the bombardment, Northcliffe had refused to get out of
bed, telling his secretary, 'If we are to die, we will die in our beds.'[29]
Northcliffe would later frequently be seen peering out from a gap in
the fence at Elmwood and down to the North Sea. His refuge must
never have felt quite the same again.

The *Daily Mail*'s theme from the very start of the war was, in
effect, that Germany be annihilated, with the charge being led by
Northcliffe himself and Lovat Fraser. But another *Mail* contributor,
H. G. Wells, disagreed.

Why, then, does this waste and killing go on? Why is not
the Peace Conference sitting now? Manifestly because
a small minority of people in positions of peculiar
advantage, in positions of trust and authority, prevent
or delay its assembling . . . I ask Mr. Lovat Fraser if it
is not his intention, and I ask your readers if it is not
their intention, to leave the German people chastened,
perhaps, but alive, independent, and in the possession
of economic resources. What is the alternative? Are we
out for a massacre of the entire German population? Do
we propose to end this war with all Germany in a sort of
prison cut off from all the rest of mankind? [30]

Northcliffe and Fraser wanted Germany crushed, penniless.
Seven weeks before the war ended, Fraser wrote under a headline
that had been used many times in the *Mail*, 'Why Prussia Must
Pay'.

We have nothing to discuss with either Germany or
Austria. We shall never discuss peace with them. We shall
drive their armies headlong, march into their country,
state the terms we intend to impose, and compel their
acceptance . . . Prussia must pay. She must pay to the
uttermost mark . . . The German is a bully and has all a
bully's cowardice . . . If we warned the Germans that for
every town they destroy in France the Allies will wipe
out one in Germany, if we named the towns we intended
to raze, if we advertised our intentions, if we told the
German armies exactly what we meant to do, I believe
the enemy would slink out of France – without knocking
another brick off a wall.[31]

Northcliffe and Fraser held a somewhat short-sighted view that is
probably best illustrated by the fate of the tiny British Channel Island
of Sark a few years later. Sark was Lovat Fraser's hideaway, about
which he wrote lovingly in the *Mail*, it was a place to potter around
drawing in his sketch pad, where he'd stroll over the beach and peer
through his round spectacles at the life forms that lived in the rock
pools – a fat chap with a moustache enjoying a smoke of his pipe.
'One goes there not to idle from mere laziness but to take breath,
to tranquillise the nerves, to stand aside and regain perspective, to
try and discern how far these marchings of great armies and these
cries of overwrought politicians really matter, to be alone with the
stars.'[32] Yet all Northcliffe and Fraser's talk of trampling the bloodied
Germans into the dirt only fertilized the soil in which Hitler's Nazis
would later grow. Just a couple of decades later German jackboots
landed on Sark and it was one of the few clumps of British turf the
Germans ever conquered during World War Two.

Then the war was over. The abdicated Kaiser was on the run and
the *Daily Mail* was branding itself 'The Soldiers' Paper' under
its front-page masthead. 'A Glorious End', the paper proclaimed on
12 November 1918.

> The armistice which was signed yesterday marks the end
> of the war and the complete and overwhelming triumph
> of the cause of right . . . It is the end of slaughter and
> suffering . . . The bravest and best are under the soil in
> France. The redeemed land holds its redeemers. The
> spring has gone out of our year with the loss of that
> 'swift and joyful generation' which welcomed the call
> and obeyed.[33]

Prime Minister David Lloyd George became a national hero, as he had taken charge of a government in disarray, and became the man who was credited with winning the war. His Coalition Government won the 1918 election by a landslide. Now all he had to do was win the peace, but Lloyd George felt he still had one heavily armed enemy left: Lord Northcliffe.

The pair had been friendly but never friends. Lloyd George had sent Northcliffe to the US to head the British War Mission, perhaps in the hope that sending him away would quieten his newspapers, and promoted him up the ranks of the peers to viscount. The Prime Minister also made him Director of Propaganda in enemy countries, so Northcliffe dropped millions of propaganda leaflets of all kinds over the German lines, which, as their battlefield positions weakened, may have had an impact on German morale. A German general even referred to Northcliffe as 'the most thorough-going rascal of the Entente'.[34] Yet despite this success, Northcliffe and the Prime Minister had fallen out – partly over an offer to become Air Minister. As an early enthusiast and sponsor of flight, Northcliffe understood the subject well but he publicly and petulantly declined the post (perhaps expecting greater office). What Northcliffe really wanted – expected – was a seat at the peace conference in Paris when the war ended, and he'd personally spelled out his demands to the Prime Minister. But Lloyd George left him behind.

Kennedy Jones had left the firm due to ill health in 1912 but later resurfaced as an MP. K. J. arranged a telegram in April 1919 signed by 370 MPs, urging the Prime Minister to 'present the bill in full' – the cost of the war – to the Germans. In a speech in Scotland, Northcliffe had earlier called for Prussia to pay 'town for town, village for village, ship for ship, jewel for jewel, picture for picture, dollar for dollar . . . she must pay full compensation for all she has . . . stolen, sacked and burnt'.[35] Northcliffe's hand was suspected in K. J.'s telegram too: making the news instead of waiting for it. For Sunny it seemed to be personal, it was always personal, and by now he simply couldn't stand Lloyd George: 'It's his big head on a little body I don't like.'[36]

The Prime Minister, though, had had enough of Northcliffe's haranguing and attempts to dictate government policy. He returned to Parliament saying he'd broken away from Versailles to deal with 'stones pattering on the roofs and crashing through the window and sometimes wild men screaming through the keyholes . . . I have come back to say a few things and I mean to say them.' Though the Prime Minister never mentioned Harmsworth by name – referring only to a 'reliable source' – he used an article signed by Lord Northcliffe the previous November which laid out his views. 'There were peace terms published in November as a sort of model to proceed on . . .' said the Prime Minister, and then, making a joke of the shelling of Northcliffe's home, added: 'There was no reparation for damaged houses – not even at Broadstairs.' The Commons erupted in cheers and laughter, MPs enjoying a supreme political showman taking the stage. Lloyd George primed his guns. Aimed. And shot down the press baron.

The Prime Minister's attack was puffed on the front page of the *Daily Mail* and reported verbatim inside, even down to the laughter – the editor Thomas Marlowe himself, perhaps, allowing the PM a free hand. The premier, punctuating his words like a conductor, said Northcliffe was

> Here today, jumping there tomorrow – there the next
> day. I had as soon rely on a grasshopper. [Loud laughter.]
> Still, I am prepared to make some allowances – even great
> newspaper proprietors will forgive me for saying so – but

when a man is labouring under a keen sense of disappointment, however unjustified and however ridiculous
his expectations may be – a man in those circumstances
is always apt to think the world is badly run. When a
man has deluded himself . . . that he is the only man who
can win the war, and he is waiting for the clamour of the
multitude that is going to demand his presence to direct
the destinies of peace, and there is not a whisper, not a
sound, it is rather disappointing, it is unnerving, it is
upsetting.

And then the war is won without him! There must
be something wrong! And, of course, it must be the
Government! At any rate, he is the only man to make
the peace! The only people who get near him tell him so
constantly, and so he prepares the peace terms in advance
and he waits for the call. [Loud laughter.] It does not
come . . . Under these conditions I am prepared to make
allowances, but let me say that when that kind of *diseased
vanity* is carried to the point of sowing dissension between
great allies whose unity is essential to the peace and
happiness of the world . . . then, I say, not even that kind
of disease is a justification for so black a crime against
humanity. [Loud cheers.][37]

At the key phrase 'diseased vanity', Lloyd George tapped his forehead,
the universal sign of madness. He had a point; Sunny Harmsworth
was losing his mind.

Alfred C. 'Sunny' Harmsworth, Lord Northcliffe, hadn't exactly
been the sanest of Mailmen for some time, and numerous stories
of his growing eccentricity had been leaking out for years. One
time during the war, when Northcliffe was angry with the picture
quality in the *Mail,* he ordered everybody involved in the process
– photographers, block makers, sub-editors – to stand in line, from
tallest to shortest. He then put the tallest man in charge. On another
occasion, Hannen Swaffer, the editor of his *Weekly Dispatch*, handed

him a proof with a bow – as a joke. Lord Northcliffe asked what he was doing. 'Bowing to a peer of the realm,' Swaffer replied. 'You don't know how to,' Northcliffe retorted. Northcliffe ordered one of his staff to show Swaffer how it was done. The man took the page proof and bowed. 'Lower still,' said Northcliffe. The man stooped lower. 'Kneel, darn you, kneel!' The man knelt. 'There you are,' said Northcliffe. 'I can make them do anything I like.'[38]

Some people, including his nephew Cecil Harmsworth King and the *Times* editor Wickham Steed, believed syphilis had damaged Sunny's mind. There is no hard evidence for this, though he did have a serious breakdown that left him incapacitated in 1910 which included a trip to Frankfurt – the centre of research into a 'magic bullet' cure for the disease at the time. Syphilis was a loaded, decadent word that was, therefore, useful to his enemies – it meant wicked sex driving one mad. His family insisted that a blood test for syphilis towards the end of his life was negative.

No matter, his mind was deteriorating whatever the cause. During a stop in Bangkok as a guest of the King of Siam in 1921, Northcliffe sent a secretary tumbling down the palace stairs when the man couldn't find a newspaper he'd requested. On another occasion around the same time, Northcliffe was with the editor of *The Times* standing by a window miserably watching the rain fall, frustrated and bored because he'd wanted to play golf. The wind blew a window blind cord and the acorn on the end hit the glass. He jumped.

'Somebody shot me, did you shoot me?' he asked.

On another evening, he asked another man on a balcony: 'How many moons do you see?'

'One,' the man replied. 'I thought so,' said Sunny, 'but I see two.'[39] Gossip was rife along Fleet Street about Northcliffe's state of mind, and he was aware of it. 'Someone has been saying I'm off my head,' he said to *Mail* news editor Tom Clarke. 'Not you, is it, Tom?'[40]

In the last few months of his life, he tore up his old Schemo Magnifico folder along with a pile of old photographs and flushed the pieces down the toilet. On his final foreign trip, he even began to assume the identity of a man called 'Mr Leonard Brown'.

'Mr Leonard Brown' was an ultra-wealthy thickset man who checked himself into a small room at the back of a French hotel in May 1922. He had been on a trip to Germany and was in Boulogne writing a series of personal observations of the defeated country. Northcliffe was certain that someone was trying to kill him and that he had eaten poisoned ice cream. A young telephonist at *The Times* called Douglas Reed was sent across the Channel to act as his secretary and had been told to expect an imperious man who must be obeyed, and that's what he found. Northcliffe was disorientated and disillusioned. He showed Reed a black silk purse he kept under his pillow: 'Look at this. It was left here for me, for Mr Leonard Brown, by a man who wouldn't give the porter his name. How do they know that I am here? You see the colour? It is the colour of death.'[41]

Northcliffe knew he was unravelling. He wrote to Lady Northcliffe in Lake Geneva, where she was staying with one of her lovers, Sir Robert Hudson, whom she later married – her ladyship had several lovers and her husband seemed not to care, so long as they were discreet (he even threatened to sack one member of staff who knew Lady Northcliffe had been caught in bed with a *Times* senior executive during a trip to Seville). The eminent physician Sir Frederick Treves, the doctor who 'discovered' Joseph 'The Elephant Man' Merrick, was also in Lake Geneva with her ladyship. 'You have with you the most distinguished medical man in the world. Will you kindly ask his opinion of my sanity?' wrote Northcliffe.

> I have begun to have doubts if it is too little work and
> too much money, or it is simply decay of my faculties;
> I do not know, but I think I am going mad. Please wire
> me at once to relieve my suspicions. I dreamt the other
> night that I had run off with Princess Mary and started a
> Boarding house at Blackpool, and she said to me: 'Thank
> you, we are doing very well.' That was a dream.[42]

In his hotel room, Mr Leonard Brown had become obsessed with the case of a murderer named Ronald True, who was sent to a mental hospital as a criminal lunatic instead of being sent to the gallows for killing a woman with a rolling pin. At Northcliffe's insistence, the *Mail* whipped it up into a scandal, alleging that True's family connections had saved him from the gallows.[43] Sunny's final campaign was to be about a madman.

Back in London, the *Mail* published the first of Northcliffe's proposed series of articles on Germany, a rambling piece from Flanders that included a conversation with a builder that the British Army said could never have taken place.[44] Northcliffe's secretary was a busy man: his master was like a broken machine in a Post Office sorting office, pinging off letters and telegrams in all directions.

The paper-thin walls that kept Sunny's thoughts inside his head had simply fallen away. One telegram to a manager read: 'Please give that suit away to some poor man tis very dirty.' Another, to *The Times*, suggested its manager become chief reporter and ordered its editor to stop walking down Fleet Street in a tall hat. Sunny sacked his golf professional for drunkenness, and his secretary Reed was put on notice for having lunch one day when his master needed him.

On the station platform the next day as he left for Paris, Northcliffe insulted railway officials, said God was a homosexual and claimed someone had tried to murder him with a Perrier bottle. The *Times* editor Wickham Steed arrived in Paris in the evening and found Northcliffe in bed in a darkened room at the Plaza Athenee Hotel, chewing a cigar and drinking a mixture of champagne and brandy. Steed later found Northcliffe with a devotional book his mother had given him in one hand and a pistol in the other – he'd thought the dressing gown on the door was an intruder. Steed tipped the bullets into his hand when Northcliffe went to the bathroom. Sunny shouted, groaned, pleaded and cursed until Steed left after 1 a.m. Steed returned at 5 a.m. and found Northcliffe with his barber. He handed Steed his second 'Incognito in Germany' article for the *Daily Mail* and 'found some passages in it so insane that I told him they must be suppressed. They referred to his revolver and his ability to shoot seven Germans at sight through his pocket. He flew into a rage when I suggested suppression of these passages, but immediately consented when I told him that people would think he was afraid of the Germans.'

The next morning they left by train for Lake Geneva to see Lady Northcliffe, and Sunny babbled incessantly to Steed for almost the entire ten-hour trip in a compartment with the curtains drawn. Northcliffe 'ended by telling some improper stories to Miss Rudge [a young telephonist]. After luncheon he said to me: "Did I go too far with that girl? Don't you think I am mad? Am I mad?"'

Northcliffe dictated telegrams that were to be sent from stations as they passed through, and as the train approached Bellegarde, the nearest station to Evian, Northcliffe 'had, or simulated, a choking fit, accompanied by dry retching. He screamed, shook his fist in my face, and seemed entirely beside himself,' wrote Steed. He was met at the station by his loyal chauffeur, Pine, and then ordered Pine to drive over the winding roads to Evian at top speed, Northcliffe shrieking from the back that they 'could all be killed'.[45] He was rude to the hotel manager and threatened the porter at Evian's Hotel Royal and called Sir Frederick Treves, the medical expert whose opinion he had sought, an old fool. William, his valet, put him to bed – where he abused Lady Northcliffe, who fled trembling to her room. He agreed to see a doctor after being told he was an expert in German poisons. The doctor promptly injected him with morphine to quieten him, but he continued to babble until 1 a.m. and had, Steed noted, by then been talking non-stop for twenty-four hours.

In the morning, the Press Lord managed to send a lucid telegram to his mother, the only true love of his life. Sunny had a strange relationship with his mother. His nephew, Geraldine's grandson, Cecil Harmsworth King, later wrote how Uncle Alfred's 'affection for his mother was embarrassing to her, and quite abnormal'.[46] Mrs Harmsworth had never been one to kiss and cuddle her eleven children, and viewed them as a burden, not a joy. Sunny would sleep in a room adjacent to her bedroom in the grand house her sons had bought her before going overseas, and he would immediately place a portrait of her on his bedroom table on ships and in hotel rooms. As soon as he arrived, he would write and cable her incessantly with messages of love.

These cables from Evian were fine to his mother but those around him began to panic, terrified that a mad telegram could be taken seriously or even be published. Northcliffe was, legally, still in complete control of his faculties and could do as he pleased. So his brother Sir Leicester was nominated by the other Harmsworth boys to rein him in. He went to, effectively, seize control of the publishing empire along with the ever loyal, by now also 'Sir', George Sutton.

Wickham Steed, meanwhile, decided he had to act and sent a cable of his own: 'Disregard Entirely And Unpublish. Tell Carmelite [*Mail* HQ] Disregard And Unpublish Any Messages Or Instructions, Direct Or Indirect, From Here Unless Signed Sutton Or Me. Sutton Arrives Late Tonight.'[47]

Northcliffe instinctively realized he was being blocked. When he instructed Steed to cable the *Times* manager – under Steed's name – saying 'You Are A Rascal And A Thief. I Will Have The Law On You. If You Don't Leave The Office Immediately I Will Come With The Police To Turn You Out', Steed sent a harmless telegram with the same number of words, which was just as well, as suspicious Sunny checked the number of words on the receipt.

Steed went to the station to collect Sir George Sutton and, while he was away, the local doctor at Northcliffe's side told Steed he had called in a nerve specialist from Lausanne – on the other side of Lake Geneva – who promptly wrote a certificate saying Northcliffe was out of his mind. Steed never met the specialist nor did he see the certificate, but a receipt for a Lausanne doctor did exist. The Harmsworths were adamant there was never any such declaration. When Steed saw his proprietor for the last time, he watched Northcliffe tell his wife: 'My dear, when I'm well again, I shall present my humble duty to the King and ask him to take back our titles . . . We shall be plain Mr and Mrs Harmsworth again.' Then he turned to Steed and started to abuse him 'with every kind of indecent insult'.[48] Lady Northcliffe buried her face in her hands and shouted at him to stop. Then it was her turn, her husband launching into an obscene monologue. Steed walked away.

At last Sir Leicester Harmsworth arrived and persuaded his big brother to leave Evian by insisting their mother wanted to see him.

There would be no more telegrams, no more articles, no more headlines. Male nurses manhandled Northcliffe on to a train, where he was seen standing in the corridor angrily looking out of the window, his fingertips pushed white against the glass.

Sunny Harmsworth lay heavily in his bed at his grand London home, the sound of whistling workmen sawing wood and banging nails drifting down from the rooftop above. He was, effectively, being kept captive by strong male nurses at his exclusive home near Buckingham Palace for the sake of his businesses until such time as he recovered – or died.

Ulcerative endocarditis, an infection of a weakened heart – generally a secondary condition caused by another disease (syphilis is not implausible) – was diagnosed, and his doctors prescribed the only thing they ever seemed to prescribe Sunny Harmsworth: fresh air. So a shed that could be spun around on a disc was under construction on the roof to take him closer to the summer air.

While the workmen were completing the shed, Sunny was a sad sight to his old friend Max Pemberton, who called to show his respects. 'The robust figure, the upright bearing, the buoyant manner were gone,' he wrote. 'I saw a stooping, wizened, shrunken old man and the first glance at him told me that he was doomed.'[49]

Northcliffe spent his fifty-seventh birthday on 15 July 1922 as a deluded prisoner in his own luxurious cage, but it'd be another full month of deep suffering before he passed away. He fasted some days and prayed aloud; often he just broke down and sat on the edge of his bed with his head in his hands. His mother Geraldine saw him only once upon his return to London, and her first born 'caused a scene'.[50] Mrs Harmsworth, perhaps remembering his many illnesses as a small boy when his skull seemed to grow way too fast for his little body, turned to his doctors and whispered, 'Is it his head?'

Sunny's grip on the world came and went. In a lucid moment, his thoughts turned to his Australian protégé Keith Murdoch and he managed to write to him to boast of the *Daily Mail*'s 'stupendous figure' of 1,735,000 copies sold a day.[51] Some days he was delusional. He promised one of his two male nurses £1,000 a year and a chicken farm, another he attacked with a fire poker. When his physician introduced him to another renowned doctor, Northcliffe exclaimed: 'One of George's bloody knights!' and pulled his revolver from under his pillow. It wasn't loaded; Steed had already taken the bullets.[52]

A mile and a half away, down by the River Thames, the Mailmen in Carmelite House were on edge. 'There was a feeling of anxious expectancy everywhere in the office,' wrote Tom Clarke. 'Reporters went about with glum faces. Even sub-editors, a much more phlegmatic species, looked up wonderingly at people who entered or left the room. Upstairs the compositors tapped away diligently at their linotypes; downstairs the machine hands got ready the giant presses . . . but they tugged at the coat of any editorial man who passed their way and whispered: "What's up with the Chief?"'[53]

The four telephone lines to his house had been cut to stop Northcliffe 'worrying the office'. But he somehow evaded his nurse guards, found a key, sneaked into Lady Northcliffe's private rooms and hid under a table to use her private line. He dialled the *Daily Mail*, hoping his Mailmen would come to his rescue. Mailman Oscar Pulvermacher took the call, another Mailman having handed him the phone gasping: 'The Chief wants you!'

'His voice was hardly audible,' Pulvermacher said. 'He wished me to give instructions designed to remove him from captivity, poor man.'[54]

It was Northcliffe's last call to the *Daily Mail*. The death shed was ready, a hole was cut in the ceiling and he was hoisted up on a stretcher on to the roof of Carlton Gardens. The strange construction was actually on his neighbour's roof, above a house, in a twist of fate, where Earl Kitchener had lived in the days when Sunny's *Daily Mail* had attacked him for ordering the wrong kind of shells.

The *Mail* carried daily updates on his condition and on the day he died it read: 'The patient's condition remains persistently grave.' It was *Daily Mail* issue no. 8218, and 1,800,000 copies were sold.

One of the last things he ever said was: 'Tell mother she is the only one!'[55]

Rain fell gently on the shelter's roof as Cecil and Vyvyan Harmsworth sat with their big brother when he died on the morning of 14 August 1922. The *Star* beat Sunny Harmsworth's first ever newspaper, the *Evening News*, to the story; Northcliffe would have been furious.

PART II

BUNNY & SON

4

Whose Mail Is It Anyway?

There was only ever one Viscount Northcliffe.

Sunny Harmsworth had several illegitimate children to more than one woman but his wife Molly never provided him with an heir, so his hereditary title fell with him into his grave. By then, though, there was already another peer in the Harmsworth realm – the first in a long line of Lord Rothermeres.

Bunny Harmsworth became Baron Rothermere in 1914 and was further elevated up the ranks to viscount as a reward for his stint as Air Minister – the job turned down by his elder brother – during the war. It was Bunny Harmsworth who was tasked to weld together the winged elements of the military and create the Royal Air Force. By the time his big brother died Viscount Rothermere was immensely wealthy, he had real political clout and he was a peer of the realm, no less. Yet Harold, always a harried and worried soul, had plunged into deep and sickening despair by the end of the war over the tragedy that befell his own family.

The slide towards despair began with his wife, Lilian, the beautiful friend of his sister Violet whom he'd married in the summer of 1893. Rothermere, unlike his father, Harmie, had wanted – and could well afford – a huge family. And this flesh-and-blood manifestation of his love for all big numbers had started well when his wife gave birth to their first son a year later and another two sons swiftly followed. But Harold wasn't the only one of Harmie's boys with whom Lilian was sharing her bed; she was also sleeping with the seventh and by far the most handsome of all Harmie's eight boys – sporty and fun-loving St John, the child said to be the most like Alfred 'the Adonis of Hampstead'. Yet St John – Bonch in the pet name stakes – was to become a tragic figure, and what happened to him was the first sign that the seventeen-year spell of almost perfect good fortune that the Harmsworth clan had enjoyed since Harmie's death was now over.

One morning in 1906, after leaving Lilian's bed at Bunny's country estate, Bonch leapt into his chauffeur-driven car and waved goodbye to his lover before clambering into the back for a lie down. A thick fog quickly began to gather, though, as they rattled over the road to the Harmsworth matriarch's mansion north of Hampstead and St John's chauffeur struggled to see. So he decided to follow the telegraph poles, figuring they'd guide them back to London. And the chances were that the poles did, indeed, lead directly to the city, but that didn't mean they stuck by the roadside. The chauffeur followed the poles straight off the road and into a ditch and Bonch lay under the car with four wheels spinning in the empty air – unable, at first, even to blink. It was a car with no roof and his neck was broken. He was paralysed for life. Worse though, for Bunny, his wife became St John's nurse and she was lost to him.[1] Harold would never have eleven children like his father.

Still, Bunny knew the Rothermere name was sure to be carried forth to future generations. He already had three sons. Except, again, good fortune had deserted the Harmsworth family and the Great War intervened. First to die was Bunny's second son, twenty-one-year-old Vere – the nephew said to be Uncle Northcliffe's favourite. It seems Sunny or Bunny might have actually pulled strings to try to save Lieutenant Harmsworth from his fate, as Vere had been offered a coveted and cushy posting way back from the front lines not long before a German shell blew him to pieces. He'd declined the offer and insisted on leading his men up and over the parapet.[2] Then Bunny's eldest boy, Vyvyan, met a similar fate. A captain in the Irish Guards, he was mortally wounded – his third war injury – at the Battle of Cambrai in 1917 and lay in hospital for months, dying shortly after being awarded the Military Cross.[3] He was twenty-three. Lady Rothermere, incidentally, might have embraced her role many years before as St John's nurse, but she never once visited her dying boy and she even showed up late for his memorial service.[4]

There was now only one son left to inherit the Rothermere name: Bunny's youngest child, Esmond, and there were dark whispers within the Harmsworth clan that handsome tennis-lover Esmond was, in fact, St John's boy.[5]

'I think one has to look on Rothermere as a very unhappy man,' wrote Bunny's nephew Cecil King, 'and after the death of his two elder sons he devoted himself to fighting off despair. So he plunged into money-making on a great scale. He was ambitious to be the richest man in the country, but thought – he told me – that he never got further than number three.'[6]

At the *Mail*'s launch Bunny had been given a quarter share in the paper that added to his magazine and *Evening News* holdings, and Sunny had also sold him his *Daily Mirror* for a pittance before the war. He was also a savvy investor. But Northcliffe did not bequeath Rothermere his controlling stake in the *Mail*. It wasn't even clear who Sunny Harmsworth actually wanted to take control of his businesses. He was a control freak to the very end and he left numerous confusing, contradictory and complex wills . . . including one that Lady Northcliffe had him sign on his deathbed which, of course, pretty much left her everything.[7] It fell to ever-loyal Sir George Sutton to wrestle sense into his master's affairs . . . and Viscount Rothermere was his master now.

Sunny had, of course, kept his penny-pinching younger brother well away from his favourite child from before she was even born – Bunny had actually done very little to earn that quarter share he was given at the *Mail*'s founding – fearing Harold would make her a whole lot slimmer and cheaper than her father desired. And Northcliffe apparently held this fear to the very end; on one visit to dying Alfred's rooftop shed, brother Cecil had thought that heavily sedated Sunny was unconscious until . . . he suddenly jerked to life and declared: 'Harold will ruin my paper! He will think too much of the money!'[8] Dour Harold, who had sold off his shares in the *Daily Mail* before the war 'and severed his connection with the paper in order to develop other financial interests',[9] later claimed that he had only ever wanted to buy the *Daily Mail* to please their mother. Nobody believed him.

Harold had competition, though, in the shape of *Daily Mail* editor Thomas Marlowe, who also wanted to buy the paper. Marlowe knew Bunny's input to the paper had been minimal, for he too had been there at the *Mail*'s birth, nursing her into the world through a cloud of cigarette smoke and filthy words alongside Sunny Harmsworth, Kennedy Jones and half a handful of others. Marlowe was the direct forebear of today's *Mail* editor Paul Dacre, being, as he was, the technician and daily living embodiment of exactly what the *Daily Mail* stood for, more so even than Northcliffe himself; Sunny's fickle energies had long been dissipated by his ownership of *The Times*. It was impossible to micromanage both papers and the pressure may have contributed to Northcliffe's eventual mental collapse.

Thomas Marlowe didn't have Bunny's kind of funds but he did have a wealthy backer in the shape of the Tory Party's election agent Sir Malcolm Fraser, who could well see the value of reaching all those voters in the middle for the Conservative cause. Yet Sutton wouldn't listen to Marlowe. In the weeks after Northcliffe's passing, Marlowe went to see Sir George, who was executor of Northcliffe's estate under the many wills, nine times to try to get him to name a price for the paper. 'I could never get him [Sutton] to agree anything,' recalled Marlowe. 'He said that there was a great deal to be done and that he was not ready to discuss it. The last time I spoke to him I said, "The truth is, Sutton, you don't want another offer." His answer was, "Well, that is the truth, I do not.' . . . I did not pursue the matter after that because I thought that it was not worthwhile.'[10] Indeed. On the very same day Sutton was formally appointed administrator of Northcliffe's estate, he had already arranged to sell Sunny's control to Bunny for a piffling £1,600,000 (around £70 million today). Marlowe recounted his story in court as a witness for one of Northcliffe's many mistresses, who sued Rothermere and Sutton claiming she had lost out as a beneficiary under one of the wills, after the *Mail* shares were sold for far less than their true value. Rothermere and Sutton also sold off *The Times*. Pragmatist Bunny saw a newspaper – then as now – that would rarely turn a profit. They didn't feel any sentimental attachment to *Answers* either – they shed the company that owned the magazines to cover Northcliffe's death duties.

Even without *The Times*, when Lord Rothermere combined his own holdings (including the *Daily Mirror* he'd already bought off his brother and, a little later, a near half-share in the ever-accelerating *Daily Express*) with Lord Northcliffe's organs he became the largest newspaper proprietor the world had ever seen.

Bunny wasn't born with Northcliffe's journalistic gene; he was simply the family's money man and a magnificent money man at that: by 1926 Bunny's love of sums had generated him a net worth of £26 million (almost £1.5 billion today).[11] Rothermere was far wealthier than Northcliffe had ever been. Sunny's business had required Bunny's blunt, ruthless force in order to thrive and, wrote their nephew Cecil King, Viscount Rothermere knew it: 'Harold told my mother after Northcliffe's death that of course Alfred owed everything to him, and that without his business management Northcliffe would never have been heard of.'[12] But, on the other hand, money men can be hired, and without Sunny's own particular genius and eye for the popular taste there would simply never have been the need for a Bunny Harmsworth.

Below stairs in the *Daily Mail* newsroom, Thomas Marlowe had to content himself with just being a journalist and not a proprietor, though he had been promoted to Chairman of Associated Newspapers by Northcliffe in 1918. Marlowe may have had a reputation as something of a brawler in Fleet Street bars in his early days as a hack but by the 1920s he had morphed into the deaf old Admiral of the British press; a grandiose snob of a man who'd sack a journalist if he didn't like his tie or the way he parted his hair.

The biggest fear in this post-war era for staunch old Tory editors like Marlowe was socialism and the rising Labour Party. After the war,

millions of men who'd killed for King and country now expected –
demanded – a greater say in affairs, and in January 1924 Labour had
formed a government for the first time under the son of a Scottish
farmhand called Ramsay MacDonald. His minority Government
didn't last long, however, and fresh elections were called later that
year. Marlowe would do whatever he could to ensure victory for the
Tories.

An opportunity arose six days before the general election of
October 1924, when Marlowe strode across the *Daily Mail* decks
and into his office, took off his hat and hung up his coat, then
checked his writing table for messages. On his desk lay a cannonball
that could blow Labour's election hopes out of the water. It was a
note from 'an old and trusted friend' that had been left there late
the previous evening. 'There is a document in London which you
ought to have. It shows the relations between the Bolsheviks and
British Labour leaders,' it said. Soon enough, the wily old hack had
two copies of the infamous document – later dubbed the 'Zinoviev
Letter' – from different sources. He sent for the printer and ordered
him to get the letter into type at once and pull a sufficient number of
proofs to supply all the other newspapers.[13]

Four days before the country was to decide on a new government,
most papers decided to publish the Zinoviev letter – especially after
the Foreign Office released it themselves, bounced into it by the
Daily Mail. Whereas other newspapers reported the letter, though,
Marlowe's *Mail* raged, screaming out loud that the letter showed the
country was in real danger of falling into communist hands:

> Everything is to be made ready for a great outbreak
> of the abominable 'class war,' which is civil war of the
> most savage kind . . . Meantime the British people, as
> they do not mean to have their throats cut by Zinoviev's
> mercenaries, must bestir themselves. They must see that
> these miserable Bolsheviks and their stealthy British
> accomplices are sent to the right-about or thrown out of
> the country. For the safety of the nation every sane man

and woman must vote on Wednesday, and vote for a Conservative Government which will know how to deal with treason.[14]

The Tories won by a landslide, though Labour's share of the vote actually increased and the election cemented the party's position as the main opposition, while killing off the Liberals as a credible party capable of winning a majority. Marlowe was certain it was the Zinoviev letter that had won the election for the Tories. 'The effect of the publication was, I think, unequalled in all the history of general elections,' wrote Marlowe in 1928. 'No single event that I have ever heard of produced such direct and definite reaction in the public mind.'[15]

Only the *Daily Herald* (the paper which would morph into today's soaraway *Sun*), edited by left-wing Northcliffe-era Mailman Hamilton Fyfe, suggested that the Zinoviev letter could be a fake. It *was* a fake. The Foreign Office's chief historian, seventy-five years later, proved conclusively that it was a forgery after studying secret documents and accessing the Soviet archives in Moscow. A future head of MI6, Stewart Menzies, even admitted in the secret internal files that he'd sent a copy to the *Daily Mail*.[16] Marlowe never backed down from his assertion that the letter was genuine but the facts prove he was either duped by the spooks . . . or complicit.

Whatever the truth, Marlowe's battles with the rising Left were not over and his next fight was with the men downstairs in the *Daily Mail* basement: his own printers. In May 1926, millions of workers were expected to walk out in a General Strike to support the already striking miners, and it was pretty clear where Marlowe's sympathies lay. 'A general strike is not an industrial dispute,' he ranted, under the headline 'For King and Country'. 'It is a revolutionary movement.'[17]

But Marlowe had a problem. His London compositors simply refused to make up the page and his printers wouldn't print it – a dumb decision on their part that played straight into the Government's hands; the dispute in the *Mail*'s press hall lit the blue touchpaper on the whole industrial-strength firework and the Government reacted with a statement claiming that 'overt acts have already taken place, including gross interference with the freedom of the Press. Such action involves a challenge to the constitutional rights and freedom of the nation . . . these negotiations cannot continue.'[18] The Government walked away from the table with the miners, which, it seems, is exactly what they had wanted to do all along.

Yet the *Mail* machine didn't even stop, it just paused a while. Many Mailmen abhorred the actions of the paper's Fleet Street printers, and print workers in Manchester and Paris let their presses roll anyway, refusing to support an attempt to dictate to a free press. Though many disagreed with Marlowe's words, they accepted that as editor of the *Daily Mail* he had a right to them. Incidentally, though Marlowe had invoked the King, he himself objected to striking miners being branded revolutionaries by the *Daily Mail*: 'Try living on their wages before you judge them,' George V snapped to coal mine owner Lord Durham during a trip to Newmarket Races.[19]

Again, typical of the British, there was no mass civil disorder, no march into Westminster by armed hordes – men who'd fought in the war wanted their rights and better conditions but there was little desire for the carpenters among them to construct the gallows. The unions called the strike off after nine days without gaining a single concession, and the miners went back down their pits to work longer hours – for less pay. And the *Mail*'s editorial that day went out unhindered, headlined: 'Surrender of the Revolution . . . Victory for the People'.[20]

Though Marlowe was all-powerful within the *Mail* newsroom, he did not own it; and it was inevitable that he would fall out with his proprietor sooner or later. Rothermere and Marlowe simply didn't seem to like each other, though they did have tragedy in common – Marlowe had also lost two sons. His first boy, Cambridge under-graduate John, had been killed when his car crashed into a cart.[21] His second son, Kenneth, was twice wounded in the war and then worked for the intelligence services and died, the cause going unreported, aged twenty-one. But, unlike Rothermere, Marlowe's personal life was set upon solid rock; Mrs Marlowe, she of the sandwiches, gave him two more sons and four daughters.

A rift opened between editor and proprietor in the mid-Atlantic in the summer of 1926. Predictably, it was over money: Bunny knew his dollars from his cents better than anybody, and he was furious when the *Daily Mail* attacked America over Britain's war debt. The *Mail* had branded the US 'Uncle Shylock', after Shakespeare's moneylender from *The Merchant of Venice*, and printed a cartoon of the sinister Jewish cliché of the day wielding a huge knife to slice away his pound of flesh through usury.[22] The *Mail* argued the debt was crippling Britain and, worse, the Germans would pay off their reparations long before the British had satisfied their debtor.

Rothermere castigated his editor in print, writing a rebuke in his *Sunday Pictorial* (later renamed the *Sunday Mirror*) – the only newspaper he ever founded – and then forced Marlowe to reprint it in his *Daily Mail* the next day. 'The *Daily Mail* jumped in at the deep end of the recent discussion on inter-Allied debts and splashed about, saying that American war debt collection methods resembled the methods of Shylock. I entirely disagree with this attitude. The opinions are those of the Editor and his staff. They are not mine.'[23]

Bunny commanded Marlowe to stop attacking the US 'and told him he should take a holiday, which he did'. On his return, they both apparently 'agreed that the old relations could not be re-established, and he resigned'.[24] It was a huge mistake and a typically heavy-handed use of the cosh by Bunny Harmsworth; Northcliffe had stuck with his half-deaf editor even when they almost came to blows – Marlowe was, after all, the only man who had properly held the title as *Daily Mail* editor up to then and he had been editor for twenty-seven years. Rothermere, in contrast, would go through seven in all before he died fourteen years later. In the meantime, Bunny did what he did best: he drove down costs and made room for more lovely fee-paying adverts. Profits increased and *Daily Mail* shares shot up in value. Bunny, the consummate money man, wrote an article in July 1929 in which he asked, 'Will Wall Street Swallow Europe?' and warned of the flow of capital from Europe to the US.

It was to prove prophetic, just three months before the stock market crash that triggered the Great Depression, the economic catastrophe that further fertilized the ground for war. A friend spotted Harold early one morning shortly after, strolling along the street near Lord's Cricket Ground. He waved hello. Bunny stopped to tell him how he had lost heavily ($40 million in a month, according to his nephew Cecil King) and couldn't sleep. So his friend invited him in for coffee, and found a lonely man desperate for somebody to talk to.[25]

Circulation was approaching the 2 million mark around this time, the target Sunny had long grasped for but never reached. However, this was less because it was a great product and more because there were greater numbers of people buying newspapers in general[26] from the ever-expanding middle classes and the increasingly literate working classes and, though he had no heir, two of Northcliffe's nephews would be at the forefront of the fight to grab these readers.

On any given Sunday before the Great War, a fleet of Rolls-Royces would crunch up the driveway to Granny Harmsworth's country estate and dozens of grandchildren would spill out on to the damp lawns as a platoon of nannies fussed after them with safety-pins and nappies. It was the dawn of the twentieth century, halcyon days for the Harmsworth clan; everything had gone their way. Even gorgeous Uncle St John was still standing, playing tennis while his elder brothers' wives tried not to get caught looking at his shorts.

Out there on the lawn trying not to get mud on their crisply laundered sailor suits, two of Mrs Harmsworth's grandchildren would become the pillars upon which Britain's popular press would rest. Neither was born to be so; both lost older brothers during the war. Cecil Harmsworth King – the son of Geraldine, the eldest sister, born between Alfred and Harold – and Bunny's only surviving son Esmond would be Mr *Daily Mirror* and Mr *Daily Mail*, the brash paper voice of the working classes and the fading paper voice of the middle classes.

To Esmond and the rest of this new generation of moneyed Harmsworths (and just as with Northcliffe and Rothermere's nine brothers and sisters), Sunny was the family's shining light – never Bunny. Once a year, for instance, Northcliffe would invite all these young Harmsworths for lunch (they all seemed to insist that *they* were Uncle Alfred's favourite) and Sunny would slip a crisp five-pound note under every plate. 'We enjoyed the lunch,' said Esmond, 'because he was absolutely charming to children. My uncle was a dreamer and not at all frightening. He was an extrovert. Father was shy and withdrawn and much more frightening.'[27] Northcliffe was a fascinating, playful and exciting character to his nephews, added King: 'Towards the end of his life he had persecution mania – the Germans were after him, and he showed me a secret catch which opened a door that would get him away if he was cornered (I think in his bathroom).'[28]

Out of all these Harmsworth nephews and nieces, it was the unlikely figure of Esmond who had emerged as the heir to the Harmsworth empire – pushed out of the middling ranks by the tragedy of the Great War. Esmond became the leader of this brand-new class of Harmsworths who really were born to better things. He was schooled at Eton and then commissioned into the Royal Marine Artillery, and he even served as Lloyd George's aide-de-camp at the Peace Conference after the war and would later tell stories at dinner parties of the Prime Minister's sexual peccadilloes at Versailles. Esmond was elected as the MP for Northcliffe's constituency by the Kent seaside at twenty-one, while Uncle Alfred was still above ground. He served inside the Tory fold for a decade, then quit Parliament to join the family firm in the late 1920s at Rothermere's right hand. Over the subsequent decade or so, Esmond was given ever more responsibility but never any real power.

It was a sense of duty, it seems, that required Esmond's presence within the family business rather than any real genetic disposition towards the newspaper trade, and he was soon crushed by his heavy father, who told him that he had to 'inherit all the sacrifices of those great personages your two elder brothers. They would have wished for you a great career and sometimes through my tears I see in the future an ample vindication for what they – and I – have suffered.'[29]

By 1935 Esmond had ascended to Marlowe's old title of chairman of Associated Newspapers (Marlowe had remained editor of the *Daily Mail* when Northcliffe elevated him). Bunny & Son were steering the *Mail* ship and there were fewer and fewer true hacks from Sunny Harmsworth's days left aboard. They could really have done with a 'proper' journalist like Thomas Marlowe to guide them through the coming stormy waters but he had long ago been thrown overboard by Rothermere.

Anyway, Marlowe died that year. He fell ill on a trip to Cape Town and passed away after an emergency operation aboard the *Winchester Castle* ocean liner as he made his way back with Mrs Marlowe to their little cottage on the Isle of Wight. Sir George Sutton was at Marlowe's memorial service at St Bride's, but there was no sign of Rothermere. And Marlowe's terse obituary in the *Mail* perfectly illustrates exactly what was now happening to the newspaper Marlowe had helped Sunny Harmsworth create all those years ago. It was just one column, crushed between huge adverts for meat extract and a new radio. 'Only BOVRIL can do it! Bovril prevents that sinking feeling and protects against colds, chills and influenza. It must be BOVRIL. Take it Daily!'[30]

Marlowe was buried at sea and, as the belligerent old Admiral of the Press floated gently to the bottom of the Atlantic Ocean bleeding true Tory blue ink as he went, the *Mail*'s voice sank with him. It'd take another four decades, and a journalist who was only a small boy when Marlowe died, before it found it again.

5

The Wrong Side of History

Bunny Harmsworth had a taste for ballerinas, and Russian ballet impresario Sergei Diaghilev liked to use his beautiful dancers to part super-rich men such as Lord Rothermere from their cash in order to fund his Ballets Russes dance company.

So Serge, as his friends called him, organized a supper party at London's Carlton Hotel specifically so dainty little fingers might open the viscount's wallet. Lydia Sokolova was given the task. She was an excellent choice, because Miss Sokolova spoke perfect English – which was not surprising really as she'd actually been born plain old Hilda Munnings in south London. But Cockney Hilda 'had no experience of extracting large sums of money from rich men'.

'I was seated between Diaghilev and Lord Rothermere. At what he judged the right moment, the "Old Man" [Diaghilev] whispered, "Now you must go and dance with him." I was very nervous and it was not until we had two dances that I summoned the courage to approach the subject. Lord Rothermere did not make it easy for me. Eventually, after a little persuasion, he said, "All right. I will do what you ask. But I want you to make it clear to Diaghilev that I am doing this for you personally."'[1]

Alice Nikitina was also there, placed far from Harold at the banqueting table, but 'that did not prevent Lord Rothermere leaving his circle and coming to ask me to dance several times'.[2] Rothermere was in his mid-fifties and Nikitina, who'd left Russia shortly after the revolution, was thirty years his junior. They'd have a fourteen-year affair, though she insisted it was never sexual. She received dresses and furs, a car, and Nikitina wasn't quite sure what to do with the gift of a five-litre bottle of Chanel No. 5 perfume – so she massaged herself with it.

Bunny was well known for his generosity and was forever stuffing cash into envelopes; his brother Cecil even told a story of Harold jamming wads of banknotes into the collection box while they were on a visit to York Minster. Secretaries carried cash to give to beggars, and the headmaster of his old school in Marylebone asked for £1,000 and was given £10,000 instead. He funded chairs at Oxford and Cambridge endowed in the names of his dead sons, and he also bought the site of the old 'Bedlam' mental hospital in south London and turned it into a park in his mother's name.

Rothermere's largesse, though, was a clumsy and blunt instrument just like the man himself. Northcliffe's generosity had been far more thoughtful, more personal. When, for instance, Sunny told Mary Howarth – the *Daily Mirror*'s first editor – that her all-female newspaper was a total failure, Alfred had opened a cabinet in Room One at Carmelite House and selected the exact brand of cigarette she preferred to soothe her. He always kept them there, just for her. Harold, on the other hand, had once sent a solid gold and gem-encrusted cigarette case to one of his sisters, who didn't even smoke. A niece he'd upset with his whining, boorish talk at a dinner party was sent a diamond Cartier brooch as an apology that was so big she called it 'The Bomb'. 'Among his mistresses I can recall a secretary who used to clatter away at her typewriter wearing a ring containing a diamond the size of a pigeon's egg,' wrote his nephew Cecil King. 'Evidently she became a nuisance, and Geoffrey Harmsworth [a cousin] told me Rothermere offered him ten thousand a year to marry her. Then there was another lady by whom he had a daughter. But most of his affairs were one-night stands with girls who were astonished to receive mink coats or diamond brooches for their services.'[3]

It seems Viscount Rothermere viewed politicians in the same crass way. They were there to do favours for and to receive favours from

– often jobs and honours for friends and family. In the early 1920s, Bunny is said to have demanded an earldom for himself and a Cabinet post for his son Esmond in return for supporting the Conservatives in his papers, but Tory leader Bonar Law declined (his Liberal predecessor Lloyd George, who sprayed honours around like a farmer spreading fertilizer, would probably have thought it a fair exchange).

Rothermere spent four months every year down at La Dragonnière, a villa he'd built among the olive groves and pine trees overlooking Monte Carlo that Northcliffe called 'a fairy-like little palace'. Bunny's ballerinas would visit him there while Lady Rothermere, a glamorous woman who looked after her figure, was 500 miles north in Paris using her husband's cash to play patron to handsome young soldiers turned poets or painters. 'Bluebell', as she liked to call herself, even financed T. S. Eliot's literary review the *Criterion*, in which he first published *The Waste Land*.

In Monte Carlo, Bunny would gamble at casinos where he'd sit back eating slices of rich pâté while watching his secretary play roulette with fat slabs of his cash. Another casino regular of Rothermere's acquaintance was Princess Stephanie von Hohenlohe. Princess Stephanie was a beautiful woman in her mid-thirties who'd trained as a ballerina before marrying and divorcing a minor Austrian prince. She liked to smoke Havana cigars – which she'd light by striking a match on the sole of her shoe.[4] One day at the gaming tables Rothermere moaned to her that there was no news for his newspapers, so she told him about the plight of Hungary, a country that had fought on the losing side during the war and had come off badly in the peace. Bunny invited the princess back to La Dragonnière for dinner – an offer that seems not to have had a sexual motive though the princess was probably willing – she had bedded countless other wealthy benefactors – and when she showed him where Hungary was on a little map in the *Encyclopaedia Britannica*, Rothermere told her: 'You know, my dear, I never realised until today that Budapest and Bucharest were not one and the same city.'[5]

In June 1927, Rothermere's byline sat above 'Hungary's Place in the Sun – Safety for Central Europe' – a typically dull bit of Bunny prose

filed from Budapest, now he knew where it was. Harold's theme was
that the handful of harassed statesmen and officials who redrew the
map of Europe after the Great War were focused on Germany, and
mistakes were made on the fringes. 'They have created dissatisfied
racial minorities in half a dozen parts of Central Europe, any one of
which may be the start of another conflagration,' wrote Rothermere.
'The hands that imposed the political conditions now existing there
sowed the seeds of future war.'[6]

He did have a point. But Rothermere soon became bored with his
Hungarian campaign, as surely must have many *Daily Mail* readers
who actually made it to the end of his articles. It was massive news,
however, in Hungary and to Hungarians no longer living in what
was once Hungary – who now lived in states created by the swift
whip of a bureaucrat's pen after the war, Hungarians now part of
Romania, Czecho-Slovakia and Yugoslavia. A viscount of the British
Empire – great victors of the Great War – had suddenly taken up
their cause. Squares and fountains were named after him, his name
was carved on a hillside, and trees and rocks were dedicated to him.
One and a quarter million Hungarians – a sixth of the population
– even signed an address in gratitude.[7] And when Esmond went on
his father's behalf to accept an honorary doctorate he was greeted
like a visiting prince by cheering crowds. Some monarchists even
thought Rothermere should be offered the Crown of St Stephen –
Monty Python couldn't write a more surreal comedy, except it wasn't
funny. Germans and Hungarians dispossessed by bureaucrats in Paris
would, indeed, be one of the root causes of the Second World War.

Viscount Rothermere spent much of his time wandering Europe
like a hyper-rich nomad with a select crop of associates travelling in a
convoy of three cars, two for the passengers and one for the luggage.
They'd stop at the roadside every so often, so that aides and editors
could swap seats when Bunny got bored with their conversation.
And if his hacks back at *Mail* HQ were having a bad day, it would
get a whole lot worse when Rothermere picked up his pen to write
a story or two for his newspapers. Finance and international politics
were his favourite themes, and from the early 1920s, the itinerant

viscount began promoting a nasty new kind of authoritarian rule called 'Fascism'.

Benito Mussolini, its founder, had, it turned out, once even worked for St John Harmsworth.[8] Before his accident, St John had been sent to France by Sunny to learn French so that he could be put to good use in the Parisian arm of the family firm, and he happened upon a restorative spring in Vergèze, near Montpellier in the south of France, with his tutor. It was a poor man's spa run by a Dr Perrier, who also bottled and sold its 'healing' water. 'There was a muddy pond with natural gas bubbling up, and a few bathing boxes round it, while quite near was a spring of beautifully clear water,' wrote nephew Cecil King. 'He conceived the idea – this *was* like Northcliffe – of pumping the natural gas into the spring water to make a sparkling table water.'[9]

Bonch never shared Sunny's taste for the printed word nor Bunny's thing for numbers, but he loved this water. So he sold his slice of the family firm and bought the good doctor's business, to the horror of his brothers. St John had a vision. He could see the new green bottles he had in mind – shaped like the Indian clubs he used for exercise – on the table of every fine restaurant in Europe. Then his car crashed, and he supervised the construction of the bottling plant from his wheelchair. The business gave him something to focus on, other than walking again. And out there among the workers moving concrete in a barrow with the soft hands of a primary school teacher was a young labourer called Benito Mussolini.

Mussolini had been earning fifty US cents a day constructing a railway on the Swiss–Italian border, then followed the work west. He couldn't go home – at the time, Benito was a Marxist agitator who'd fled Italy to dodge his National Service, a crime that could get a young man shot two decades later after iron-chinned Benito had passed through a spell as a journalist and newspaper founder, turning ever harder to the right until he became the world's first Fascist dictator.

Or, to put it another way – as the *Mail* did in an editorial just a few months after Northcliffe's death, when his Fascists became 'The Saviours of Italy': 'The rescue of Italy from the Bolsheviks by the unselfish devotion of the Fascisti is not only a romance in itself; it is also one of the most important events of our time.'[10]

It was clear, then, from the start where the *Mail*'s sympathies lay. Whereas Russia's Communist leader Lenin, Rothermere himself wrote in September 1923, was a criminal who 'took hold of a backward country and smashed it to pieces', Mussolini's Fascists were 'manifestly inspired by more exalted motives . . . This young, vigorous, ardent Italian did more than save Italy. In my judgment he saved the entire Western world.'[11] Bunny Harmsworth was driven by a cold fear of the Communists; the Reds after all wanted to tear down a system that had served arch-capitalists like him just fine. Though Bunny did accept in his article that the British were rather fond of a hard-won thing called 'democracy' – designed precisely to check the rise of these nasty dictators.

Five years and several signed articles in Mussolini's favour later, Bunny met his hero in Rome and found him hard at work at an oak table in the corner of a grandiose office that had 'the air of a sacristy'. Just like Northcliffe, Il Duce also liked an oversized room to work in. Indeed, Northcliffe's passing seemed to have left a void in Bunny Harmsworth's life that could somehow only be filled by dangerously strong men like Mussolini. 'I am proud of the fact that *The Daily Mail* was the first newspaper in England, and the first in the world outside Italy, to give the public a right estimate of the soundness and durability of his work,' wrote Rothermere. 'In articles published at various times I have expressed my own profound admiration for what Mussolini has accomplished . . . There can be no doubt as to the verdict of future generations on his achievement. He is the greatest figure of our age. Mussolini will probably dominate the history of the twentieth century as Napoleon dominated that of the early nineteenth.'[12]

Six hundred miles north of Rome in Munich, a weird Austrian corporal was also watching Mussolini with adoring eyes; Adolf Hitler was incandescent that the German peoples had lost the war and he too, just like Bunny Harmsworth, admired the way in which these Italian Fascists had taken absolute power. Soon enough, his

Nazis were on their way to such power too. So Lord Rothermere dispatched his favourite correspondent – himself – to Germany in 1929 to find out more about this new force, his byline sitting over a piece headlined 'Will the Republic Endure?':

> Many people in this country still feel very bitterly towards Germany. Our generation can never forget the loss of precious lives and the incalculable suffering and impoverishment which German ambition for world dominion imposed upon us. That is a feeling I fully understand, for my own family losses were terrible and unforgettable. But we must not forever dwell upon the bitterness of bygone days. Our duty now is to build up a better understanding between all European peoples for the future. I know that the people of this country wish strongly and sincerely to live in good relations with their German neighbours across the North Sea. We British have never been good haters.[13]

Rothermere went to Munich the following year and began to fully embrace the Nazi cause with an article headlined 'Germany and Inevitability – A Nation Reborn'. It was a heavy story, exploring the theme that the young were taking control of the nation, led by forty-one-year-old Hitler. 'The older generation of Germany were our enemies. Must we make enemies of this younger generation too?'[14]

Hitler thanked Lord Rothermere personally for his support and Bunny's piece was reprinted verbatim in the Nazi party's own newspaper, the *Volkischer Beobachter*. It was a sea change from Sunny's day, when Northcliffe had been enough of an enemy of the German state for them to dispatch a destroyer to shell his house. After Rothermere's words were published, Mailman Rothay Reynolds was immediately granted personal access to Hitler, who told him he'd read the article 'with the greatest astonishment . . . Lord Rothermere possesses the true gift of intuitive statesmanship'.[15] Bunny later sent Hitler a photograph of himself mounted in a solid gold Cartier frame, as a present. On the reverse was said to be a copy of his article.

Rothermere was roundly attacked in the press for this 'Nation Reborn' piece and responded in kind a week later, writing that it had 'startled and shocked the old women of three countries – France, Germany, and our own'.

> It was bound to do so, for it told the truth about the latest phase of the greatest development going on in Europe – *the rise to power of the young generation which has grown up since the war.* A new idea invariably produces this effect upon the pompous pundits who pontificate in our weekly reviews and those old-fashioned morning newspapers whose sales and influence alike sink steadily month by month towards the vanishing-point. The wiseacres who conduct these out-of-date organs of our Press can see no further than the edge of their own desks. Their minds are set immovably in the mould of pre-war ideas. Because they are stiff-jointed they think the whole world has lost its power of movement. They are incapable of realising that new and powerful forces are at work in Europe,and that the future of this country depends upon our proper understanding of them.[16]

Princess Stephanie, Bunny's friend from the casinos who had first roused his curiosity for the Hungarian cause several years before, was, by now, well connected with the Nazis – the princess at one point even had a sexual relationship with Hitler's handsome personal adjutant – and she was very much playing both sides. In 1933, the year Hitler came to power, British intelligence circulated a note from their French counterparts, who had found documents in her flat in Paris in which the Nazis ordered her to persuade Rothermere to campaign for territory lost to Poland after the Great War, for which they'd pay her £300,000 (something like £19 million today). Rothermere himself was also paying her an annual retainer of £5,000 (around £314,000 today) to liaise with the Nazis.[17]

Viscount Rothermere filed frequent dispatches from German soil and, as he puttered along in his usual three-car motorcade in the early 1930s, he saw something fluttering upon the roofs of farmhouses in the distance like poppies in an open field: the new flag of the Fatherland. The swastika is an ancient mark that symbolized luck or 'auspiciousness' to Buddhists and Hindus. It was a symbol chosen and put in a white circle on a blood-red background by Hitler's own fair hand, the same hand that would bring war again to the world, staining the once peaceful swastika symbol forever with the blood of innocent women and children. Likewise, Bunny's support for the Nazis would also leave its own indelible stain on the *Mail*'s masthead.

As he sat in the back of his Rolls-Royce, Rothermere must have felt sure he was on the right side of history. He'd finally prove he had his big brother's editorial gene and he was doing what true reporters did: he was on the road seeing the story for himself. No matter that he was in Germany as a guest of the Nazis, seeing what they wanted him to see. No matter that he was travelling with a convoy of staff and staying in the plushest of hotels, eating in the most expensive restaurants. Harold reached out for words, for weighty phrases that he'd blend with historical details someone else could check for him later, his secretary being jolted around at his side, pen scraping mis-shapes on his pad. The Hitler miracle had yet to fix the roads; it'd be a while before his vast armies were ready to mobilize.

'On a visit which I am paying to Northern Germany I find the signs of the new Hitler spirit as manifest in the most out-of-the-way villages as in the largest cities,' Bunny wrote from 'Somewhere in Naziland' for the *Mail* in July 1933. 'Across the heavy-laden fields of corn one sees the Nazi flag flying from the roofs of lonely farmhouses. Almost every bicycle met on the long, straight roads bears its swastika pennant, and through the picturesque streets of the little country towns stride the sturdy, brown-shirted young men – and their brown-frocked girl helpers – who have taken over the rulership of Germany from their ineffective elders.'[18]

Bunny hit back at those who claimed the Nazis used foul means over fair in the same article, headlined 'Youth Triumphant'.

> They [Nazi critics] have started a clamorous campaign
> of denunciation against what they call 'Nazi atrocities,'
> which, as anyone who visits Germany quickly discovers
> for himself, consist merely of a few isolated acts of
> violence . . . which have been generalised, multiplied,
> and exaggerated to give the impression that Nazi rule is a
> bloodthirsty tyranny.

Germany, he added, had been 'rapidly falling under the control of its alien elements. In the last days of the pre-Hitler regime there were twenty times as many Jewish Government officials in Germany as had existed before the war. Israelites of international attachments were insinuating themselves into key positions in the German administrative machine.'[19]

Sir Leicester, arguably the only genuine journalist in the Harmsworth clan after Northcliffe, loathed Harold's policy towards the Nazis. During a lunch with the *Mail*'s editor – Lord Rothermere's fifth – W. L. Warden in the early 1930s, Sir Leicester said the campaign was alienating Jews and Jewish advertising and also long-term *Mail* readers who had joined Northcliffe in being suspicious of Germany from the start. 'Northcliffe had conducted this campaign for years before the war, and the war itself, provoked by Germany as it was, had been the great justification of Northcliffe's campaign,' he wrote in his diary. 'Upon this campaign and the wise direction Northcliffe gave the papers throughout these years and during the war I felt, and always had felt, that the strength of the *Daily Mail* and its reputation was based. To reverse this policy and adopt one of unnecessary friendliness with Germany and Hitler, and Hitlerism worship, would be contrary to the instincts of British nationality, and would inevitably react unfavourably, and perhaps disastrously, upon the circulation of the *Daily Mail*.'[20] George Dawson, the editor of *The Times* (who had been editor for a while under Northcliffe's ownership), simply thought Rothermere 'a joke'.[21]

Bunny Harmsworth, however, was not alone in being an enthusiast for the Fascist cause – there was a sizeable minority in Britain that shared his support for Hitler,[22] and despite Sir Leicester's concerns his writing actually seemed to have little direct impact on the paper's circulation. Maybe then, as now, many readers simply skipped the comment pieces altogether and neither read nor cared about Rothermere's opinions. Germany is, after all, a foreign land and Hitler did not dominate most people's minds until war was fast approaching.[23] Former Prime Minister Lloyd George, for example, also became an admirer and even met the Führer in 1936, referring to Hitler as 'the greatest German of the age'.[24] He thought it a good thing that strong men like Hitler were in power, saying 'a powerful statesman is in himself a guarantee of peace'. The Führer was doing in Germany what Lloyd George had wanted to do in Britain – he was curing unemployment and making his country strong again. The former PM even gave the Führer the message that 'public opinion in Great Britain was to an increasing degree showing more and more understanding for Hitler's position and the one anxiety of British public opinion today was to bring about the closest co-operation between the two countries'.[25]

At the same time as boosting the Nazi cause, Rothermere did appreciate its dangers – he warned *Daily Mail* readers that Britain was a 'fifth rate power' that needed to re-arm and he worried that German bombers could obliterate Tyneside, 'that great centre of Socialist pacifism',[26] in a single evening. Strength was the best way to avoid war, and the sky was the key. Britain needed aircraft and Rothermere even paid for the development of his own bomber.

Rothermere was also privately informing the Government of what he had learned about Hitler and his regime, urging politicians to heed the threat of war and to re-arm. In October 1934, he wrote to then Chancellor of the Exchequer Neville Chamberlain to warn him that 'the oligarchs of Germany are the most dangerous, ruthless men who have ever been in charge of the fortunes of a people of 67,000,000 in number. They will stop at nothing. Violent as they were on 30th June [the purge that saw many of Hitler's perceived political enemies executed in the 'night of the long knives'] in internal politics, they will be equally or more violent in external politics.'[27] And in May

1935, he wrote to the Prime Minister, Ramsay MacDonald, saying he had 'built up a fund of some good will' with Hitler and 'if in the coming emergency days an informal, semi-official conversation between him and me can serve any national purpose, I place my services at the disposal of the Government'.[28] He also claimed he'd resolved to use 'the language of butter because these dictators live in such an atmosphere of adulation and awe-struck reverence that the language of guns may not go nearly as far.'[29] Bunny Harmsworth was a complicated man and, whatever he said in private to British politicians, his words about the Nazis published in the *Daily Mail* were far more treacle than butter.

England, of course, had her Fascists too. And Bunny also used his *Daily Mail* as a mouthpiece for *their* cause, seeing them as a possible antidote to the loss of Britain's Empire. The British Union of Fascists was founded in 1932 by the British strong man Bunny so craved: a handsome, womanizing, über-ambitious toff called Sir Oswald Mosley.

'Hurrah for the Blackshirts!' wrote Bunny in January 1934. 'Britain's survival as a great power will depend on the existence of a well-organised Party of the Right, ready to take over responsibility for national affairs with the same directness of purpose and energy of method as Mussolini and Hitler have displayed . . . That is why I say, Hurrah for the Blackshirts! They are a sign that something is stirring among the youth of Britain.'[30] The paper even printed the address so young readers could sign up, and a noticeable increase in the middle-class membership of the British Union of Fascists was noted in places such as Leeds, for instance, whose 2,000-strong membership was partly generated as a result of the *Mail*'s call.[31]

> The folly of this anti-Blackshirt campaign – when it is
> not deliberate falsehood – lies in the fact that it stresses
> minor and infrequent aspects of a great movement as if
> they made up the whole. Our Socialist Press, for example,
> is constantly denouncing what it calls 'the horrors of the
> concentration camps' . . . blood-curdling stories of Nazi

brutality which are being circulated at the present time. That isolated outrages may have occurred in Germany is possible. But in comparison with other revolutions far smaller in scope the Germans have set the world a model of moderation.[32]

After a love affair that lasted a few months, Bunny turned away from the Blackshirts. There were ugly clashes between Blackshirts and Communists at a rally and, as Sir Leicester had warned, it was damaging something Bunny understood far more than politics: advertisers were uneasy. Although Mosley claimed it was specifically Jewish advertisers who stopped Rothermere 'at the point of an economic gun', Rothermere dithered. Mosley met Rothermere in a London hotel bedroom to discuss the way ahead, and found Bunny lying on a narrow brass bedstead. 'I'll let you know, I'll let you know,'[33] Bunny said, but soon stopped the campaign.

At the end of 1934 Viscount Rothermere positively glowed with admiration when he finally met Hitler for the first time along with his close entourage: Göring, Goebbels and Ribbentrop. Smitten Bunny sat down at his hotel desk in Munich on Christmas Eve and began to write up his impressions for his *Daily Mail*.

> What magic has restored hope to the German hearts, given to German eyes the flash of courage and self-confidence, and magnetised this mighty nation until one feels in its midst as if one were in a gigantic power-house? Hitler. That is the whole answer. Without Hitler none of this would have happened. With Hitler no limits can be set to the developments in Germany that may yet surprise the world. During the past week I have had several opportunities of talking and listening to this unique leader of his fellow-countrymen – not only in the formal atmosphere of the Chancellor's office but beside a glowing log-fire after luncheon as the short winter afternoon faded into darkness, or in the spacious but

simple suite of public rooms at the Chancellery, decorated
to his own quiet taste, where he entertained myself and
some of his more intimate collaborators to an after-dinner
concert of that German music which is his only
relaxation. There is something in Hitler's personality
which photographs him instantaneously and indelibly
upon the mind. His eyes have remarkable powers of
magnetism; his low-pitched voice is eloquent and
persuasive . . . It gives me special satisfaction to testify to
this from the city [Munich] where the Nazi movement
was born, and where, two and a quarter years before
Hitler came to power, I was the first outside the ranks of
his own followers to make a public prophecy of his
ultimate triumph . . . As I have said before I now repeat,
that nearly all the news regarding the Nazi regime
published even in our most responsible journals is pure
moonshine. These have spread, for instance, the
impression that German Jews lead an almost hunted
existence. Yet in German hotels and restaurants I have
frequently seen merry and festive parties of German Jews
who showed no symptoms of insecurity or
suffering . . . We and the Germans are blood-kindred.[34]

Article after article signed by Viscount Rothermere in support of
the Fascists rained down on his *Mail* readers for year after year, in
addition to the countless bits of news that the paper carried covering
the rising tide of world events that would eventually spill over into
war. Harold Harmsworth seemed mesmerized by Adolf Hitler;
if Bunny had kept a scrapbook, it'd be packed with newspaper
cuttings and snaps of him standing alongside the Führer and the
Nazi hierarchy. As Hitler rose to absolute power and his henchmen
began assembling the machinery that would lead to another world
war and the Holocaust, Rothermere's pen blundered on. And if he
knew of the dark events behind the scenes – and, despite Bunny's
knife-wielding ways, the *Mail* still had the remnants of the fine

foreign newsgathering system Sunny had created – he chose to ignore it.

In June 1935, Bunny's public Hitler-worship reached its peak under the headline 'Adolf Hitler at Close Range', accompanied by a complimentary sketch drawing of the most infamous face in history. Bunny described a man who dressed simply and didn't drink or smoke, a vegetarian who loved dogs. And he apparently adored children, did Adolf Hitler.

> After unusual opportunities of observing Herr Hitler at
> close range, both in private conversation and by a corres-
> pondence extending over many months, I would sum
> up his personality in two words. He is a practical mystic.
> In him is found the rare combination of dreamer and
> doer. Like Oliver Cromwell, Joan of Arc, and the Prophet
> Mahommed, he draws his inspiration from a hidden
> light not shared by his fellow men. Hitler is in the direct
> tradition of those great leaders of mankind who appear
> rarely more often than once in two or three centuries.
> He is the incarnation of the spirit of the German race.[35]

Rothermere repeatedly urged the British to get into bed with Germany in print. 'Natural sympathies, due to ties of race and instinct, are fast developing between the British and German nations,' he wrote in July 1936, '. . . the close association in international affairs of two such mighty States as Great Britain and Germany would create a force that no aggressor would dare to challenge.'[36] A year later, alongside a picture of himself standing proudly at Hitler's side, Rothermere wrote that 'I am what the textbooks of philosophy call a "pragmatist". Such people do not ask themselves "What is the ideal solution of this difficulty" but "What is the best practical solution?" . . . Let us rid ourselves of the delusion that Hitler is some sort of ogre in human shape. I have been his guest at Berchtesgaden, and had long conversations with him there. He has assured me of his desire to meet the British Government halfway.'[37]

In March 1938, Hitler reached down to his map and rubbed out the border with Austria, pulling the nation of his birth into the Third Reich. And inside Germany, the ever-increasing persecution of her Jews since Hitler first came to power exploded on Kristallnacht – 'night of the broken glass' – when the Nazis unleashed an orgy of violence in which Jewish synagogues and businesses were destroyed. Around 30,000 Jews were disappeared into concentration camps. As 1938 continued, the *Mail*'s sub-editors seemed not to want to dirty their own hands with any more of Rothermere's words. Stories bylined 'Viscount Rothermere' began to just be tagged 'Some More Postscripts' or 'Further Postscripts', with no effort applied to write a catchy headline. But, as tensions escalated, the adoration didn't stop, as one article from May 1938 attests:

> Herr Hitler is proud to call himself a man of the people, but, notwithstanding, the impression that has remained with me after every meeting with him is that of a great gentleman. He places a guest at his ease immediately. When you have been with him for five minutes you feel that you have known him for a long time. His courtesy is beyond words, and men and women alike are captivated by his ready and disarming smile. He is a man of rare culture. His knowledge of music, painting, and architecture is profound.[38]

Among all the adoring words over the years, Rothermere had indeed spotted the major faultline running under Europe between the wars: Czechoslovakia, the country forged in the embers of the First World War, where at least half a million Hungarians now lived, as well as more than 3 million Germans. Bunny had no time for the Czechs and signed many articles about the country that could 'be elbowed out of existence overnight'.[39] According to him, Czechoslovakia was a fake state 'contrived in the interest of the Czechs, a crafty race'.[40] 'Most blunders in life have to be paid for. The blunder of creating that synthetic and spurious state called Czecho-Slovakia may well cost Europe another war.'[41]

In February 1937, Rothermere wrote that 'the immense development of armed strength in Nazi Germany now threatens [the Czechs] with retribution . . . The dragon's teeth that the Czechs have sown are sprouting all around them in a crop of deadly dangers.'[42] He was correct. In September 1938, the British Prime Minister, Neville Chamberlain, sacrificed the German-speaking part of the country in the name of peace, signing an accord promising that their two countries would not go to war. Lord Rothermere sent a telegram to his friend: 'My dear Führer, everyone in England is profoundly moved by the bloodless solution to the Czechoslovakian problem. People not so much concerned with territorial readjustment as with dread of another war with its accompanying bloodbath. Frederick the Great was a great popular figure, may not Adolf the Great become an equally popular figure. I salute your excellency's star which rises higher and higher.'[43]

As war fast approached, even Princess Stephanie the spy urged Rothermere to restrain his effusive support for the Führer, telling him in February 1938, 'You must be very careful in future. I do not see how it will be possible for you, under these new conditions, to continue to support Hitler in future and at the same time serve the interests of your own country.'[44]

German troops marched into the rest of Czechoslovakia on 15 March 1939 and Europe was on the brink of war. Most British people who had held a degree of support for Hitler's Germany in the mid-1930s had long since turned away.[45] But not Rothermere. Records released in 2005 revealed that Lord Rothermere's support for the Nazis was, even this late in the day, tantamount to treason when he wrote to congratulate Hitler, urging him to capitalize on his 'triumph' . . . with a march into Romania.[46] The documents had been intercepted by British intelligence in the possession of Princess Stephanie's Hungarian lawyer at Victoria station; she was suing Rothermere for breach of contract after he had cancelled her retainer. On the printed page, Rothermere really was like a bunny rabbit caught in Hitler's hypnotic headlights and, with the war just four months away, there was simply no stopping his pen:

He is supremely intelligent. There are only two others
I have known whom I could apply this remark – Lord
Northcliffe and Mr. Lloyd George. If you ask Herr Hitler
a question he makes an instant reply full of information
and eminent good sense. There is no man living whose
promise given in regard to something of real moment I
would sooner take. He believes that Germany has a divine
mission and that the German people are destined to save
Europe from the designs of revolutionary Communism.
He has a great sense of the sanctity of the family, to
which Communism is antagonistic, and in Germany has
stopped the publication of all indecent books, the production of suggestive plays and films, and has thoroughly
cleaned up the moral life of the nation. Herr Hitler has a
great liking of the English people. He regards the English
and the Germans as being of one race. This liking he
cherishes notwithstanding, as he says, that he has been
sorely tried by malicious personal comments and cartoons
in the English Press. I was talking with Herr Hitler some
eighteen months ago when he said, 'Certain English
circles in Europe speak of me as an adventurer.' My reply
is: 'Adventurers made the British Empire.'[47]

A month later, there was finally some good news for the *Mail*'s
sub-editors who had to write the headlines for Rothermere's stories.
'Further Postscript', 17 June 1939: 'Readers of *The Daily Mail* owe
me a vote of thanks for relinquishing its control.'[48] He'd handed over
to his son Esmond and these were just the fading embers of his *Mail*
regime.

Britain declared war on Germany after Hitler's troops invaded
Poland in September 1939. There was still a war to win, but the
entire editorial floor of the *Daily Mail* must already have felt a little
liberated. They didn't have to publish any more of their proprietor's
bullshit.

6

Faster Than the Mail

Esmond Harmsworth had a ghost over either shoulder, constant reminders that there had once been two boys ahead of him in the line of succession for Sunny Harmsworth's folded-paper throne. 'In his room at Northcliffe House hung portraits of his two elder brothers killed in the First World War,' said Arthur Wareham, one of the ten *Daily Mail* editors during Esmond's reign.

> It is said that these two sons were the favourites of the first Lord Rothermere and that Esmond, who was to inherit the newspaper empire, received little encouragement and sympathy from his father. Perhaps this helps to explain the mixture of diffidence and hardness in the character of the second Lord Rothermere. Wealthy, powerful, one of the handsomest men in the country with his slim height and noble head, he . . . failed to make the mark on the country's affairs which might have been expected of him.[1]

For the *Daily Mail* to kick on towards a fresh future and renew itself as the leader in its field, Esmond had to somehow become an amalgamation of both Sunny and Bunny Harmsworth. But he found he was neither. He wasn't a natural-born journalist and mischief-maker like Uncle Alfred nor a gifted money-man like his father. Esmond may have been the boy to inherit Northcliffe's Room One – his big room for big ideas . . . but Esmond didn't seem to have many ideas, big or otherwise. Years earlier, Esmond had told a friend he'd stop all the *Mail*'s political campaigns, focus on the weather and make the paper 'damn boring'[2] . . . which is not precisely what happened; the paper still employed intelligent and actively engaged journalists who got on with the job day-to-day without ever even meeting the paper's gangly and reticent proprietor. They could handle a news story as well as anybody. But he *did* change its tone, its voice. The single most crucial factor in Esmond's era was the fact that he didn't share his father and uncle's lust for real political clout, nor did he have Sunny's passion for hyperbole – Northcliffe's noisy need to be provocative in print, to be noticed and to be one of the men truly in command of his country. Esmond had no desire at all to 'make' the news.

So, unlike his father and uncle, Esmond kept his thoughts and opinions in the drawing room where they belonged and out of the pages of his newspapers (there are only a handful of articles in the *Daily Mail* archive signed by this Harmsworth, yet he ruled for over three decades, and none of these are even remotely controversial). Esmond knew he was no journalist and, also crucially, he had seen at close quarters the rank stupidity of his father's support for Hitler. All he had to do was glance out of his office window during the Blitz to see how bad Bunny's judgement had truly been.

London was being reduced to rubble and Nazi jackboots seemed sure to follow – goose-stepping their way down Fleet Street through the ash of the second Great Fire of London towards St Paul's. The Blitz began in September 1940 and would last until the spring of 1941. France had fallen that May, and thousands of boats had set sail to rescue almost a quarter of a million Allied troops who had retreated to the shores of Dunkirk. Britain was badly wounded, weak and in retreat. She stood tall, bloodied but alone. She could not now, surely, win this war.

Esmond's father Lord Rothermere wasn't even in town. He had accepted a request from his old friend and government minister Lord Beaverbrook (more of whom later) to head off on a mission to America seeking support for his country's cause, but fell ill and was unsteady on his feet in New York and on the Canadian leg of his trip. So his doctors suggested he went down to Bermuda to rest; he took his granddaughter Esme – who was in New York – with him, telling her he needed to get into an area where sterling was the currency. Bunny was sad and gentle, she said, a seventy-two-year-old man worried about events on the other side of the Atlantic. He was diagnosed with dropsy – swellings caused by excess water. His health worsened and he was taken to hospital; he liked to have Esme by his bedside because she reminded him of his mother.

Harold Sidney Harmsworth died in hospital on 26 November 1940 and, though he had insisted in print during his flirtation with Hitler and Mussolini that he shared their abstinence, his post-mortem revealed signs of cirrhosis of the liver – just like his father and grand-father. Viscount Rothermere's body didn't join them, alongside Northcliffe and their mother, in the family plot in north London, though. Bunny was buried on Bermuda.

There were many obituaries but perhaps the final words on Bunny Harmsworth are best left for his favourite German: Adolf Hitler had, several years earlier, said he thought Rothermere 'one of the very greatest of all Englishmen. He is the only man who sees clearly the magnitude of the Bolshevist danger. His paper is doing an immense amount of good. I have the greatest admiration for him.'[3]

A little over a month after Rothermere's death, in the early evening of 29 December 1940, around 120 tons of explosives and 22,000 incendiaries fell on London. At least 125 people died. In the lanes around Fleet Street, tins of printer's ink detonated as firemen fought back the firestorm. The *Daily Mail* had been warning about war from the air since the birth of manned flight, and fire now licked at St Paul's Cathedral, a church that had risen from the burnt-out shell of the first cathedral, which had been ravaged by the first Great Fire of London almost 300 years before. Herbert Mason, the *Daily Mail*'s chief photographer, was on the paper's roof with his camera, trying to find St Paul's in his viewfinder through all that smoke. Journalists like Bert are paid to rush to war zones, but this time the frontline was home. 'I focused at intervals as the great dome loomed up through the smoke,' he said, but the 'glare of many fires and sweeping clouds of smoke kept hiding the shape. Then a wind sprang up. Suddenly the shining cross, dome, and towers stood out like a symbol in the inferno. The scene was unbelievable. In that moment or two; I released my shutter.'[4]

Ads had stopped covering the front page of the *Daily Mail* the previous September,[5] so Bert's photograph was to dominate page one of his paper on New Year's Eve 1940 and help define a terrible epoch as St Paul's stood inside a hoop of smoke. 'War's Greatest Picture: St Paul's Stands Unharmed in the Midst of the Burning City,' read the caption. It was the 125th attack of the Blitz and things looked grim.

'Hitler meant to start the second Great Fire of London as the prelude to an invasion,' wrote Mailman Noel Monks, the paper's Air Correspondent. 'The New Year invasion was to have followed.' However, the British weather came to the country's aid that night, gathering wind and clouds that forced the 1,000-strong bomber squadron home. It wasn't just London that the Nazis set ablaze. Strategic cities around Britain were pummelled and around 40,000 civilians lost their lives, half of them in the capital. But in the same New Year's Eve edition of the *Mail*, beneath the picture of the smouldering City and resolute St Paul's, there was a spark of hope that would catch afire soon enough – and raze the Nazi nightmare to the ground. '100 to 1 Backing for Roosevelt,' the paper said. 'President Roosevelt is "tremendously pleased" at the reaction to his speech in which he pledged more aid to Britain and declared that the Axis could not win the war.' The 'Arms Flow Has Begun', added a Mailman in New York.

Northcliffe House, a palace to the printed word Bunny Harmsworth had built in the mid-1920s but only ever visited a handful of times, was damaged during the Blitz and Mailmen formed a bucket chain to empty water from the basement so the presses could roll. It became a barracks for journalists, with camp beds for editors and technical staff. The *Mail*'s Manchester facilities became vital. And readers were encouraged to share their copy instead of putting it down for the dog. It was a slim read. Paper shortages shrank it to four pages and columns increased from seven to eight to pack in more information.

One toiler inside Northcliffe House at the time was Arthur Wareham, the sub-editor in charge of the front page, a *Mail* lifer who would rise to become editor. 'We became masters in the art of compressing a mine of information into the tidy wartime newspapers,' he would say after the war. 'This lesson in the economy of words was invaluable and as a result there is no doubt the post-war daily journalism has been superior to the brand we inflicted on our readers before 1939.'[6]

When Germany's ally Japan did Britain a huge favour in December 1941 by attacking the US Navy at anchor in Hawaii – finally pulling the Americans into the war at Britain's side – Wareham hit back against the Japanese in the best way he could. 'Pearl Harbor was the night that changed the course of the war,' wrote Wareham. 'Up to then I had been sending off a brief cable every day to a Japanese newspaper, the *Hochi Hochi Shimbun*, containing the highlights of the day's war news. The message I sent on the night of Pearl Harbor was too rude, I am afraid, to be repeated here but it ended the contract in no uncertain way.'[7]

During the Second World War the *Daily Mail* was physically a thin paper and, as with the First World War, the women's pages and the fluffy features were the first to be jettisoned to make room for news. Most of the *Mail*'s editorial women had worked in these areas, but towards the end of the war a formidable female hack called Rhona Churchill was in the field, and filling the paper. Ms Churchill spoke German and slipped on an American uniform to travel with the US Army. And as the Americans pushed the Germans back to their own western border, she was proof that there was at least a sliver left of Sunny's populist touch two decades after his death. 'My instructions were to ignore the battle stories and roam at will concentrating on getting in among the German civilians and writing factual reports,' said Ms Churchill.

I think the *Daily Mail* was the first Fleet Street newspaper
to adopt this policy and it must have taken courage and
foresight. I was lucky enough to have this very fertile
field almost to myself until the war ended . . . It was
mid-winter and I went out to Aachen [the first German
town to fall to the Allies] each day in an open jeep in
search of a story, and each day returned with a winner.
Somewhat naturally, I became a bit unpopular . . . Our
newspapers were reduced to four pages by newsprint
rationing, and it was thought I was hogging more than
my fair share of the newsprint available for war stories.
But it wasn't my fault. My job as roving reporter was to
supply the *Daily Mail* with all the copy I thought they
might want, and the system worked too well. Every
day I found just what the *Daily Mail* wanted – a good
human-interest story.[8]

As the Third Reich fell after five years of war, though, it was clear
that the *Daily Mail*'s voice had indeed changed – calmed, even – and
the second Viscount Rothermere, Esmond Harmsworth, was being
true to his word. Though the *Daily Mail* was an effective newsgathering machine during the Second World War, it did not launch
the loud campaigns of its founding fathers nor try to apply a firm
hand upon government policy. There was no call for heads to roll,
no demand for a different kind of shell to be used at the front, and
Esmond kept his name resolutely out of the paper. Paper supplies
were short and maybe there was no space for noisy campaigns, but
the tone continued when it ended. Esmond was never going to
become a fresh mix of Sunny and Bunny Harmsworth, and the *Mail*
was sailing along nicely as 'just' a newspaper that reported the news
instead of trying to make it. But, unfortunately for a generation of
Mailmen, just up the road on Fleet Street proper another man had
Sunny's editorial instincts and the brutal business acumen of Bunny
in abundance: a Canadian called Max Aitken, owner of the rival
Daily Express.

The *Daily Express* was founded in 1900 by a man who had long travelled in Sunny Harmsworth's slipstream. Arthur Pearson had won a *Tit-Bits* competition during the peak of the battle between George Newnes's magazine and Sunny Harmsworth's *Answers*, and his prize was a job in the *Tit-Bits* office; but, like Alfred, he ached for more and soon created his own magazine to compete with both *Tit-Bits* and *Answers*. He joined the newspaper game four years after Harmsworth had founded the *Mail* but eventually sold up when he began to go blind and his listless *Express* was selling fewer than 500,000 copies a day. Aitken stepped in and bought it, in secret, bit by bit.

Max Aitken was a mischievous little imp of a charmer who'd been nicknamed 'Moccasin Mouth' by the other boys in his hometown in Canada. One even quipped that if God had made Max's mouth any bigger, he'd have had no space left for his ears. Aitken's father was a fierce Presbyterian minister with fire-and-brimstone eyes and long black sideburns who had sailed out to the New World from Scotland (just like Rupert Murdoch's grandfather). Papa Aitken's strict morality wasn't for Max, though, and his boy became a millionaire by the age of twenty-five through ruthless cunning and the manipulation of other people's money. When a dodgy Canadian cement monopoly exploded into a scandal in 1909, he sold up and sailed away to Britain, pockets bulging with loot.[9]

Sunny Harmsworth spotted the threat from the *Express* soon after Aitken began to exert control but, by then, Northcliffe's mind was already too diminished to do anything effective about it. And Bunny, in a truly witless move, fell for Aitken's radiant charm; he bought around half the *Daily Express* shortly after his brother's death and began to, effectively, fuel a paper chasing the same ever-expanding middle market of readers as his *Daily Mail*. Max Aitken, like Sunny Harmsworth, had created his own school newspaper as a youth and he dipped in and out of journalism as a young man before turning his hand to making money on a grand scale. As Bunny drove down costs and opened up space to the adman in the *Mail* and the paper became gloomy and pessimistic and stuck in the past, Aitken exercised his

ultimate control of the paper and began to invest in the *Daily Express*.
He dictated its political line and filled it full of gossip and intrigue; it
was the first to carry a crossword and he had been the first to shed the
ugly classified ads from the front page, something Bunny couldn't
bear to clear away from his *Daily Mail* because of the cash they
generated. Aitken, who became Lord Beaverbrook, blew life into the
Express, giving it his energy and his ruthless vigour. The paper fizzed,
it sparkled, it was optimistic, wicked and humorous, and it looked
to the future – just like the first days of Sunny Harmsworth's *Daily
Mail*. Aitken's *Express* was faster, cleaner, crisper and sharper than
the *Mail* – an easier read for a newspaper market that was expanding
rapidly. It was simply a better newspaper than Bunny & Son's *Daily
Mail*. And Beaverbrook, crucially – just like Northcliffe – was never
in it for the cash. Canadian cement had already made him hugely
wealthy. 'I run my papers purely for propaganda,' Aitken later told a
Royal Commission.[10]

Indeed, Max Aitken had long shown he was a far cannier political
operator than both Bunny and Sunny Harmsworth had ever been.
He was elected as a Unionist MP in 1910, not long after arriving
in the UK, and became Minister for Information (from the House
of Lords after being ennobled) and Chancellor of the Duchy of
Lancaster – with a seat in Cabinet – in 1918. And a dozen years later,
Beaverbrook and Bunny Harmsworth infuriated three-time Prime
Minister Stanley Baldwin over a crusade for free trade between the
countries of the British Empire. Baldwin was livid over an article in
the *Daily Mail* in which the paper implied that Baldwin – Leader
of the Opposition at the time – was unfit for government because he
had squandered his family fortune. Baldwin had thought of suing for
libel but instead attacked Rothermere and Beaverbrook at a public
meeting with a killer phrase from his cousin, the poet and writer
Rudyard Kipling: 'What the proprietorship of these papers is aiming
at is power, but power without responsibility – the prerogative of the
harlot throughout the ages.' Beaverbrook's political instincts were so
much sharper than those of the Harmsworths, and he never fell for
Hitler like Bunny Harmsworth. The *Express* stayed broadly neutral.

Aitken also held several posts in Churchill's Government during the Second World War.

In 1922 the *Express* sold only a third as many copies as the *Mail*, but it overtook Sunny's darling within a decade and by 1939 it was selling 2.5 million copies a day – a million more than the rattly old *Daily Mail*.[11]

Bunny's grandson Vere, who was born in 1925, just as the *Express* was starting to catch the *Daily Mail*, said: 'Beaverbrook was a natural journalist and he understood the whole situation instinctively. He hired away from the *Daily Mail* all the top journalists, all trained by Northcliffe and of course the managers on the *Daily Mail* were under my grandfather's instructions, cutting this and cutting that and . . . pushing down the journalists. And Beaverbrook said essentially, "What do you want to work there for? Come and work for me and I will give you more money."'[12]

After the war, there was yet another factor driving the best Mailmen into Beaverbrook's arms: Vere's stepmother, the new Lady Rothermere – a lady many staff began simply to call 'the Monster'.

Esmond's second wife Ann was prone to making the kind of telephone call that every editor dreads the most: the one from the proprietor's wife offering advice or suggesting stories and campaigns for his paper or friends he should hire. Some thought control of the *Daily Mail* was actually in Lady Rothermere's hands, not her husband's. Rothermere's managing director after the war, William McWhirter, told a colleague: 'Esmond will come to the office in the morning and announce something with a tone of finality, and you know perfectly well where it has come from. Then you set to work to argue against it, all the more forcibly because you know that his pride is involved and that he will have to go home and explain to Ann why it can't be done.'[13]

Esmond had always been, like Uncle St John, very popular with the ladies. His first marriage to Vere's mother, Peggy – who had, in fact, first been promised to dead brother Vyvyan – ended badly on the grounds of Esmond's serial adultery: at least two dozen co-respondents were named in their long-drawn-out divorce proceedings. And though Ann Charteris, who became his second wife, was not a conventionally beautiful woman (her enemies said she was 'hatchet-faced'), she had a strong and deeply sexual hold over her men, and during her years with Esmond he wasn't the only man she took to bed. Ann, who was married when she began her affair with Esmond after he offered to rub oil on her back during a holiday in Austria in the late 1930s, also began sleeping with Ian Fleming in 1939. She married Esmond after her soldier husband was killed towards the end of the war but she continued her sexual liaisons with Fleming (even having dinner with him the night before her wedding to Esmond).

Fleming was more to Ann's taste than Esmond; he was the feckless Eton-educated scion of a wealthy merchant banking dynasty until war came and he joined the intelligence service and found his calling. And the future 'James Bond' thriller writer had a thing for kinky sex and pornography, of which he had a fine collection. As one girlfriend described it, they were 'variations on a theme about flagellation . . . books about women dressed up as a schoolmistress in lace collars, standing over manacled men with a whip.' 'I say,' he asked one girlfriend as she flicked through. 'Are you getting a kick out of that?'

Ann was only too happy to join him in bed for sessions they called their 'bruisings', in which they'd whip each other with 'raw-cowhide'. 'You have made bruises on my arms and shoulders,' he wrote to her. 'All this damage will have to be paid for some time.' He liked to give her twenty lashes, 'ten on each buttock'. She also wrote a 'poem' to Fleming on one of his inevitable, for the British upper classes of the era, trips down to the French Riviera. 'This dear familiar face is not accustomed to neglect, and still has the capacity to make other men erect. So if by chance you meet a pretty Biarritz slut, just pause for thought and hesitate before you stuff her up, etc.'

Fleming was also Esmond's friend. He would wander down from Boodle's gentlemen's club in St James's to Warwick House, where the Rothermeres lived in London, for dinner or to play bridge. If Esmond was away or at the office Fleming would invariably find his way upstairs and into Ann's bedroom. After one of their sessions in 1948, she wrote to Fleming: 'I hope you are safe at home and missing your black bitch [Ann] and I long for you even if you whip me because I love being hurt by you and kissed afterwards.'[14]

Esmond, on the other hand, truly irritated his wife. Ann was an aristocratic snob of the Charteris clan – her father was the second son of a minor earl – and it greatly upset her sense of the order of things to learn that Esmond liked to spend time with the middle classes. Esmond enjoyed 'tennis tournaments and dances in Eastbourne', she wrote to her brother Hugo – whom she manoeuvred into a job on the Continental *Daily Mail*, 'and I think he genuinely prefers that CLASS [her capitals] of society to our CLASS of society'.

Lady Rothermere also blamed the mess the *Mail* had become on Esmond. 'The *Daily Mail* can never be anything but a muddle,' she wrote to Hugo, 'for even in the unlikely event of Esmond finding perfect lieutenants, the perfect lieutenants will be in the impossible position of quicksand power and no final responsibility; how can you completely trust or indeed help any person who will within cautious limits inevitably listen to the advice of the last acquaintance he meets?'[15]

'The Monster' also didn't care for the *Mail*'s smartly dressed, fair-haired and athletically handsome Stanley Horniblow, who had been editor since 1944. Maybe, as a true aristocrat, she didn't like his accent; Aussie Stan had, somehow, developed the plummy English voice of the upper classes, maybe from the newsreels. So Horniblow was pushed out in 1947 and replaced by one of 'Annie's boys'. Frank Owen was a former *Evening Standard* editor and ex-MP who had been as fierce an anti-Nazi while working for the *Daily Express* as Bunny had been a fan.

Tom Pocock, a Charteris family friend, became a Mailman at Lady Rothermere's insistence shortly after Owen's appointment and found the *Mail* editor 'a bit wild'. Owen was six foot four tall, with broad shoulders and 'very macho and tough with dark hair sprouting straight out of his forehead'. On his first day in the job, Owen asked this new hire foisted on him from above for ideas. Pocock had suggested a feature on folk who had terrible jobs yet enjoyed them. Dustmen, for instance, were 'always smiling and singing'.

'So you think you would enjoy their jobs?' said Owen. 'Why?'

'Well, perhaps when they're opening dustbins, they're always hoping they'll find a diamond necklace.'

'That's right, Tom. Life is a dustbin. You go out and find me the jewels.'

That first lunchtime in his new job he bumped into Owen on the stairs. 'Come and have lunch with me,' said the editor. So they went to El Vino, the famous Fleet Street wine bar, and on to a posh restaurant 'with some friends he had picked up and we didn't get back to the office at all'.

> We ended up with some glamorous women in low-cut dresses in the Milroy nightclub. There were two wonderful dance bands. We were sitting there in the dark, bottles all over the tables. His link with the office was a white telephone among the bottles and every now and then a dispatch rider would come clumping into the night-club with page proofs for the *Daily Mail*, and the wine waiter would come over and shine his torch on it. Frank would read the proofs, ring up his night editor and tell him what to do. This went on until four in the morning. I thought 'Gosh, I never knew Fleet Street was like this.'[16]

Owen's former-showgirl wife turned heads when she visited the office, as did his mistress, who would pop into the building during office hours. The editor would then disappear for hours, only to reappear flushed with his shirt unbuttoned to the waist. When asked where he'd been, he'd reply: 'Sunning myself on the roof.' Then Owen fell out with Lady Rothermere; as *Time* magazine reported in June 1950, 'it has long been common knowledge in Fleet Street that the real boss wears a petticoat'.

For several years, pretty, vivacious Lady Ann Rothermere, 36, has tried to run the *Mail* from Warwick House. Without consulting Editor Owen, she often summoned staffers to her home to assign stories or suggest new features . . . Owen fought back, but fought a losing battle. In recent months, eight top editorial executives and writers and two directors have been fired or quit. Last week, as fed up with Warwick House as Warwick House was with him, Frank Owen quit.[17]

Finally the *Daily Mail* staff were saved from 'the Monster' when Esmond discovered Ann was pregnant with Fleming's child and they divorced. Ann, who joked that it was 'the death of the golden goose', married Fleming, and the day after their wedding Fleming sat his bruised backside down to work on *Casino Royale* at his house in Jamaica. His first novel featured a spy called 'James Bond' – a name the keen bird-spotter had borrowed from the author of an exhaustive study of Caribbean birds.

Despite the drift, the *Daily Mail* did still have some of the finest talent in Fleet Street in the post-war period and one of them in particular, Vincent Mulchrone, may well have been the most gifted newspaper writer the trade has ever seen. The 'King of the Intro' would craft the first paragraph of a newspaper story into a thing of real beauty. 'The news story must be the only human activity,' explained Mulchrone, 'which demands that the orgasm comes at the beginning.'

Mulchrone was one of the very few so-called 'Fleet Street Legends' who was actually worthy of the term; he would sit crumpling up sheets of paper and write out his intro longhand in pencil, said colleague Peter Lewis, until 'the words gave off an exciting fizz – like the sound of the foam when the first wave runs up the dry sand'.[18] He could sum up an entire story without need for anything much more than one paragraph, often under pressure in a stiflingly hot cable office in some dangerous trouble spot, yet could still find the deceptively simple detail that somehow illustrated the whole. It was always a *human* detail. People ultimately care about people not things – a fact often lost on many 'heavy' journalists, lesser writers, who really do believe *they* are more important than the story.

As Winston Churchill lay in state in January 1965, for instance, Mulchrone summed up the nation's grief in less than forty words: 'Two rivers run through London tonight and one of them is made of people. Dark and quiet as the night-time Thames itself, it flows through Westminster Hall, eddying about the feet of the rock called Churchill.' And when one of the architects of the Holocaust went on trial, he painted in the banality of evil in just a couple of sentences: 'As the bells of Jerusalem rang nine today the Jews offered their prisoner to the sight of the world – a desperately lonely, balding monster who has a new suit and a cold in the head. The local tailor who made the suit specially for Adolf Eichmann did not, perhaps, put his best skill into it.' Just like those of Ernest Hemingway – incidentally, also a former newsman – there is a lot of human information eddying beneath those simple words. Mulchrone's words simply demanded the reader kept on reading, even if they did not know what the story was about. For example: 'When the poor but honest die, all that remains personal to them can be – and with weird frequency is – contained in a cardboard shoebox.' And 'I was shaving waist deep in the Areguma, a pastry slice for a mirror, when this cannibal swam down the river and grabbed my ankles . . .' Or 'Wielding my fearless pen like a tin-opener, I now return to the worrying subject of pineapple chunks', to 'It is my firm intention, some time during the second half of my life, to do something about the wonky handle on the sitting room door.' And 'I don't mind being fat. And even less the fact that I'm unfit. But I hate like hell being 40. Which I have been now for one whole day. I'm sitting here, a fat, 40-year-old fool, watching a fold in my flesh on the back of my hand which refuses to go down.'[19]

On another occasion, in the summer of 1966, rugby league fan Vincent wrote the perfect paragraph to sum up a football match later that day, the World Cup Final: 'If the Germans beat us at our national game today, we can always console ourselves with the fact that we have beaten them twice at theirs.'[20]

Any reporter who has written for both a popular newspaper and a broadsheet knows how much easier it is to work on a broadsheet – broadsheets, of course, have more space. To tell the same story with fewer words is a tough skill few can truly master; it generally took talented sub-editors to actually form a tabloid newspaper (the work they used to do can truly be seen nowadays online as ever more reporters file clumsy and cluttered stories – full of 'txt msg' grammar, spelling mistakes and typos – straight to their web pages with very few costly subs making the whole product sing in time and tune).

Arguably Vincent Mulchrone – just like with George Warrington Steevens at the very start of the *Mail* story – defined exactly what Sunny Harmsworth had originally wanted his paper to be (before Lord Northcliffe's thirst for power, his ownership of *The Times* and his German obsession dissipated his energy and diluted his populist touch). The best of daily popular journalism is rarely given the respect it deserves, as Vere Harmsworth, who'd become the third Lord Rothermere, explained of Mulchrone: 'He felt in some ways, paradoxically, that he was a failure as a writer because he confined his talents to daily journalism, which is read, crumpled up and thrown away. It did not occur to him that what he achieved could only be accumulated over the years through daily written journalism, a more direct and immediate communication from writer to reader than either books, on one hand, or television on the other. He took tremendous pride in his craft but he simply did not know how good he was.'[21]

Yorkshire-born Mulchrone began most working days before midday with champagne in the back bar of the Harrow pub – a paper aeroplane's throw from the *Mail*'s offices (the bar is now named after him). But he was mostly on the move, and Mrs Mulchrone, recalled their son Patrick, 'could get in and out of Heathrow like threading a needle'. 'One time when he was coming in from somewhere exotic and going out to somewhere cold, and there was no time to get home, my mother was rung from some far-flung place and told, "Pack all my cold gear, my heavy gear." And he unloaded his suitcase on the floor of the arrivals building while she shovelled the lightweight stuff in. We three boys stood in our dressing-gowns watching my mother transfer hot-weather kit from a suitcase into a bag.'[22]

Though he adored the *Daily Mail* and resisted plenty of overtures to join the *Express*, in common with many reporters on right-wing newspapers, Mulchrone was no Tory. 'He always was tortured by the fact that he was writing for a Tory newspaper,' said Vere. 'His heart really was on the left.'[23]

Mulchrone may not have realized how good a writer he was, but he thought a true reporter 'the happiest animal on earth' and the *Daily Mail* had 'opened doors that would otherwise be barred to one so obviously devoid of any talent but the rough cunning and low-born persistence required of a reporter'.

> No other trade would have paid one to swim at
> midnight in Alice Springs, or fish Loch Ness for its
> Monster with a bottle of Malt for bait, or open National
> Tequila Week (a purely personal fiesta) in Mexico City,
> or marvel at grey Jerusalem flushing apricot in the dawn.
> When the barricade went up in Algiers the thought
> came, too, that it would be neither sweet nor fitting to
> die for one's intro . . . You can feel yourself growing the
> extra skin. This explains, in part at least, why journal-
> ists live, and drink, and move together . . . Diabolical
> phonies abound. I have never known one fool a group
> of journalists . . . I wouldn't want to be anything other
> than a reporter.[24]

When the sixties really started swinging in the autumn of 1963, John, Paul, George and Ringo welcomed Vincent to take an inside peek at the biggest showbiz story there has ever been. 'This Beatlemania, I wondered what it was all about,' he wrote in October 1963. 'The divisive forces which have been tearing at the nation's loyalties in the past week might be crystallized in one vital question: "Would you let your daughter marry a Beatle?"'

If you haven't heard of them you're either deaf or a High
Court judge . . . Depending on your age, or whether
you suffer from hardening of the opinions, they are
raves or knaves, living idols or false gods . . . They are
shatteringly honest, incredibly modest, immediately
friendly, with apparently no thought for the importance
of the person they are speaking to . . . Above all, they are
refreshing: they are fun; they are kind. I feel better about
life for having been in their company.[25]

Beatle John Lennon, incidentally, was a *Mail* reader in the 1960s.
A fact that perhaps belies his middle-class roots growing up in the
Liverpool suburb of Woolton – with his aunt Mimi, not with the
mother and father who deserted him – for the man who later wrote
'Working Class Hero'. Lennon picked up the *Mail* in the first week
of 1967 and used it to write the song 'A Day In The Life' that closed
the *Sergeant Pepper's Lonely Hearts Club Band* album: 'I read the news
today, oh boy . . .' In its edition of 7 January 1967,[26] the *Mail* published
a story about the death of Tara Browne – Lennon's friend and an
heir to the Guinness black beer empire – who had been driving with
a girlfriend through the sedate midnight streets of Kensington at
106 m.p.h. not too far from what would later become the *Mail*'s
current headquarters and smashed into a parked lorry: 'He blew his
mind out in a car, he didn't notice that the lights had changed . . .'
Another story in the *Mail* that day was a fairly dull little yarn headlined
'Holes in the Road' – 'There are 4,000 holes in the road in Blackburn,
Lancashire, or one twenty-sixth of a hole per person, according to a
council survey.'[27] Now, whichever Mailman penned this classic bit
of throw-away newspaper filler couldn't have had a clue that he was
helping inspire one of popular music's all-time classic songs: 'I read the
news today, oh boy. Four thousand holes in Blackburn, Lancashire,
and though the holes were rather small, they had to count them all,
now they know how many holes it takes to fill the Albert Hall . . .'
The 'cultural revolution' that was happening, or appeared to be
happening, led by Lennon's Beatles in the late 1960s, was handled

in a fairly mild and non-reactionary manner by many comment writers in the paper. A few months before John Lennon curled up with his *Daily Mail* on his little sofa in his huge mansion to compose 'A Day In The Life', Mailman Hugh McLeave, the paper's science correspondent, took a cool and detached look at the dropping of acid. 'LSD has a notorious reputation among the living-for-kicks addicts. But clinically it has a deep significance in the concept of mental chemistry.'

> How would you react if, lying wide awake, you had
> a mental playback of the Crucifixion in all its detail?
> Or you could hold an imaginary dialogue with Plato
> in Ancient Greece? Or relive the time you spent in the
> womb and the process of your own birth? . . . This
> compound, synthesised before the war, is helping the
> doctors to peel off the layers of the mind in the way
> that a housewife peels an onion . . . LSD has convinced
> many scientists that schizophrenia and similar illness has
> a chemical cause; if they can find what has gone awry in
> mental chemistry they might cure these diseases. So it
> may be there is a seventh or an eighth veil of conscious-
> ness which these drugs can strip away – to make the
> breakthrough which would revolutionise mental health.[28]

When Mick Jagger received three months in jail for possession of amphetamines and Keith Richards got a year for allowing cannabis to be smoked at a party at his home (both sentences were soon quashed on appeal) at the start of the so-called 'summer of love' in 1967, the paper opined, under the headline 'Pushers, pills and penalties' on the Comment page: 'The real point about the trial of the two Rolling Stones is that drug-taking has now been shown up for what it is – a national problem in urgent need of attention.'

> Opinion is sharply divided on whether the sentences will
> have the intended effect. Some say it will make martyrs

of the two youngsters. Others retort that a lesson was needed to deter those who are hovering on the brink of drug-taking . . . At present there is all too little agreement on the basic facts. For instance, which drugs have what effect?[29]

Vincent Mulchrone's effervescent opening words, Hugh McLeave's detached scientific writings and the mild worries about cannabis use among the young by the paper's leader writers were not enough to save the *Daily Mail*, though. She was, at heart, a dull old dear. Esmond had under-funded and under-promoted the paper and industrial strife had blighted the parent company's profitability – in common with the rest of Fleet Street – for years as the men who actually made the physical thing often sought unreasonable conditions for themselves and tried to resist irresistible techno- logical change. The print unions ruled Fleet Street – possibly more so than the proprietors – through what were called 'old Spanish practices': absurd working rights in which cash payments could be demanded for the remaking of a page on deadline or for covering for mysteriously absent colleagues – machine-room minders would even enter false names on worksheets to gain a payment. Some printers, consequently, were paid far more than the journalists; it was very much a closed shop (employees had to become members of the relevant union) and the chances of a skilled craftsman getting a post on Fleet Street were pretty slim – jobs were passed down from father to son. Strikes were endemic. In April 1955, for instance, national newspapers disappeared off the streets for almost a month after a pay dispute between 700 members of the electricians' and engineers' unions and the Newspaper Proprietors' Association – which Lord Rothermere had chaired since the thirties. It cost the industry £3 million (something like £70 million today). Big news events the Fleet Street papers missed included Prime Minister Sir Winston Churchill's resignation, the Budget and the announce- ment of a general election. As Rupert Murdoch put it, years later, the print unions 'had a noose round the neck of the industry, and they pulled it very tight'.[30]

So the *Daily Mail* was struggling to make a decent profit. And then, of course, there was the *Daily Express*. The second Lord Rothermere was as completely and utterly blindsided by Lord Beaverbrook as his father had been before him. Even his mother, 'Bluebell', had warned Esmond of the danger: 'I am convinced that Beaverbrook has only one dominant aim in life, perhaps a quite natural one, which is to place his paper ahead of yours! Therefore I do most emphatically warn you against this man and ask you in full seriousness to weigh up the reasons which prompt him now and will in the future to make all kinds of overtures to you, believe me none will be prompted by the desire to really help you – of this I am certain.'[31]

Esmond did not heed his mother's warning and personally fell for Max Aitken's big smile and seductive charm. Years later in 1962, Esmond, for instance, even hosted a lavish party to mark the eighty-third birthday of his 'friend' Max. Most of the other newspaper proprietors looked on as Beaverbrook sat on Rothermere's plush settee in the first-floor drawing room of his Warwick House home with Sir Winston Churchill on one side and Harold Macmillan on the other. The old man was presented with a birthday cake that had a music box and a skating rink on top of the icing and his birthday present was a huge solid silver tea tray engraved with the signatures of every guest . . . a platter more than big enough for Esmond's head. Beaverbrook later wrote Rothermere a note thanking him for a bash 'exceeding in glory all my many birthdays'.[32]

As he ate his slice of cake on the comfortable sofa under a huge chandelier alongside two former Prime Ministers, Beaverbrook may have reflected how, decades earlier, he had declared that the two newspaper groups were 'locked in a death grapple'. And this fight to the death must have seemed almost done in 1962 to those ex-PMs and London's other newspaper proprietors. The vivacious *Express* was at the peak of its powers. It was selling almost 4.5 million copies a day, an astonishing figure and nearly twice what the *Daily Mail* has ever achieved in its entire existence. Arguably, all of those readers should – and could – have been *Daily Mail* readers had it remained anything like the paper its founding father had originally intended (though, to be fair, newspaper readership was vast in this era, with many house-holds taking more than one paper every day – even the limp *Daily Mail* was selling around 2.5 million, while cousin Cecil King's *Daily Mirror* was well on its way towards its peak of over 5 million).

Around the same time as the Beaverbrook bash, the *Mail*'s gossip columnist and film critic Quentin Crewe asked Rothermere why the *Daily Mail* was 'so gloomy'. Esmond replied: 'My father was a gloomy man, I think that's the reason.'[33] Bunny Harmsworth might have been dead over twenty years by then but he still cast a long dark shadow over the *Daily Mail*.

Neither of the first two Rothermeres seemed capable of grasping it, but Sunny Harmsworth's formula was, fundamentally, very simple: give the target audience – the middle classes of whichever era – exactly what they wanted. The *Daily Mail* could have trounced the *Daily Express* if either Rothermere had managed to keep things fresh by finding – and sticking with – the right editor while allowing him the freedom to edit without interference. Esmond actually made a botched attempt to sign an editorial wunderkind called Arthur Christiansen from the *Sunday Express* in 1930 to edit his *Sunday Dispatch*, but Beaverbrook persuaded the twenty-six-year-old hack from Merseyside to stay inside his firm and soon appointed him editor of the *Daily Express*, which Christiansen led, for two decades, through its meteoric circulation rise. Beaverbrook also later poached Ted Pickering, who followed Christiansen as editor in the 1950s, from the *Mail*.

The *Daily Mail* entirely lost its way under Bunny & Son – Esmond would appoint an editor to take it upmarket and when that didn't work, he'd fire the man and then head half-heartedly the other way. Yet up the road Beaverbrook had simply followed a refreshed version of Sunny Harmsworth's original formula and reaped the rewards of a massive circulation (it sold fewer than 500,000 copies a day when he bought the *Daily Express* five decades before and progressively found 4 million more people happy to buy it every day).

Beaverbrook had once declared: 'I shall go back to New Brunswick and retire a failure if I don't succeed in killing the *Daily Mail*.' The

Mail wasn't quite dead yet, but it was seriously ill when Beaverbrook died just two years after his birthday bash at Esmond's plush London home. Max 'Moccasin Mouth' Aitken was sent back to Canada in a box and his ashes were interred underneath a head-and-shoulders bust in the town square in Newcastle, New Brunswick, beside the spot where he sold newspapers as a young boy; many people thought the *Daily Mail*'s obituary was all but set in type.

It looked as though the newspaper that would speak to and for tomorrow's middle England was the *Daily Express*, not the *Daily Mail* . . . unless the next Viscount Rothermere, Esmond's son Vere, could somehow become an amalgamation of grandfather Bunny and great-uncle Sunny Harmsworth.

PART III

THE MAIL PILL

7

Win a Pub

There was a new boy in Postal Bargains.

He was very tall, frightfully posh and awfully handsome – a young chap who looked like an Italian gigolo from one of the movies of this 1950s era, turning the heads of the female staff in the little-loved annexe of the advertising department of Associated Newspapers with his high cheekbones, cleft chin and fine mane of curly hair. The men noticed him too as they prepared special offers and prizes to try and boost circulation, for a different reason: he was the son of the boss, the heir to the Harmsworth folded-paper throne – the second Lord Rothermere's only son: Vere Harold Esmond Harmsworth. Or 'mere Vere', as his caustic chums at Eton had called him.

Few people thought Vere was very bright. Some thought he was plain lazy. When he was evacuated to the US as a teenager during the Blitz for a brief stint at Kent School in Connecticut, for instance, a business associate of his father's remarked that he was 'supremely good' at three things; sitting, eating and sleeping. He loved life in the US though, especially his school. 'I got back to Eton in 1941 and I did very well for the first year and then this awful negative atmosphere of British education seeped into one. One became sort of brain dead.'[1]

Vere was a rare thing among old Etonians: he failed to gain a commission as an officer, serving his entire four-year National Service stint in the ranks. Yet it proved to be a good thing and would serve

him well in the future. He liked these working-class lads from tough
cities like Newcastle, Liverpool and Glasgow. And they liked him.
'You see,' he said later in an oblique interview with the *Observer*,
'when you're standing above a tree, you can only see the branches
and the leaves but when you're underneath the tree, and you look up,
you can see all the things inside the tree – and that's a very valuable
experience.'[2]

Lord Rothermere, Vere's father, hadn't planned a newspaper future
for his son. 'I remember when I was a small boy, riding,' Vere told the
BBC. 'My father had a most beautiful house in Kent and used to take
me riding in the mornings. I remember him telling me that my
future would be as an officer in the Blues or the Life Guards and
what a wonderful life it was, hunting and shooting and fishing
and all this sort of thing. And I listened to this with a sinking heart and
utter horror at the dreadful prospect that lay before me.'[3]

It was abundantly clear to anyone who understood Fleet Street
that Esmond Harmsworth did not have ink in his veins . . . but Vere
did; he adored the family newspapers and joined the family business
as fast as he could, first at a paper mill in Canada for a couple of
years before arriving on Fleet Street in Postal Bargains. Male staff
sniped. Female staff adjusted their frocks and hair. Vere was hot, posh
and . . . loaded. His father did his best, however, to keep him away
from the actual editorial side of the firm, sending him off to the West
Country for a stint as a sales rep, where he'd talk to newsagents and
suppliers instead of the drunkenly debauched hacks of Fleet Street.

Then he moved to the senior management of the *Daily Sketch*,
a paper Bunny had bought when he and Beaverbrook had carved
up another minor media empire in the early 1920s and shared the
spoils. Harold sold it on but Esmond later bought it back to compete
– ineffectively, as it turned out – with cousin Cecil King's *Daily
Mirror*. Vere loved the little *Sketch* though. It was a much leaner,
swifter operation than the *Mail*.

One day in the mid-1950s Vere came up with an idea for a competition – perhaps inspired by the ultimate dream of those working-class
army pals – in which one lucky reader would 'Win a Pub'. Newspaper

promotions need words, they need to become a fake story, and it often falls to the features department to turn these sugary freaks into actual stories for people to read in their paper as if somebody hadn't paid for the space. The *Daily Sketch*'s features editor at the time was David English – an editorial whirlwind in his mid-twenties. The pair pulled on their jackets and went off to do some research in various pubs, and became firm friends. A dozen or so years later, they'd be two sides of a freshly minted *Daily Mail* coin: the perfect editor on one side, the perfect proprietor on the other.

David English adored his grandpa Alf.

It was Alf who stirred in him a love for newspapers, a passion that would elevate him to the side of the most infamous of Britain's Tory Prime Ministers even though Alfred Brazenor was a staunch Socialist and union leader who drove a tram.

David English's father died in 1930 when his boy was only three months old and Alf, for his part, had lost his only son in the final weeks of the First World War. So Alf lavished his only grandchild with love and attention. White-haired, fun-loving Alf and boisterous, friendly David would play cricket out on the lawn with the children of guests at the family-run hotel in Bournemouth. Those were idyllic days, until war came again in 1939 and invasion seemed imminent; tank traps and land mines were sunk in the sand, great spools of barbed wire rolled out along the beach and the pier walkways were blown up so the Germans couldn't land their boats. A hotel was no longer such a good trade, so the family let the business go and moved to a little house.

Everything was scarce in town, including footballs. So Alf picked up his needle and thread, grabbed a few strips of old leather and sewed them up – magically – into footballs, and became a hero to all the boys of Bournemouth. Alf had been a London saddle-maker – from a long line of saddle-makers – until the motor car killed forever man's need for the horse.

Grandpa Alf was also, crucially, a newspaper reader who took three from the newsagent every day: the *Daily Herald*, the *News Chronicle* and the *Daily Mail* – one Socialist, one Liberal and one Tory. 'I was fascinated by the look of them,' English told Harmsworth biographer S. J. Taylor. 'When the war came, you read them avidly, the maps and vivid battle accounts. It was fascinating for me to see three papers and how they dealt with different stories.'[4] English kept bundles of them under his bed, and would revisit them – long after their news had gone stale.

'He became obsessed with newspapers,' Tony Burton, a friend from English's first days in Fleet Street, told the author. 'And he loved and admired his grandfather. It was his grandfather who led him to the idea of everything, of laying out a paper – of reporting. The whole kit and kaboodle.'[5]

English's mother, Kitty, had worked as a secretary on Fleet Street and told stories about the reporters she'd encountered there, and the family would watch movies about hacks in trilby hats. An older boy left school for a job on a local paper and English 'sort of hero-worshipped him a bit', and wanted to follow him out of school and on to Fleet Street.

> My mother was absolutely furious. She wanted me to go
> to university. She changed all her stories about Fleet Street
> and then it was all, you know, doom and gloom and Fleet
> Street was nothing but full of drunks and ne'er do wells
> and people in deep debt. But I was encouraged by my
> grandfather, who felt that I should write and do what
> I wanted to do. My grandfather was very courteous, he
> would never fight with my mother, he would be magis-
> terial with his lovely mane of white hair. He would say,
> 'I think the boy should do what he wants. Let the boy
> do what he wants.'[6]

Alf's boy got a job on the *Christchurch Times* shortly after the war. A local weekly newspaper is the single best training-ground there has ever been for a journalist because they have very few staff and only one press day, so a young hack has to cope with everything from town hall meetings to football reports to minor and major crime. 'Death knocks' are also an important rite of passage for most young reporters on any decent local paper; the news editor would scan his paper's death notices in search of bodies to turn into stories and send the office junior out to knock on the dead man's door. They tend not to answer but their next of kin do. It can be tough, walking up and pressing a doorbell knowing you are intruding upon grief, but it is also great experience of how to cope with a difficult situation and emerge from an address with a notebook full of quotes from which to construct a story. English would speak 'to the widow and his children, I learned to relate to people in grief. I was surprised that people were so grateful. But I learned how to handle difficult circumstances. It's a wonderful sort of grooming school, finishing school really, how to relate to people.'

Chris Rees was a friend of English's from their days together as fourteen-year-old Sea Cadets at the end of the war, and Rees was set on a job as an electrician until his friend infected him with his enthusiasm for the words trade. 'Any little thing at all got the same level of commitment, even the shipping forecast,' Rees told the author. 'He put his whole being into the job. I think that's why he became so successful.'[7]

English moved to a big local daily on the south coast and then on to Fleet Street in 1951. 'He got a job on the *Daily Mirror* by the age of twenty, by lying about his age,' said Rees. 'He added a year because you had to be twenty-one in those days before they'd hire you.'[8] And so a dapper young man who'd somehow managed to dodge his compulsory eighteen-month national service arrived on Fleet Street as a seasoned operator with four years' worth of wear on his reporting shoes before the university boys had even hung up their books.

Esmond's cousin Cecil Harmsworth King was in charge of the public company that owned the *Mirror* at the time (he didn't own it himself – he had been a senior manager when Bunny sold it off in the early 1930s when it began to fail as a picture paper on account of every paper printing photographs by then). King had refocused the paper and aimed it at the working-class market and, with the help of Welsh editorial genius Hugh Cudlipp, the *Mirror* would go on to sell almost 5.3 million copies a day – a world record. Cousin Cecil's downmarket *Daily Mirror*, however, horrified the snobbish Harmsworths, according to King. His extended family were 'desperately anxious' to conceal their humble beginnings. 'Popular newspapers were the source of their wealth, their power and their titles but they did not want to be reminded of this.'[9]

By the time David English was starting his career, Cecil King's *Daily Mirror* was the mightiest working-class paper of the day, in the same way Beaverbrook's *Express* dominated the middle-class market. And the *Mirror* was always hiring (and firing).

Tony Burton was another young reporter making his way in Fleet Street at the time. Burton and a reporter friend, Des Lyons, were sick of living in a flea-pit boarding house so, one day in the early 1950s, they decided to find somewhere nicer to live. They went to look at two empty beds in a two-bedroom flat in Dulwich, south London – two beds to a room. Another young hack was already living there.

'My first memory of David English was him sitting down with drumsticks and banging away "bum bum bum, bum bum" on a coffee table in front of the fireplace,' Burton told the author. 'His charm got you immediately.'[10] English was 'a bit of a dandy, a Teddy Boy' who cared about his appearance and always made sure he had nicely cut hair. The flatmates became close friends. And, boys being boys, they liked to meet girls.

'English wasn't much of a drinker but he loved to dance and one day he insisted that we go dancing at the Hammersmith Palais,' said Burton. 'Des was reluctant but he drove us there in his clapped-out Austin Seven; one of the doors had to be held closed. While we danced with various young ladies, disgruntled Des just sat drinking. And when we gallantly decided we would escort two young ladies home he reluctantly agreed to take us. David and I sat in the back with a pretty girl on each of our laps and kept calling him "chauffeur" in a lordly fashion while directing him which way to go. Crossing Barnes Common we ordered him to stop so that we could continue "getting to know" the girls. As we strolled into the bushes, Des took off, giving us a two-finger salute.'[11] They thumbed a lift home in the rain off the actor Richard Attenborough, who was passing by in his Rolls-Royce, recalled Burton, after a late-night radio gig.

One night, the flatmates decided to have a party in their flat and it proved to be an event that perfectly illustrated David English's tenacity, a vital trait in any reporter. Des was a mean razzmatazz piano player, and English ordered a piano. 'They couldn't get the fucking thing up the stairs so he got some sort of a crane and they brought it in through the window!' said Burton. 'This was so typical of David English – other people would just have given up. But no, he decided he'd *got* to have that piano so Des could play at the party.' He also demonstrated his guile by getting girls to come to the party. 'David put a notice up at the Adelphi Theatre on the Strand where the Tiller Girls were dancing, inviting all the girls round to this party. And a bunch of them came!'[12]

The Tiller Girls were a famous high-kicking dance troupe at the time, and one would later become Mrs English (though Irene Mainwood wasn't actually at that party). 'I shared a bedroom with David to which he brought Irene for a sleepover,' said Burton. 'She said her first memory of me was a hairy arm emerging from the bedclothes to find and light a cigarette.'[13]

They married in the early 1950s on the south coast and English would remain tethered to Irene his whole life. But his career was on rockier ground. 'David didn't get on with the *Mirror*'s news editor Ken Hord – nobody got on with Ken Hord,' said Burton. 'And David's connection to the *Mirror* was actually above the news editor, and I think Hord resented that.'[14] Worst of all, the news editor didn't like the youngster's socks. 'I won't have reporters wearing white socks,' he told him, 'go home and change.' Hord put a note on the newsroom notice board saying he'd been forced to discipline a young reporter for not being dressed well enough to represent the *Daily Mirror* and 'any more sartorial aberrations by this man will result in dismissal and anyone else who indulges in sartorial aberrations will be fired as well'.[15]

English soaked up Hord's abuse for a couple of years, then quit, thinking he'd find another staff gig elsewhere. He didn't, and he was forced to freelance. Initially, English and Burton set up their own press agency, but it soon failed. So Burton joined the *Mirror* up in Birmingham and English worked for a now defunct left-wing Sunday paper called *Reynolds News* for a while and was soon up to mischief in search of a scoop.

Bags full of post, back in the day, would be just dumped off trains and left on the platforms at railway stations unguarded until someone from the Royal Mail came along and took the bags away to be sorted. Maybe English's news editor had seen the fat bags of mail himself at Euston station on his way into work, but anyway, he suggested his most enthusiastic young reporter should go 'and steal a mailbag, they're just lying about, bring it back to the office. Nobody will stop you.'[16] It would be a front page for sure.

The young hack lined up his body just like they did in the movies, scooped up a fat bag of letters and scurried off up the platform towards the taxi rank trying to look innocent . . . maybe working out his intro on the way. If he got back to the office, triumphant, he could rummage through a few letters and add in some great detail. 'The mail that didn't make it through.'

English was a nice, newly married middle-class boy from the seaside and a great reporter . . . but he was a crap thief. Likewise, poor Reg Coote, the photographer assigned to the tale, was twenty years older and carrying a heavy camera. English and Coote must have looked curious thieves to the pair of bored inspectors who spent their lives watching humanity hurry through Euston station. It was a criminal act big enough to make the *Reuters* news wire in September 1952 when David and Reg stood up in court a little while later. 'English was about to enter a taxi when the officials ran toward him. At that moment there was a flash from Coote's camera. English explained it was a stunt "to prove that mails at mainline stations were not properly guarded" and added, "This incident has now proved to us we were wrong."' The magistrate said it was 'a silly thing to do' and dismissed the case.[17]

English soon joined the *Daily Sketch* and rose rapidly through the ranks of the paper's pared-down staff to become the assistant editor in charge of Features. Vere Harmsworth, the future third Lord Rothermere, became his friend but not his boss; Vere didn't work in editorial – his father wouldn't let him anywhere near those dirty hacks. The *Sketch* was a good little paper, if never in the *Daily Mirror*'s league. The snobbish, upward-facing side of the Harmsworth clan were never comfortable in what they saw as the rough end of the market. But at least the *Sketch* wasn't dragging its heavy past into the future like her big sister the *Daily Mail*.

One *Daily Sketch* reporter was Barry Norman, who later became famous as a presenter and film reviewer. 'David English sent me off to cover the war in Cyprus when I was very young,' Norman told the author. 'And I wrote a pretty crappy piece and he rewrote it beautifully for me. It was a very good read but it didn't bear a very strong resemblance to the facts I'd put in my far duller story. The *Sketch* was a bit like that, though, as a paper – never let the facts get in the way of a good story.'[18]

He was an excellent features editor but the executive path bored young David English and he longed to get back on the road. So in 1959 he flew to New York to work for the ailing *Sketch*'s struggling sister paper the *Sunday Dispatch*. English was back where he wanted to be, 'at the ring side of history'.[19] And he was having fun. On one occasion he tested out a new drug that was supposed to stop people getting drunk on a collection of twins. One twin took the pill, the other didn't. The experiment soon dissolved into drunken brawls that spilled out into the street. The fun didn't last for long though; the *Sunday Dispatch* was getting battered by Beaverbrook's *Sunday Express* in the same way the *Sketch* was being battered by the *Mirror*, in its market, and Esmond closed it in June 1961.

English and his wife Irene wanted to stay in the US and English had a strong reputation as a good operator, so he soon found a job on the *Daily Express* in New York. He had a reputation as a ruthless competitor with gimlet eyes but he also showed a human side. When a reporter on a rival publication, for instance, was too petrified to go and see a giant worm – several feet long – that a man kept as a pet in his apartment, it could have been an easy scoop for English, seeing as the competition was too scared to even knock on the man's door. Yet both reporters lied to their bosses, saying the Peruvian monster wasn't home. He also began to pen a column of American miscellany that was viewed as a huge success.

There were two David Englishes, politically, in this early part of his career: the one who sailed to the United States listing to the left and the one who returned listing to the right. David English had started out – just like Grandpa Alf – as a Socialist and had even been an official for the National Union of Journalists, while his wife Irene was in the performers' union Equity. But then they began to be pushed to the right by America's free market and all the lovely stuff it could provide for even the average person – from cars as big as boats to refrigerators as big as tombs. By 1963 the former NUJ man even helped create a strike-breaking newspaper when all the other papers disappeared off the streets after the print workers walked out.

It proved to be a great learning experience for the future editor: he learned what happened if he fused the efforts of American and British journalists, and it also taught him about getting the paper printed beyond the reach of the strikers and how to do dodgy distribution deals with – as English told the tale – a Mafia don who controlled the drivers' union. 'I went to see a man called Waxy Gordon,' English reminisced three decades later. 'He had some office on Broadway. Anyway, we did a deal which of course virtually took away all the profits, but allowed us to go on producing the paper.'[20]

There's a problem with the precise truth and accuracy of this anecdote, though. In actual fact, the real-life mobster Waxey Gordon was long gone from the Mafia scene by then[21] – he'd died in Alcatraz prison a decade before – and, maybe, English was embellishing a story for effect. A fictional Waxey, however, did appear on TV in the mob series *The Untouchables* shortly before English's paper appeared. All the newspapers came back after four months and the paper, like Waxey, melted away.

Then David English suffered the curse of many a top reporter after almost five years in the States with the *Daily Express*: he got promoted. The *Express* called him home in 1965 to become foreign editor, hoping some of his natural chutzpah might rub off on the rest of the staff. One of those infected by English's natural exuberance for the newspaper trade was Louis Kirby, who would later become his long-term deputy editor on the *Daily Mail*. 'The first time I saw David English,' wrote Kirby, 'was on a *Daily Express* cinema advertisement: the very picture of a powerful foreign editor, issuing instructions, shouting down the phones "Write it! Write it!"'[22]

It wasn't just the sky in England that seemed so lead-lined on English's return; post-war Britain was a grey and drab, drizzly, cold-water and outside-loo kinda place – dragging the weight of her past into the future like horsemeat. The British Empire had long ago expired, though many clung – some still cling – to the corpse, but Queen Elizabeth II embodied a fraction of the importance of Queen Victoria.

Mr & Mrs English wanted to bring home some of that American sparkle, that freshness, a lifestyle from the dominant world power, a place where it was perfectly acceptable to beam a big smile and say 'Have a nice day' – even if you really didn't mean it. 'As he climbed the journalistic ladder he and Irene moved from a modest home in Orpington to an upmarket house in Chislehurst where he would throw terrific parties, sometimes with David in charge of a roulette wheel,' said Tony Burton. 'What a host. When visiting I would be taking a shower and he would hand in a martini for me to drink while soaping up.'[23]

The Englishes had always aimed to become independently wealthy, added Burton. 'David was determined to make enough money outside of Fleet Street so he could afford to say "fuck you" and walk away if he had to,' he told the author. 'So he and Irene set up a laundrette business, and they made a lot of money. Irene was a very elegant, beautiful lady. And the joke at the time was that Irene – who was actually running this laundrette business – cricked her back carrying all the little coins from the machines to the bank each day.'[24]

English also turned his entrepreneurial flair to what he knew best: the newspaper trade, by setting up a free local newspaper business in south London. 'The little paper was doing okay,' added Burton. 'Then English got a call from Rupert Murdoch, who had just arrived from Aussieland and was starting to make his moves in England. "I wanna buy your little newspaper," Murdoch told him. "No thanks," English replied, "it's not for sale." "Look," said Murdoch, "you know I've got loads of money. If you don't sell it to me, I'll set up a competing paper and knock you out of the ring."

'And English, being a realist, said, "Well, how much will you pay?" And it was a decent amount – he wasn't being screwed, it was a fair amount. So, rather than get into a fight with Murdoch, he said, "Okay." But he didn't like being intimidated like that, as you can imagine, but that was his first encounter with Rupert Murdoch.'[25]

After his spell as a newspaper proprietor and a few years as the *Daily Express*'s foreign editor, everybody who was at least half a hack knew David English should be the editor of the *Daily Express* as it continued its domination of the middle-class mass market. He was, by far, the paper's most talented executive, yet when Beaverbrook's son sacked the editor, another man got the chair. Beaverbrook had only been dead a year or so, and his feckless playboy son, also called Max Aitken, was seemingly set on steering the *Express* off a cliff. Ann Leslie was a junior *Express* hack at the time. She had fallen into journalism while working out what to do with her life after Oxford University and it was English who made her realize journalism was her calling. As she told the *Independent*:

> He had a slightly spivvy, gossipy and manipulative
> charm – but if he lost faith in you, a terrifying coldness.
> I, like many of his staff, was both thoroughly alarmed
> and thoroughly exhilarated by him. I became a foreign
> correspondent largely because he had unshakeable faith
> in me – when others, understandably, didn't. He sent me
> on a story in Guyana and I blew it. The macho thugs on
> the foreign desk jeered: 'We told you so, David. Girlies

can't hack it!' When I wanted to run the New York bureau
the then editor refused on the grounds that 'You can't
have a WOMAN running a bureau!' David would say,
'When I'm editor, you can run any bureau you want.' I
realised that he would never become editor because the
proprietor was Sir Max Aitken, Lord Beaverbrook's son,
who only knew and cared about power boats and women.
When I resigned I was summoned to Aitken's office to
explain why. Among my reasons was that his decision not
to make English editor would eventually prove to be the
downfall of the *Express*. And I was right.[26]

David English was made associate editor instead in 1967, a
creature in the strange middling ranks, under the editor himself
yet senior to department heads – often a clutch of highly ambitious
hacks who would happily headbutt a rival to death if it would win
them a Sunday shift on the rota to actually edit the paper. By 1969,
the drive to be an editor by the age of forty was racing up to meet
him – English was thirty-nine – and down by the river at Associated
Newspapers, his pal Vere's power was increasing.

Vere arranged for English to be appointed editor of the ailing *Daily
Sketch* on the recommendation, partly, of another mutual friend –
its editor, Howard French (who was promoted on to the Associated
Newspapers board). Jean Rook was the *Daily Sketch*'s woman's editor:
'David English was the most demanding and inspiring editor I have
ever worked for,' wrote Rook in her autobiography. 'A massive ideas
man, everything he magically Midas-ed – and he touched every page
of the paper – turned his staff's output to gold. He never doubted his
newspaper's influence, or his own strength . . . English, we knew, was
too big to be satisfied with the small *Sketch*.'[27]

When he joined, the *Sketch* was being battered in its market by
the *Mirror* and it was about to take another hammering by Rupert
Murdoch's rising *Sun*. Its boyish editor blew oxygen into it, pumped
hard on its chest and managed to turn it into a lively little read.
But the *Sketch* was doomed. Meanwhile, the Harmsworth family's

flagship *Daily Mail* drifted in the newspaper doldrums with no wind in her broadsheet sails either.

There was a flicker of hope for the *Daily Mail*, though, in the shape of a small team of girls led by Shirley Conran who were working hard trying to get the *Mail* moving again by creating a paper – within the paper – that women wanted to read. Conran had first worked on the *Mail* in the early 1960s, writing about homes and design, before being poached by the *Observer* to create a woman's page, where she found that 'the *Observer* was very much a man's world and in that world of men, I could do whatever the hell I liked – because none of the men on the paper ever actually read my page. So I got away with murder. It was a sophisticated and sexy page,' she told the author, 'not sexy in the lewd sense – sexy in the same way any woman's magazine today is sexy. And that's why the *Mail* wanted me back.'[28]

Conran's old boss, a gentle Mailman called Gordon McKenzie, persuaded her to return and Conran thought she'd be doing a similar page for the *Mail*. But McKenzie had bigger plans. 'It was a top secret project they just called "the rabbit", nobody else knew anything about it.'[29] Features chief McKenzie and Arthur Brittenden, the broadsheet *Daily Mail*'s final editor, planned to launch a tabloid for females – tucked inside the broadsheet *Daily Mail*. What to christen this 'rabbit' proved to be a struggle. 'Everybody said the obvious name is *Femail* – with an "i", as in *Mail* – but it was so damn obvious, everyone just thought, "Let's not call it that." And then Arthur got a little note from Lord Rothermere [Esmond] saying he'd been talking to some of his friends over dinner and he'd had what they had all thought was a rather wonderful idea – we should call the new magazine *Femail*. So everyone concerned with "the rabbit" said: "What a brilliant idea! Let's call it *Femail*!"'[30]

The first sixteen-page tabloid *Femail* was launched in October 1968, with Conran resplendent in a glam-looking picture byline above a huge photo of a topless long-haired model in jeans . . . the snap taken from behind (bare breasts would be left to Murdoch's *Sun*); sex was a firm part of the *Femail* formula from the start. Inside was a feature on 'The Fertility Pill' by that bomb-proof old hand from the war days Rhona Churchill. As Conran wrote on the miniature *Mail*'s first front page:

> The things women are supposed to want to read about
> are generally decided upon by a man. In this magazine,
> as in our other women's pages, we are writing for a real
> woman . . . She doesn't want to compete, to be equal,
> she knows she's different. She's not interested in women's
> rights, but she's concerned about women's wrongs,
> especially if they happen to affect her . . . She thinks about
> men but not all the time. She's interested in sex but not
> all the time . . . She's as bewildered as a chameleon on
> a tartan rug, trying to be wife, mother, mistress, chauf-
> feur, cook, washer-up, accountant, general dogsbody
> and, sometimes, wage-earner . . . She jumps from crisis
> to crisis, shoulders family problems, and does a lot of
> thankless work that bores and exhausts her. She tries. She
> knows what doesn't interest her, whether it's politics or
> football, and doesn't want to feel guilty about it. Now and
> again she wants a good gossip. Like us.[31]

A new *Daily Mail* could be built upon this kind of content. Forty-three-year-old Vere, who had been vice-chairman of the company's board since 1963, spotted it immediately. But it'd take a new era – which was imminent – before the overladen *Mail* mothership could change course.

By now Fleet Street was not the road down which magazine-boy Sunny Harmsworth had rolled his brand new *Daily Mail* cannon in May 1896; it was not a street populated with tired old gentlemen who barely noticed the change that had come through the fug of their own cigars and self-regard. And by now Esmond, the second Rothermere – who was, after all, only two years younger than the *Mail* itself – was a relic from a bygone era.

By the end of the 1960s Fleet Street was a raucous, drunkenly dangerous place. But the dull *Daily Mail* wasn't even at the party. It was a seventy-three-year-old middleweight in a land bristling with younger, lighter, faster, far more vicious pugilists led by a young Australian called Rupert Murdoch. And the *Mail* had lost its voice long before. It had changed direction so many times, its staff barely knew right from left. It didn't seem to be for, or against, anything in particular. It didn't know who its readers were – or should be. The *Mail* had been milked for money by the first Rothermere and startled off course by Beaverbrook's *Daily Express*. It was testimony to the newspaper Sunny Harmsworth built that the *Mail* survived the first two Lord Rothermeres at all. By the end of 1970 its circulation was in decline and the combined financial losses with the *Sketch* were over a million pounds (£14.5 million today). Something had to be done.

Overpaid accountants said the wise move was to merge the *Mail* and the *Express* newspaper groups to make a mid-market monster. So a meeting was called between Lord Beaverbrook's son Max – who declined the title upon his father's death – and the second Lord Rothermere to decide whether a marriage could be arranged between the two press dynasties. Vere was there too, watching horrified from the sidelines. The *Daily Express* was the senior partner now in Fleet Street and any new daily beast could only have been named 'the *Express* & *Mail*'. It looked like it was all over for the Harmsworths of Fleet Street, a fate that would befall the bloodline of every single other press baron including, soon enough, Beaverbrook's family. At this summit, Esmond had been prepared to let the *Mail* go but wanted to keep the *Evening News*, the first newspaper the Harmsworth brothers had owned. Aitken's lawyer refused, insisting any deal had to be for the whole company. So Lord Rothermere saved his single most important contribution to the *Daily Mail* story until the very last moment; he washed his hands of the whole sorry mess, resigned and sailed away on a long holiday to South Africa at the age of seventy-two with his third wife, a Texan beauty almost exactly half his age.

Vere was given total control, and if 'mere' Vere Harmsworth had somehow received Uncle Northcliffe's *Daily Mail* DNA, maybe the paper could be saved.

8

A Compact Double-act

Vere Harmsworth gathered with his top managers and David English, his number-one editorial guru and the man he thought could revitalize the *Daily Mail*, in a cold and musty, dank oversized room with cracked windows and flaking walls; Room One, Great-uncle Northcliffe's 'big room for big ideas', was tatty by now, just like the attic where Sunny and Bunny Harmsworth had met with Kennedy Jones under a cracked skylight to work out what to do with the *Evening News*. This time, seventy-seven years later, it was the *Daily Mail* that was in deep trouble.

Problem after problem became apparent, starting with the paper's voice: the *Mail* didn't have one. It sounded like a sad old dear yearning for the past, an old lady they had to somehow make young again, positive and buoyant. The paper needed 'a sort of Victorian evangelism', the advertising manager, Brian Henry, had said in a memo, 'which seems to combine the virtues of hard work with a belief in personal salvation and rewards in this life as well as the hereafter'.[1] But, most of all, the *Mail* needed a young and vigorous new editor. And Vere already knew, of course, who it would be. The *Daily Sketch* editor David English was brash and bouncy, full of vim and mischief, but he was also, underneath, a slightly Puritanical man[2] who believed absolutely in the family and was loyal to his wife, unlike so many in his trade, and he was also loyal to his friends. He was perfect.

Vere was lucky English was at the meeting at all because, around the same time Esmond had sat down with Beaverbrook's son to discuss merging the two newspaper empires, Aitken had finally woken up and done what he should have several years before: he had offered English the editor's chair at the *Daily Express*. English, though only editor of the silly little *Sketch*, turned him down and went skiing with his wife and children. It seems it was a decision taken out of loyalty to his good friend Vere, and perhaps he knew better things were on their way. Plus Max Aitken Jr was no Lord Beaverbrook, in the same way as Esmond was no Northcliffe. Beaverbrook's boy had already proved, to many, he was a fool. Vere must have, surely, seemed the better bet – a better boss. When David English returned from the ski slopes, Vere was in full command of the *Mail*: he swiftly appointed English editor.

English thought sport and television needed to be handled better and the *Mail* needed outspoken, readable columnists with crisp and sensible opinions. It also had to have a clear political stance. It needed a cleaner look and the best photographs had to be selected with greater care, displayed better and bigger. The *Mail* should be, in a way, the *Daily Express* when it was at its best under Beaverbrook in the 1950s. English saw *Mail* readers as 'traditional without being reactionary; who are believers in the individual being independent; who are ambitious (not yet rich, they hope to be some day) and who very much believe in this country. This does not mean they are all fuddy-duddy colonels; there is still a "British is best" attitude among the young and the working class as well as the middle class.'[3]

Long-term Mailman Noel Barber wrote a story introducing the new editor to the paper's readers over a photograph of a clean-cut young man who commuted in to work each day from Chislehurst, eleven miles to the south of London. 'Though politically a Conservative, he is flexible, and feels that "It is not necessary to take a preconceived stance on every issue that comes up,"' wrote Barber. 'After newspapers, David's passion is boating and sailing, and when he gets a day off the family heads for Ramsgate where they berth their sea-going motor-cruiser called *Dinan*, a name made up of family initials. Does this picture of a young, middle-class family remind you of anyone? It does me – it reminds me of a typical *Daily Mail* reader.'[4]

Young Sunny Harmsworth had been of the middle classes too, an earlier version from the later Victorian era, and he was about to help out his *Daily Mail* from beyond the grave. It all came down to a little pill. Alfred C. Harmsworth had been forever fretting over his health. Even as a boy, there was always something wrong with him and he armed himself against sickness as an adult. When Lord Northcliffe, for example, sailed off for a world tour, the year before he died, his medicine chest was better stocked than some hospital wards: he had opium and phenacetin alongside vegetable laxative, soda mint, bromide, potassium permanganate, chlorodyne, calomel, zinc sulphate, mustard leaves, iodoform, caustic pencil, a thermometer, suture silk and needles, bandages, plaster, lint and a water-sterilizer. Sickly Sunny Harmsworth, the five-star traveller, also had snake-bite lancets because, well, one just never knew.

It was this morbid self-obsession that led to a new word entering the newspaper lexicon: tabloid. The word was invented towards the end of the nineteenth century by a medical salesman, to mean any medicine compressed down into a small pill – a 'tablet' with the Greek suffix '-oid'. During a trip to the US, Alfred was invited by journalist Joseph Pulitzer to publish the perfect newspaper on 1 January 1901, the first day of the twentieth century. (Sunny Harmsworth was fascinated by America and visited the US twenty-two times in an era in which it was a five-day trip each way by steamship.) He took hold of Pulitzer's *New York World* and cut it physically in half. Harmsworth had noticed that people folded their papers, to avoid sticking their elbows into the nose of their neighbour on the bus or train. Some just cheated, and only read the headlines and the sub decks – so Sunny ordered that stories written for the *World* that night should be no longer than 250 words.

'All the news in sixty seconds,' he wrote. 'The *World* enters today upon the Twentieth or Time-Saving Century. I claim that by my system of condensed or tabloid journalism, hundreds of working hours can be saved each year.'[5]

Sunny christened this strange, experimental newspaper a 'tabloid'. It didn't catch on. The next day the newspaper was printed in its usual broadsheet form.

By 1971, 'tabloid' meant a pair of breasts peeking into your personal space instead of a broadsheet reader's elbows. Vere Harmsworth hated the word. A tabloid was read by a bloke as he sat on the toilet with a hard hat laid on the cistern or at the wheel of his parked white van or black cab as the radio blared out David Bowie and the solo wares of the broken-up Beatles. Tabloids were made for the men with the small hat size that Sunny Harmsworth had found so curious. The word was the very definition of downmarket. They were sensational rags that people of a certain class instinctively didn't trust. The new breed of post-war, middle-class readers Vere was aiming at would never allow a 'true' tabloid into their home. Never. And Vere knew that the adman didn't want these unwashed hordes either; they had no spare cash. The adman wanted nice folk with their own car parked on their suburban driveway and money to spend on new carpets and package holidays to Majorca and double-glazing. Twenty-three 'new towns' had sprung up all over Britain to help rehouse people whose homes had been bombed during the war and to clear away city centre slums. Vere, who had worked in the company's circulation department as a sales rep, thought they were populated with just the sort of people who should be reading his new version of the *Daily Mail*.

Nevertheless, the actual physical size of a tabloid newspaper was clearly the way to go. Compressing and condensing the old *Mail* into a new pill was the magic formula. They were 20 per cent cheaper to produce than a broadsheet and yet could earn exactly the same advertising revenue. Bunny would have loved the numbers; a tabloid page was physically half that of a broadsheet, yet the bill the adman sent out wasn't reduced by a single penny. A page is a page, was the adman's phrase. And half of the tabloid *Mail*'s revenues had to come from ads for the paper to be viable. Lastly, studies showed that readers simply liked the smaller format better. Readers spent more time reading them; tabloid-sized newspapers were – as their inventor

Sunny Harmsworth had realized seven decades before – simply easier to hold and easier to read.

That word, though, 'tabloid', was proving to be a real dilemma for designing a new *Daily Mail*, as Brian Freemantle, who was to be the new paper's foreign editor, told the author: 'Saying the word tabloid was a bit like saying "fuck" in a monastery. We agonized over that. But the fact was that we were going to go down to tabloid – there you are, you see, I used the word – yet the last thing we ever wanted to be was a tabloid. So, what to call it? We went round and round the houses on that. And finally we chose the word compact.'[6]

'Compact' was all about the size and compression of information, not sensational celebrity headlines and soft-porn. Vere wanted to line the paper up for women, specifically young mums. And female readers were already familiar with a pared-down *Daily Mail* thanks to *Femail*. But this aspirational young lady didn't want nipples poking her husband in the eye every morning while her 2.4 children tried not to dribble milk down their neatly pressed school uniforms, the paint drying on the walls of her new kitchen. Vere Harmsworth was certain that the female of the species was the last great, untapped newspaper market – and they'd take their husbands with them.

Sunny had aimed originally for the female market but he had not really succeeded; it was the clerks that bought his *Mail*, not women. If his paper had truly found its female voice, he would never have felt the need to create the all-female *Daily Mirror*. 'Northcliffe's *Daily Mail* was aimed at the lower middle-class,' explained Vere. 'The *Mirror* discovered the working class. Women are going to save this paper. We have to direct ourselves at women right through – not to producing a women's paper but a paper for women. The difference is subtle; you don't publish a lot of women's pages, you give a news coverage that women want to read; that way you hold your men readers too.'[7]

These women, it was presumed by the adman, also controlled the family purse. The meeting in Room One broke up and they knew the way forward. Everything was going to change. Everything. There was no hope for the *Daily Sketch*, they'd shut it down and merge it with the *Daily Mail*. The new paper was to be a tabloid's size without containing 'red-top' material; it was to be given a new voice without having a tabloid's loud and sometimes foul mouth. It would appeal to women and advertisers. The plan was pretty bold and possibly pretty stupid. At the time, a 'serious' tabloid was absurd – these readers didn't exist. It could be crushed from above by the higher-brow broadsheets, knifed in the ribs by the still-strong broadsheet *Daily Express* and chewed from below by the red-tops. Mick Shields, Vere's long-term managing director, would say of the proprietor at the time: 'The chairman is twice as clever as he looks but only half as clever as he thinks.'[8]

'Mere' Vere was about to start a war on three fronts and was either the playboy buffoon many thought he was, or Sunny's genes had finally bubbled back to the surface inside a living, breathing Harmsworth.

Whatever Vere would prove to be, David English simply bounded away to form a newspaper he wanted to read, that he wanted to edit, around Vere's vision. However, he was far better prepared than perhaps anyone in such a position had any right to be – he'd had a head start. English had spent the preceding two years growing a new brain for the *Daily Mail* in the Harmsworth family shed down the bottom of their immaculate lawn. Inside the little-loved *Daily Sketch*, English had assembled a talented young team. Through sheer charm and force of character, English had persuaded many to quit the mighty *Express* for the *Sketch* – a paper some presumed to be doomed. And now, these brand-new Mailmen raised in Beaverbrook's stable had until the first Monday of May 1971 to build a new paper from the sky down, the *Daily Mail*'s seventy-fifth birthday. Brian Freemantle was one of them. He had known David English for two decades and they'd both been reporters on local papers on the south coast before meeting up again in Fleet Street, where Freemantle worked under English on the foreign desk of the *Daily Express*. When English went to the *Sketch*, he took Freemantle with him as foreign editor. It was a grand-sounding job title but by that point in the *Sketch*'s decline, it barely had a foreign department at all.

'I went across to the *Mail* as the foreign editor,' he told the author. 'It was a defacto takeover of the *Mail* by the *Sketch*. The news editor of the *Sketch* went across as news editor of the *Mail*. The picture editor went across from the *Sketch* to be picture editor of the *Mail* . . . all the department heads were *Sketch* people. It caused a lot of bad feeling between the *Sketch* and the *Mail*.'[9]

The *Mail*'s editor, Arthur Brittenden, agreed over lunch with Vere at Claridge's that he would continue editing the old broadsheet *Mail* as English prepared and tested the new paper in parallel. He even helped compile a hit list of his staff whom he felt the new *Mail* could live without. There were a lot of them, and what followed was a period of bloodletting dubbed 'The Night of the Long Envelopes' in Fleet Street mythology. It came as a shock to many Mailmen and Femails to learn that they were the ones getting the boot; it seemed to some that all that was changing was one word on the *Daily Sketch*'s masthead. It was actually the *Daily Mail* that was to die.

Barry Norman was by now the *Mail*'s star showbiz writer. 'We were all told one Friday that redundancy notices were to be given out that night,' he told the author. 'And we all gathered around at about nine o'clock at night in the newsroom and then, you knew if you were called in to see your head of department you had a long envelope waiting for you. And I was called in, and I got one.'[10] Within a couple of years, Norman was established as a big BBC name and would review movies for twenty-six years, starting with *Film '72*. English later claimed he'd tried to persuade Norman to stay, which was, said Norman, 'a total lie. I'd never talked to David English about that at all . . . But I was soon kind of glad I wasn't there any more because it wasn't the kind of newspaper that I'd been used to working for. It was much more like *The Sun* or the *Mirror* than like the old *Daily Mail* or the then still-broadsheet *Daily Express*. I had a lot of admiration for David, I think he did a very good job on the new *Daily Mail*. But he wasn't a man I would trust. I mean he was very affable, good company . . . but I wouldn't turn my back on him.'[11]

At the same time as the mass redundancies, the new paper was being precision-planned in absolute secrecy and several trial-run 'dummies' of the new tabloid had been made in Amsterdam. The building was packed on the Sunday evening when the floor rumbled and the mighty presses rolled on the first tabloid *Daily Mail* just like it had all those years before for Sunny Harmsworth. The paper had a good scoop with the splash 'Spy Scandal in Britain's Defence HQ'; a Soviet wiretap had been found on a phone line at the Ministry of Defence. And on the leader page, the aged paper was already sounding a lot like Sunny Harmsworth too.

> Welcome to the new *Daily Mail*. Today, 75 years after
> the birth of Northcliffe's *Daily Mail* – the paper that
> pioneered popular journalism – another generation of
> British newspapers is born . . . we aim to give you more,
> much more in the new *Daily Mail* than a paper that is easy
> to read and handle in the train. We believe that people
> are also looking for a new style of journalism . . . To be
> serious without being glum, to entertain without being
> trashy, to catch the flavour of these swirling times. With
> your encouragement we can do it. For a newspaper is only
> as strong as the support of its readers for whom – and to
> whom – it speaks. We want the new *Daily Mail* to be like
> a conversation between friends. [12]

Yet despite all the planning, something *had* gone horribly wrong. The new *Daily Mail* looked like an invite to a wake, not a birthday party, on Monday, 3 May 1971, just a day shy of the paper's actual seventy-fifth anniversary (it would be weird to have a relaunch on a Tuesday). 'As soon as it began to come off the press there was a great moan of "Oh fuck, what have we done there?"' said Brian Freemantle. 'We had put this black border, these boxes, around the text on the front page. It just looked so wrong, like a big funeral notice. It looked crap. It seems so silly and not very important now but it was such a huge thing at the time. We fixed it within a few days. The effort that went into that first edition was Herculean but the reader would never have known by looking at it.'[13]

The compact *Daily Mail* looked exactly like what it was; a broadsheet crushed down to tabloid size. Unlike Rupert Murdoch's relaunched *Sun*, the new *Mail*'s character was not born fully formed. The two personalities, that of the *Sketch* and that of the *Mail*, simply didn't gel. At first, it was neither one thing nor the other. If it was going to survive, it had to become something entirely new and quickly.

Vere invested in a huge advertising campaign but to little real effect, because every other paper was also spending big at the time. Viewers were slapped about the face with screaming ads for newspapers during every TV ad break for months, and they were hounded through the pages of their papers with promotions and competitions and exclusive after exclusive; even the *Guardian* – in its 150th anniversary year – joined the fray, the broadsheet trying to steal readers from the ever-lumbering *Times*. Nevertheless, the first two months of the new *Mail*'s life saw circulation climb back over the magic 2 million mark, where Northcliffe always felt it belonged. But these new readers were phantoms, and they vanished as quickly as they had arrived. Circulation had been given a boost by subscribers to the *Sketch*, who had been moved over automatically from the dead paper to the new *Mail* by their newsagent. Most soon left for the bright red waters of *The Sun*. But of far greater concern to the *Mail*'s management were the readers of the old *Daily Mail*, who deserted the new paper in favour of the still-broadsheet *Express* in their droves.

Management reckoned that the new paper needed a circulation of at least 2 million for the numbers to work, but by the end of 1971 circulation was down to less than 1.5 million, a perilous low. The numbers were so low that senior Mailmen thought about what they'd do if it failed, or if Vere stopped propping it up with Harmsworth cash and headed for sunnier climes like his father. Brian Freemantle had already had a couple of books published and decided he would write full-time. 'Everyone was taking out as much insurance as they could in case it collapsed,' he said. 'David English, in fact, planned to go and buy a hotel in Bournemouth. Doomsayers said it would die the death, and it was a very shaky start. We lost a lot of readers and it took us a long time to pick them up again. But there was also an awful lot of excitement. Because it was new. And that excitement was pretty well established and stayed with us.'[14]

It took nerve to stick with the change and English admitted his own confidence cracked a little, even suggesting to Vere that the answer might be to race downmarket to compete directly with the *Mirror* and the ever-rising *Sun*. 'I went to Vere,' English said, 'and he said no. He said we've got to keep the same course. He said the old *Daily Mail* never kept its nerve and that was the trouble. It kept changing tack. It would do something and then if that didn't work it would do the opposite and that didn't work either. He insisted that we should stick to the plan.'

Vere's resolve was admirable . . . but circulation kept on falling. 'It's all right for you,' Vere said to English one day when the numbers had taken another tumble, 'whatever happens, you can still be a journalist and have a wonderful life. I'll be a failed proprietor who will never be able to work again.'[15] It was well over a year before the paper truly began to stabilize and stopped shedding readers.

A fresh ad campaign was launched that set out why 'Every woman needs her *Daily Mail*' and, finally, the two-year-old newspaper found her voice. This *Mail* was certainly female. 'So that you are not just a good listener at parties,' said the ad. 'So that you can interrupt your hairdresser once in a while. So that in the evening you can tell him a few things he might have been too busy to learn during the day. So that you are not just another pretty face, Every Woman Needs Her *Daily Mail . . . And Every Man Knows Why*.'[16]

David English was a man who knew 'why' and he also knew every single person in his newsroom. As a young editor he seemed to have time and energy for everyone – from the Chairman of the Board down to even the most junior members of his staff, and many loved him for it. Standing on the lowest rung of the editorial ladder, for example, were the messengers, gangs of teenage boys who had been part of every newspaper's DNA since heavy printing presses had first crushed their metal faces against long sheets of paper. Messenger boys (some were, in fact, adults) flitted in and out of newspaper offices and the warrens of the City and beyond, not entirely unlike the Dickensian thieves in *Oliver Twist*, picking up and dropping off copy and messages instead of picking pockets, and they answered, ultimately, to the editor instead of Fagin. Charlie Whebell was the *Mail*'s own Artful Dodger, given a 1970s upgrade. Having left school at fifteen, teenage Charlie was a 'bovver boy' with hair shorn to the bone. He stood resplendent in the newsroom among Mailmen and Femails in his Ben Sherman shirt, Levi Sta-Prest trousers and Doc Marten boots. David English took a shine to Charlie immediately.

'I thought I was the bee's knees,' he told the author. 'I was a very, very cheeky – "aw-wite my san" – Cockney boy at the time. Arthur Brittenden was the editor when I started and I used to see him walking around the office but he would never speak to a messenger boy like me unless it was, you know, "Boy! Get me a tea!" Then David English took over and we all got a 100 per cent pay rise. Can you imagine? Bosh! Without even asking for one. And then he just started talking to me one day. He asked my name and we had a chat, and I thought: "Blimey, the editor of the *Daily Mail* is speaking to me!" David English knew everyone and everything in that newspaper; he knew what the messenger boys were up to, he knew what the chairman was up to – he was aware of everything.'[17]

David English was also in no way shy around the women on his staff, as Anthea Disney, one of his long-term executives, explained. She had not been a reporter long on the dying *Daily Sketch* when David English arrived as editor and pulled her aside, handing her a book called *Black Like Me*. All David English's best ideas seemed to come from America, and the book was a late-1950s tale of a man who travelled through the then segregated Deep South of the US, medically swapping the privileged skin tone of the white man for that of the black. He suffered everything from the threat of violence to the indignity of not being allowed to sup from a water fountain. English – ever the editorial enthusiast – thought the same ruse might work in Birmingham, with Anthea as an Indian. She was young and keen, so she found a doctor in Puerto Rico who could help turn her skin dark with medication and she lay naked on his roof, parting her hair regularly to tan her scalp and making sure the sun got between her fingers and toes, to make sure she looked right. It worked, and in early 1970 she spent weeks in a cold-water flat in the middle of winter in the Midlands, getting abused almost every day. But the stunt made her famous and she was front-page news and a popular talk-show guest. She was even applauded whenever she went for an Indian meal, and didn't have to pay the bill for months. It took over a year for her skin to return to normal.

'David was always very comfortable working with women,' she told the author. 'He wasn't remotely phobic about it as a lot of guys were in those days. He wanted energy and he wanted ambition and he wanted a sense of fun. He was a great editor to work for. I think he tried everything out at home on Irene; his formula was to target the paper at himself and his family. If they liked it, a mass of similar people would too.'[18]

Like Sunny Harmsworth, David English – the middle-class boy done good – was great at understanding what his readers wanted and, again like Harmsworth, he was a man most often described as 'boyish'. He had the enthusiasm of a young boy but also the cruelties; his name would become a byword for a Fleet Street bully, of which there has been a long tradition.

'David was a very good editor,' said Brian Freemantle. 'He had a huge amount of energy, he would bounce around the room in the mornings when he came in. He always seemed to be in a hurry. But he did rule by fear, actually. He did frighten people. Not that he fired people. He wasn't an editor who fired people. He didn't bully me. I think you've got to let yourself be bullied to an extent. He wasn't a tyrant. And I was always going to leave and write books, so his power over me was fairly limited – the only way you can really frighten someone is if you think if you fuck it up, you're going to get fired.'[19]

Anger, though, says Disney, was just a tool. 'David was very feline. You had to understand that he'd always be probing you to find out where your weaknesses were and if he could find them and if you responded and you were frightened of him then – God help you. He was a bully, but in a very charming way. And very controlling. But he didn't have an unpleasant personality. He wasn't always swearing at people.'

Disney was sent to New York but then returned as features editor while still in her twenties. 'English would like to do that; he would like to put a young woman into that job, that had always been occupied by men in their fifties, because he'd enjoy seeing everybody else deal with it – and also see how that person would deal with it.'[20] Disney's immediate boss was Gordon McKenzie, the man who had helped find the way forward for the new *Mail* with *Femail*. Some, such as Shirley Conran, thought McKenzie could have been editor; and maybe English knew it too. But, said Brian Freemantle: 'Gordon was way too nice to be a *Mail* executive.'[21] English would target McKenzie without mercy and would, added another Mailman, Stewart Steven, 'blame Gordon for the rain'.

It was like a school playground. 'After we got the features pages to bed at night for the first edition,' said Disney, 'English would be sitting on the back bench and he'd call Gordon and I over – Gordon was a sweet, sweet, gentle Scotsman. We'd go over to the back bench and Gordon would put one foot in front of the other saying, "Ah here we go – he's gonna give it to us." And I would say: "Gordon, if you have that attitude when you go over there he's gonna do it. Don't let him. Call his bluff." David could be very cruel. He'd sit in the middle of the back bench with all of his backbench guys around him, and he would say things like "So, do you think this is a great features page, Miss Disney?" And I would say: "I don't think it's a great features page but I think it's a good features page for the first edition." "You do? And what are you gonna do with it for the next edition?" And you just had to hit back: "Why don't you let me go do it, or fire me?" He'd laugh and go: "Okay. Go do it." You had to stand up to him, you just had to. But David was fun, incredibly charming and funny. And a terrible gossip.'[22]

English's friend and long-term deputy Louis Kirby said English 'could be wickedly impish. Whenever he heard an amusing anecdote about a colleague, or rival, he would wait for an opportunity to rehash it when he could create the most devastating effect.'[23]

By the time the compact found its voice after a couple of years, the physical make-up of the newsroom staff had changed. It got younger, as older hands left and new hacks arrived. 'I was the first new guy that English recruited for the *Mail* after the Night of the Long Envelopes,' Mickey Brennan, who'd just won Photographer of the Year for his pictures in *The Sun*, told the author. 'I got a call from English: "Can we have a discussion?" So I went round there and he said: "How much are you earning at the moment?" I stuck ten quid on it and said: "Fifty quid a week." And English – he had this horrible cringeing voice – said: "Well, I can only afford to give you £70 a week" . . . and I nearly bit his fucking hand off.'[24]

'I was still just a boy,' said messenger Charlie. 'But I didn't feel so young in there any more like I had in the old broadsheet *Daily Mail*. It felt like a young newspaper.'[25]

Young David English also always made time for a party. As the very first edition of the very first issue of the new *Daily Mail* came off the presses, he started what was to be a long tradition. He invited everyone into his office for a drink. 'The editor had two very big offices, one was his work office and the other, opposite, was for entertaining,' said Charlie. 'And I was having a drink with Janet Street-Porter who worked on the fashion desk at the time and I remember David English talking to everybody and congratulating everyone. I don't remember much after that . . . I got very very drunk.'

Whenever there was an excuse for a shindig – a birthday or an anniversary – David English would open the drinks cabinet and Vere would often be there, too. 'I was up and down, up and down, getting Mr 'armsworth a drink all the time,' said Charlie. 'All the journalists were obviously wary of him because of who he was. But us messenger boys were just ordinary Jack-the-Lads, and we didn't even know.'

Another reason to crack open the drinks cabinet was to celebrate a scoop, and there was a plentiful supply for English's revitalized paper from the start. The *Daily Mail* was, for example, the first paper to really grab hold of a massive pharmaceutical scandal after the father of a girl born with neither arms nor legs walked into the *Mail*'s office in the winter of 1971.

David Mason told the stunned editor about a 'wonder drug' that seemed to help with everything from coughs to insomnia; the German inventors had actually found it impossible to kill laboratory rats with it. And thalidomide was considered so safe, pregnant women took it for morning sickness . . . with catastrophic side-effects. During almost every day in the first few weeks of pregnancy it could cause a different deformity in the unborn child – if an expectant mum took it on day twenty-four, for instance, the baby could be born with no arms. If she took it a few days later, the baby would be robbed of its legs. Thousands of babies died worldwide.

Thalidomide was marketed by the British whisky-, gin- and vodka-maker Distillers until it was taken off the market in late 1961. But 180 million tablets had been sold worldwide, destroying or damaging over 100,000 babies.

Mr Mason told English he was effectively being blackmailed into accepting a pay-off as part of a cover-up by Distillers. 'Scandalous' was the front-page headline just before Christmas 1971. 'I remember discussing it at the time,' said Brian Freemantle. 'And it wasn't a fitting word, it wasn't a bad enough word – a big enough word.'[26]

The *Mail* came under pressure to stop any further articles, with threats coming from all sides – including the Government's lawyers – as court proceedings were active and reporting the story could be *subjudice*. Other parents also attacked the *Mail*, as they wanted to accept the settlement that David Mason was blocking. English's attention moved on and he pretty much let the story go (but the *Sunday Times* editor Harry Evans stuck with it, finding a way around the legal problem by focusing on the families).

Scoops were a good sign that the paper was getting back to where it belonged, and everybody at Associated Newspapers knew, scoops or no scoops, that Vere had absolute confidence in his editor and that editorial was entirely English's domain; editorial was king. Like his forebear Sunny Harmsworth, Vere kicked the management into the backrooms and, said English, 'let me and my people have the best offices and the best expenses – and the circulation went up'.[27] Editors at Associated Newspapers, English said later, were blessed with being totally free to choose their own staff. But only God could choose the proprietor.

Down at the bottom of the *Daily Mail* hierarchy David English was also still making his presence felt. One day English pulled his favourite messenger boy aside. 'So, Charlie,' he said, 'what are you going to do with the rest of your life? Stay looking like a bovver boy with not a thought to what lies ahead, or are you actually going to do something positive?'

'I don't know, Mr English,' Charlie replied. 'To be honest with you, sir, I don't know what I'm gonna do.'

'What would you like to be?' English asked.

'Well, I'd like to be one of those,' Charlie said, pointing to the reporters. English looked over at the toilers, as they compressed or inflated themselves – depending upon their character – at suddenly being in the editor's line of sight. Charlie had joined the *Mail* straight from school and had zero qualifications and, of course, the *Daily Mail* editor knew this already, having spoken often to the boy. 'Okay, I give you my word. If you can get me an English A-level at night school, I will get you a job as a journalist.' Whebell thought he was kidding but the editor stared hard at the boy and said: 'Oh no, I mean it.'

A year went by, Charlie's hair grew and he went to night school, where he learned shorthand and how to type. 'I got an A-level in English, and I went up to him and I said: "Here it is, Mr English." And I gave the certificate to him. And within a month, he'd got me a job on a local paper.' Whebell spent most of his career on the *Daily Telegraph* and then moved to the United Arab Emirates as production editor on the *National*, the country's national newspaper. 'If it wasn't for Sir David English I've really got no idea what I'd be doing now. I'd probably have ended up working in a factory – Fords of Dagenham. I owe that man everything. He saw something in me that I certainly didn't see in myself.'[28]

9

How to be Different

Regular readers of the reborn *Daily Mail* may well have been mildly bemused when a culinary column called 'Instant Gourmet' suddenly appeared, offering recipes on 'Ancient British Dishes', and then promptly vanished after only ever offering up one dish. 'Rook Pie' didn't sound too tasty either, with the main ingredients being four rooks ('use only young birds') and hard-boiled eggs:

> Skin and draw rooks. Lay the birds on their breasts, cut down each side of the spine and remove back-bone as this makes the birds a little less bitter . . . Not a dish one would want every week – but on occasions tolerable in the right company.[1]

In May 1972 David English had insisted, furiously, that space be made in his paper for this cryptic recipe. It was his revenge against Jean Rook, his star columnist who had defected to the evil *Express*, to which the *Mail* was still losing readers. She had betrayed him. Rook was the self-proclaimed 'first lady of Fleet Street', who'd been a columnist and woman's editor on English's *Sketch* before it took over the *Mail*. Rook's *Mail* column ran on a Wednesday and began with the headline: 'Introducing a very important lady in your life . . . The lady has views. The lady will amuse . . . The lady makes news – Jean Rook, the *Mail*'s new columnist.'

'You've seen the headline and already you're asking a question,' she wrote, 'what's this column all about? It's about you. And me. What I think about British Rail (!!), David Frost (!!!) and university students (!!!!). What makes me think that my broad and sometimes bloody minded views are worth reading? The fact that thousands of women write to tell me that I've said exactly what they think.'[2]

Rook's chatty style and rather silly rhetorical questions would become the template for this kind of writing, satirized so perfectly by *Private Eye* as the columnist 'Glenda Slagg'.

> We've really got woodworm in Olde Englande, haven't we? The rot truly is setting in. I was maddened – weren't you? – to read about bulldozers crunching down a 1490 Hertfordshire farmhouse while 'weeping villagers' and protesting policemen looked helplessly on . . .[3]

Rook, a lass from the West Riding of Yorkshire, wasn't afraid of saying what was on her mind and her writing seemed to somehow perfectly embody the opinions of a certain kind of Briton: the lower-middle-class housewife. 'Talking about nuisances, what secretary can't tell when her boss has had a row with his wife?'[4] or Prince 'Philip's pearls of wisdom often drop with a clang. But what do we want . . . a stuffed Duke who daren't open his mouth?'[5]

The *Mail*'s top Femail seemed very 1970s glam in her byline photo, but in the flesh she looked, dressed and acted like a brassy blonde barmaid from a pub on Hull docks; she had a boxer's jaw, wore leopard-print outfits, had exploding hair and a permanent sunbed tan. John Junor, the fifty-three-year-old predatory womanizer who edited the *Sunday Express*, liked to have pretty young females on his staff and it was his lunch invite that led Rook away from the *Mail*. But when 'J. J.' saw what the forty-one-year-old Femail-in-chief looked like in the flesh . . . he recommended her to the editor of the *Daily Express* instead.

'Once your name is worth selling, the trick in Fleet Street is to walk from one side of the pavement to the other for more money,' wrote Rook in her autobiography but she added that there were other reasons to be tempted away.

> I was disturbed to find the *Mail* an unhappy ship, right from its spectacular launch. Perhaps because of the *Sketch/Mail* merger – at the start, two people for every one job, and one bound to lose it – it was a back stabbing staff. And, given half a chance, your *Mail* colleagues would stab you front and sides for good measure. The *Mail* whined, and griped, and could never raise a smile at its earnest self . . . even under ever-inspirational English, I wasn't enjoying what should have been the Total Tabloid, but was in fact a greyish, moaning publication, with such vicious in-house politics that the walls ran blood.[6]

It was a slap across the face for the *Daily Mail* editor; his paper was aimed at women and to lose his star female columnist to his deadliest rival was a nightmare. David English needed to find a replacement and he needed to find her fast. English knew more than most that there's nothing more pointless than a columnist with no opinions – the *Mail*'s top Femail had to appeal to the housewife, she had to leap to judgement, because that's what real housewives did, in real life. Most people don't pause and ponder, they don't police their thoughts and their language when sharing a cup of tea or a glass of wine with their friends. And English, from day one, wanted his paper to be 'a conversation between friends'.

The *Mail* is a newspaper and a product, not a court of law. Never mind depth or 'truth', Rook's replacement had to be bloody entertaining; she had to be absolutely sure of what she was absolutely sure of – at least for the moment or two she sat at the typewriter. Jean Rook had been a natural. She could file 1,000 words armed with the flimsiest of 'facts' and she may even have felt it all for real, for a while at least. It quickly became a formula, though, but Rook's readers loved her for it. She'd instinctively known how to pander to their prejudices without challenging them – if a *Mail* reader wanted a sermon over breakfast she could subscribe to *Church Times* instead. English had conjured Jean Rook up himself on the *Sketch* in the first place, and he could do it again; he'd write the bloody column himself if he had to. But maybe there was another solution.

Probably David English's single greatest gift as an editor was as a spotter and promoter of talent. Ian Wooldridge, for instance, had been a revered cricket writer for a decade before English gave him a full-blown sports column in 1972 – he covered ten Olympic Games for the paper, several football and rugby World Cups, numerous heavyweight boxing bouts and he spent many a sunny and not-so-sunny afternoon at Wimbledon – he was a master of the written word like Vincent Mulchrone, and far more than 'just' a sports writer: Wooldridge's twice-weekly columns were read by people who didn't even care that much for sport. Another columnist was the dapper gossip writer Nigel Dempster, who pointed his pen at the marital foibles of playboys, royalty and the mildly famous for his 'Dempster's Diary' column.

English had inherited the urbane Wooldridge, who had started out on tiny weekly newspapers on the south coast alongside English and Freemantle, from the old broadsheet *Daily Mail*. Quick-talking and charismatic deputy *Mail* diarist Dempster – who had been a vacuum cleaner salesman as a young man – was also promoted from within when English's first two choices as diarist didn't work out.[7] Dempster had been on a New York stint at the time, after falling out with his predecessor, where he scooped an interview with a drunk Richard Burton about his break-up with Elizabeth Taylor.

It was English who realized these two writers could do a lot more than that which they'd been asked, and he pushed them firmly and permanently out front. Their columns became two of the three pillars upon which he set his new *Daily Mail*. He needed the third after Rook's defection to the *Daily Express*.

And one of the heads sitting there quietly among all those typewriters in the *Mail* features department was an unremarkable thirty-seven-year-old Femail from Lancashire, looking out from under eyebrows like McDonald's archways: Lynda Lee-Potter. She was on a day off when the call came.

'Our features editor phoned up and said the editor wants you to come in and do a column, and I said "Oh, right",' she wrote. 'I went in and did it. Every week I thought somebody else would probably take over.'[8]

Nobody ever did. Lynda Lee-Potter, Wooldridge and Dempster were all in place within the first couple of years of the new paper and would underpin the *Daily Mail* until serious illness and the grim reaper scythed them away three decades later, within a few years of each other.

'When he [English] first asked me to be a columnist, he told me a column was like a microcosm of a newspaper. "You need to make people laugh, make them think, make them cry and make them cross."'[9]

Lynda Lee-Potter's style – based on Jean Rook's template and forced upon her in person every Tuesday evening in his office by her editor before her column went to press – is utterly woven into the fabric of the paper. Lee-Potter *was* the voice of the paper, speaking directly to Vere's target audience: middle-class mums and housewives. Yet when Lee-Potter had first joined the broadsheet *Mail* in Gordon McKenzie's features department, she had been a writer of tame little tales and did not seem by nature to be as sharp, witty and bitchy as Fleet Street's foul-mouthed and raucous busty barmaid Jean Rook. Lynda had fully expected to be one of those fired like so many others – all eight *Femail* writers, for instance, had been executed – when it merged with the *Sketch*. But English saw something he liked in this suburban housewife Lynda Lee-Potter – or Lynda Berrison, as she'd called herself in her short-lived days on the stage.

Born into the Higginson family in the Lancashire mining town of Leigh, Lynda was northern and working class just like Jean Rook (Rook had been raised by an engineer and a cinema usherette on the direct opposite side of the country). Lynda Higginson was the granddaughter of a coal miner who had earned a little extra spare cash by running an illegal bookmakers from his front room. Her father had also started out down the pit but climbed free to become a painter and decorator. Lynda and her mother always dreamed of being 'posh' and, after Leigh's all-girl grammar school, eighteen-year-old Lynda headed south to the Guildhall School of Music and Drama.

'I got on the train at Warrington with a Lancashire accent,' she wrote in her autobiography, *Class Act*, 'and got off at Euston without it, which meant I had to speak very slowly for a very long time. My fellow students were mostly middle-class and I kept my background to myself. I described my father as a painter without adding "and decorator". This made things very tricky when people asked what kind of pictures he painted. "Sort of abstract," I said.'[10]

Shortly before she graduated from the Guildhall she also worked at a coffee shop near the Whitehall Theatre, where the actor-cum-manager Brian Rix was about to stage a 'Whitehall Farce' called *Dry Rot*. She auditioned and won a part. Rix later described her as an 'awkward, snub-nosed girl' and said it was her croaking voice that won her the part. 'She was awful,' he concluded.[11]

Lynda left the stage when, in 1957, she married a student doctor called Jeremy Lee-Potter, the elder son of Air Marshal Sir Patrick Lee-Potter, pulling her into the upper ranks and skipping the middle classes altogether. Her husband got a job as an RAF doctor and they moved to Aden (now Yemen), where she started writing for the local paper about life as an expat housewife. When they returned to England, she joined the *Mail* and became, for the most part, an interviewer, with the disconcerting technique of scribbling shorthand in a notebook on her lap while never taking her eyes off her subject. Then Jean Rook flew the *Mail* nest, just as youngsters such as Rod Gilchrist, another rising star on English's rejuvenated paper, and Lee-Potter were settling in for a thirty-year stay.

'Lynda was a great believer in taking your opportunities when they came along,' Gilchrist told the *Guardian*.

> She had been writing a series of personality interviews called Face to Face. They were almost always warm and unprovocative. That was her style in those days. But that was not what Sir David wanted; he wanted sharp claws and blood to be drawn, and Lynda was to become the

new 'she cat' of the media, and take on Jean Rook of the
Daily Express and, by God, she had to beat her. It was
not Lynda's natural forte. But the genius of David was
that he knew what Lynda should be telling the readers
of his newspaper even if in those days she didn't. Lynda
would emerge shaken from her meetings with Sir David,
and in need of a glass of red wine with her friends. Of
course it didn't take her long to learn. And along with
Nigel Dempster and Ian Wooldridge she became one
of the three stars on whose bylines you could sell the
paper.[12]

Lynda Lee-Potter of the *Daily Mail* and Jean Rook of the *Daily
Express* vied for the title but there was really only ever one First Lady
of Fleet Street and she wasn't even a journalist. Margaret Thatcher
was a politician and David English's kinda gal. They had a lot in
common, both were nuclear-fuelled among coal-burning colleagues,
and both came from humble lower-middle-class backgrounds. And
the new *Mail*'s political voice needed to be crisp and clear: the paper
– unlike English – had been born a Tory and has never faltered from
the Conservative cause (at election time).

Margaret Thatcher, too, had always been a Tory. By the age of
twenty-one, the grocer's daughter from Grantham was already
chairman of the Oxford Union Conservative Association and in
the election of 1959 won the safe Tory seat of Finchley – right in the
heart of Harmsworth country, next to where Northcliffe himself is
buried in north London. Unlike almost every other Tory hack in
Fleet Street, David English 'talent-spotted' her early. Thatcher was,
of course, a great story for a paper aimed at females: a woman's bid to
be leader of her party and maybe one day – mad as it sounded – even
Prime Minister. English and Thatcher first met and became 'affably
friendly' in 1970, when he was still editing the *Sketch* and she was
Education Secretary in Ted Heath's Government.

A year later, and 'Thatcher Thatcher Milk Snatcher' was being
savaged for taking free milk away from schoolchildren and Jean

Rook, at the end of the *Mail*'s first year as a tabloid, defended her, writing:

> Come off it Mrs Thatcher . . . Let's see you hit back with
> a bit of the snooty, steel-blue-eyed bitch! . . . I do wish
> Mrs Thatcher would stop behaving like the frail, pale,
> Most Misunderstood Girl in the School. I do beg the
> Education Minister not to snivel into her initialled lace
> hankie that 'you don't know what it's like when everyone
> hates you'. Show some spunk Margaret . . . You've got it
> in you. In fact I'd say you've got it in you to be quite a bit
> of a snooty, hard-hatted, steel-blue-eyed bitch. Show us.[13]

A few months later Lynda Lee-Potter was less effusive; she wrote up a fairly flat and unconvincing interview – probably because she was flatly unconvinced by Thatcher (some colleagues suspect miner's daughter Lynda was never really a Tory), writing: 'She doesn't look like a girl who used to serve behind the counter of a grocer's shop in her school holidays.'[14]

When Thatcher challenged Ted Heath for the Tory leadership in 1975, the *Mail* was the only paper that said – out loud – that she was going to win. The number-one Mailman couldn't stand Heath, and Heath loathed David English in return. The pair even had a bust-up at a lunch in Room One over the lack of uncritical support for the Government by the supposedly Tory *Daily Mail*, Heath objecting to the fact that the *Mail* had on occasion actually agreed that the striking miners of the 1970s did have a legitimate grievance. And when the *Mail* editor asked Heath exactly how he thought the paper could help his government, Heath 'curtly responded' that English could start by sacking parliamentary sketch-writer Andrew Alexander, 'whose views, [Heath] snapped, were completely negative'. Heath was never invited again.[15]

Mail readers born into working-class families but who now found themselves part of the easily outraged centre of British society could maybe – with a little gentle persuasion – become Tories too, just like

David English, and hurl the Labour Party of their parents' generation into the abyss. 'We supported her for many reasons,' said English, 'maybe because she was a woman. But she had new ideas and the Tory party needed new ideas.'[16]

Vere Harmsworth – the toff who liked to call himself a 'nobleman' – backed his editor's support for Thatcher but, just like Lynda, Vere didn't seem to like Thatcher much at all. Some thought Vere suspected that Thatcher's favourite newspaperman was always likely to be Rupert Murdoch, and Thatcher would gain far more from the *Mail*'s backing than the *Mail* would. When she was invited to Northcliffe House for a similar lunch to the one Vere gave Ted Heath, Vere stood her up – he was on a plane to Paris. Thatcher became, arguably, the woman who would make the single biggest impact upon Fleet Street – and, indeed, kill the street off as a place of work for a multitude of journalists – in 1986 when she'd help Rupert Murdoch smash the print unions.

The *Daily Mail*'s exciting, invigorating and hugely demanding new editor had to find any way he could to make his 'compact' newspaper stand apart from those filthy tabloids at the newsagents, and one way of staying a step or two upmarket from the 'red-tops' was to have a healthy supply of foreign news in his newspaper. Which was great for David English; as a former Washington correspondent and ex-foreign editor of the *Daily Express* he adored news from overseas anyway. And the Holy Grail for any foreign correspondent after the Second World War was to find a living, breathing Nazi who had somehow managed to evade the hangman's noose – or their own cyanide pill – when they lost the war.

At the end of 1972 Brian Freemantle, the fresh *Mail*'s first foreign editor, was enjoying a rare and well-earned Friday off. It had been a tough couple of years for Freemantle and all the other Mailmen and Femails who'd brought the paper back from the brink; the *Mail* would never now become a withered appendage of the *Daily Express*. So Freemantle was at home in bed in Southampton on the south coast with a delicious long weekend ahead; he planned a nice lunch and a

drink or two with Mrs Freemantle out in the countryside after she got
back from a strange job she'd been called out on at the last moment.
Maureen Freemantle was a freelance make-up artist and had gone to
help out on an unusual top secret TV shoot that was being filmed
locally . . . far away from the loose lips of the London media set.

As the *Mail*'s former foreign editor, and now novelist, told the
author at a café in London's Sloane Square forty years after the event
– enjoying every delicious detail more so even than sips from his
wine glass – it was not going to be the relaxing day away from the
office he had hoped for.

Mrs Freemantle, he explained, had laid out her equipment in front
of the TV studio's dressing-room mirror. It had been an early start,
and groggy Maureen nearly spilled her brushes when six Nazi storm-
troopers stomped into the local television network's make-up room.
They had all the attire, the black SS outfits and the death's-head
daggers, and Maureen could see that the wardrobe department had
done a sterling job. She loved a good war film but for this commission, unusually in her line of work, she hadn't been given a shooting
script and none of the other girls knew what it was all about either.

'Wow, this looks terrific!' she said to her Nazi as he sat in her
make-up chair. 'What are you doing?'

'Oh, it's top secret,' the actor replied. 'We're doing an advert for
Sunday night.'

Out came Maureen's brushes. 'Ooh really, what for?' she said
through a cloud of powder.

'Well, we had to do it here in a provincial television studio because
it would've leaked if we'd done it in London.' Maureen started to
prepare the SS man's face, a little powder here, a little black pencil
to help bring out the evil inherent in those dark eyes: 'What would
have leaked?'

'Well, don't tell anybody,' whispered the fake Nazi, 'but it's an
advert for the *Daily Express*. They've found Martin Bormann in Latin
America.'

Now, no newspaper has yet managed to find a Nazi mass-
murderer reclining on a beach in South America sipping a Bacardi,

and Bormann was just about the biggest Nazi fish there was left to find: the Führer's Private Secretary, no less. Nailing one of Hitler's henchmen and bringing him back to face justice was every foreign editor's fantasy. Imagine the circulation boost that could bring! Equally, every foreign editor's worst nightmare was to find that the enemy – another newspaper, the *Express*, say – had found a Nazi mass-murderer reclining on a beach sipping a Bacardi.

'Really? Ooh, that's nice, dear,' said the wife of the *Daily Mail*'s foreign editor with a dash of powder. The guy looked the part and he'd pass for an SS murderer for the cameras, no trouble at all. 'I'm just nipping out to the loo,' she said. There was a row of telephones on the wall outside.

Mr Freemantle was still in bed, enjoying his Friday off, having worked the previous Sunday so his deputy could have a Sunday away from Fleet Street. The phone rang.

'Uhh,' he grunted. 'Yes?'

'I think you're fired,' Maureen said.

'Uh? Why?'

'The *Express* have found Martin Bormann in Latin America . . .'

Brian Freemantle, the foreign editor who had failed, hung up the phone on his wife . . . and called the editor who had failed. 'It's the only time I have ever spoken to an editor when I was stark naked. I got David English at home and I screamed down the phone: "The *Express* have got Martin Bormann!"'

'Where?!'

Silence.

'Fuck knows! I don't know. I don't know. Somewhere in Latin America, obviously.'

Freemantle phoned the *Mail*'s US bureau chief, Dermot Purgavie, in Costello's bar, Manhattan, and ordered him to 'round everyone up! I want you all in South America. Now!'

'You what?' replied Purgavie. 'Whereabouts in South America?'

Silence.

As Freemantle explained, years later, he was still standing naked with his telephone in his hand at his Southampton home. Purgavie on the other end of the line stood – on the other side of the Atlantic in a bar – with a glass in his hand.

'Fuck knows!' Freemantle told Purgavie. 'I don't know. Go to Buenos Aires! That's a hub. Buenos Aires. That'll do.'

'I sent everybody and their dog to Buenos Aires. Got a load of people in the office and we began ringing all the stringers from Colombia down to Patagonia trying to get any sort of reaction . . . we were like a fucking tsunami going through South America.'

The *Daily Express* still had the best foreign staff in Fleet Street, and they even had their own man in Argentina for just this sort of eventuality. 'Dermot gets to Buenos Aires and the *Express* had a guy there then called Jack Conlan, whom he knew.'

Purgavie called Conlan and said: 'Hello, Jack.'

'Hey, Dermot,' Jack replied. 'What's up?'

'Well, it had to happen I suppose, didn't it, eh?'

As Freemantle explained, the confused *Express* correspondent at first had no idea why Purgavie had called or even what the hell the chief Mailman in the States was going on about, but soon realized he was being pumped for information.

'Yeah . . .' said Jack, 'I guess it did . . . ?'

'Yeah, we've got a big thing going,' said Dermot, 'but I just thought I'd give you a call.'

The two ace reporters danced around the subject of runaway Nazis in general and Martin Bormann in particular. Purgavie put the phone down, getting nowhere, because there was nowhere to get to – the *Daily Express* never did *find* Martin Bormann. But the *Express did* have a slightly dodgy book by a man who said *he* had found Hitler's most trusted henchman. The only information the *Mail* had was from Maureen Freemantle's fake Nazi in a Southampton TV studio. Nothing more. Then, after speaking to Mailman Purgavie, the *Express* reporter in Argentina thought that the *Daily Mail* had the scoop of the seventies. He called his foreign desk back in London: 'The *Mail* have found Martin fucking Bormann!'

'Where?!'

Silence.

'Fuck knows!'

The Bormann story bounced back and forth, back and forth – feeding back upon itself like a transatlantic phone call down a bad line – and the *Express* soon went into panic mode, as its foreign editor, Stewart Steven, *was* actually constructing a story about Bormann at that very moment from an entirely inaccurate book by writer Ladislas Farago. 'So now the *Daily Express*, who know they haven't got him really – they only have this crap book – they think the *Daily Mail* have got the real thing!' chuckled Freemantle. 'And this whole thing compounded itself and went round and round and round.'

Startled and afraid they'd been scooped, the *Daily Express* scrapped their TV ad and rushed the publication forward from the Monday to the Saturday, hoping they could get the revelation into print before their number-one enemy, the *Daily Mail*. And the *Mail*'s top team, of course, still thought the *Express* had their hands on the chief living Nazi. 'In the office of the *Daily Mail* as we waited for the first editions to land,' said Freemantle, 'we were literally gripped by diarrhoea. All of us. And we got a copy of the *Express*. And we read the intro on the *Express* story, it read something like: "Usually reliable sources last night claimed that Martin Bormann had been found in Buenos Aires . . ." And we knew it was a phoney. It made the *Daily Express* look ridiculous.'[17]

The 'usually reliable source', it seemed, was only the half conversation between Mailman Dermot Purgavie and the *Express*'s man in Argentina. It was a symptom of the *Daily Express*'s ever-steepening decline, and the story itself is illustrative of the insanity that grips Fleet Street whenever there's a sniff of a 'world exclusive'. 'But can you imagine that? What were the chances of the wife of the foreign editor of the *Mail* getting told the *Daily Express* had found Martin Bormann by an actor in a Southampton TV studio?'

The boring truth was that Bormann never did make it to sip that Bacardi on a beach in Argentina or anywhere else. After escaping from the Führer's bunker in May 1945, he'd bitten into a cyanide pill rather than be captured by the Soviets and was buried in a shallow grave beside a Berlin rail track. DNA tests on a corpse found years later confirmed the skeleton was his – complete with shards of glass in its teeth from the lethal capsule.

There was an afterword to the Bormann saga, though, that was to deliver David English another vital cog for his *Daily Mail* machine. The architect of the *Express*'s Bormann yarn was Stewart Steven – born Stefan Cohn in Hamburg, the son of a German Jew who escaped Nazi Germany with his family and arrived in Britain before the Second World War – and, despite what was viewed by many on Fleet Street as a catastrophic cock-up, Steven's career was far from over. He was soon poached by English and would become his deputy on the *Mail* and then the successful editor of the *Mail on Sunday*, before ending his career as editor of the Rothermere-owned *Evening Standard*. What's more, though, the defection of one of its most important players to the *Mail* was symptomatic of the *Express*'s decline and it also revealed another English modus operandi: stealing talent from the *Daily Express* was a great way of undermining the enemy; whether or not English actually required their services on the *Mail* was often a side issue. He'd always find something for them to do.

It also revealed how important overseas stories were to the 1970s *Daily Mail*. A reader of the print edition of the *Mail* today would search in vain for regular space set aside for foreign news, but David English loved to splash on a good foreign story.

Even better than a good foreign story was a good showbiz tale with a foreign twist, as Anthea Disney found out when she was sent to the south of France early in English's reign to cover Mick Jagger's wedding to pregnant Nicaraguan beauty Bianca Pérez. 'It was in the days of communicating by Telex,' Disney told the author. 'And I went to some awful little Telex office and sent a message back to Brian Freemantle saying something like: "*Daily Mirror* has five reporters, *The Sun* has eight, even the *Telegraph* has two. You have me. What to do?"' The young reporter, her skin now returned to its natural shade, waited and watched the technicians hovering over their machines, bemused by the shifty-looking Fleet Street horde that had descended on their pretty little seaside town. 'And then the answer came back, it was just two words . . . "Walk Tall".' So she did. 'I got the story, of course I got the bloody story. But that was pure David English.'[18]

The root of the man was in reporting. David English was a great newspaper hack, 'an operator' in Fleet Street parlance. 'All good editors should be envious of their reporters,' English said, 'because they are sent to the ringside of history and have the opportunity to bring human drama to life.'

Ann Leslie, the paper's award-winning foreign correspondent, would call the *Daily Mail* in London to file her story from some faraway hotspot with mortar shells and fighter jets screeching overhead. But the call, invariably, would not be fed through to the foreign desk or the copy takers – it would be the actual editor *himself* who would pick up the call and let out a mischievous giggle before shouting down the crackly line: 'So, tell me, what's going on, I want to know everything!'

'Not just the story I'd be filing, but my adventures with drunken Kalashnikov-draped thugs, cross-eyed secret policemen, local tarts, the whole colourful, if often deadly, galère of characters who adorn the world's troublespots,' she wrote in the *Daily Mail* after English's death in 1998.

> He adored the sheer fun, the crazy derring-do of foreign
> corresponding – because that's where he'd made his
> name – and deeply envied those in his employ, like me,
> who were out on the road, which he had long left, but
> continued yearning for. I was there when the Berlin
> Wall fell and, after having worked for days with no more
> than a few hours' sleep, I rang him to complain about
> how exhausted I was. 'Listen, my darling, you have an
> immense privilege to be there at a moment of history.
> In fact, you should be paying me for the privilege,
> not me paying you!' I could only agree. (And I half-
> expected David, being David, to send me his bill.) He was
> mischievous, brilliant, funny, dangerously charming, and
> intensely loyal and generous-hearted to those he trusted.[19]

Perhaps David English's favourite kind of story of all was a foreign scoop mixed up with a bit of mischief, a good old-fashioned Fleet Street stunt – preferably with him orchestrating the whole thing. As his favourite foreign reporter Ann Leslie said, the *Mail*'s editor still itched to be out there on the road and he'd jump on a plane whenever he felt he could. In the spring of 1975, for example, as Saigon was about to fall into the hands of the Vietcong, the US had convinced the whole world that once American forces had gone, the communist troops arriving from the north would seek retribution on the locals who'd been the Americans' hosts. It was feared that the Vietcong would show little mercy to abandoned babies in orphanages, especially those born to Vietnamese women who'd had sex with US soldiers. These babies were fairly obvious, as some were black and others were clearly Caucasian. US forces were actually airlifting children out while the British Government dithered about what, if anything, to do.

'I saw a paragraph about a priest in the Midlands somewhere,' said Brian Freemantle, 'who'd appealed for someone to get orphans out of a particular orphanage he had in Vietnam. And I said to David, "Let's see if I can rent an aircraft and get the kids out." And he said, "You'll never do it. I bet you five pounds you can't." Then, of course, he claimed the credit for it when it worked.'

Within a few days, English told his readers of their plan on the front page of the paper by saying the *Mail* would offer a 'raft of hope' through these deep 'seas of despair'. 'The big problem was getting an aircraft, because we were going into a war zone,' said Freemantle. 'British Airways wouldn't do it. British Midland did it in the end. But they said, "Yeah, you can have the plane and you can have the crew but our insurance won't cover it." So I insured it through a syndicate at Lloyds of London. I can't remember now exactly how much it cost, but it was an astronomical sum of money.'[20]

Vere's managers must have winced when they got the bill, but they wrote the cheque. Yet there was still a problem: the Mailman on the ground in Saigon, defence correspondent Angus MacPherson, had found only sixteen orphans, not the 150 he'd been asked to find, and it would likely take at least two years to get the official clearance for them to leave Vietnam. The Vietcong might well be due in three weeks or so but the Mailman's editor was due in three days. MacPherson and aid workers frantically scoured the city for orphan babies to fill the plane and, eventually, they rounded up ninety-nine. Twenty or so weren't technically 'babies' – they were aged between five and fourteen – and many, it turned out, weren't even orphans. They had simply been left at orphanages temporarily by their parents who thought they'd be safer there.

Next came those pesky exit visas. The paper asked the British consul general in Saigon, Rex Hunt, for help. 'There was no doubt that I was being used,' Hunt said. 'I could guess what the *Daily Mail* would say about the Foreign Office if we didn't help. But I thought it was for the good of the children.'

The plane landed in Saigon with the *Daily Mail* editor on board and Hunt was 'surprised' when English spoke 'sharply' to MacPherson because he hadn't quite found the 150 babies he'd 'ordered'. The BBC correspondent Brian Barron was there too, and described English as 'a shabby General Custer galloping over the horizon to save kids in need'. Another reporter present, *New Statesman* correspondent Richard West, thought the whole affair 'a disgusting sham'. West never believed that the Vietcong would seek vengeance on innocent children and described English as 'the star of the airport ceremony' in a combat uniform inscribed with the words Bao Chi, meaning 'journalist'. English had even learned to pronounce 'Bao Chi' correctly, said West, unlike other hacks who would often unwittingly label themselves 'dog shit' in Vietnamese if they simply said the two words as written.

'The *Mail*'s Mercy Airlift' was front-page news for the *Mail*, of course, and the paper devoted six more pages to it inside. Evergreen reporter Vincent Mulchrone, a father of three, wrote the main story with MacPherson from inside an orphanage: 'We ourselves – and anybody who called – were invited to help with the bathing, powdering and feeding . . . Not all the children had the olive-coloured skin of the Vietnamese. Several were obviously sons of negro GIs, who would grow far taller than the average Vietnamese, and would always be marked men should the entire nation fall to the Communists.'[21] Some of the numbers written on the backs of the babies to identify them for the blanket visa had rubbed off in the sweltering heat and nobody knew who they were.

Brian Freemantle, David English, Vincent Mulchrone and the other Mailmen on the plane helped six doctors and nurses feed the children and changed nappies on the long flight to Heathrow. 'It would have been so easy to have wanted to adopt these children,' said Freemantle, 'or to have got deeply involved because they were so frail.'[22] Most were suffering from malnutrition, and thirty-four were ill enough to be kept in hospital. Three died.

A hostile press reception awaited the *Mail* 'mercy mission' crew when they landed at Heathrow. 'We came in for a lot of stick at a press conference when we got back, saying it was just a stunt,' said Freemantle. 'Well, yeah, it *was* a stunt. But it was a stunt that worked and it got 100 kids out of Vietnam who were in *real* danger. It was also partly just "Fleet Street"; other papers attacked us because they'd not thought of it first.'[23]

Freemantle quit the *Daily Mail* shortly after the orphan airlift scoop to focus full-time on writing books. On his last day, there was a huge leaving party that was kicked off by gossip writer Nigel Dempster jumping up on to the foreign desk wearing a mask and cape, tights and a T-shirt with the name 'Captain Schizoid' sprayed across it. 'Because I used to commute up and down from Southampton,' said Freemantle, 'David turned his office into a railway carriage and everyone dressed up, Gordon McKenzie was dressed up as a station master. David loved giving parties. And he gave me a wonderful one.'[24]

Some hacks were also dressed up as Vietcong soldiers as they all fell out of the main entrance to Northcliffe House down by the River Thames, and David English, with a nod to a Saigon street scene, stood between the sticks of a rickshaw and proceeded to pull Freemantle up Carmelite Street and on to El Vino, the famous wine bar on Fleet Street itself that had been a haunt for journalists from well before the *Daily Mail* was even born.

As the hacks celebrated at El Vino, just across the road a bronze bust of Lord Northcliffe stared benevolently down Fleet Street from outside the church of St Dunstan-in-the-West. Northcliffe had shared the same taste for mischief and foreign news as David English, but his bust, unveiled in 1930, had spent four grim decades forming a green patina and watching helplessly as the first two Rothermeres ruined his paper. By 1975 the *Mail*'s circulation, after a rocky relaunch, had stabilized at around 1.7 million – almost the same number it sold when Northcliffe died – while the *Express* was losing readers rapidly. Now, at last, Sunny Harmsworth – the boy who liked to make the news instead of wait for it – would surely have been pleased; his *Daily Mail* was back on song.

10

Tall Stories

David English must have felt humiliated.

The pioneering, campaigning and boldly successful father of the 'compact' *Daily Mail* had been well on his way to becoming a living legend – even his diarist was beating the best political writers in Fleet Street to scoops; in the spring of 1976 Nigel Dempster predicted that Prime Minister Harold Wilson, who had Alzheimer's, was planning to step down. Yet there the revitalized paper's editor was, a year after Wilson had indeed quit, searching for the *Mail*'s other parent, Vere Harmsworth. So he could resign. The wheels were being ripped off English's career by the British car industry – in the days when Britain actually had one, albeit an unwieldy and clumsily amalgamated heavy load carried by the state.

Only a handful of people knew anything about the *Daily Mail*'s 'scoop of the century' until one evening in the spring of 1977 English came out of his office and ordered that the front page of the next day's paper be scrapped to make way for a special story. He handed the text to the 'splash sub', Nick Morrison. 'There you are,' English told him, 'I bet you've never had to sub a front page like that before?'

'Yes I have,' Morrison thought. 'And the same man's byline was on the story.'[1] English had poached Morrison, like so many others, from the *Daily Express*, where, a few years before, he had prepared the *Express*'s front page to receive another 'scoop of the century' – it had been the tale about Martin Bormann. Both stories began with the three words 'By Stewart Steven'. Steven, of course, had also been poached by English and was by now the third most senior man on the *Daily Mail*.

The paper had a letter from Lord Ryder, the chairman of the National Enterprise Board, to the chief executive of British Leyland, Alex Park, which suggested that Ryder condoned or even master-minded millions of pounds in 'slush money' – for the paying of bribes – to obtain overseas orders. The source had seemed strong to English, but was soon arrested for fraud, as the letter was a forgery and a sloppy one at that. The struggling Labour Government wrung the scandal for all it was worth and Steven had little choice but to resign. Yet, it later turned out, the substance of the story – about bribes and corruption – was broadly true (though there was no proof Lord Ryder himself had ever been involved). Angry MPs demanded English's head roll too, and his position seemed untenable, so he wrote his letter of resignation and went to see Vere.

'It never entered my mind to let David English go,' Vere told Harmsworth biographer S. J. Taylor,

> not for a solitary second. There was a great furore in the House of Commons demanding that David English should be dismissed. But they could demand whatever they liked. It wouldn't get anywhere with me . . . It was a good news story. And if British Leyland hadn't been bribing the Arabs or whoever, well, then, they bloody well should have been, like everybody else has to do. You can't do business in those parts of the world if you don't.[2]

Vere may have declined his resignation, but English did feel the need to write a long letter of apology to his readers the day before his forty-seventh birthday in 1977, which he published in full in the paper:

> . . . the *Daily Mail* is a newspaper which reflects much of what is fine and decent in our country. It is not only

a good newspaper, it is a great newspaper. It has courage
and humanity. It has understanding and compassion. Yes,
it fights hard and it attacks relentlessly when it believes it
should. And sometimes it is human and gets things wrong.
And occasionally it is misled and gets things very wrong.
But it is not dishonest. It is not dishonourable. It does not
deliberately set out to smear people. It does not concoct
lies, or twist facts, or invent incidents . . .[3]

It was a blow to the paper's soaring confidence after six years of
unmitigated success. The paper had got something horribly wrong –
and rather amateurishly and publicly wrong at that – and was now
facing a potentially massive bill for libel.

Yet Vere stuck with his editor just like Northcliffe had done with
Thomas Marlowe all those years ago. The first two Lord Rothermeres
had viewed their editors merely as hired hands, to be changed on a
whim: they went through fourteen between them. Vere would only
ever have two, and his second editor (as of early 2017) is still there.

Technically, during this period of the *Mail*'s recovery, Vere still
answered to his father, Lord Rothermere, even though Esmond had
washed his hands of the whole sorry mess that the Harmsworth
newspaper business had become when he handed over to his son in
1971. Esmond remained chairman of the Daily Mail and General
Trust (DMGT) parent company, while Vere was chairman of
Associated Newspapers – that is, the company that owned the *Daily
Mail* was itself owned by DMGT.

But Esmond's involvement in the paper's affairs was minimal.
Indeed, while spending three months on holiday in South Africa after
walking away, he didn't even know the *Daily Sketch* had been closed[4]
and 1,733 of his employees had been made redundant,[5] including his
host, the paper's South Africa correspondent, Peter Younghusband.
Esmond remained chairman of DMGT but Vere was in charge of the
newspapers as chairman of Associated Newspapers.

Esmond was also weakened by Alzheimer's disease in his final years
and died, aged eighty, at his home in London shortly after returning

from a trip to the south of France with his wife and young son, Esmond junior, in the summer of 1978. The Rothermere title passed to Vere, though the hereditary principle did not sit well with the third viscount – he had even considered rejecting the title, just as Lord Beaverbrook's son had done. 'You could call it vanity, I suppose,' Vere told a friend. 'But it means changing my name to somebody else's, and I think I've made a name for myself.'[6]

Change was coming too in Westminster. Margaret Thatcher had made such a name for herself since taking over as Tory leader in early 1975, with the *Mail*'s backing, that it looked as though she could actually secure victory for the Conservative Party and be Britain's first female Prime Minister. The seismic political shift to the right for which the reborn *Daily Mail* had been aligning itself for its entire existence was about to come to pass.

By the time the general election was called in 1979, David English and Margaret Thatcher were firm friends and political soulmates. Two weeks before polling day, which coincidentally was to be held on the mini-*Mail*'s eighth birthday, David English sat down to interview his friend. Thatcher raised the spectre of a Socialist state reminiscent of Orwell's *1984* rising slowly, Labour taking freedom away 'by stealth until you get to the position which no nation would tolerate if they saw it coming but suddenly it is there'. She alleged that everybody would become council house tenants and every worker a government employee; ordinary people would become dependent upon the state for everything.

> At the beginning of the peak period of the campaign, Margaret Thatcher is looking good and feeling great. She poured out the drinks – a gin and tonic for me and a scotch and water for herself – took a sip and settled back. She looked remarkably untired for someone who starts work at seven and finishes after midnight. I said, 'Well, I seem to be able to get by on five hours' sleep a night.' She replied, 'Well that's very lucky. But there is a trick to it; you have got to get one good night – eight or nine hours'

solid sleep – once a week. That puts all the energy back
into the bank. That's my secret.'

Being a mother and handling crises in the home was great training
for a Prime Minister, she said. Yet Labour had painted her as an 'Ice
Maiden', not a mother of two children, wrote English:

> a woman they project as cold, indifferent, insensitive and
> out of touch with ordinary people. The personal attacks
> on her are going to get rougher in the days ahead. 'It's a
> political thing, trying to pin those labels on me,' she said.
> And then she grinned, a good old-fashioned grin, enjoying
> a joke. 'You know they can never forgive me for having such
> an ordinary background. They're so angry about that.'

Maggie Thatcher was the nice girl you knew from the corner shop
who stood for the exact same things as David English's *Daily Mail*:
she'd cut taxes, put money back in people's pockets and reduce waste.
Bunny Harmsworth would have adored her. It was an act of faith,
she said:

> that if we give people the chance with their own money.
> If we put the ball at their feet, a great number will take
> it, start running and score some goals. This is the way to
> break out . . . I now believe we can fight for victory. And
> make our country great again. I'm fighting to win . . . and
> win we shall.[7]

'It's history – a woman takes over No 10. Prime Minister Maggie!'[8]
was the headline on 4 May 1979 – the eighty-third birthday of
Sunny's *Daily Mail*: David English may have started out as a Socialist
but the *Mail*, like Maggie, was born a Tory.

It's awfully difficult to proclaim oneself a 'Messiah' in the information age.

Pesky journalists tend to demand proof, a photograph perhaps, of this well-connected chap actually walking on water; they would seek interviews with witnesses to his miracles and medical evidence to prove that the sick had been, for a fact, cured by his hands. The red-tops would almost certainly uncover an ex-girlfriend or two or maybe a criminal record along the way, and they'd find out exactly how much cash his new church was generating and query why an ascetic needed a big house in the country with a swimming pool sunk in the lawn and a Bentley on the drive.

David English's *Daily Mail* could never be accused of lacking ambition, and the paper's next fight was with a man some thought was truly a messenger of God, a man called Sun Myung Moon who had once declared: 'He [God] is living in me and I am the incarnation of Himself. The whole world is in my hand.'

Reverend Moon, or 'humanity's saviour' as he liked to be known, was born to a peasant family in what is now North Korea, and claimed to have had a vision at the age of sixteen in which Jesus asked him to set up God's kingdom on earth. The crucifixion was actually – Jesus told Moon – an unfortunate error, and had he lived, Jesus would have married the perfect wife and created a 'pure' family. Moon's mission, of course, was to complete this task himself with the second Mrs Moon. His Unification Church became known in the 1970s for its mass weddings, in which thousands of identically dressed strangers married one another in huge ceremonies in front of their 'true parents', Mr and Mrs Moon. Moon's missionaries headed out across the world and were accused of 'love-bombing' – flattering and brainwashing – impressionable youngsters into joining the Moonies cult. Members were also encouraged to break all contact with their friends and family; unluckily for Moon, one new church member was the nineteen-year-old son of one of David English's neighbours, and English took it personally.

Moon's followers may well have believed their leader was 'the perfect human being', carrying a message direct from God, but the low-church Methodist editor of the *Daily Mail* wasn't convinced. To David English, Moon simply attacked the most important institution on God's earth: the family. In May 1978 the *Mail* accused the Moonies of being 'The Church That Breaks Up Families'. English penned the piece himself, recounting the tale of his neighbour's son being picked up by 'love bombers' outside a railway station in San Francisco while on a hitchhiking trip across the USA before taking up his place at Oxford University:

> Almost immediately they began the thought control process, which ended inevitably with him coming under their complete control. In the weeks that followed, I saw first hand the seeds of disintegration take root and tear that family apart. Michael, the son, stopped writing to his family after one missive telling them he had found a new kind of life.

Michael's parents travelled back and forth to New York and found their son working as a street seller for the Moonies and then working up to ten hours a day as a labourer on one of the church's building projects. 'I did not bring up my son to work to the point of exhaustion to make one of the richest men in the world even richer,' his father told the *Mail* editor. 'And as for his happiness? How can I tell whether he is happy or not? I can only tell you that he's a zombie, dehumanised it seems to me . . . incapable of giving or receiving any affection. Capable only of repeating endless slogans.'

English's neighbour wasn't the only family to tell a similar story – many others had written to the paper. The *Mail* launched its campaign, and the British branch of the Moonies sued for libel.

Early in the proceedings, the paper could have settled the case for a few thousand pounds and an apology and not risked losing an estimated million pounds in a libel action. And the Moonies could afford a long-drawn-out court battle; the church's global income was tens of millions of dollars a year. It owned properties across the US and businesses around the world that included various newspapers, a ski resort, a golf course, hotels, a football team and even a ballet company.

Vere, now the third Lord Rothermere, and his editor decided to fight because settling the case and apologizing, wrote English, 'would have been a cheap and easy way out. But the real cost would have been our professional pride and the betrayal of our readers. Campaigning newspapers do have to live dangerously.'

The case went to the High Court . . . and the Moonies lost. The court even went a step further and recommended the church's tax-free status be investigated, as it was a political organization, not a charity.

'The *Daily Mail* is a family newspaper, which means it cares passionately for those values of family life that bring so much to ordinary people in this country,' English wrote. 'Yesterday, the *Daily Mail* won a great victory for those values.'[9]

Although it was a case fought in the English High Court against a movement originally founded in South Korea, the Moonies story was essentially an American tale. Moon had moved to the States in 1972 and lived in an eighteen-acre compound in Irvington, up the Hudson River from New York City in a house that had a ballroom and a bowling alley, two dining rooms (one of which had a pond and a waterfall) and a kitchen with six pizza ovens. His church owned several properties and companies in the US, including the New Yorker Hotel in mid-town Manhattan. Moon was also later sentenced to eighteen months in prison in the US – for tax evasion and conspiracy to obstruct justice.[10]

English, the former Washington correspondent for the *Daily Express*, had never quite let America go. David and Irene had never really wanted to leave in the first place, and they returned to the States whenever they could to visit friends or to ski in Colorado. 'He was a great – a total – lover of America,' said Brian Freemantle. 'Too much a lover of America actually because he sort of copied from American newspapers.'[11]

David English had once been the master of American miscellany when he wrote a column from the US for the *Daily Express* in the 1960s, and he wanted to try and replicate this for his *Daily Mail*. So London-based Mailman James Gibbins was sent, for a three-week stint, to Washington, partly to provide the same kind of crisp little items for the paper that illuminated life stateside in the late 1970s. And young Gibbins, who'd won an award in his early days as a reporter in Scotland, came up with some crackers. He arrived in America in the early summer of 1978 and soon found a brilliant tale that Sunny Harmsworth would have adored: a hat story. There were beggars outside the White House and Gibbins wrote that 'every one who approached me hand out-stretched, was wearing a bowler hat'. The hats had been given by a city draper to a welfare organization, he explained, who later gave them away 'to bring dignity in head gear to the city'.[12] It must have been fascinating to see destitute men who slept in doorways begging for change in black bowlers beloved by English City gents – and these sartorially elegant vagrants would have made a fantastic photo but, unfortunately, there wasn't a picture.

Another Gibbins scoop soon followed. The Secret Service was on the lookout for a potential 'gatecrasher' at a NATO summit – disgraced former President Richard Nixon.[13] It was a great story, and the other British hacks in the US were immediately harangued by their foreign editors back in Fleet Street; how the hell could they miss such a story? Gibbins even got a front-page splash out of the – Nixon-free, he never did appear – NATO summit: 'Jim Callaghan emerged last night in the unlikely role of the new Iron Man of the NATO alliance.'[14] Gibbins was proving to be a better hack in the States even than his famous editor.

He came up with another cracker about President Jimmy Carter, stating that he was a wreck, had backache and migraines and couldn't eat or sleep. The First Lady, Rosalynn, 'she of the beguiling smile', was according to Gibbins 'increasingly regarded by Washington insiders, men and women who have studied the shifts and nuances of supreme power for decades, as the de facto President'. Something had to be done. This was an emergency for the Democrats with an election just over the hill – 'clinical injections had failed' and 'three top psychologists, and any number of sociologists and demographers' advised Carter to take drastic action. There could, of course, be but one solution, the President had no choice – he had to grow a beard.

'Image-makers hired to fathom how Jimmy Carter can grow "giant-sized" with a public that views him as a presidential pygmy,' wrote Gibbins in June 1978, alongside a sketch of a bearded Carter, 'have decided that one-inch can do the trick – a tuft of beard. Just enough to convince Americans and the world that there are shades of the wisdom of Abe Lincoln here.'

Gibbins wrote that Carter at first snarled 'Are you crazy?' when told of the idea and 'other equally bizarre face-savers', but was 'trying it on' with close friends and 'may well' even have discussed it over breakfast with British Prime Minister Callaghan.[15] Maybe Jimmy and Jim did in fact discuss beards over bacon and eggs, but the other hacks in America had had quite enough of James Gibbins and his 'scoops'. White House bums in bowlers? The President growing a beard? They denounced him to their bosses as a barefaced liar.

An American reporter named Jim Srodes wrote it all up for the *Washington Post*. Srodes himself was a little worried it might all be an elaborate spoof, a genuine attempt at satire, until he phoned the *Mail*'s foreign editor, John Moger. 'We did send Mr Gibbins to Washington briefly,' said Moger. 'He is one of our best feature writers and he did a good job for us. The *Mail* prides itself on its reputation for accuracy and so if you say it's all fantasy, that is you saying so and not me.'[16] Srodes unpicked a dozen Gibbins stories under the headline 'The Faker of Fleet Street – the tale of a foreign correspondent who went too far in inventing stories'.

The *Washington Post* did give Gibbins a right of reply in which he stated: 'I stand by everything I wrote about America.'

> The Post, acting for a press gang in the worst sense of the word, struck me a vast psychological blow which robbed me, at least so far as its readership goes and possibly far beyond this, of the 'credit card' vital to my survival as a professional journalist: my integrity. Indeed, the repercussions of this attack so far indicate that I might well be left penniless for life.[17]

A letter from Gibbins was also printed soon after in *Press Gazette*, the trade magazine for British journalists, shortly before he departed the *Daily Mail* staff. 'I wish to announce formally that I am not the Faker of Fleet Street,' he wrote,[18] though he didn't deny the *Post's* story – he did write a 'rebuttal', which he'd sent to every newspaper office in London. And those beggars in bowlers had been there, he insisted. The other Washington hacks simply didn't like him, that was the problem.

> I decided to roll up my sleeves rather than rest my elbows on the bar counter of the Press Club. Journalism by hand-out wasn't for me. A bad mistake, I now see. I knew I was rocking the boat, of course – it never occurred to me that the other occupants would throw me overboard and leave me to drown.[19]

America was the second most important territory for generating content for the pages of the *Daily Mail* newspaper and David English wanted someone he rated highly, somebody he could trust to run his paper's US operations to make sure this kind of thing never happened again. But his choice, Simon Winchester, wasn't born to be a Mailman – his byline simply belonged within the tall, wide-open space of a broadsheet.

English now had a problem with the *Mail*'s reputation in America, though, especially among other journalists, and Winchester – who'd studied geology at St Catherine's College, Oxford, and was a seasoned foreign correspondent with a solid reputation – could bring some intellectual ballast to the *Mail*'s listing ship in the USA.

'I was in Delhi and I got this call from David English, who I knew quite well,' Winchester told the author, 'and he said, "Simon, I've been reading in the papers it's rather hot over there at the moment."'

'Yes, David,' said Winchester. 'It's very, very hot indeed.'

'How many air conditioners does the *Guardian* give you?'

'You've got to be joking? I think there's one.'

'Well, quite. So, it's miserable working for the *Guardian*, isn't it?

They don't pay you enough. We, however, would pay you a heap of money if you came to work for us in New York.'

'Well, David, that's sweet of you but I'm just not a *Daily Mail* kind of chap.'

'Well, there's a seat reserved for you tonight first class on British Airways 145 from Delhi to London. Come and have a chat.'[20]

Winchester spent a few days being wined and dined at the Savoy before finally saying 'why not'. He was duly appointed US bureau chief of the *Daily Mail,* though he had to work his notice on the *Guardian.* Coincidentally, he was sent to Bangladesh on a story, where he met Jim Srodes among a press pack of other hacks. He told them he was joining the *Mail,* to which Srodes replied: 'You're an idiot for going to the *Mail* and I'll show you why.' He went off to find his copy of his 'Faker of Fleet Street' story and showed it to Winchester.

Even so, the *Guardian's* Simon Winchester – now a successful author – became a Mailman at the end of the 1970s. But it didn't take him long to realise he'd made a huge mistake. 'They hated me after about three months,' he said, 'because I was clearly some pointy-headed, pompous Oxbridge ex-*Guardian* man. And they started doing things that they knew would get up my nose.' The foreign editor, still John Moger, wanted to send him to California to see what a load of British union officials got up to while visiting the golden state on a fact-finding mission, and his *Guardian* nose smelled a dull but worthy kind of tale: 'Oh, that's interesting, John, to do a comparison of English and American workplace practices? That would be fascinating!'

'No,' Moger replied. 'That's not what we want you to do. We want you to follow them surreptitiously to all the nightclubs and strip clubs they go to. And just do a "number" on them.'

'And I said: "John, come on. I'm not holier-than-thou but . . . what if they don't go to any? And anyway I don't want to be following people around like that." He said: "It's an 'Editor's Must' – you've got to do it."'

Another 'Editor's Must' that Winchester was asked to write up from the US was a study by 'a thoroughly disreputable eugenics organisation saying, essentially "Black People Are Stupid – It's Official!" This was measuring intelligence on a very skewed basis and it was an utterly discredited survey. And of course the *Mail* – David – wanted to run it big. Something with some academic credentials showing that black people were not as bright as white people.'

'Editor's Must' is a phrase that has struck fear in many a Fleet Street hack, meaning a direct order from the Führer which cannot be declined – a stick often used by department heads to get reluctant reporters to do as they're told. The *Mail*'s highly paid US bureau chief struggled with his conscience on both these stories for under five seconds: 'I refused to write these pieces. And then things got very nasty indeed.'

Winchester was finally saved from his *Daily Mail* hell by the Pope. The pontiff was in New York, and where the Pope goes the press pack follow; among them was a friend from the *Sunday Times* called John Whale, who asked how it was going on the *Mail*. 'I'm having a miserable time,' Winchester replied. 'I'm being paid heaps of money by the *Mail* but they're just asking me to do all these weird stories which basically, and I know I must sound very naive in saying this, but they're not true! I mean I am being asked to write things that have no truth in them at all.'

The *Sunday Times* religious affairs correspondent would prove to be a saint for Simon Winchester. He walked away to a phone booth. 'And then he opened the door and beckoned me over. And he said: "Take this phone call."' On the line was the legendary *Sunday Times* editor Harry Evans, who said: 'I understand you're not happy working for the *Mail*?' He offered the Mailman a job, and Winchester resigned. But English had a shock for him yet: he was going to hold him to the notice period stipulated in his contract – one whole year. 'That was pretty wretched,' said Winchester. 'That year was horrible.'

As he endured his long goodbye from the paper, Winchester got to see up close just how the supreme Mailman operated when English attended the Republican Party National Convention in Detroit in July 1980, which saw Ronald Reagan anointed as the party's nominee to run for president. There was a suggestion at the time that ex-president Gerald Ford could run for Vice-President on the Reagan ticket, but George H. W. Bush joined Reagan instead. Ford was, apparently, being prevented from running by his wife Betty, who was a struggling alcoholic and would be unable to handle the stress of her husband's return to frontline politics.

'So it was at about ten or eleven at night in Detroit,' said Winchester, 'that would have been about four in the morning in London. And David said, "I'm going to dictate the following copy for you to take down." And it said, basically, "In an exclusive interview with a weeping Betty Ford, she said under no circumstances am I going to allow my husband to run as nominee for vice president."'

Winchester paused, looked up.

'David,' he asked, 'did you see Betty Ford?'

'And he said: "No, no. It's entirely fiction. But this is going in as an 'Editor's Must'." And it was this personal interview. I mean, it was complete fiction. Of course, I just sent the copy over. But that was David really, I mean, never let the truth get in the way of a good yarn. I hated what he did. But as a man he was so amusing. David and I always got on well personally – even years later after I left. But it was a pretty damn dishonest ship he was captain of.'[21]

Indeed. And a level of dishonesty was exactly what was required when English's *Daily Mail* lost out in a bidding battle with other newspapers to secure the rights to the big books of the day – political, celebrity or royal biographies that could often deliver a full week's worth of scoops and scandals (but cost a great deal of money as a consequence).

'We did a lot of stealing of books,' one former Mailman told the author. 'We might lose out on the rights but that didn't stop us, we'd just launch an undercover operation to get hold of the manuscript without actually buying the rights. It was like cops and robbers and we got very good at it. One of the best techniques was to find out where the printing took place, which was often abroad, and someone would arrive as a prospective client asking to have a look around the print plant. And you'd get a tour and you'd have your cover worked out – like who you represented and so on – and then on the tour, if you were lucky, you'd ask to see a few samples of stuff they'd printed and hopefully you'd find that elusive biography and you'd just put it in your bag.'[22]

Back at the *Mail*'s office, the place would be alight with excitement at having a book full of scoops in their hands a full month before the rival paper planned to run their stories. But there was still a problem; they had to find a way to cover up where all these juicy tales had come from – they couldn't just say they were from the book they'd failed to buy, that would be theft.

'Sometimes the best way was to take the stolen manuscript and commission another book off the back of it, a very quick book that would be written in a week with all the best stories in, which would basically be attributed to "friends" or other anonymous sources, and get a tame publisher to publish it, then buy the serial rights and run the best stories from it in the *Mail* before it was in the *Sunday Times* or whatever. And that was very hard for anyone to trace. It was very clever and, of course, it was illegal and immoral but it was a hell of a lot of fun too. It was all very "Fleet Street" of the day though – those playground games. And David English loved all that.'

An example of just how dishonest David English could be personally, however, did not emerge until 1988, when English wrote a piece in the *Daily Mail* about his experiences as a young *Daily Express* hack in the US in the early 1960s. Everybody, so the cliché goes, could remember precisely where they were when they heard the news that John F. Kennedy had been assassinated. Not David English. He told his readers a quarter of a century later that he was in Dallas, Texas, the day Kennedy died in November 1963. But he wasn't, he was 1,600 miles away, having a coffee with the office Telex operator George Valinotti near the *Express* HQ in New York City.

> Selected by Lord Beaverbrook, a long time crony of the
> Kennedy clan, to be his man at the new Camelot I had
> by patronage and connection become part of the inner
> press circle which the Kennedys courted so assiduously.
> It was a heady, intoxicating spell they wove around us,

corrupting with charm and grace, mesmerising with a
dazzling imperial vision of America's role in the world and
disarming us with inside information which always put
them in a good light. And all along with humour, style
and grace unknown before in political America and exceptional even to the highest standards of Europe. As the
youngest member of this elite club I could hardly believe
the providence and luck that had put me there . . . We
lived and travelled well, we President's men in the White
House Press Corps in brand new special planes. We were
cossetted and flattered. We were part of the system. And
so that November we went to Texas because the President
was going. None of us would have deigned to have set
foot there but for him. For we knew from him and his
brother Robert that there was more than something
rotten in the state of Texas.[23]

It was wonderfully evocative stuff, with the *Mail*'s editor painting
in words a full-colour picture of a wonderfully gifted, heroic even,
young reporter – himself – right at the centre of things. But unfortunately, he had not been personally 'selected by Beaverbrook', as
Max Aitken senior was an old man riddled with cancer by then and
he died only six months after Kennedy. The *Express* didn't even send
anyone down to Dallas with the President, probably because Ross
Mark, the *Express*'s accredited White House correspondent, was on
holiday. It was not as mad a decision as it seems in hindsight, given
that the President was there for the start of his re-election campaign
and the business end was another full year away.

Dozens of English's fellow hacks from the era knew English had
made all this up – because they had also been working in the States
or receiving copy from the US on the *Express*'s foreign desk at the
time. 'That was, to my mind, the most astonishing thing to have
done,' chuckled English's good friend and the reborn *Mail*'s first
foreign editor Brian Freemantle, who had left Fleet Street a decade
before to write novels, 'because so many people immediately knew it

wasn't true! I mean, Kennedy was shot and so was Oswald but David English wasn't where he said he was when it all happened. I knew he wasn't there, many people knew he wasn't there – when *he* was hitting the keys *he* must have known he wasn't there for fuck's sake. You know, if you're gonna just tart a story up a bit – don't do it with a story that is blatantly, blatantly, blatantly, blatantly not true. I saw his story the day it appeared, and called a friend on the *Express*, David Eliades, and said, "What the fuck's this about?"[24]

David Eliades knew more than most; he had worked for most of his career as a senior editor on the *Express* foreign desk and he knew who was where and when. The day he received the call from Freemantle in November 1988, he was in the *Express* office reading the same piece with utter astonishment – alongside a retired *Express* reporter, Robin Stafford, who was the man who had actually written the initial J. F. K. story from Washington while English dashed to the airport to get down to Dallas. English's story was a great read, a well-spun yarn. It continued:

> So I witnessed the whole unbelievable scenario spiralling out of control in a frenzy of hysterical violence, culminating in Lee Harvey Oswald being shot down a few feet from me in the basement of the Dallas police headquarters.[25]

The blood of Kennedy's mortally wounded murderer pumping out across the concrete towards our intrepid reporter's nicely polished shoes was a wonderfully evocative image. Again, though, it was not true. Though English was by now, at least, actually in Dallas – he was covered in soap suds in his hotel room, very close to Dallas police HQ. 'David did a very good job picking up the story when he landed in Dallas and everything else,' said Eliades. 'And then he was rung in his hotel room by the head of bureau at the time, Henry Lowrie.

'"What are you doing then, David?", Henry asked him.

'"Well, I'm having a shower at the moment."

'"So, you're not watching television?"

'"We don't have televisions in the showers here, Henry."

'"Well, I should check it if I were you because the man who shot Kennedy has been shot dead in the police station just below you . . ."'[26]

Twenty-five years later, dumbfounded *Express* colleagues Eliades and Stafford stood around a copy of the *Daily Mail* trying to work out what to do and Eliades decided to write a rebuttal for the next day's *Daily Express*. But the paper's editor and head of news decided not to print it, saying, 'We can't use this. We'll have blood on the streets!'[27] Just like the New York Mafia 'going to the mattresses' in a mob movie, *Mail* and *Express* reporters would have gone to war – shooting ink at each other across every story, across every page. It could have got messy.

Yet somebody in the *Express* office (not Eliades) *did* leak the spiked story to the satirical magazine *Private Eye* and, when friends asked how he was going to respond to the *Private Eye* accusation, says Eliades, English simply replied: 'Well, I think I told that story so many times I was there – I actually believed it.'

'Lots of people have hypothesized about why English did it,' said Freemantle, 'and the main theory was that he sort of elaborated his story over the years with Harmsworth and went and got himself trapped. He got himself into a situation that he just couldn't get out of. He felt he had to write it.'[28]

'The popular story that reached me – because I was the one that wrote the offending piece that ended up in *Private Eye*,' said Eliades, 'was that he had told the story to Rothermere so many times that when the anniversary came up he told him, "You better write that story you've told me so many times." So, he had to do it. But, I have to say, I worked with English for many, many years on the *Express* and never knew of him consciously inventing a story. Apart from this one about the Kennedy assassination but, well, you couldn't go much bigger than that though – could you!'[29]

From his earliest days as an editor rewriting young reporter Barry Norman's copy as features editor of the *Daily Sketch*, to later claiming he had tried to persuade him to stay on at the *Mail*, to claims to having met a long-dead New York mobster and 'interviewing' Betty

Ford – David English certainly seems to have had somewhat of a 'flexible' relationship with the truth. Nobody but David English and Vere Harmsworth can know for sure what other stories were shared between them, and they're both long dead now. But Vere had absolute and unwavering faith in – and unwavering *loyalty* to – his friend and editor.

Yet Vere did have his secretive side, just like Sunny Harmsworth. And one secret he kept from his editor was a whopper: he was planning to found a brand-new newspaper . . . and David English knew nothing about it until Lady Rothermere found a phone number in her husband's suit pocket. She thought he was having an affair and asked the *Mail*'s editor to investigate, so English dialled the number – a man answered. English asked him his name, and he replied 'Bernard Shrimsley' – deputy editor and then editor of Rupert Murdoch's relaunched *Sun* and then editor of the *News of the World*. English hung up; he worked out in an instant what was happening.

Rothermere had often talked of taking the fight to the once-mighty *Sunday Express*, now staggering around the builders' yard at Trafalgar House. It makes economic sense to own a morning, an evening and a Sunday newspaper, to ensure that those expensive printing presses are never idle. Rothermere had, in fact, wanted to buy the *Sunday Times*, which Murdoch scooped him to – largely because Vere didn't want to be lumbered with the heavy loser *The Times*, which came as part of the deal.

He decided to start his own Sunday paper instead, without David English, and he asked Shrimsley to be its launch editor. It was a disaster.

The *Mail on Sunday* was a dull and grey baby when it was born in May 1982 and it didn't look like she could survive in what was soon to be a full-colour newspaper world. Even a huge news story couldn't blow life into the *Mail*'s little sister, and you don't get many stories bigger than a war – Britain was fighting one 8,000 miles away over a clump of barren rocks that was home to 1,800 people and 400,000 sheep; the Falklands to the British, Las Malvinas to the Argentinians.

'While the launch date of the *Mail on Sunday* drew closer and as we were assembling a staff for the big day,' wrote the paper's deputy picture editor, Alun John, 'Mrs Thatcher was assembling a task force to sail to the South Atlantic.

'Just as our own D-Day day arrived, so did the British forces in the Falklands. Editor Bernard Shrimsley was pleased: "I love a war," he said, "There's never any argument about what to lead on." The first paper was not a great one. It didn't really set me alight; it didn't set the readers alight, either.'[30]

The sixty-four-page paper's arrival was 'the first new national Sunday paper in 21 years' and its first front page was pure Rule Britannia: 'Mission Accomplished' was the headline, after the RAF bombed the airport at Port Stanley in preparation for invasion. Unlike the daily, she was an ugly-looking thing. Her masthead was shoved over to one side and there wasn't even a picture of a stealthy-looking British Vulcan bomber, just an old agency photo of Argentina's dim leader General Galtieri riding a donkey – into a war few of his people wanted. It was to prove an apt metaphor.

Shrimsley, with Vere's approval, had decided against simply turning the *Mail on Sunday* into a twin to the daily. Common currency in the newspaper trade of the day was that readers wanted a longer, fatter read of a weekend as they reclined in a comfy chair after a heavy Sunday lunch with their feet propped up on the dog. The *Mail on Sunday*'s typeface was small and tight – it looked more like a broadsheet. And pictures had to be kept to a minimum because the antique presses used to print it couldn't cope.

Worst of all were the paper's sport pages. May is the best month of all in a football-mad nation. Prizes are won, trapdoors down to lesser leagues whip open and hearts are broken. Most games were played on a Saturday – making Sunday the day to savour the victory or suffer the loss in delicious detail. In 1982 Liverpool clinched the then First Division title for the thirteenth time and the England team were packing their boots for the World Cup in Spain, having failed to even qualify in 1974 and 1978. The FA Cup too still mattered and was only a couple of weekends away. Lots going on, then – it should have been a doddle.

Yet the *Mail on Sunday*'s back-page splash was . . . the roller-skating world championships in the Netherlands. Maybe it was a stroke of luck that not many people actually read the thing, as Associated Newspapers had no choice but to renovate and reuse ancient presses and these 1938 dinosaurs couldn't pump out enough papers. Its target circulation was 1.25 million but it collapsed to 700,000 after six weeks. The paper, as it stood, could not survive. So Shrimsley was sacked in under three months and a new editor 'abseiled to the rescue' from upstairs: David English.

The first working day on a Sunday paper is Tuesday and, when Alun John showed up after Shrimsley's departure, the ex-editor's office looked 'like a crime scene'. The staff shuffled in at the normal conference time and soon enough the door swung open and in walked Rothermere plus English and some of his senior hands from the *Daily Mail* – deputy editor Stewart Steven, showbiz chief Rod Gilchrist and a thirty-three-year-old news editor called Paul Dacre.

'Most were in dark blue suits, white shirts and restrained ties. You could cut the tension with a knife,' said John.

> Rothermere announced that Bernard had been fired.
> 'He had to go. He has not given us the paper we needed.'
> He told us from now on the *Daily Mail* would take over
> and David English would edit both the daily and Sunday
> papers. Changes would follow and we would be informed
> about them. 'Let there be no mistake,' said Rothermere,
> 'The *Daily Mail* is now in charge.'[31]

Outside the editor's office sat young reporter Sue Douglas. 'So the A-Team came down,' she told the author. 'It was Roddy Gilchrist, Paul Dacre and a few others. And I remember Roddy jumping up on to a desk in a block of six desks, and saying, "We're taking over!" Can you imagine? I remember just thinking, "What the ffffuck?"'[32]

As English's cartoon pirates took control of the listing *Mail on Sunday*, David English skippered both papers, sleeping in his office on a camp bed and working from 9 a.m. to 1 a.m. – spending half of his time on the daily, half on the Sunday. He was fighting hard to save the paper but, in fact, some thought it was actually jealous English who'd kept the wind from her sails from the start, denying the *Mail on Sunday* access to the *Daily Mail*'s talent that could save her like typewriter-wielding shipwrights. The only way Lord Rothermere could rescue the *Mail on Sunday* was to make the man who wanted to sink her its protector. A smart move indeed – nobody seemed to call Rothermere 'mere Vere' these days.

The paper was cleaned up visually and relaunched with *Daily Mail* talent hived off to help the stricken sister. New sections were added, plus a magazine called 'You', edited by a gifted journalist called John Leese. Editing two papers was too much for one man though, so Rothermere found another editor close to home. Mailman Stewart Steven, who had quietly rejoined the paper after resigning over the British Leyland fiasco, was appointed editor of the revitalized *Mail on Sunday*. Steven often joked about his pair of monumental journalistic failures to his new staff.

'Gradually David faded into the background,' said Alun John.

> Stewart was an excellent editor, the best I've worked for. I instantly hit it off with him in two ways. First, I supplied him with an autofocus camera for his holidays, complete with an ample supply of colour film, which I would collect from his secretary on his return and make sure was promptly processed and returned. Second, he could not understand how to work the video recorder in his office and I would be summoned to set it to record his choice of programme most days. This gave me a little privileged access and we occasionally chatted about office events as I punched in the channels for the video. Stewart's greatest gift as an editor was a supreme confidence in his own ability to become the greatest newspaper editor the world has ever seen.[33]

Steven turned out to be an excellent *Mail on Sunday* editor but would never become editor of the *Daily Mail* – though many saw him as English's obvious successor. English, who was by now editor-in-chief of Associated Newspapers (apparently after receiving an offer from Murdoch to join News International, which he declined out of hand), wasn't going anywhere soon. As he celebrated his first decade in the *Daily Mail* editor's chair in the summer of 1981, it was clear to most on Fleet Street that the *Daily Mail* was the mid-market master, not the decelerating *Daily Express*. By the end of the 1970s the *Daily Mail* was only 50,000 or so short of the magic 2 million circulation mark. The *Daily Express* was actually still slightly ahead with a circulation of a little over 2 million – a fact that failed to disguise that its sales had, effectively, halved since Beaverbrook died in 1964. The *Express* had followed the *Mail* down the tabloid track in the mid-1970s before being sold off to the property development company Trafalgar House. Bricks and mortar were their trade, not ink and paper and truculent hacks and despotic editors. Beaverbrook's baby was on her slow slide to nowhere.

But Lord Rothermere's *Evening News*, the newspaper that had turned Sunny Harmsworth from a magazine boy into a newspaper man in 1894, was also in trouble at the time. Beaverbrook's former company had also owned a London evening newspaper called the *Evening Standard*, which, after a long-drawn-out process taking several years, Vere eventually bought outright from Trafalgar House. Vere merged the two papers and the *Evening News* disappeared off the streets in 1980; this was no time for sentimentality – the *Standard* was simply the stronger paper read by middle-class Londoners beloved by the admen (the *Evening News* did reappear briefly in 1987 as part of a London newspaper price war).

It was, as a consequence of the *Express*'s decline, easier than ever for the *Mail*'s editor to make the case for his favoured journalists to defect to the *Mail*. But the *Express* was not his only target and English could charm just about anyone into working for his beloved *Daily Mail* from up and down Fleet Street. The writer Keith Waterhouse, for example, had spent his entire national newspaper career on the *Daily Mirror*, until he decided he didn't like the paper's disreputable new owner Robert Maxwell in 1984, and, when the rest of Fleet

Street heard Waterhouse was about to leave, Sir David English –
himself once a *Mirror* reporter – invited him out to lunch.

'I knew David from the beginning of my days in Fleet Street as a
man who got great fun out of journalism and made it, therefore, fun
for everyone else to read,' said Waterhouse.

> He thought that newspapers were there to be enjoyed,
> while at the same time informing the readers to the hilt.
> I once saw him, in New York, when he was editor of
> the *Daily Mail*, snatch a telephone out of a reporter's
> hand and dictate his own version of a story which he
> did not think was being well told. David poached my
> column from the *Daily Mirror*, having heard that I was
> unhappy under the lash of Cap'n Bob Maxwell. Several
> other papers were after it but David took me to lunch
> at the Savoy Grill where we talked about everything but
> column-writing. But that morning he'd had a *Daily Mail*
> column prepared as an exact replica of my column in the
> *Daily Mirror*. Nothing was said. I was hooked, and he
> knew I was hooked. He was a superb newspaperman, and
> a superb newspaper chief.[34]

Another English swoop was for Richard Addis, who had
first planned to be a monk, surely the rarest of entries on any
Mailman's CV; he even spent two years after Rugby school as a novice
at the Community of the Glorious Ascension in Devon, and had the
habit of wearing a monk's smock at Cambridge – until the delights
of university life eventually got to him. Rothermere took a shine
to Addis when he worked on the Londoner's Diary column of the
Evening Standard. Addis was soon poached by the *Sunday Telegraph*,
where he rose to be deputy editor. One day English invited Addis to
lunch at the Savoy Grill – English's usual table, of course.

'English had oodles of charm,' Addis told the author, 'but I was
so nervous I couldn't drink my drink because my hand was shaking
so much. So I had to do this elaborate thing where, whenever he

looked away, I had a quick glug – usually with two hands – and brought my head right down to the glass. His style was, basically, "What are you earning? I'll double your salary if you come. I want to make you . . ." – and he'd create some amazing job title – "and the contract will be delivered tonight and I'll give you two days to make up your mind." It was a great sales technique. English basically made me an offer I couldn't refuse – invented a job and doubled my salary – and that was my first meeting with him, it was very, very overwhelming for a young journalist.'[35] Addis would go on to be the *Mail*'s number three before being poached to edit the fading *Daily Express* in a bid by yet another set of new owners to revitalize the paper. Tina Brown, editor of *Vanity Fair*, then the *New Yorker* and founder of the *Daily Beast* website – and wife of former *Sunday Times* editor Sir Harold Evans – was wooed by English and also, briefly, joined the *Mail*; 'David English gives great hire,' she said.[36]

English still had a problem in the US though, now that Winchester had failed to fit into a Mailman's tights, and in 1979 he decided he needed another fresh hire to hopefully fix his American problem for good. His sights fell upon a tall, slightly awkward *Daily Express* reporter in New York called Paul Dacre. They met for lunch and it went well, with English telling Dacre about how the *Mail* was by now far superior to the lost *Express* and he needed a new bureau chief. A few hours later Dacre was standing at a newsstand in the foyer of the *Daily News* building pretending to read a magazine, its famous big old globe perched in the background. He'd just taken a call as he sat at his desk in the *Express*'s office four floors above, with instructions from a man (David English) to do exactly that. Dacre recalled that 'the phone went and this man with a kind of disguised voice said, "If you go down to the foyer of the *Daily News* building to the magazine stall, something will happen." I felt something being slid in my pocket, I turned around and saw David English scuttling off into the crowd. What was in my pocket was a full, typed contract with David's own type of typing mistakes, outlining the terms of the job and the offer. I was totally impressed by this.'[37]

Dacre signed up and became a Mailman; he would rise through the ranks to replace English as editor a dozen years later and has now been the editor himself for over two decades, longer than English and nearly as long as Thomas Marlowe. Just like the contrasting personalities of Sunny and Bunny Harmsworth, Dacre is a very different kind of man to David English: whereas English was exuberant and extrovert, Dacre is awkward and shy – especially in the company of women. Whereas English started his climb from a weekly newspaper as a teenager, Dacre is the son of a star writer on the *Sunday Express*, attended a nice school and went to university.

Nevertheless, despite their differences, Marlowe, English and Dacre were all fairly typical middle-class boys of their era done good. And the key factor that defines whether one was middle class or not in the second half of the twentieth century, perhaps more than any other, was the house one grew up in.

PART IV

KING OF
MIDDLE ENGLAND

11

Daily Mail Country

Middle England has a brown door.

It's a nice enough varnished wooden door to a nice enough red-brick house with mock Tudor beams and a short driveway leading to a small garage. It has a nice front garden with an untamed hedge that screens it from a pleasantly wide street called Brookdale. Brookdale, in Arnos Grove, north London, is firmly in *Daily Mail* country, suburbia. The street could be the setting of any number of classic British sitcoms set among the British middle classes: from *Terry and June* and *George and Mildred* to *One Foot in the Grave*. Paul Michael Dacre, editor-in-chief at Associated Newspapers, was born in London on 14 November 1948 and grew up on Brookdale,[1] the eldest of five boys. He has often stated how crucial Arnos Grove was to his rise from the suburbs to take the crown of King of Middle England.

'Its inhabitants were frugal, reticent, utterly self-reliant, and immensely aspirational,' Dacre once said. 'They were also suspicious of progressive values, vulgarity of any kind, self-indulgence, pretentiousness, and people who know best.'[2]

Before the 1930s, Arnos Grove was in London's hinterland until the brick and concrete of the ever-expanding city spilled north along the banks of the Underground. Indeed, the Tube line is only a tennis ball's throw from the back garden where the Dacre boys could hear trains squealing to a halt coming into the station at the top of their road. Arnos Grove is near the northern tip of the Piccadilly Line that slashes London from Heathrow airport to Cockfosters, passing through Holborn on the way; which was handy for Dacre senior, as Holborn is just a short walk to Fleet Street, where he worked.

Peter Dacre had started out in Yorkshire,[3] the son of a joiner who survived the trenches of the First World War only to be killed in a building site accident when his son was just six years old. Dacre senior left Batley Grammar School at sixteen for the *Doncaster Gazette* and landed a few years later in London, where he worked briefly as a personal assistant to Lord Beaverbrook himself and also joined the Press Lord's *Sunday Express*. He'd stay on the paper for almost forty years.

Dacre senior was the paper's US correspondent just as rock 'n' roll erupted. He was even the first British journalist to interview a young singer with snake hips by the name of Elvis Presley. Upon his return to London, show business and feature writing became his newspaper passion,[4] which was fortuitous, as it was possibly the best time there has ever been to be a showbiz writer – the Beatles and the Rolling Stones and a multitude of lesser bands were on their way and there were only two channels on the television, which each commanded truly vast audiences. The *Sunday Express* was huge then too, selling around 5 million copies every Sunday on the back of a very simple formula: its staff always kept the reader in mind – in every single sentence, on every single page – just like those on Sunny Harmsworth's *Daily Mail*. It was never pompous, verbose or pretentious and would always use the throwaway detail such as 'the house with the yellow door'[5] that helped paint an instant and clear picture in the reader's mind. The paper existed to intrigue and to entertain just as much as to inform.

Paul Dacre had his father's newspaper gene; he would sit with his dad at the dinner table in Brookdale every Sunday and they'd dissect that week's edition of the *Sunday Express*. The paper was, Paul Dacre often said later, his journalistic 'primer'. Peter and Paul Dacre adored newspapers and journalism but the son would become a very different journalist, a very different man.

INTERESTING. EXTRAORDINARY. AMUSING.

ANSWERS TO CORRESPONDENTS

☞ ON EVERY SUBJECT UNDER THE SUN. ☜

No. 3. [Entered at Stationers' Hall.]   **JUNE 16TH, 1888.**   [European Postage, ½d.]   Price 1d.

"ANSWERS" IS PUBLISHED EVERY WEDNESDAY MORNING.
The trade can obtain the paper from all wholesale agents, and from the office,
26, Paternoster Square.

THE QUEEN'S PRIVATE LETTERS.

R. S. PINKERTON writes:—"I have in my possession what I believe to be a private letter from the Queen to a deceased lady of high rank. The letter is written on small rough paper, but it bears no crest, address, or date. It is, however, fortunate that there is a watermark with the date (1855). The letter fell into my hands in rather a curious manner, and though I have no intention of selling it, or making its contents public, I should like to know if there is any way of finding out whether it is genuine. Does the Queen underline many words, and is she careless of her punctuation? How does she sign herself? Also, where could I (if I felt so disposed) find a purchaser?"———— From an examination of several undoubtedly genuine letters from Her Majesty, which are to be seen in several collections of autographs, we should say that there is a probability of our correspondent's example being a genuine one. The

Extraordinary Prize

FREE CONTINENTAL TOUR.

STRANGE EXPERIENCES.
Do women live longer than men?
CURIOUS FACTS.
Crossing sweepers' fortunes.
INSIDE A NEWSPAPER OFFICE.
Narrow escapes from burial alive.
WHAT HAS BECOME OF TICHBORNE?
The world's postcards.
STRANGE THINGS FOUND IN TUNNELS.
Can snakes kill pigs?
TERRORS OF TOP HATS.
A delicate question.

THE STRANGE THINGS FOUND IN TUNNELS.

"RINGDOVE" writes:—"Your correspondent 'Norseman' is wrong when he says that things found on railway lines and in tunnels are the property of the finder. They belong to the railway company until claimed. You would find it worth while to make a list of the remarkably strange things found in tunnels. As a railway clerk, I know that the most extraordinary things are found."———————"Ringdove" is right. Some enquiries at leading stations proved that the strange things found in tunnels would form a very curious collection.

From the tunnels of the Underground Railway in London there are every month brought to light lost and stolen property of every description. It is strange, too, that so many people select this line for depositing their old letters.

All along the line the platelayers and other workmen find tiny scraps of paper, and occasionally the passenger has not troubled to destroy, but has thrown the letter away entire. There is evidently a popular belief that these tunnels are never visited, whereas as a matter of fact

ABOVE: *Answers to Correspondents* magazine. The first edition in June 1888 displayed Alfred C. Harmsworth's fondness for the royals, taste for a grim tale and his desire to see a German thrown from a train. (Adrian Addison, courtesy of the British Library)

LEFT: The young magazine entrepreneur turned newspaper mogul Alfred C. Harmsworth, known as Sunny to his parents and 'the Adonis of Hampstead' to his admirers. He is depicted here, *c.* 1900, shortly after he founded the *Daily Mail* newspaper. (© Culture Club/Getty Images)

ABOVE: The first *Daily Mail* of 4 May 1896. So much more enjoyable and easier to read than its rivals, its staff kept the reader foremost in mind from the very start. (Adrian Addison, courtesy of the British Library)

ABOVE: Young Esmond Harmsworth stands between his uncle, Lord Northcliffe, and father, Lord Rothermere, in 1915. Esmond became sole heir to the Harmsworth publishing empire following the death of his two elder brothers in the First World War. (© Hulton Archive/Stringer/Getty Images)

ABOVE: The first Viscount Rothermere was, declared Adolf Hitler, 'one of the very greatest of all Englishmen… His paper is doing an immense amount of good'. The pair met on several occasions, including here in 1937 at the Berchtesgaden. (© ullstein bild/Getty Images)

LEFT: Esmond Harmsworth sits resplendent in a vice chancellor's cap and robes. However, by the time this photo was taken in the 1950s, the *Daily Mail* was being soundly beaten by the *Daily Express*. (© Baron/ Stringer/Getty Images)

LEFT: David English, photographed here in 1971, was the hottest hack on the *Daily Express* of the 1960s. He would later become the boyish editor of the Harmsworth-owned *Daily Sketch* and go on to rescue the *Daily Mail*. (© PA Archive/PA Images)

BELOW: It was Buddhist billionaire Vere Harmsworth who decided to appoint David English to the editor's chair, and to change the *Mail* from broadsheet to tabloid. By the mid-1970s, the threat from the *Daily Express* had been seen off. (© Frank Barratt/Stringer/ Getty Images)

ABOVE: *The Daily Mail*'s newsroom in Carmelite House on the Thames embankment near Fleet Street, 1913. Sunny Harmsworth would often stride through his newsroom handing out cigarettes and quietly issuing instructions to his editorial staff. (© PA Archive/PA Images)

ABOVE: David English on the microphone over 70 years later with senior executive Paul Dacre (sitting with arms crossed), as the paper prepared to pack up and leave Fleet Street forever. (© Clive Limpkin)

LEFT: Twenty-two-year-old Paul Dacre – future *Daily Mail* editor – after his college newspaper won an award. As the son of a *Sunday Express* showbiz writer, Dacre always knew he wanted to follow his father into the newspaper trade. (© Leeds University Library)

BELOW: Pictured here in 1980 in El Salvador, a shirtless Paul Dacre enjoys a poolside meal with other journalists. (© Michael Brennan)

HOUSE SERVICE

Memo from............ PAUL DACRE ....

To.................. MR. STEWART PAYNE ....

November 23rd ....19...82

Stewart,

There was obviously a full moon the

night you did these expenses. Please

cut them or, alternatively, return them

and give me the pleasure.

HOUSE SERVICE

Memo from............ PAUL DACRE ....

To.................. MR. STEWART PAYNE ....

January 6th ....19...84

I would have spoken to you, but as you are
not here I am sending a memo:

I don't know whether you were badly briefed,
but your copy on watches for all train
drivers was woefully thin.   Seven paragraphs
on a story of this importance - it ended up
on most front pages apart from our own -
is just not good enough.

ABOVE: David English brought Paul Dacre to London as deputy news editor and
though he quickly rose through the ranks, the still painfully shy news editor's
preferred method of communication was by internal memo. (© Stewart Payne)

LEFT: Paul Dacre took over from David English as *Daily Mail* editor in 1992. He is pictured here arriving at the Leveson Inquiry in 2012. (© Stefan Rousseau PA Archive/PA Images)

  Bobby's baby brother has a name! Cole Jacob Scott and we are all in love! 💚💚 #myboys

↩ 79   ⇄ 83   ♥ 341   •••

He has a name! The former Girls Aloud singer, 34, and her husband, 34, announced their second child's moniker via Twitter on Friday

The name is likely to resonate with the star's best friend and bridesmaid Cheryl, 33, who is pregnant with her first child with One Direction hunk Liam Payne, 23.

Cole was Cheryl's surname when she was married to first husband, footballer Ashley Cole, between 2006 and 2010.

SHARE THIS ARTICLE

Share

RELATED ARTICLES   ‹ • ›

 'You're going to be honorary UNCLES?' Lorraine awkwardly...

 Pregnant Amy Childs displays her baby bump in a...

Confident and happy Danielle Lloyd parades her enviable...

'Can't wait to find out if you're pink or blue': Pregnant...

The couple split acrimoniously amid multiple allegations of cheating on his part.

Cheryl tied the knot with French businessman Jean-Bernard Fernadez-Versini on the island of Mustique in July 2014 - but the pair split just 18 months later in

passing

▶ On Santa's naughty list! Chloe Khan suffers a nip-slip as she struggles to contain her surgically-enhanced assets in skimpy festive fancy dress

▶ Richard and Moody: Television's favourite couple go for a casual look as they enjoy a date day at a London pub Not in the festive spirit?

▶ Pregnant Zara Tindall proves there's no hard feelings as she chats to ex Richard Johnson at Ascot racecourse (but wears her husband's name on her badge)

▶ 'Burst into tears and pick up everyone remotely involved': Kate Beckinsale and Michael Sheen celebrate as daughter Lily, 17, gets into college

▶ The Apprentice's Frances Bishop flaunts her curves in TWO black bikinis as she soaks up the sun in Dubai following her boardroom disappointment

ABOVE: The future is digital. Newspapers are dying in print, but the *Daily Mail* is thriving globally online. *MailOnline*'s success has been driven partly by celebrity stories that run down its infamous 'sidebar of shame'. See pp. 324-374. (© *MailOnline*)

'Peter was a lovely man,' Barry Norman, also a showbiz reporter of the era, told the author. 'Paul is a much harder, much tougher character than his dad. His father was a much gentler, much quieter man.'[6]

Lifelong *Express* hack David Eliades, who knew both father and son well, agrees. 'I liked Peter Dacre very much. He wasn't Paul, I can tell you. He was a very different sort of man. Peter was very softly spoken, unobtrusive. The most daring thing I ever saw him do was jump on the open platform of a London bus and nearly kill himself because he didn't get his foot on it properly and he was dragged along Fleet Street! He was a nice chap to spend time with, to have a drink with. He was a big noise on the *Sunday Express*. He was very talented, he even wrote lyrics for popular songs; famous singers sang them.'[7]

Paul Dacre later chose one of his dad's songs – a Bing Crosby number for which Dacre senior wrote the lyrics called 'That's What Life Is All About' – as a request on *Desert Island Discs*, the quintessentially English BBC Radio Four programme that has, so far, been his only broadcast interview. 'My father was a great newspaper man but he was also a frustrated newspaper man because his great love – his first love – was writing songs and lyrics to songs.'[8]

Dacre junior was focused firmly upon print from the very start, as he showed as editor of his school magazine at University College School in Hampstead. One edition of *Compass* that Dacre devoted to the evangelical American preacher Billy Graham, who was in the UK at the time to host a handful of mass revivalist meetings that were something of a phenomenon in the mid-1960s, was to prove to be a vital lesson. 'Doubtless influenced by the possibility that they might view my A-Level essays in a more benign light, I asked several of the most intellectually impressive masters to attend a Graham gathering and write about their impressions,' he said in a speech in 2008.

> It was a journalistic disaster. Without exception, their words were ponderous, prolix and achingly dull. The issue went down like a sodden hot cross bun. Lesson

2

MAIL MEN

One: Brains and education have little to do with the
craft of journalism which is to ferret for information
and then explain it clearly, informatively and above all,
entertainingly. Journalists are born, not made,
and all the media schools in the world won't change
that. Also: dull doesn't sell newspapers. Boring doesn't
pay the mortgage. In the next issue, I discreetely secreted
a couple of expletives into an article. It was child's
stuff . . . but they got me into terrible trouble with the
headmaster. The magazine, needless to say, sold out but
my relationship with the school was never quite the
same again. Lesson Two: Sensation sells papers.[9]

Dacre may have been finding his journalistic direction with
Compass, but he was best remembered by some fellow pupils as
a shy and gangly boy who could balance a tennis ball on the end
of his foot.[10] As fellow pupil Michael Sadgrove, now the Very
Reverend Dean of Durham and a committed *Guardian* reader, told
the author: 'I remember Paul quite clearly from UCS days as we
were exact contemporaries. What made him stand out was his flair
for sports and games, particularly rugby – enviable in someone like
me who was an abject failure in this respect. He did not strike me
as particularly an academic star, nor do I recall that he excelled in
music or the arts. I recall him as being on the quieter side; I would
not have foreseen that he would one day be the editor of a national
newspaper!'[11]

'Paul loves to reminisce about the London of his youth,' said one
Mail insider. 'Arnos Grove, getting on public transport, his days at
University College School. These days, he's rarely outside W8 or
SW1. He can get very misty eyed about the London of the sixties
and seventies.'[12]

Sadgrove and many of Dacre's contemporaries from his school
went up to Oxford and Cambridge universities in the mid-1960s
just as 'Flower Power' was about to burst into full bloom. But Paul
Dacre went to Leeds, his father's hometown.

This was the late 1960s, an age of protests, and thousands of students would head down to London to march around the capital making their voices heard. Every student in the land, it seemed to some in Middle England, had turned into a 'bloody Commie' overnight; they were squandering tax payers' money on paint for silly placards when they should have been in the library working out how to put the Great back into Britain. The *Mail* itself commented, after a violent demonstration outside the US Embassy in London in March 1968, that as 'Students start looking on the whole police force as a Fascist organisation out for blood, the rest of the country sees the whole student body as a bunch of irresponsible hoodlums.'[13] A 6ft 3-inch shaggy-haired English student called Paul Dacre was marching with the best of them, as he later told the BBC.

> Like most sensible young people of that age, I was
> left-wing, and of course we went to London on
> anti-Vietnam marches. And we all chanted – and for the
> life of me I'm not quite sure why – 'ho ho Ho Chi Minh'.
> They were wonderfully heady, liberated days. Quite what
> we were protesting about I'm not too sure in retrospect.[14]

It was newspapers that drove him, though, and not the left-wing politics of his fellow Leeds University students Jack Straw and Clare Short, who both went on to become prominent figures in Tony Blair's Labour Government. Dacre edited the *Union News* and seems to have been one of the few students of this era who never learned how to roll a joint. He did, however, run an interview with a student who had, under the headline 'The delights of getting stoned'. His paper was sympathetic to gays, immigrants and homeless families and even called on students to help in 'breaking down the barriers between the coloured and white communities of this town'.[15] He put pretty female students he dubbed 'Leeds Lovelies'[16] into his paper just as Rupert Murdoch was about to start his infamous page three on *The Sun*. Dacre's wholesome lasses were, of course, fully clad. Jon Holmes, now a sports agent, was one of Dacre's student reporters:

It all seemed to me at the time a proper, grown-up
journalistic experience and I thought it only right that
every day should end with the consumption of vast
quantities of alcohol in the 'local' – in our case, the union
bar. It was just along the basement corridor from the
newspaper office, which was filled with cigarette smoke
and lavishly equipped with a couple of typewriters. Not
once did Dacre join us for a pint.[17]

Union News won best newspaper at the National Union of
Students awards of 1969 and Dacre, aged twenty, posed for a photo
in a tweedy jacket and a sweater over a check shirt, looking a bit like
Shaggy off Scooby Doo.[18] 'He came in about a week later after it had
been announced,' added Holmes, on Radio Four, 'and said: "We've
won the award, I'm gonna cease to be editor now. I'm gonna get a
degree – I'll see ya." That was it. I never saw him again. He never
called in the office, he never said: "Brilliant! Let's all go out for a
drink or anything." Nah. Just "That's it. On my CV. Cheerio."'[19]

It worked. Straight after getting that degree in English, Dacre
secured probably the best job any young journalist of the day could
possibly have hoped for: he joined the staff of the still-massive-selling
Daily Express as a graduate trainee in Manchester in 1970.

A young photographer called Mickey Brennan remembered
meeting Dacre for the first time on a story outside Manchester
University shortly after Dacre became a 'proper' journalist for the
first time, and he wasn't impressed: 'He was so young and eager like
some big fucking Labrador puppy. I remember looking at him and
saying "Oh, piss off"; he was just some bumbling twerp. And he's
possibly the clumsiest man I've ever come across . . . He'd just left
university and he'd not done any time on the locals or anything like
that, which would make it like a "grace and favour" job that he'd got
on the *Express* . . . thanks to his father's connections.'[20]

Photographers often get the best insight into reporters on the road,
crushed together as they so often are inside bars, cars and hotels –
tanks even, in a war zone – and Mickey Brennan would weave in and

out of Dacre's life for the next decade or so, but Brennan never quite rated him as a hard news man.

Dacre's lack of experience of the hard graft of grinding out stories for a local paper was a real disadvantage when it came to earning the respect of the other newspaper hands; the journalism trade of the early 1970s was not quite so flooded with graduates as it is today. Though just a pup compared to the hoary old hacks of the day, eager Dacre took some real risks in the name of a story during the height of 'the troubles' in Northern Ireland. One day Dacre found himself in an IRA area of Belfast interviewing a Catholic girl who'd been shot in the kneecaps for dating a British soldier:

> I rushed off to see her and she was in a Republican
> stronghold area and I was jolly foolish because I knew
> that you had to clear these things in advance with the
> relevant godfathers. Anyway, I got to see her and she was
> a lovely girl and it was such a tragic story and it was a
> great, great interview. I came out of the front door of her
> council flat absolutely exultant and out of the shadows,
> out of two alleyways on either side, this whole group of
> men emerged and kind of pinned me against a wall with
> guns pressed against my ribs. And all I could think was
> what a fool I'd been and I kept chanting, 'Look, feel in
> my right hand pocket, it's my press card. It says I'm a
> journalist!' And this went on for about 15 minutes and
> eventually more men came and phone calls were made
> and they let me go.[21]

Dacre was soon called down from the provinces to continue his learning on Fleet Street itself, where he flourished on the *Daily Express*'s features desk inside the same black art-deco building where his father was writing stories for the Sunday paper. But it seems he didn't quite have his dad's gentle showbiz touch. After a story about the Scandinavian leg of a tour with Paul McCartney's band Wings, someone – it may well have been a fan – was so incensed that they sent a solid rebuke, recalled Mickey Brennan: 'Dacre told me many times how he received a box back at the office, a chocolate box or something with "from Linda and Paul" written on it – and he thought it was a "thank you", you know, a gesture from McCartney and his wife. So he opened it up . . . and there was a big fucking turd inside!'[22]

Paul Dacre's bosses had a far higher opinion of his work, though, as, not so long after, he was sent to the US to cover the Jimmy Carter election of 1976. Just as it had done with David English sixteen years before, Dacre's time in the States would go on to define him. He would stay in the country for six years, mostly working from a desk inside the *Daily News* building in New York City, another – this one a thirty-six-floor skyscraper – art-deco monument to the printed word in which the pirates of the British Press had moored themselves. The *Daily Mail*, *Daily Mirror* and *Daily Express* all rented space in the building. Fleet Street was an ocean away, and by the time the first editions came out in the late evening in the UK most expat British hacks were operating on 'Costello's time', i.e. they were working out of the infamous hacks' bar that was all the pubs of Fleet Street compressed into one long and dark cave, just a few blocks from their desks.

Most journos from back in the day had a tale or two to tell about Costello's Bar and Grill – it was a memorable kinda place. A shillelagh, a tough piece of wood, that Ernest Hemingway had bent around an Irishman's head hung over the cash register and there were famous photographs of Marilyn Monroe sitting in a booth looking up at drawings *New Yorker* cartoonist James Thurber had made to pay off his bar tab. Thirsty journalists would step in from the light and the traffic of East 44th Street and be greeted by the bartender, Fred Percudani, a frightful chap who would yell across the packed bar at his demanding Fleet Street clientele: 'Just wait, you Limeys, everything round here's done by hand!'

'For us Brits the Zero-Hour was around 6pm,' wrote photographer Mickey Brennan, who washed ashore on Manhattan Island ahead of Dacre in 1973. 'Most nights the two pay phones would ring

– remember, this was long before mobiles – and a mad dash to grab them usually involved someone from the *Mail, Express* or the *Mirror*.'[23]

On the public side of the bar, an expat German called Herbie waited on the Costello's clientele with his own inimitable kind of service, complete with a German accent that sounded like it was straight out of a war movie. 'Herbie shuffled around in a filthy suit with soup stains and dribble caked on it, serving food,' added Brennan. 'He would arrange a set-up – knives and forks, napkins – with the bread rolls in his pocket. The ladies didn't like that. The beautiful Anthea Disney, then the *Daily Mail* US correspondent and bureau chief, refused to be waited on by Herbie. [I] couldn't blame her really after she and I saw him leaving the bar one afternoon with a dead chicken hanging from his pocket.'

'One day Herbie was serving a lady lunch when she complained about her lumpy mashed potato,' recalled another expat, Ian Bradshaw. 'Herbie, using his great paw-like hands, scooped it up off her plate and disappeared into the kitchen, only to reappear with another handful of mashed potato which he slammed down in her gravy splattering her suit. It didn't pay to complain.'[24]

Polite Paul Dacre, the tall young chap with hair long to the collar who always seemed to wear a pin stripe suit even on a hot day,[25] didn't quite fit in at Costello's. David English's old friend Tony Burton, by then working on the *Daily News* and a Costello's regular, never warmed to the well-spoken young man from the *Express*. 'I never felt comfortable with Paul Dacre,' he told the author, 'he was never "one of the boys". And the funny thing was, I kept getting mixed up and calling him Peter, his dad's name . . . apparently he didn't like that.'[26]

'Paul didn't hang around in the bar so much,' added Anthea Disney. 'He was a dogged and ambitious young kid who was eager to please. And he would do anything – do whatever he needed to do, "scruples" was not his middle name. Paul Dacre was just interested in his career . . . and was eager to get out of just seeming to be his dad's son.'[27]

The relationship between father and son was soon in trouble itself, though; Dacre's parents had, by now, divorced, and when Peter Dacre

married his new lover in 1979[28] it must have come as a seismic shock
to his eldest boy, who had such a profound belief in the nuclear
family. 'I think Paul was very contemptuous of his father,' Phil Finn
Jr, another New York hack, told the author. 'I probably shouldn't say
this, but Peter was always reputed to have had affairs and what have
you and didn't treat the family well as such. Whereas Paul and [his
wife] Kathy have always been totally devoted.'[29]

Whatever the relationship with his father, there were other journalists to guide him along this part of his career and one man, more
than any other, seems to have been crucial: Dacre's boss, Brian Vine.
Rotund and ruddy-cheeked 'Vino' could be found most evenings
holding court in Costello's in a crisp Savile Row tailored suit and
with a monocle pushed into his left eye 'for opthalmic reasons' – even
though it was obvious to all that the glass was clear. His English voice
booming across the bar, Brian Vine looked and sounded every bit
like an English m'lord on a drink-sodden vacation in the Big Apple,
especially to the locals. However, it was all a deceit, and Vine was
probably one of the best operators the newspaper trade has ever seen.
Vino had scoop after scoop to his name, and he had even helped
to track down Britain's most wanted man, the runaway Great Train
Robber Ronnie Biggs, in Brazil in 1973.

'New York Magazine wrote a story profiling Vino's lifestyle,' said
Mickey Brennan, 'which included a luxurious apartment on the East
Side of Manhattan, a weekend house at the end of Long Island, one
very large Cadillac motor car – company owned – and a boat. He
also had a couple of very slow racehorses.'[30]

Vino, however, didn't take to Paul Dacre and would often refer
to him as 'my fucking tea boy'. As Express foreign desk stalwart and
English's friend and former colleague David Eliades, who happened
to be in New York on a visit in the late 1970s, explained: 'Dacre was
just a soldier [a junior hack] in New York when I dropped in on the
office one day, and we went to the bar [Costello's] and we were sitting
there and I suddenly noticed that Paul wasn't in the company. So I
went and sat with him for the rest of the evening and talked to him
because the others didn't really get on with him very well; they used

to refer to Dacre as "pin head". Brian was a big, bumptious man, and a great friend of mine and there was a clear animosity between Dacre and Brian Vine. It was rather tragic really because I liked Paul, I thought he was a very nice young man.'[31]

Phil Finn Jr was another hack who weaved in and out of Dacre's life during these years; Dacre and his wife Kathy would often have dinner at the Finns' apartment, where Dacre liked to relax with his socks pointed to the air on a reclining chair Finn had in his living room. And Finn had no doubt that Dacre's time in New York was preparing mild-mannered Dacre well for what was to come.

'I think the biggest single influence on Paul Dacre was Brian Vine,' he told the author. 'Many of the facets of Dacre's life and the way he acts now were obviously learned from Brian Vine, he learned a lot of those "wrinkles" from Brian. But Vine was a far, far superior journalist to Dacre and Brian was a bit contemptuous of him really. I think that working in New York, if nothing else, he got a lot of steel. I would credit Brian Vine with instilling that in him, giving him that hard edge. I think Dacre saw that if he was going to do anything in the newspaper world he had to have a lot of Brian Vine in him.'[32]

To some in New York City, Paul Dacre was often an unwitting and unwilling figure of fun. One story has Dacre all in a fluster after Fred the barman handed him a Jewish yarmulke skullcap one afternoon when he walked into Costello's with the Jewish office secretary.[33] But the worst times for Paul Dacre were when Jean Rook, the *Express*'s lantern-jawed and perma-tanned star writer, showed up in town with her leopard-print dress squeezing out her chest. Her welfare would fall to Dacre, the office junior. And prudish Dacre – so the Costello's story goes – once even had to shop for tampons for the First Lady of Fleet Street after the airline lost her luggage.

'She'd call Costello's and he'd panic,' Mickey Brennan told the author, 'and he was a real fucking panic merchant in those days, I can tell you, of the first order. His voice would quaver – he had this oscillating voice when he was scared – and so when she called the pub, he'd go "Oh, oh my God" and he'd run and push anybody out of the way to grab the telephone. And, of course, we'd take the piss out of him mercilessly. The craic in the pub some nights was quite mighty and Dacre was a target for a lot of that piss-taking, you just could not help it. But he never gave it back, he just wasn't smart enough on his feet in that way. He had this silly upper-class twit kind of an attitude, like he was above it all. Plus, well, he just wasn't a humorous bloke . . . but we all found him fucking hilarious.'[34]

Even outside Costello's, Paul Dacre would have to endure the occasional ribbing, such as the day he went horse riding in New Jersey with his wife, Mickey Brennan and Neal Travis, a witty gossip writer on Murdoch's *New York Post*. The party watched the riding school staff struggle to push clumsy Dacre up on to his horse. 'The saddle hadn't been tightened properly and of course it slipped and he went underneath the horse, and the horse took off!' said Brennan. 'And we're all standing there pointing and pissing ourselves laughing; Kathy Dacre too. There were only two creatures who weren't laughing: Dacre, and his fucking horse.'[35]

During another period out of doors, Mickey Brennan took a snap of a shirtless Dacre eating lunch by a hotel swimming pool in El Salvador, where they'd both been sent – an unstable country that eventually bubbled up into civil war. It was also regularly rocked by severe weather . . . and earthquakes.

'We were only in El Salvador a short time and we didn't exactly have a dangerous time, in fact we rather enjoyed ourselves,' said Brennan. 'But we were there during a big earthquake and it frightened the shit out of me, I'd never been in an earthquake before and it was quite a big one. Our rooms were on the fifth floor and, fuck me, Dacre was on the same floor but by the time we got down to the ground floor he was already there, sitting by the pool! He must have got down there in record time. The fucking earthquake was still going on, the swimming pool was still making waves.'[36]

It was far safer back in the *Daily News* Building, where Paul Dacre had a reputation as something of a studious journalist. Dacre would work far longer than anyone else perfecting a feature, agonizing over every word. Yet no matter how hard the *Express* staffers worked in New York, back in Britain the paper was on its long slide to nowhere, and by 1979 the *Daily Mail* was rising to take control of the middle ground that the *Daily Express* had dominated since the days of Beaverbrook and Bunny Harmsworth.

David English had by now, for sure, noticed Paul Dacre, and one day in 1979 the top Mailman was in New York and he invited Dacre to lunch. English's *Daily Mail* was by now simply a better newspaper than the *Daily Express*, English told him. The *Mail*'s time had come again. So Paul Dacre became a Mailman in the autumn of 1979, the clumsy contract appointing him as the *Daily Mail*'s new New York bureau chief.

'It's difficult to understand really what personally attracted David English to Dacre initially,' said *Express* hack David Eliades, who knew both men well, 'because David was flamboyant and he liked to roll his sleeves up and get involved but Paul was very much more laid back and shy.'[37]

Perhaps only Dacre and English knew the truth, but it's a fact that the *Mail*'s New York bureau had been floundering for years, and Simon Winchester had spent an unhappy year failing to squeeze into a Mailman's tights before handing over to Dacre and joining the *Sunday Times*, a paper to which he was far more suited.

'I was obviously a lame duck by then,' Winchester told the author, 'but I got on perfectly well with Dacre. I was astonished to find he was appointed the *Mail*'s editor a decade later or whatever it was, because he never struck me as anything out of the ordinary. He was a rather mild-mannered, perfectly pleasant guy. Unremarkable. He's become transformed into something that I just don't recognize; talk about the rise of the mediocre personality!'[38]

Paul Dacre's byline in the *Mail*'s own archive reveals that features were still his forte. In October 1979 he wrote a story about executions in America being turned into a soap opera. 'At times this week, it was difficult, if appalling, to resist the thought that the man who convulsed to death in a Nevada death chamber was not a full paid up member of Equity.'[39] And Dacre, who was still only thirty but already somewhat of a puritan, disapproved of American couples exploring their sex lives on TV – shows that highlighted 'a grotesque trend seeping insidiously across American television and mirroring a disturbing social malaise'.[40]

Dacre also wrote a column for his new paper, similar to the one that had helped turn David English into a star reporter on the *Express* in the 1960s. Dacre's version, though, wasn't considered a great success. 'I don't think that worked,' said David Eliades. 'David English was a spectacular New York column writer and Dacre just didn't have the same touch. He was more of a features man.'[41]

Paul Dacre was not born to be a George Steevens or a Vincent Mulchrone – few, to be fair, are – and Dacre himself began to accept that he was never going to be the greatest writer of his generation. He was, as he told the BBC, approaching a crossroads.

> For the first ten years in journalism I did wonder whether my career would be pursuing the writing course but frankly I reached a point – and I was a very good writer – I reached a point where I realized I was never going to be a very great writer. I think if I had stayed as a writer I would have ended up as a frustrated chap contributing less and less as I got older. And I decided at that stage to go down the executive path, and I haven't regretted it.[42]

It was just as well, as only fifteen months after he became a Mailman, Dacre was recalled to London to become deputy news editor, one of the lowest rungs on a very tall ladder to the top. Around the same time, the *Mail*'s correspondent in Rhodesia, George Gordon, had actually turned down the much bigger job offer to be the news editor; it was an office job and he hadn't become a journalist to get stuck in an office.

'Suddenly it was all collapsing in New York,' Gordon told the author, 'so I had lunch with David English at the Savoy and English said, "Dacre's coming back and I'd like you to go out to New York as the bureau chief." He said things hadn't quite worked out for Dacre and he simply didn't want him there any longer.'[43]

Several expat hacks in New York – including Finn, Eliades and Brennan – had a fairly low regard for Dacre's actual abilities as a news reporter. He was viewed as a feature writer and interviewer rather than as a great Fleet Street 'operator' (whereas English had very much been regarded as a top-notch hack in his day). And, it seems, the supreme *Mail* being must have agreed.

'Dacre never had much of a news sense,' added George Gordon, 'and all right, it was a sort of promotion – I guess – for the New York bureau chief to be made deputy news editor, But I know English never thought much of Dacre's news sense either. And that's a Dacre failing, I think, even now as editor. Dacre had impressed English as a writer and with his good academic background but in English's estimation he lacked on that "cut and thrust" Fleet Street experience that New York needed. He was a very good interviewer; he was good on the features. But it was at the height of a circulation battle with the *Daily Express* and the *Express* had a formidable team in New York.'[44]

On 10 October 1980 – a month shy of his thirty-second birthday – the *Daily Mail* published Dacre's final 'America' column; he'd miss 'Oyster stew at Paddy's clam bar before a fight at Madison Square Garden' but would be glad to be free of junkies in the street, born-again Christians and 'American women's seeming obsession with orgasms . . .'[45]

So Paul and Kathy Dacre and their two boys readied themselves for their return to the UK, tying up a few loose ends such as ridding themselves of the family's vacation home in the Pocono Mountains. New bureau boss George Gordon tried to help out: 'I took a whole bunch of UK hacks up there to see if anyone wanted to take it over [from the property's occupants]. However, when we saw the agent she told us there had been a problem: the local sheriff had arrested [Dacre's] previous tenants . . . they'd turned the basement into a pot [cannabis] production facility.'[46]

Mailman Dacre returned to Fleet Street in the autumn of 1980. It would take another dozen years of tough climbing to reach the top; he'd work double-time, fourteen hours or more, on most days. Paul Dacre was hooked on hard work and headlines and had been since his student newspaper days.[47] But first he had to get up off that first rung, and somehow survive a national tabloid newspaper's news desk, a dangerous furnace that has vaporized many a promising executive career over the years. Some Mailmen of the day suspect that English was testing the news judgement that was thought to be Dacre's biggest weakness.

Dacre rolled up his sleeves and joined a handful of junior news editors assigning reporters to stories and sending them back again and again to knock on a door, this being the *Daily Mail* – as well as reading every last sentence in a tall stack of newspapers and magazines, keeping tabs on the wires and sifting agency copy and tips from freelancers. They would then process these fought-for words after they were filed and feed them into the fire – where they might be either incinerated or come out on 'the stone' as a double-page spread, the highest compliment for any tale in the *Daily Mail*.

The news desk performs all these duties with the constant fear that a bomb might go off in the editor's office; no matter how good the news desk is, something always tends to go wrong. Life, such an untidy business – even for Mailmen – sometimes simply gets in the way: the idea may have been ridiculous in the first place (it is not unheard of for a Fleet Street editor to order the pursuit of a story that actually came to them in a dream), the tip-off from a member of the public or a freelancer may have been false, the target may not be home or the address may be wrong, another paper may have got to them first or simply bought them up as an 'exclusive'. Yet the editor isn't interested in reality. Every evening, the news editor's success or failure is there to be weighed and measured against the rest of Fleet Street in the shape of all the first editions of every other newspaper sprawled out over his oversized desk. If *his* paper doesn't have the best stories – and the best versions of the same stories every other paper has – the best editors will want to know why, right NOW! The news editor is the man – always a man, on the *Daily Mail* – who has to keep the furnace burning, he is the one who has to answer for all the human frailties of his innumerable staff and freelancers.

It's a damn tough job, especially under an ultra-demanding editor like David English. Many journalists, including English himself, wisely dodge the news desk altogether and find other routes to the top. Yet Paul Dacre wasn't even the news editor, he was just the deputy and desperately unhappy at being just a number two[48] to rising English protégé Rod Gilchrist.

It turned out Dacre could take the heat, and he survived, thrived and then began to rise; soon enough, English moved Gilchrist across to Showbiz and promoted Dacre to news editor. If it had been a test, Dacre had passed; he was in his early thirties and had found his calling. Dacre had always been destined to be a man in an office.

Then the polite and mild-mannered boy from the suburbs began to morph into an expletive-spouting monster; his favourite word became 'cunt', a word that would have been like a bullet to a blue sky in Arnos Grove. Context, though, is important; this was the norm in the Fleet Street of the day.

'We all took a tremendous amount of shit in those days from executives,' said the *Mail*'s crime reporter Tim Miles. 'Dacre would call us a "load of cunts" or "a shower of cunts". It was always "cunt this" and "cunt that". He did like the word "cunt".'[49]

Tim Miles was probably the best reporter on Dacre's newsgathering team, a true Fleet Street 'operator' whose byline stood above some of the biggest stories of the 1980s, from the Brink's-Mat gold bullion heist to IRA bombings. And he could have bylined himself 'Air Miles' for all the travelling he did on the *Mail*'s account: he was in Zimbabwe for Robert Mugabe's election, covered the assassination of Swedish Prime Minister Olof Palme and was in Tripoli when bombs fell on 'the mad dog of the Middle East', Colonel Gaddafi. A British drug smuggler told Mailman Miles from his Malaysian prison cell how 'they'd never hang him' . . . only for the chap to swing from the neck until dead a few days later. David English rated him highly and his news editor rated him too.

'It's often said of Dacre that he's a bully, and maybe he is,' he told the author. 'I made it very, very clear that I wasn't gonna take any shit from him. I would accept criticism but I certainly would not be bullied. There were one or two reporters who just couldn't take it, life became too miserable for them under Dacre, and they left. But I'm sure it was never personal: it was just that he wanted to get the best out of people and the best story. There was bombast, there was bluster, [and] there were very, very tough dressings down – "bollockings" – if you didn't get things right. Yet beneath all that bombast and the bluster, I have to say, is a good heart. He always cared very much if people had family problems, he gave people time off if they did have a family problem. He was solicitous about those who were having some kind of problem either with wives, children, whatever it was.'[50]

Miles would sometimes see a lanky figure striding headlong down the road towards Fleet Street marching on towards his future. 'I would give him a lift and I guess I got closer to him than a lot of people because he was in my car. We'd talk about what had gone on the day before, stories. But he didn't gossip, he didn't ask me about what I felt about other people in the newsroom – he wasn't looking for tittle-tattle. It was all about the story. The story. I wouldn't say we were close friends – I found him a bit of a loner, he's a self-contained man who is above the fray most of the time, and I don't think he makes friends easily. But I wouldn't personally do the man down. He's not the bad man – the evil man – that some people want him to be.'[51]

Dacre, of course, still had to answer to one man: David English. Everyone bowed before David English.

'As a young reporter when I arrived on the *Mail* in the late seventies,' added Miles, 'I was very much in awe of David English. It was always said of English that he could do everything on a newspaper better than anybody else – layout, subbing, writing . . . he was a brilliant writer. I mean you paid a lot of deference to English, he was the "supreme editor".'[52]

Paul Dacre received his fair share of 'bollockings' from this supreme *Mail* being, as did Tim Miles. But reporters tended not to have to endure daily red-faced rows from Dacre, the *Mail*'s new news editor. His preferred method of communication was by internal memo. And so, every day by the swing doors to the early-1980s *Daily Mail* newsroom, reporters would approach a wooden rack screwed to the wall and gingerly push their hand into a square hole with their name on it.

'The first thing you did when you came in for your shift was to check your little pigeonhole for a house envelope,' reporter Stewart Payne told the author. 'And you'd let out a deep sigh when you saw one. As chances were it was a bollocking memo from Paul Dacre.'[53]

Reporters would watch Dacre standing in his glass office behind the news desk as he mumbled these endless memos to his furiously scribbling secretary . . . even though he was often only a few yards from the living, breathing hack he wanted to address.

'He didn't really walk down into the newsroom to brief you on a story or anything, someone else on the desk would do that,' said Payne. 'He looked embarrassed, almost, if he had to have a conversation. He would just kind of make a stab at it – a classic one would be "Christ, old man, that's a dreadful tie" – and he would grab your tie and hold it up as if he was going to cut it. And you'd just think, "That's probably his attempt at being friendly." Dacre just couldn't talk to you in an easy-going way. A memo was safe. I suppose you could say it was cowardly but I never really thought of him as a coward – just awkward and clumsy around other human beings . . . [A memo] could be succinct and devastatingly deliver the point and he didn't have to actually talk to the person.'[54]

In the days before equally devastating emails, house envelopes began flying back and forth with the senders and recipients just yards apart, the messenger boys throwing them into pigeonholes like croupiers tossing out cards. 'You couldn't just collar Dacre and say, "Paul, can I have a word?"' said Gill Swain, one of his few female news reporters. 'So everyone had to enter the memo-sending game to get their point across. As a woman, I found Dacre very good to work with professionally but absolutely impossible to communicate with on any other level.'[55]

Partly as a result of the memo-sending, the *Daily Mail* secretaries became oddly powerful creatures, led by Ina Miller – the editor's secretary, a semi-regal figure. 'Ina was very, very grand and was always heavily made up, with her hair piled up on top of her head,' reporter Stewart Payne told the author, 'and she walked with the posture of a titled lady. She was very "glam" – frighteningly so.'[56]

'She was stuck in a time warp, a 1950s throwback of Elvis movies and American diners,' added 'Barry'. 'One *Femail* writer even pitched an idea in conference for the paper to do a makeover on her, to bring her up to date into the 1980s. [The reporter] didn't last very long after that.'[57] Queen Ina and the other secretaries were never shouted at nor treated shabbily, and seemed to have more authority than most of the hacks on the paper. However, the deputy editor's secretary had a name that would land any company straight into court these days. 'Stewart Steven's secretary was a black lady – an Asian-black lady rather than African – and everybody called her "Sooty" . . . to her face,' Stewart Payne told the author. 'She even referred to herself as Sooty, it was her name. I mean, even in the late 1970s when I joined the paper – when people were nowhere nearly as politically correct on issues of racial discrimination as they are today – even then, I felt acutely embarrassed addressing a black woman as Sooty.'[58]

Out in the newsroom, there were frequent comedy moments at Dacre's expense; one day, the news editor thought he was talking to a Mailman in Scotland called Jimmy Grylls but was actually on the line to the Tory MP Michael Grylls (father of TV adventurer Bear Grylls). 'Dacre picked up the phone and he just started barking down the line a tirade of swear words and instructions, thinking it was his reporter,' said Payne. '"We need to fucking do this that and the fucking other, you cunt, and fuck this and cunt that", and I'm waving at him horrified. Eventually he breaks off and I say, "Paul, that's Michael Grylls the MP you're talking to, not Jimmy Grylls the reporter!" And the line was still open, and he started shouting, "Oh, I'm a cunt! I really am a fucking cunt! What a stupid fucking cunt I am." And then he starts apologizing profusely to this bemused MP on the other line. He was so clumsy, and he just didn't listen to people. He would just sort of bluster in, especially when he was under pressure. He never broke under pressure but he was like a bull in a bloody china shop.'[59]

Every day at around 5.30 p.m., a gentle hour or so of calm would fall over the newsroom when Dacre and all the other executives shuffled into English's vast office for afternoon conference and some of the braver reporters actually dashed out for a 'Conference Quickie', CQ in code; they'd leave their jackets on the back of their chairs and grab a beer or two in the upstairs bar at the Harrow across the road. A few months before, when Dacre was usually still left outside the editor's door with the rest of the plebs as a lowly deputy, he'd watched his reporters indulge in this quaint Fleet Street custom.

'CQs were absolutely fundamental to the *Mail* newsroom culture when I was there, especially to the more "risky" [those not cowed into staying at their desks for fear of retribution] reporters,' said Payne. 'Dacre knew all about CQs and he started to resent it when he became news editor. If you can't see them then they must be up to no good was his prevailing attitude.'[60]

Then the calm would be broken by a stampede of flustered executives stumbling out of English's office, spiking stories and setting off a flurry of phone-bashing and door-knocking to stand up the stories and ideas that the editor now demanded appear in *his* newspaper. Dacre would often send two reporters at a time on the same tale.

'He'd shout over just as you went out the swing door: "And I don't want you two cunts holding hands!"' said Payne. 'Meaning, you were supposed to virtually work against each other. Divide and rule was very much the *Daily Mail*'s underpinning philosophy and there were a few reporters who absolutely swallowed the *Daily Mail* bible, one guy had absorbed it so much that if you were sent out on a story together he wouldn't even talk to you; he wouldn't even tell you where he was going! Some reporters were just totally driven by the *Daily Mail* and weren't great company as a result. You ended up working against each other, and Dacre liked that. He thought it'd achieve a better result because you'd be stabbing a colleague in the back at the same time. Whereas, of course, most of us were good mates . . . and we didn't do any of that stuff.'[61]

One old hand who experienced this 'creative tension' was English's friend from the days when they had both walked two young girls into the bushes on Barnes Common in the 1950s: Tony Burton. He worked on the *Mail* in London for a few months in the late eighties, and then in New York.

'There was some press conference going on with Rolls-Royce up in the Midlands. And the news desk suddenly called me over and said, "Hey, get up there now!" wherever it was, two or three hours north of London. I knew I was going to be late so I hurtled up there, and found the *Daily Mail* already had a reporter on the job. And I was fucking furious because I risked my life and licence to get up there, and they were just playing games. English was responsible for this philosophy, to send two reporters on the same story to compete with each other and whoever did the best job – it'd be their story that was carried in the paper. It pissed me off big time though, stupid fucking games. I didn't give a fuck if they wanted to use my version or not, to be honest.'[62]

Hoots of laughter could be heard out in the street coming down from the upstairs bar of the Harrow most evenings, with one hack or other usually doing a perfect impersonation of their boss the news editor.

'We all used to laugh at him,' said Payne, 'more behind his back than to his face. He was rather a comical character, although he would hate to be seen that way I'm sure. He was often imitated. If you went across to the Harrow someone would always be relaying the Paul Dacre story of the day. I didn't dislike Dacre though, I actually found him rather funny because he was so bloody clumsy and oafish – I just thought he was silly at times, buffoonish. Not intentionally, that's just how he came across. But I didn't think he was a dickhead.'[63]

Every now and then, Dacre would actually appear in the bar himself.

'He would stand at the bar and he'd clip the guys on the shoulder and bumble (in a voice like an Eton schoolmaster) "h-aargh, you cunt . . ."' recalled Swain, 'and his conversation didn't seem to consist of anything much more than that really. So I would hover on the edge trying to find a way of getting into this "conversation" . . . but on the level of – "h-aargh, you cunt!" I couldn't really find a way in.'[64]

Another reporter did find a way to reach Dacre, though – with his fists. Allan Hall, who is now a *Mail* freelancer in Berlin, had been a Mailman on six-month rolling contracts in the early 1980s (many reporters joined the paper on such deals, which would sometimes turn into staff jobs) before leaving to join the *Daily Star* after Dacre told him he didn't think he had what it took for a coveted staff position. A little while later Hall happened to be in the Harrow on one of the rare evenings when Dacre was also there, as another reporter who was there that night explained: 'Allan was at that time a staff reporter on *The Sun* and chuffed to bits because he had just been told he was going to be the *Sun's* new man in New York. He'd been in a pub all afternoon, with his colleagues as you did in those days, waiting for a jury to come back in an Old Bailey trial. So he was completely pissed. Allan clocked Dacre and just . . . he just went for him, shouting: "You said I didn't have 'the *Daily Mail* sparkle', you cunt!" And he biffed him one in the face! Dacre was completely bemused by it. I don't think it really hurt him, he didn't fight back or anything and a couple of reporters pulled Allan off him . . . He didn't hit the cunt hard enough in my view,' growled the ex-Mailman, 'we all thought Allan was a legend after that. But Dacre, to be fair, is not one to hold a grudge – the paper has given Allan a lot of work since as a freelance.'[65]

Dacre may not have been comfortable in company over in the Harrow pub but he was certainly comfortable inside the *Daily Mail* office, where he was on the rise. In the late summer of 1985 he was promoted to the role of assistant editor in charge of both foreign and home news, and then English moved him across to run the features department – the beating heart of the *Daily Mail*. News by its very definition comes and goes, whereas features, generally, require more time and thought. And he was soon joined in conference by Tim Miles, who later followed him into the news editor's chair; promotion into the executive ranks, so often the curse of the best reporters.

'I was on a foreign job in 1987 and David English was in Milan,' said Miles, 'and he actually summoned me to come and see him in his hotel there and offered me the news editor's job. "It's time for you to move up and mature a bit and become a *Mail* executive, Tim," he told me. English could be very flattering, very persuasive. And I took the job, quite honestly, reluctantly – because I enjoyed life on the road. So, I was duly appointed news editor . . . and I fucking hated it.'[66]

Miles was one of those reporters who liked to go for a beer or two in the Harrow of an evening, but he soon realized this was not the done thing for an executive when Dacre pulled him aside one day and offered him some advice, telling Miles, 'Look, you can't really go out drinking with these guys any more. You're the news editor. You've got to put distance between you and reporters because all they're going to do is give you a hard time over a story that didn't get in or a story that was cut. And your relationships are going to founder.'

Miles ignored his advice. 'And I spent every evening getting shafted about why a story didn't get in or why a story was cut or why those expenses were cut,' he laughed. 'So the dynamics of the relationships did change. But I wasn't prepared to not drink with reporters – my friends – because I'd become the news editor. And I also wasn't prepared to rip these people to pieces [in the office]. I was a reporter myself, I knew how easy it was to fuck stories up and how stories could go sour on you and not from lack of trying or lack of expertise or ambition. It's just that shit happens. If a reporter was lazy or indolent or cocky, yeah, sure, I could give a bollocking with the best of them. But I understood the frailties and difficulties of being a reporter which often weren't recognized by Dacre and English.'[67]

Miles was never going to battle Paul Dacre for the editor's chair. He didn't want it. An office – though it may be a mighty big office with a secretary or two – was to Tim Miles, and to many a hack since newspapers began, just a dungeon with better decor. However, this wasn't the case with Paul Dacre, who by the end of the 1980s had again been promoted, this time as an executive on the back bench, where he joined the clutch of key lieutenants and senior sub-editors alongside David English who actually put the newspaper together – these are the people who finally decide which story goes where with which photograph, have final copy approval, and write or green-light the headlines before the pages are sent off to be turned into a physical newspaper by the workers in the press hall.

'I sat for months looking at the grey heads on the back bench,' said Miles, 'with absolute dread, thinking, "I don't want to be here, I don't want to be here . . . I don't want to be here in another ten years' time;

I don't want to turn into one of those guys." So, I quit after about eight months as news editor and left the paper completely.'[68] Miles soon joined a new full-colour newspaper called *Today* that Rupert Murdoch had bought and that was aimed squarely at the mid-market *Mail* and *Express* (unsuccessfully, in the end – it closed after less than a decade), and English never spoke to him again because of his betrayal.

English's talent-spotting skills were, of course, not infallible, and Tim Miles's fellow Mailman Stewart Payne (they also shared a house) had already proven to be a similar test for Paul Dacre. Payne had staggered in one morning after being up all night partying in mid-1985 and was called into Dacre's office. 'So I go in, still feeling horribly hungover and expecting to get the bollocking of my life and he's saying, in a sort of droning voice almost like he'd rehearsed it and without looking at me – in a kind of reverie: "Well, young Mr Payne, I see a great future here for you. I have been very impressed with your work recently and your commitment. Therefore, I think it's time for you to move on and I'm making you television correspondent." And I was open-mouthed; not only was I *not* being bollocked – and Dacre was somehow completely oblivious to the fact that I had been as pissed as a parrot at work, he was quite blind to some things that might be obvious to other people – I was being promoted! I didn't trust myself to say anything very much because I was so hungover. So I came out. And the guy I had been on the piss with all night had come in on shift and he asked how I'd got on at work after such a late session. And I gasped: "I've been made the TV correspondent!" And he fell about laughing, saying, "But you've not got a TV!"'[69]

Word quickly spread throughout the office, with much amusement, that the *Mail*'s brand-new television correspondent didn't have a TV and actually loathed the whole business of showbiz – a department he was now based in. Someone quietly informed the news chief of this fact and Dacre called Payne into his office a few days later and asked: 'How the fucking hell are you going to be the television correspondent if you don't have a TV set?' Dacre turned it around, however, quickly deciding a television virgin was actually a great choice for television correspondent – as he could watch telly with fresh eyes. So the paper rented him a set, which Payne watched for a few miserable months while his mates back on the news desk ribbed him mercilessly about the fluffy stories he had to write – about which he had not a clue; he'd even have to head to the library to check on even regular TV faces such as 'Orville the Duck'. Dacre watched all this from the far side of the room with a look on his face that said, 'I rammed that square peg into that round hole but why isn't it working?' Payne quit and joined *Today*.

Unlike Payne and Miles, though, Paul Dacre wasn't going to be leaving any time soon, especially seeing as there were only a few rungs left on the ladder to the editor's hallowed chair itself. Those hours and hours of hard work were finally paying off. He had long wanted to be an editor, he confessed in a speech years later: 'Not just wanted, if I'm being honest. Hungered. Lusted with a passion that while unfulfilled, would gnaw at my entrails.'[70]

Yet there were several Mailmen ahead of him in the pecking order. If David English had decided to go and open a B&B on the south coast, there was only one Mailman that Lord Rothermere would have chosen as the paper's supreme editorial being at the time: Stewart Steven. Steven had made the *Mail on Sunday* an even bigger seller than the *Daily Mail* after gently nudging it upmarket 'against the inclination of senior colleagues' (i.e. English). The Sunday paper was a different, slightly more thoughtful and edgier newspaper than her elder sibling. In Vere's eyes Steven was almost, but not quite, on a par with editor-in-chief David English.

Sue Douglas was Steven's protégée on the *Mail on Sunday* until English forced her to move to the *Daily* and work under Dacre running the features department. In true English fashion it was actually, in effect, two people doing the same features editor job.

'Dacre and I were set against each other like two ferrets in a bloody bag,' Douglas told the author. 'David was designed to set people against each other and he really believed in that creative tension. But he would stir it up so much that it was actually disruptive. He was very female, bitchy.'[71]

For a while, it looked as though Sue Douglas could even one day compete with Dacre for the editor's job on the *Daily Mail*, if Lord Rothermere decided to appoint a Femail to run a newspaper aimed broadly at women. Meanwhile, Dacre was striving to improve his vocabulary, as one former colleague explained to the *Independent*; he would drop words such as 'schadenfreude' and 'hubris' into conversations and stories without, apparently, fully understanding their meaning: 'I used to think he was reading the dictionary from A to Z because every day you would get a new word and a consecutive new letter from the alphabet.'[72]

Dacre also had a weakness for showy French and Latin phrases such as 'bien pensant', 'sine qua non' and 'au contraire' – he would later even invent his own words for his enemies such as 'quangocrats', the 'liberalocracy' and 'the Subsidariat'.

'Dacre wanted to be "the intellectual",' Douglas told the author. 'And I think where he and I ever got on was that I could play that card because I actually *was* an intellectual, and I ended up marrying one.'[73] Douglas's partner at the time was the writer and historian – and presenter of TV documentaries – Niall Ferguson, a man she'd met when she'd been sent up to Oxford University by David English on a 'talent-spotting' expedition. Mr and Mrs Dacre would attend dinner parties with brainy types at Douglas's basement flat in Islington.

'I'd got a first in biochemistry, which Dacre was slightly in awe of,' she added, 'and I knew loads of clever people. I think Dacre was actually always in awe of the clever, north London intelligentsia, and because I had that card he was quite respectful of that but he didn't really like it at the same time, so we got on all right.'[74]

Intellectual or not, the talk in the pub at the end of the 1980s wasn't so much about Dacre's brain power but more about how he seemed to actually be morphing into David English in conference; some even began to call him 'Little David'.

'Paul Dacre was wise,' said Douglas, 'he kept his head under the parapet and he was a good David English disciple; he followed – he followed and he followed and he followed. He modelled himself on what David was – even down to the jokes, the voice inflection, the way he sat in his chair. Everything. And it was completely sycophantic and revolting. It was like a Hydra, you know, with him growing out the side of David English. But it worked, David liked that. And Dacre knuckled down, he worked damn hard.'[75]

'Dacre definitely did do the David mannerisms, absolutely. Yeah, he did,' chuckled 'Terry', another senior *Mail* executive and daily conference attendee. 'A very high squeaky laugh and all of that. English found that very flattering, I'm sure.'[76]

Yet Paul Dacre and David English were vastly different characters: English was exuberant, creative and devious by nature, whereas Dacre was naturally restrained, shy and quiet. It remains a mystery to some fellow Mailmen as to why English pulled him aside to be his protégé, while others believe he never really did; all that hard work simply put Dacre in the right place when the right time came along.

'I don't think David ever really encouraged an heir apparent,' said Sue Douglas. 'David was so completely "the King", I think there was kind of a weird bit of him that didn't want anybody to be as good as him. Paul Dacre never did anything that made me particularly go "wow!" He was always very mainstream safe. Dacre would always steer straight. And I think David liked that – because then he could be the stardust. And one big difference I've noticed over the years between Dacre and English – then and to this day – is that Dacre never writes anything [under his own byline]. English was a good writer and would byline himself on the front page on the really big, important story; he'd actually write the seismic splash himself. But I can't remember reading a single thing Paul Dacre has ever written.'[77]

Great writer or not, heir apparent or not, as the 1980s turned into the 1990s it didn't really matter because it looked like fifty-nine-year-old David English would be sitting in the *Daily Mail* editor's chair for quite some time.

12

Scorpio Rising

David English was by far the strongest and most secure editor in 'Fleet Street' as he approached the anniversary of his second decade in charge of the *Daily Mail*, largely because he had cornered the female market in a way Sunny Harmsworth had never done.

Over half the *Daily Mail*'s readership were women and, of course, the country was still being led by a female *Daily Mail* loyalist; Margaret Thatcher was English's firm friend and neighbour. The supreme *Mail* being lived just down the road from Downing Street, in a house said to have been bought for him by Rothermere, and would often pop in for chats, and English was there in the early hours of the morning for three of the most special parties for any Tory: her general election victories. In *Daily Mail* headlines, Margaret Thatcher was usually referred to as Maggie but never Peggy nor Madge; short forms have to fit the personality or they just don't stick. Likewise, even as a young man nobody ever seemed to refer to David English as 'Dave' and certainly never 'Sir Dave', which is what he became in 1982 as a personal reward for his newspaper's help in returning the Tories to power. 'She looks after you,' English said of Thatcher. 'She'll make you a bloody sandwich if you want one.'[1]

Thatcher would also help her friend get a passport for a South African athletics prodigy if he wanted one, especially if the girl could run awfully fast in bare feet for Britain. Sports columnist Ian Wooldridge had written a piece about seventeen-year-old Zola Budd, who was running world record times at middle distance in her native South Africa but could not compete in the 1984 Olympics because her home country was banned due to apartheid. As Wooldridge recalled later:

> The article contained one piece of information I lived
> to regret revealing: she had a British grandfather . . .
> 'Brilliant,' cried David English, our editor of the time.
> 'Because of the British family connection she shall run
> for us.' By 'us' he meant the *Daily Mail* first and Britain
> second. He was a dynamic boss with a strict sense of
> priorities.[2]

The bemused teenager who ran without shoes would become another of English's celebrated 'stunts' – making the news instead of waiting for it like the Vietnam orphans airlift a decade before. The *Mail* editor flew the Budd family over and settled them in a house near Guildford with some minders – his reporters. He called the Home Secretary, Leon Brittan, and her citizenship was granted in ten days. Other newspapers, especially the *Daily Express*, were aghast at the speed with which the runner had attained a passport that could take months or even years in similar cases. One of Miss Budd's minders was Mailman Stewart Payne, who recalled the first time she ran on British soil: 'We were planted in the press conference to ask innocent, mindless questions to stop other much more pertinent questions being asked. So, we were told to say things like "How did you find the track, Zola?" and "How are you adapting to the weather conditions, Zola?" While others were desperately trying to ask her "How come you're here in the first place, Zola?"'[3]

The youngster suffered terrible homesickness and her father soon squandered the money the *Mail* were paying for the story, but she did run for Britain in the 3,000 metres final barefoot at the 1984 Olympics in Los Angeles where she tangled legs with America's Mary Decker, who fell to the ground. Zola came seventh to boos from the American crowd (and apparently made sure she did not come within the medals, as she knew she'd be harangued on the podium).

It was the *Mail*'s real political clout, through English's friendship with Thatcher, that put Zola Budd on that track. Yet Thatcher's number-one media man was never actually Sir David, and he wasn't even English. It was an Australian who would never willingly kneel before the Queen: Rupert Murdoch. Thatcher's union-bashing policies of the 1980s had helped Murdoch free all of Fleet Street from the yoke of the kingpins in the press hall when he sacked 6,000 striking print workers one day in 1986, and moved all his newspapers overnight to a state-of-the-art facility that simply didn't require them. The *Mail* joined the exodus that followed and set up shop at the end of 1989 in an old department store in posh Kensington, west London, with Harrods owner Mohamed Al-Fayed as the landlord. The location was mainly David English's choice – the editor-in-chief didn't want to head east to the docks like Murdoch's News International and both the *Mirror* and *Telegraph* groups. As Lord Rothermere's relative Vyvyan Harmsworth – who helped coordinate the move as head of corporate affairs at the DMGT parent company – told the author: 'David English liked the area and was very much against going to Docklands because he felt it would disconnect the journalists – especially those on the *Evening Standard* (a city paper) – from London. And I think that was the right choice in the end.'[4]

All the lovely new technology meant things could be done so much more efficiently, but it had little impact on the philosophy that underpinned the *Daily Mail*, as the top Femail of the day explained. 'I wouldn't say the paper was consciously nasty,' Sue Douglas told the author, 'it wasn't. But the paper did play to the prejudices of its readers – which is a very, very different thing; a calculated thing. It's to sell newspapers to these people. And English was utterly brilliant. He had this feral instinct for the prejudices of the British middle class. So we would reflect that in the paper. Some of us didn't like that and railed against it but the paper was successful because it held a mirror up to these readers so they could go: "See? Look! I'm right!" It was sexist. Racist. Every other -ist in the book. But not – probably not

– in a really nasty way. It reflected society, the *Mail*'s part of society anyway. And if you look at it coldly, you have to say that if it's nasty – then so is that element of society. If it didn't reflect its readers back at them, it would not be profitable. It really is that simple.'[5]

Yet this reflection was often given a good polish. For instance, a *Daily Mail* advert of the day featured a female barrister wearing a legal wig, with a handsome young chap trailing behind her carrying her papers. The message being that *she* was the boss. But the truth inside the *Mail*'s new office was somewhat different. Sir David would suggest a feature on how housewives 'always' lose a single sock in the washing machine,[6] to which most of his male execs would nod in excited agreement and chip in with ideas of how to handle the piece.

'The paper did absolutely bugger all to empower women on any level,' said Douglas. 'And yet the packaging was "we're listening to you". Utter bollocks. There was even a man editing *Femail* at the time! The truth was that we seemed to be listening and pandering to a female audience – powerful women read the *Daily Mail* and they read the *Femail* bit, and all this guff – but it simply wasn't true. I think women read the *Mail* as a newspaper and maybe look at *Femail*, but some of the "sexier" bits of *Femail* – though they might be, and I use the word loosely, "interesting" to women – by and large it was just an excuse to do things for men. A headline as a question like "What do I do if my husband is unfaithful?" – that's what the men in the office wanted to read because it was men producing those stories. It was a complete joke.'[7]

The office culture, too, seemed still to be stuck in the early 1970s. Sir David's old pal Tony Burton observed the dynamic between English and his senior staff from the safe position of a close friend. He attended conference one day and watched Sir David harangue his features editor.

'He had the news conference first and that was fine, and then they all left and the features editor Sue Douglas came in. There was just the three of us and I sat there and listened while she put up ideas and one after another he brutally destroyed them – and I don't know if he was showing off to me or he didn't like her or what but I felt like walking out it was so fucking horrible and embarrassing. And I should have done. I really didn't like what was going on there and it was partly English. He was too tough. He would screw people big time.'[8]

Sir David's daily conferences were sometimes, somewhat disparagingly, called the conference of 'the nodding dogs',[9] because of the way his top Mailmen all fought to agree with their master most forcefully and laugh the loudest at his jokes. But these 'nodding dogs' were getting more chances these days to sit in the big chair and actually drive the machine and make their mark on the paper. By the time he turned sixty in May 1990, English was taking much longer holidays and he would also involve himself in the wider Associated Newspapers business that should have been of little concern to the top editorial man. He loved, for instance, to personally organize the annual *Daily Mail* ski show, which was a promotions affair and not something that should have overly concerned the editor-in-chief. But skiing was his passion.

There were at least four top Mailmen who'd prowl the brand-new utilitarian carpet outside the editor's office, desperate to take command of the paper in his absence; they all seemed to dress the same and spoke alike. 'I used to think of the group of editors below English as dangerous denizens of an aquarium created and supervised by him,' Tony Burton told the author, 'partly for his amusement, as he watched them circling for a kill.'[10]

The vibe on the editorial floor would sizzle when the supreme *Mail* being Sir David stepped out of his office and mingled among his senior men on the back bench, a big cat with very sharp claws. The picture editor would even soothe him with sweets he kept in his top drawer, seemingly for that very purpose. 'English would almost flirt with the picture desk,' said Stewart Payne. 'It was all a bit pathetic really.'[11]

There tended to be two seats beside Sir David's throne on the back bench that would be filled by his two most trusted men that day, and one afternoon English whisked one chair away for a laugh and awaited the arrival of deputy editor Jonathan Holborow and the

Mail's number-three man of affairs, Paul Dacre. 'English hid behind a column,' insider 'Barry' told the author, 'to see how Holborow and Dacre would react to find only one chair.'[12] Several of English's top men were in on the joke, as English tittered and giggled like a schoolboy, but, unfortunately for the spectators, it was all handled in a rather gentlemanly way; neither Mailman sat down.

Mailman 'Terry' was another executive who observed the editorial jungle like a naturalist in a sensible tie instead of a sunhat. 'It was all hugely entertaining for us on the sidelines watching all this silly positioning of the senior guys,' he told the author. 'Paul Dacre wasn't David English's only favoured child; he had other favourites who were very powerful within the *Daily Mail*. And definitely, until the last minute, any one of them could have been editor. It's too clean and convenient to say that Dacre was the chosen one. Maybe he was, but he wasn't the *only* chosen one. That just wasn't David English's style.'[13]

It did begin to become clear, though, to some, that if anyone could edit the paper as well as Sir David, it was Paul Dacre. Dacre had shown from his days as news editor that he understood the philosophy, politics and culture of the *Daily Mail*.

'The main memory I have of Paul Dacre,' said Gill Swain, 'is him sitting at his desk in the new *Mail* building in Derry Street and leaning right back with his hands on his head pushing his hair back saying – in a sort of posh, mumbling growl – "oorrr, ooor, must do this, we must do this". And everybody around him on the desk would be sitting and concentrating and reading stuff, getting the nitty gritty done. Dacre would always be sitting back having the strategic thoughts, which is why he became the editor, I guess.'[14]

Unlike Sir David, Dacre was most certainly not comfortable in the company of women, and some Femails would use his discomfort to their advantage in a way they could never do with English. 'I used to sit on [Dacre's] desk in a very short skirt and sit ever closer, invading his private space,' said one writer. 'He used to lean back at such a dangerous angle I thought he was going to fall off his chair. He could cope with screaming, violence and bullying, but he just couldn't cope with a little coquettish girlie behaviour. A lot of women used to do that on the paper.'[15]

There was nothing coy about Sir David's behaviour when it came to wooing Maggie Thatcher at election time, though, when he effectively handed his paper over to the pumping out of Conservative propaganda. One Mailman explained to the *Guardian* how, during Thatcher's 1987 campaign, it had felt as if they were all working in Tory HQ: 'One day, after Labour had scored a particularly good point against the Government, one of English's deputies stood up in the newsroom and had shouted: "We must hit back! We must hit back!"'[16]

Thatcher had won in 1979, 1983 and 1987, and she had her sights firmly fixed upon the new decade as she sat down with Sir David for one of their frequent fireside chats published in the *Mail* under English's byline.

> As a young mother Margaret Thatcher lived through
> the ruinous social revolution of the Sixties. Today she
> dedicates herself to removing the last vestiges of that
> decade's influence from our national life. The Nineties,
> she says, can bring fresh and better values to Britain.[17]

Maybe fresh and better values were on their way, but Margaret Thatcher and Sir David English would not be the people delivering them. It was Europe, which, then as now, was the fault line running under the Conservative Party HQ, that would shake the Tory tree in 1990 and see Thatcher fall to the ground. Sir David didn't share Maggie's ingrained and instinctive dislike of Britain's Continental partners; he was committed to the European cause, as he told the *Independent on Sunday*: 'I fell out with her politically because I am a Europhile . . . We enjoyed a good argument and agreed to disagree.'[18]

Other Tories disagreed with Maggie too, including her longest-serving Cabinet minister, Geoffrey Howe, who was exasperated by Thatcher's intemperate anti-European rants and resigned: 'Sir Geoffrey the Assassin', the *Mail* called him on its front page in

November 1990.[19] And in the same edition of the paper, Lynda Lee-Potter also had a dig at the falling PM for starting to look decidedly regal.

> What we wear often reveals how we feel. On Monday
> night before her 'We will not be defeated by friend or
> foe' speech, the Prime Minister wore a voluminous velvet
> cloak with a huge stand-up collar. She looked just like
> Queen Elizabeth I, who ruled for 45 years. Maggie clearly
> feels she herself has only just begun. And I suspect she
> believes, like royalty, only death should have the power to
> dethrone her.[20]

However, it was all over for Thatcher and her reign ended a few days later, when she was knifed by her own Cabinet. The *Mail* proclaimed in an editorial – probably written by the editor himself – that she was 'Too Damn Good for the Lot of Them'.

> Betrayed and rejected by her party, Margaret Thatcher
> gave up her power yesterday . . . Still strong. Still sound.
> The great oak has been brought down. The fall of
> Margaret Thatcher has the full dimensions of tragedy. The
> woman who has given so much and done so much for
> Britain felled, not by the democratic will of the people,
> but by the desertion of her own party supporters. Bitter?
> Of course, we feel bitter.[21]

It was a shuddering blow to Sir David; his reborn *Daily Mail* and Maggie Thatcher had risen together. But Thatcher's demise was nothing compared to what the English family were facing at home, just down the road from where Maggie was packing her bags: Lady Irene, English's beloved wife, had been stricken with Alzheimer's disease.

One day in the early 1990s, English's oldest friend, Chris Rees, picked up the phone to an utterly disconsolate Sir David. 'David was really cut up when he rang me he'd had to do what he didn't want to do which was to have Irene committed to a nursing home because she was a danger to herself, wandering the streets and so forth. "This is the worst day of my life. I've just had to call the people and have her taken to a nursing home," he told me. And he was truly distraught. They were extremely close, Irene and David. Extremely close.'[22]

They were also extremely loyal, say friends, with there never having been any suggestion that Sir David had strayed; a newspaper editor can sometimes exude a raw kind of sexual power that some women find attractive. 'David adored Irene,' said Tony Burton. 'I mean, who knows what really goes on but, no. No. I think he was completely faithful.'[23]

'David was crazy about Irene,' agreed Anthea Disney, 'and he was very close to his kids. He was very much a family man. David loved gossip but that didn't mean he wanted to do anything on his own behalf. I would be stunned if you told me he had an affair with anybody. Stunned. It just didn't seem to me to be part of his DNA.'[24]

The last time Tony Burton saw the stricken Irene was on a sailing trip in Chris Rees's boat on the Solent, the strait that separates the Isle of Wight from Southampton, the city on the south coast where the Englishes had married in 1952. Rees and Burton moored the boat. 'I remember David and Irene walking away down the dock ahead of us after we had tied up, he had his arm around her and her head was on his shoulder,' said Burton. 'They looked like the loneliest people in the whole world. I suspect David's enormous success had turned to ashes in his mouth and he would have tossed it all in the water if it would save Irene.'[25]

Before Sunny Harmsworth founded the *Daily Mail* he'd tested the journalistic theories he'd formulated in the magazine trade within the pages of the *Evening News*, the first newspaper the Harmsworth family had ever owned. But by the time Paul Dacre was ready to step up and become an editor himself, a century later, the *Evening News* had already been dead a decade, swallowed by the *Evening Standard*. It would be, for Dacre, a similar kind of testing ground.

By 1991 Bunny's grandson Vere owned the *Evening Standard*
outright (after first co-owning it with the group that controlled
the *Express*) and it had become 'the voice of London', edited by 'a
newspaperman's newspaperman', the founding editor of the *Mail on
Sunday's* You magazine,[26] John Leese, who answered to the editor-
in-chief of Associated Newspapers: Sir David English. But Leese fell
ill with cancer and retired in March of that year (he died six months
later).

The *Standard* needed a new man at the helm, and when Paul Dacre
was informed by Sir David English and Viscount Rothermere that
he was to be appointed its editor he was, understandably, ecstatic.
There was, after all, no sign that Sir David was going to leave the
Daily Mail any time soon.

> It was a tremendous moment in my life. I mean I'd
> worked for the last twenty years with the objective of
> becoming an editor, I desperately wanted to become an
> editor. And the *Standard* was a wonderful paper. It was
> one of the most exciting moments of my life . . . I know
> this sounds slightly silly, but I actually went back to Arnos
> Grove and I went to walk round the house where I had
> grown up as a boy. And walked the area that I knew so
> well . . . those are the forces that created me.[27]

It's worth taking a step back in time at this point, to walk through
the doors of that suburban Dacre home of the late 1950s and early
1960s where, on any Friday evening, a demonic little Glaswegian
called John 'J. J.' Junor was likely to leap from Dacre senior's briefcase
and ruin the family's weekend. J. J. was the heavy-handed, autocratic
editor of the *Sunday Express* and Peter Dacre's boss.

> My father would come home on a Friday night and he'd
> have written his article for that week with the carbon
> copy black in his briefcase and I'd rush for it and there
> were Junor's notes scrawled on it. It'd either say absolutely

brilliant or rubbish. And if it was rubbish and it didn't
go in the paper that weekend it was a rather a gloomy
atmosphere in our household.[28]

Junor was, by almost all accounts, a monster. He was a hard-
drinking, workaholic womanizer who would often bawl his journalists out like a drill sergeant and even had buzzers fitted to the desks
of his senior men so he could zap them as required; everyone else
would know who'd been buzzed due to the fact that they would leap
from their chair. The 'seedy gargoyle' also 'propositioned the wives of
almost every member of his staff', wrote former *Sunday Express* hack
Graham Lord, whom Junor invited to his home and on his boat even
though Lord was only a junior employee; it was Lord's wife he was
interested in. J. J. would ply Lord with brandy to remove the obstacle
between his urges and Lord's wife: 'J. J. would grope her at every
opportunity and had once chased her along a corridor. The endless
huge glasses of calvados had been the old goat's attempt to knock me
out so that he could ravish my wife.'[29]

J. J., according to his own daughter, Penny Junor, had a
'fundamental dislike of women' – to J. J. there were only two types
of female: sluts or virgins.[30] Junor may have been a hideous human
being but he seemed to be the perfect editor for the *Sunday Express*;
his crisp and simple editorial approach articulated the fears and
foibles of Middle England so well that it generated a peak circulation
of somewhere around 5 million copies every Sunday. Paul Dacre
has often said he believes Junor's *Sunday Express* to have been one
of the best newspapers there has ever been. J. J. was famous for
reading every single word in his paper and running it through a
simple mental filter; if he couldn't understand what the reporter had
written, then the reader most certainly wouldn't. And J. J. himself
got to vent his anachronistic views on these readers in a column of
his own that romanticized a tiny little town in Fife, Scotland, called
Auchtermuchty, a place where men who wore hats or had facial
hair were not to be trusted and where if they drank white wine they
were 'poofters'. J. J. hated Socialists, immigrants, social workers and

intellectuals and he would never knowingly allow a homosexual into the pages of his newspaper.

'J. J. was a bigot who instructed his staff never to trust a man who smoked a pipe or wore a beard, hat or suede shoes,' wrote Graham Lord. 'He believed that Aids was a fair punishment for buggery.'[31]

His *Sunday Express*, though, didn't have much space for actual news, and most of the intros were 'dropped' – meaning there'd be layers of icing before the reader got to the actual cake in the third or fourth paragraph. Paul Dacre loved it: 'The paper was warm, aspirational, unashamedly traditional, dedicated to decency, middle brow, beautifully written and subbed, accessible, and, above all, utterly relevant to the lives of its readers.'[32]

John Junor – alongside his father, David English and Brian Vine – shaped Paul Dacre's understanding of what it took to create a successful newspaper.

Back to the spring of 1991, and the euphoric freshly crowned *Evening Standard* editor Paul Dacre now had the opportunity to stamp his personality on a newspaper in the same way J. J. had a generation earlier. But the *Evening Standard* staff were not quite so excited about his arrival.

'Everybody was absolutely terrified because he'd got "a reputation",' Anne de Courcy, a writer on the *Standard* at the time, told the author. 'And the joke that went round was that somebody had sent a message to the *Daily Mail* to ask, "Hasn't *anybody* got a good word to say about Paul Dacre?" And they got the reply: "No, but his mother is reconsidering . . ." But I liked him immediately, I immediately warmed to him. The *Evening Standard* was put together like a series of magazines – because the people who came to it had worked on magazines – and when Paul came I thought, "Oh, how wonderful. Working on a newspaper again." He immediately revitalized it.'[33]

The readership of the *Standard* Dacre inherited was mostly male, so the new editor sought to recalibrate it to appeal to women by adding lifestyle pages which soon boosted the female readership by 60 per cent. He also thought it was 'in danger of becoming just a little too twee and its appeal was to too narrow a social band of people',[34] so he broadened its outlook. And the advantages of state-of-the-art technology meant that the new editor could tear apart up to ten pages even late into the afternoon, meaning the paper's final edition was still pretty damn fresh and warm even as the morning papers were starting to put their pages to bed. It impressed a lot of people in 'Fleet Street', including the owners of other newspapers.

'He was a very good editor of the *Standard*,' *Evening Standard* senior staffer 'Kevin' told the author. 'It was a good mix because he was this rather crude militaristic leader in charge of a bunch of highly intelligent, argumentative, eccentric people, who made the *Standard* work. And the two went together well. They needed him, and he probably needed them. To help him further his career.'[35]

These were very good days for Paul Dacre and some of the *Standard* staff actually warmed to the man himself, preferring Dacre to his boss Sir David. 'David English was always considered a nasty piece of work by people on the *Standard*,' *Standard* staffer 'Kerry' said. 'He created such an awful atmosphere on the *Mail*, most people at Associated would much prefer to work on the *Standard* over the *Mail*. Paul was a very sharp editor and a much nicer man than English I thought but, the funny thing was, he had no social skills whatsoever. He was always very awkward.'[36]

Less than eighteen months after taking the helm, and in a time of recession, the paper's vigorous and brutally hard-working editor had increased its readership by 26 per cent. Magic numbers for any newspaper owner. And the biggest beast in 'Fleet Street' was about to take a bite out of any dreams Sir David might have had of hanging on as *Mail* editor for much longer.

The Times would soon be in need of a new editor, as the incumbent, Simon Jenkins, wanted to go back to being a full-time writer. And Kelvin MacKenzie, the editor of *The Sun* – a *Times* stablemate within Rupert Murdoch's News International – recommended Dacre to executive chairman Andrew Knight as a good choice for the top chair at *The Times* after noticing the change in Dacre's revitalized *Standard*. 'The idea came to me from Kelvin,' Knight told the author, 'but it immediately chimed with what I – and many people –

observed anyway in the *Evening Standard* at the time; Paul's editing verve shouted from the paper every day.'[37] Knight picked up the phone and later arranged for Dacre to come round to his house in Hampstead and meet Rupert Murdoch, a meeting at which Dacre showed his respect for the position of *The Times* as the 'newspaper of record' and the need to maintain the paper as a high-quality broadsheet 'while stressing he could make it more aggressive in getting stories and making waves with campaigns'.

'Our concern was that he did not see *The Times* as a downmarket tabloid, scrapping in the tabloid market. He went out of his way to demonstrate that that was not how he saw it. Editing the *Standard* or the *Mail* was one thing, Paul said, [but] editing *The Times* would be quite another. However, he would bring aggression to the broadsheet market which he thought was missing. I had pre-briefed both Rupert and Paul, we sat around a dining table, and the meeting was totally one of like minds . . . Rupert simply made it clear that if Paul wanted to be editor the offer was there.'[38]

Indeed, the son of Lord Northcliffe's favourite Australian was firmly of the mind that Dacre was about to join his empire. 'I have great respect for his abilities,' Murdoch said later; 'he agreed to leave then and come and edit *The Times* and I was extremely pleased.'[39] Out of courtesy, Dacre insisted on speaking to Sir David first before signing any contract and soon found the editor-in-chief in a meeting with a royal contact and reporter Ann Leslie at a hotel bar near the *Mail*'s HQ. They had a drink and English insisted Dacre speak to Lord Rothermere first before joining *The Times*, but the proprietor had gone fishing and was uncontactable as he was in the middle of a lake – in Iceland. Sir David had to think fast on his feet: he couldn't let Rupert Murdoch – of *all* people – take his top man, especially a man who was proving to be such an exceptional editor of the company's *Evening Standard*. So English decided to step aside and give his job to Dacre, as he knew that would keep him in the firm and away from Murdoch. But first he had to clear it with Lord Rothermere, who had by now returned to his home in Paris. Sir David flew out to meet him and the two friends who'd saved the *Mail* two decades before sat down for lunch at Le Vaudeville brasserie to talk again about change, their faces reflected back and forth at each other 10,000 times in the famous old establishment's massive mirrors.

Dacre had kept Murdoch waiting for almost a week when Lord Rothermere finally arrived back in London to formally offer Dacre the *Daily Mail* editorship, and Dacre asked if he could spend an hour with his wife discussing whether to turn down *The Times* in favour of the *Mail*. Paul Dacre, like John Junor, is famous for reading every word in his paper, and maybe during his hour or so away to think about Vere's offer he saw his future written there in the stars. In the *Standard's* horoscope that day, Scorpios were experiencing 'what may be the most powerful few days of the year for you. Do not be distracted from events that could revolutionise your life.'[40] The hour came and went but Dacre hadn't returned, so Sir David went and found him and the pair returned to Lord Rothermere's plush sixth-floor office. Dacre agreed to turn down *The Times*.

On the other side of London there were no hard feelings for Paul Dacre. 'I cannot fault how honourably he behaved,' Knight told the *Sunday Times* at the time. 'He was straight throughout. He made it absolutely clear that he very much wanted to do the job but had tremendous loyalty to David English and Lord Rothermere. I feel sad but I don't feel let down. Paul Dacre was very firmly of the view that he was coming because he couldn't see David English stepping down.'[41]

'I jested that our consolation prize was a £2 million aggregate increase in Associated's salary bill,' Knight added later.[42]

Sir David would later spin one of his own inimitable yarns around the whole saga, about how he had selflessly stood aside for Dacre – insisting his own promotion to Lord Rothermere's role as chairman of Associated Newspapers that resulted from the reshuffle was only an afterthought when he and Vere had sat down exhausted at the end of a very long day. That was not, as was so often the case with David English, strictly true; Dacre insisted he'd never have taken his mentor's chair if it had put Sir David on the dole and Lord Rothermere had actually suggested English replace him as chairman many months previously. Vere was, of course, still ultimately in charge; he was the proprietor and he remained chairman of the parent company.

English had been twenty-one years in the top chair, not quite as long as Tom Marlowe but still, a good innings. The paper announced the changes to its readers in July 1992, quoting Sir David as saying:

> I am tremendously honoured . . . To start as a cub
> reporter and end up as chairman of a great national
> newspaper group is an achievement beyond anything
> I believed possible. But it can happen in Fleet Street.[43]

Meanwhile, as part of the reshuffle, Stewart Steven had been forced to leave the *Mail on Sunday* to take over from Dacre at the *Standard* – while Sir David's other most-favoured Mailman, Jonathan Holborow, took over the *Mail on Sunday*. Steven burst into tears when the staff 'banged him out' – an old custom of the Fleet Street printers, where they'd bang metal plates when a colleague retired – when he put his final edition of the *Mail on Sunday* to bed on the Saturday night. Steven only agreed to take over the *Standard* after Lord Rothermere reassured him it was his personal wish and not just the machinations of Sir David English, a man Steven had known for over three decades and whose feline instincts he understood only too well. Insiders believed that Steven may have been a little too gifted an editor for his own good.

'There is no love lost now between David English and Stewart Steven,' one source told the *Sunday Times* after the reshuffle. 'When the *Mail on Sunday* overtook the *Mail* in sales, English became very jealous of Steven's success.'[44]

As the editors began to settle into their new chairs and a massive new office was being fashioned for Sir David English, the new chairman of Associated Newspapers, some speculated that Dacre may have learned the most important lesson of all from his *Mail* master and played a superb game to get his hands on the *Mail*. 'I don't think many people have played along Rupert Murdoch and

Andrew Knight,' a source told the *Sunday Times* at the time. 'Dacre wanted a particular job and he has now got it.'[45]

Long-serving Mailman 'Terry' believes English and Rothermere only really had one thing in mind. 'The most important thing to them was that Murdoch didn't get one over on them,' he told the author. 'It was a panic measure. I don't think the idea was ever that he'd get the *Mail*. I think the plan was for Dacre to edit the *Standard*.'[46]

13

The Pencil and the Knife

Sir David's *Daily Mail* was on the slide by the time Dacre squeezed his lanky frame into the captain's chair and reached for the controls; it was selling around a quarter of a million fewer copies at the end of the 1980s than at the start, yet, still, the formula was just about right. The *Mail* needed recalibrating for the 1990s but it would have been madness to make major changes.

As the decade went on, the Tories would be on the slide too, just as Labour would re-emerge as a genuine political force capable of actually winning a general election under its young leader Tony Blair. Thatcher, of course, had already gone by the time Dacre was appointed editor of the *Mail* and, three months before Dacre took over, Sir David had helped shepherd John Major in for the Tory Party's fourth successive term.

Change was coming, but Paul Dacre's political instincts seemed – like those of so many middle-aged, middle-class men – to be nudging him out ever further to the right the older he got. It was life in the United States in the 1970s, the same as David English in the 1960s, that had first turned Dacre from a mild student Socialist to a true Tory believer thereafter. 'If you don't have a left-wing period when you go to university, you should be shot,' Dacre told the *British Journalism Review*.

I don't see how anybody can go to America, work there for six years and not be enthralled by the energy of the free market. America taught me the power of the free market, as opposed to the State, to improve the lives of the vast majority of ordinary people. I left a Britain in 1976 that was ossified by an us-and-them, gaffers-versus-workers mentality in which a tribal working class was kept in place by subservience to the Labour authorities who owned their council homes, to the unions and the nationalised industries. Mrs Thatcher, in what was a terribly painful process, broke that destructive axis, empowered the individual and restored aspiration and self-reliance in this country. And, I suppose, if there are two words that sum up the *Mail*'s philosophy, they're 'aspiration' and 'self-reliance'.[1]

By the time he took over the leadership of the aspirational and self-reliant editorial staff of the *Daily Mail*, Dacre was a firm Thatcherite, more so even than Sir David and certainly more so than *Mail* proprietor Lord Rothermere. Yet Dacre was entirely unconvinced by the Tories under John Major and he thought the paper's role in the 1980s as a mouthpiece for Conservative Central Office had been way too cosy. 'The Tories had been great in power but they were exhausted,' Dacre said. 'They were decadent. I don't want to sound arrogant but I did have very little time for John Major. I thought he was a very weak man. And the *Mail*, it came as quite a shock to the Tories, became very critical of the Tory Party. Very, very critical.'[2]

An old town in the Netherlands called Maastricht was the epicentre of a rupture in the Tory Party that also forced clear blue water between the *Mail*'s Eurosceptic new editor Paul Dacre and its Europhile editor-in-chief Sir David. In the early 1990s, a collective of Euro-technocrats had gathered in Maastricht to truly start the process of trying to weld Europe together with a document called the 'Maastricht Treaty'; the treaty created the European Union out of the old European Communities and would eventually lead to the euro.

While still editor, pro-Europe Sir David's *Mail* had mostly been supportive of these ever-closer ties to Britain's Continental partners, but Dacre wasn't keen. Many Tories didn't – and still don't – agree with the erosion of British sovereignty and feared that the UK would potentially become just a small state within a United States of Europe. The tectonic plates under the Tory heartland were rubbing up hard against each other and seismic activity was set to continue, like those under the Pacific, in perpetuity (even post-Brexit, there are Tories who still think Britain should be part of Europe – David Cameron's replacement as Prime Minister, Theresa May, voted to remain).

Dacre had only been editor of the *Daily Mail* for two months when Britain was crushed between the cogs of the European Exchange Rate Mechanism (ERM) – a device to keep each member state's currency valued within set limits linked, of course, to the German mark as a prelude to joining a single currency. The Prime Minister and his Chancellor, Norman Lamont, spent the 'Black Wednesday' of 16 September 1992 trying to prop up sterling by buying billions of British pounds with foreign currency reserves on the markets. Interest rates leapt to 15 per cent and the Government had little choice in the end but to pull sterling out of the ERM and let the pound find its own level.

The aftershocks nearly toppled Paul Dacre out of the *Mail* editor's chair a year later when his judgement came into serious question after he backed a Tory Party rebellion against the Prime Minister. In an unguarded moment – typical of John Major, caught on camera – the Prime Minister had branded a handful of his Cabinet ministers as 'the bastards' ahead of a confidence vote over the tediously dull yet combustible implications of the ratification of the Maastricht Treaty. The ringleader was a vain, ambitious young politician called Michael Portillo, a strange man of half-Spanish, half-Scottish extraction who seemed to be wearing someone else's face and it didn't quite fit.

'The Dacre call was that Major would be dumped and the front page of the *Mail* that day [suggested that]. It wasn't "he's gone" because we didn't know that but it implied that Major was finished,' senior Mailman 'Duncan' told the author. 'And of course Major won the vote. It was a bad, bad call and I felt that day that Dacre's job was on the line; he was very, very dejected and downcast. My guess is that English and Rothermere called him upstairs that morning and warned him that the *Mail* couldn't get things so wrong.

'He'd fucked up, badly. His news judgement was just plain wrong. It was never what was likely to happen. It was what he *wanted* to happen. He desperately wanted Major to be defeated and he allowed that desire to cloud his actual news judgement whereas English was much too clever to let that happen. Whenever English launched a campaign, he'd only do the campaign once he'd been absolutely, categorically, told it was definitely going to happen by his friend Mrs Thatcher. So, the paper would come out with this massive campaign and sure enough, four days later, it would be announced that, whatever it may be, a tax cut or whatever – was happening. And then it would be "How the *Daily Mail* Won the Battle". It was a great insight into how to do campaigns actually; you must only do campaigns when you've already won them because newspapers can't be made to look like they didn't make a difference.'[3]

Tensions were emerging between *Mail* father and *Mail* son, and it began to seem to some Mailmen and Femails that maybe the machine Sir David had built entirely to fit himself was a little too blunt and brutal in the clumsier hands of the younger, less experienced and far more uptight new editor.

'Unlike at the *Standard* where Dacre had thrived, at the *Mail* you had "the Drone Army" who were just too obedient and didn't have enough personality to create real fun, or real sparks,' added Mailman 'Terry'. 'What they needed was a David English, mercurial and unpredictable and brilliant, and awful – all at the same time. And they got – they've still got – Paul Dacre. A very, very different kind of man.'[4]

The changeover from English to Dacre had all happened too quickly for some *Mail* people of the day, and many had thought, though Dacre was nominally editor, English would actually still be in charge as editor-in-chief. But English stepped back and did allow his new editor a free hand because, as he explained to the *Independent* at the time, 'I helped build up the culture of editor power; I didn't want to destroy it.'[5]

Some Mailmen thought the still-supreme *Mail* being simply had far more important things on his mind as Irene descended into dementia, so Sir David let go and settled into his big new office upstairs and busied himself with strategic projects within the company such as Teletext – news and information on a TV screen at the touch of a button – and its small, disparate television interests (few spotted the internet as the existential threat to newspapers it was to become; Britain's first digital newspaper, the Electronic *Telegraph*, didn't even launch until the end of 1994).

While Sir David was upstairs thinking strategic thoughts, downstairs his Mailmen were pining for him. 'Dacre was just so incredibly different to David English,' sighed Mailman 'Duncan'. 'David loved the world and revelled in delving into all sorts of worlds. He loved politics, he loved skiing. He loved all sorts of things. I think David English was just a much happier guy. He had much more fun. English saw life as a great big party that he just wanted to be at; wherever the fun was, he wanted to be there right in the middle of it – preferably organizing it. I felt Dacre just saw life – the world – as an awful, threatening place where he wanted to be in his bunker. Firing salvos out, you know – blowing up his enemies. That bunker mentality. English was always laughing and always full of mischief and he was, you know, very engaging. If truly a bastard, on occasion.'[6]

Yet Dacre, say some who were there, was actually a cautious editor at first precisely because he was working under his boss's nose; it took about a year or so before he really began to get a firm grip on the editorial controls and as the months passed, his strength and his confidence increased.

'You began to detect the underlying view that if English had done something, it was a bit crap,' Mailman 'Terry' told the author. 'It was no longer a good excuse to say, "Well, David English always used to do it this way." It would be "I'm not David English, I'm not doing it that way." And I think his relationship with English started off very much as the devoted son and then ended up very much the un-devoted son. It was all very predictable really. The proud, prickly Dacre didn't want to be seen as the lesser editor to English. At the *Mail* there was always this "cult of the editor". It's a very culty place; there's this feeling that being an editor is a mysterious thing only for a genius and everyone said English was a genius, and Dacre wanted to be the bigger genius. A bigger, better editor. A more successful editor.'[7]

'I suspect towards the end,' Dacre himself admitted, 'when I was getting stronger and he was getting older, there were tensions – there always are between men at that level.'[8]

Some of those close to Sir David began to see these very tensions for themselves as, behind the scenes, English started to voice quiet dissatisfaction with the tone of Dacre's paper, or at least its editorial vision. A couple of years after the handover, Sir David made one of his frequent trips to America and met up with the *Mail*'s New York bureau chief, George Gordon, the man who had replaced Dacre and finally solved English's American problem. English had his doubts about the *Mail*'s new editor, telling Gordon: 'I didn't think I could do more to take the circulation higher, but maybe Dacre can. I don't much like what he has done to the paper, but he is getting results.'

'He asked me what I thought,' Gordon told the author, 'and I said I didn't like it either. The paper was fanatical about celebrity trash and rife with hysterical right-wing columnists. In New York, one felt the *Daily Mail* was publishing "the Orpington man's" [a 1960s term for the lower middle classes] views on how the US should be run. Dacre once said in morning conference, "Don't ask George Gordon, he'll only give the American point of view."'[9] George Gordon was ushered into retirement and replaced in New York with a Dacre man not long afterwards.

The paper, a year after Dacre took charge, also published an extraordinary headline for an editor who took great pride in reading every word in his paper – 'Abortion hope after "gay genes" findings'. Scientists in America, wrote reporter Jason Lewis, said they had discovered definite evidence of a genetic link to homosexuality: 'isolation of the gene means it could soon be possible to predict whether a baby will be gay and give the mother the option of an abortion'.[10]

It was enough to incite a small reaction in Middle England, with a couple of readers writing in to the Letters page, at a headline implying that people were waiting for a cure to stamp out homosexuality. 'I take tremendous offence to such careless interpretation of facts,' wrote Andy Seale. 'As a happy young gay man, from a loving family, it is appalling to think that an opinion-forming national newspaper should be allowed to assume people would want to find a cure for homosexuality as a matter of course. Headlines like this feed ignorance, fear and hatred to a population . . . gay people are not aliens.' Another reader added: 'I abhor the implication that parents would choose to have their unborn child aborted just because the foetus carried a gene which predisposed it to be gay. How can the *Daily Mail* stand by such a homophobic and insensitive headline?'[11]

Out on the editorial floor, Dacre was very much proving to be 'insensitive' to some of his staff as he prowled his domain. The word 'cunt' remained his favourite expletive, to be fired at anyone who displeased him. Yet 'cunt' is such a bullet of a word; to be called a 'cunt' in anger to one's face generally elicits a proportionate response, unless, of course, the person calling one a 'cunt' is one's boss – the man who decides on one's career prospects and the salary that pays off one's mortgage. The new editor of the *Daily Mail*'s rants would come to be dubbed 'the Vagina Monologues' by his staff – after the stage play of the same name – because nobody else could get another word in when Dacre went off on one.

'There was a glass box where the editor in charge of features used to sit, about the size of a billiard table,' said former Mailman 'Terry'. 'And if you were lucky, you'd get to see the windows vibrate when Dacre was in there with some poor unfortunate person that was getting a really bad row. The glass would just shake a little bit. You couldn't really hear but you could see the red face and everything, so we used to monitor that. It only happened about once a month and was always quite exciting, like a big thunderstorm or something, a geological event – a weather event – that we'd look forward to.'[12]

Mailmen and Femails who had never suffered under Dacre when he ran the news-desk were getting used to this new creature who had arrived to take total control of their newspaper. Some, such as features hack Jane Kelly, thought the man she'd known as the gauche yet pleasant enough chap who ran the features department (features was always calmer territory than news) had turned into a monster. 'As soon as he got made *Mail* editor he changed so much,' she told the author. 'I've never known anyone change so much actually. I'd heard he'd been a terrible tyrant when he was on the news desk but I hadn't seen that myself and now he was just a tyrant to everybody. All the time.'[13]

The back bench of senior Mailmen felt the worst of the blunt force of Dacre's tongue.

'Dacre was doing the traditional thing towards the end of the day where he's looking at proofs and bollocking everyone for the headline not being good enough,' 'Duncan' told the author. 'And he called someone a "cunt" and one of the few women on the subs desk looked up and so he said, "No. Not you, you cunt. Him!" You know, he'd get it so wrong sometimes. But that was kind of the charm of Dacre.'[14]

Another writer of the day found people once favoured by English were having a tough time proving themselves to the new boss.

'I didn't like Paul Dacre,' 'Roy' told the author, 'and Paul Dacre didn't like me. I think it was because I'd been an English appointment, I was an English man not a Dacre man. And he was such a strange bastard, I used to watch him just before the first edition went to bed and he was like a fucking ape – screaming and swearing, shouting at the subs and the back bench . . . he would scratch his back so hard, he actually bled. The paper was always late off the stone because he'd commissioned far too many things for the number of pages and he couldn't make up his mind which story was the one he wanted. The other pieces would just be chucked in the bin, all that effort and expense for nothing. A good editor? A strong editor? Or an editor who didn't know what the fuck he wanted until the last second?

'I was never afraid of him, I thought he was rather absurd and a lot of other people did too, especially the more senior hands from the English days. Some of the younger guys who came through were in awe of *the* editor though and they began to become a version of him themselves in a way, some of them. Fine. But I found them absurd too and rather pathetic.'[15]

Mail executive 'Terry' would sidle up to the editor with page proofs for the next morning's paper printed off on long rolls, with each story folded neatly on top of the next.

'I remember the fury with which he would edit stuff on paper,' he told the author. 'You went along with your stories and he would go "No! No! NO!" and he would start scrubbing it out, and the bits underneath would then get the marks from the one on top, going through the top bit of paper to the next bit of paper. Often the pencil would go clean through the paper and start ripping it to pieces. And there'd be quite a lot of stabbing with the pencil. It was all very physical the whole thing. It was incredibly hard sometimes to piece together exactly what he actually wanted you to do when you walked away holding these shreds of paper!'[16]

Dacre later answered the frequent accusations of bullying himself in an interview for the *British Journalism Review*, when the interviewer, Bill Hagerty – himself a tough and highly respected national newspaper editor – asked him if he was 'the ogre so often depicted by his critics':

> 'An ogre!' he cries, followed by a hoot of laughter that
> rattles the windows. Well, perhaps tyrant is a better word,
> I suggest? 'Tyranny? I'm privileged to be surrounded by
> a hugely dedicated and talented bunch of professional
> journalists. The day I tyrannise them into silence is the
> day this paper will die. Look, newspapers are all about
> energy. I like to feel I lead from the front and I work as
> hard as anybody, if not harder. There's not a job on the
> paper I can't do and I work with them [his staff] very
> closely. I think if you were to ask them, honestly, they'd

say he's a big-mouthed, loud-mouthed tyrant, but he does his fair share and he gets the paper off at night and we all go home pretty proud of it. Yes, there's a lot of shouting and a lot of swear words, but it's never personal.[17]

By the middle of the 1990s Dacre's *Daily Mail* circulation was on the rise due to his fresh, features-led approach. The numbers were also boosted by an influx of readers from the mid-market *Today* newspaper, which was killed off by Rupert Murdoch at the end of 1995. At the end of 1993 he launched a magazine of TV listings, soft gardening and cookery features to be slipped into the Saturday paper. The front-page blurb the day before launch promoted it as 'WEEKEND the magazine that makes your weekend last all week'.[18] Saturdays began to get extra-special attention, with strong double-page spreads being commissioned especially or held back to make the Saturday paper really shine.

Dacre's paper was winning awards too. The successes were trumpeted in the paper in February 1996 as 'Awards hat-trick for the brilliant *Mail*'; the paper won two separate National Newspaper of the Year titles and was acclaimed as 'Medium of the Year' by the advertising industry. It was just ahead of the paper's 100th birthday and the gongs marked 'one of the most dynamic periods in the paper's 100-year history. Circulation last month soared through the two million barrier, notching up the *Mail*'s highest January sales for nearly 30 years.'[19]

The choice of 'nearly thirty years' as the benchmark was, surely, significant; in an article that actually quoted Dacre himself, it was a date from *prior* to English's reign, which had begun twenty-five years before. It was a message from *the* editor, perhaps, that the apprentice had now truly become the master. And, again, another newspaper proprietor liked what he saw in those numbers. In a 'cloak and dagger meeting one evening', the owner of the *Daily Telegraph*, Conrad Black, offered Dacre the editor's chair on Britain's leading broadsheet. And Black didn't much mind Dacre turning him down and using his offer 'to better his own lot' on the *Mail*, but found his 'self-righteous public claims that he had dismissed our overture' tiresome. Dacre had actually, wrote Black, 'enthusiastically accepted the job in principle'.[20] The events were not entirely dissimilar to how Murdoch had thought he had secured Dacre's services for *The Times*.

By 1997, there was no doubt who was in command of the *Daily Mail*, and after almost five years at the wheel, Dacre was to show exactly how strong an editor he had become by writing a headline that has come to define his career. It was a landmark in the British media.

The *Daily Mail* is not a court of law nor even a police force, yet it was about to accuse five men – in bold capitals across its front page – of being murderers.

Stephen Lawrence, the victim, was a strong and healthy boy – as well he should've been; he was only eighteen. And as he stood at a south London bus stop with a friend in April 1993, he could reflect upon his hopes and dreams as his whole life stood before him. On occasion, he helped his plasterer dad out, doing a bit of work on houses here and there, but he was aiming higher and he wanted to actually design those houses himself by becoming an architect. He was bright, aspirational and self-reliant. Stephen Lawrence was a *Daily Mail* kind of boy.

It was a testament to how fit he was, said the pathologist, that he managed to run over 100 metres from that bus stop as pint after pint of blood pumped out of his body from a pair of deep knife wounds that had both severed arteries; it was testimony to the long and healthy life he might have expected, had he not been murdered by a gang of white thugs – for being black.

Five white youths were duly arrested not long after Stephen's murder but the investigation stalled and they were released, with the Lawrence family accusing the police of racism and corruption. It took time and a twist of fate before Dacre actually lifted the murder case into a fully fledged campaign by his paper for justice for Stephen Lawrence.

Shortly after Stephen's death Hal Austin, at the time the paper's only black reporter, had initially struggled to get the news desk interested in the story; it at first had seemed to be just another south London murder, perhaps gang-related. There had, in fact, been at least two racially motivated murders and several stabbings[21] in the area in the months before Stephen's death that received far less coverage than the Lawrence murder was about to receive. The Lawrence murder did not cause a massive reaction within the *Daily Mail* newsroom until a connection was made by Stephen's dad, Neville Lawrence, a link that made it personal for Paul Dacre in the same way the Moonies had become personal for English when it involved a neighbour's son a generation before.

Mr Lawrence had done some plastering work on Dacre's Islington home a while before Stephen was killed, but he only realized his client was the *Daily Mail* editor after he and his wife Doreen met Nelson Mandela in May 1993, a month after Stephen's death. As Mr Lawrence told the BBC: 'There had been a riot the weekend before and the *Daily Mail* had this story about the riots and in the middle of that story there was stuff about Stephen and the fact that we had met Mandela.' And Mr Lawrence wasn't too pleased when reporters from the *Daily Mail* arrived at his door to try to interview him. 'The first thing I said to them was: "Why did your editor put my family in the middle of all that violence, we are not about violence."'

Still furious the next day, he picked up the phone – after realizing from reporter Hal Austin that the polite gentleman whose house he'd helped fix up was the editor of the paper that had so annoyed him.

> The following morning I rang the *Daily Mail*'s office
> to speak to Paul Dacre. He said to me: 'Neville, I didn't
> know it was you.' I said: 'But Mr Dacre, you've met my
> kids. I used to take my children to places where I work.'
> He had met Stephen and [his other son] Stuart.[22]

Stephen's family did see three of the men in court for murder (the charges against the other two were dropped) after bringing a private prosecution, but they were acquitted in April 1996 through lack of evidence. Many decent police officers and journalists feared that they had now, for sure, got away with murder, as the 'double jeopardy' rules at the time meant they could not be tried again.

The next legal hurdle left for the accused men to face was surely a formality. All violent deaths are subject to an inquest by a coroner to establish how the person died, and the inquest into Stephen's death was held before a jury at a coroner's court in February 1997. It was a proceeding through which the men smirked and refused to answer questions while protestors gathered outside, hoping to see some kind of justice served. And, in a way, it was – as the jury went way beyond their instructions and, after only half an hour's deliberation, ruled that Stephen was unlawfully killed 'in a completely unprovoked racist attack by five white youths': effectively accusing the men of murder. The coroner, though, couldn't do much about it as this was only an inquest. He was not a judge presiding over a murder trial at the Old Bailey – his role was only to record a cause of death. True justice seemed blind to these boys.

Immediately after this inquest, however, their luck changed.

A man wielding a different kind of raw power sat in his office as big as a classroom, a fat pencil in his hand instead of a knife, and watched a report on the evening news on the TV of the jury's rapid decision and how the men had refused to answer any questions. Paul Dacre was furious, along with thousands of other viewers, thousands of *Daily Mail* readers. Dacre knew the details of the case well, of course, and he knew Neville Lawrence personally. And he had also had lunch with a senior police officer earlier in the week of the inquest and the police chief 'very eloquently told me it was his personal opinion they were as guilty as sin'.[23] Fury at the sheer injustice of the case had been brewing in the *Mail*'s conferences, and Dacre's mind, for some time.

Dacre finally snapped. Personal connection or not, few people are prepared to act as judge and jury in a murder case, yet the outraged editor of the *Daily Mail* was prepared to do exactly that. The criminal justice system had singularly failed over many years to deal with these men and it was time for *his Daily Mail* to act on Stephen's behalf. He pulled a newspaper make-up pad across his desk and began to scratch out a headline with the kind of marker pencil used in newspaper offices for over 100 years: 'MURDERERS,' he wrote. 'The *Mail* accuses these men of killing. If we are wrong, let them sue us.'[24]

> I showed it to the senior sub-editors. There was a kind
> of nervous laughter but then contempt of court is drilled
> into every newspaper executive's thinking. And this was
> contempt of a cosmic order. They obviously thought I was
> mad. Someone muttered libel and I remember snapping –
> 'The bastards haven't got any reputation to lose.'

There is a central tenet of the legal process, drummed into all journalists, that restricts what the media can report on active cases (i.e. when a suspect has been arrested and charged) – in case the information published could impact upon a future trial; a potential juror could have already convicted the accused person before he even shows up for jury duty because the accused had already been found guilty in the press. Many court cases have collapsed because information was published which meant the accused could not expect to receive a fair trial. For a newspaper, or anyone, in fact, to break this rule is contempt of court – journalists have been jailed for contempt in the past. But the Lawrence case, at this point, was technically not 'active' – nobody was currently charged and facing a trial.

'I remember Paul saying to the lawyer, can we do this, can we do this?' one long-term Mailman told the author, 'and the lawyer said, "Yes, yes, you can." And Paul didn't seek Sir David's or Lord Rothermere's approval, as far as I'm aware they only found out about it the same as every other reader did – when they read the paper.'[25]

Love or loathe the *Daily Mail*, support or deplore Dacre's decision – it took supreme confidence to publish that headline that night. Dacre could, he feared, have been jailed himself, with the five men he'd accused of murder laughing at him from the other side of the iron bars. And the father of David Norris, one of the men he accused, was the son of notorious south London gangster and drug baron Clifford Norris; tabloid editors bleed too. Yet if they actually did sue, the *Mail* would get the chance to challenge in court their actions and whereabouts on the night Stephen bled to death and effectively put them on trial for murder. The editor had a lot to think about before he sent the page off to the printers; if this story backfired, then tomorrow the career to which he had dedicated his entire life would be cat litter, just like that day's newspaper.

> The paper was due off at 9.45 p.m., and by now it was
> 9.30 p.m. – the loneliest time of the day for any editor
> when only one man can make a decision. Of course,
> I was desperately aware of the enormousness of what
> was being proposed. It's not up to newspapers to accuse
> people of murder or act as judge and jury . . . After about
> five minutes on my own, I walked back on to the floor.
> The 'Murderers' page was made up with an alternative
> front page next to it. The mood was electric. 'Let's go,'
> I said. 'You can always come and visit me in jail . . .' I
> went home and rang my wife to tell her what I'd done
> and how dangerous the men concerned were. As always,
> she totally backed me. That night I took a sleeping pill.
> Despite it, I woke up at four o'clock in the morning – the
> time when all the decisions of the previous day suddenly
> assume terrifying proportions. I was drenched in sweat
> and convinced my career was over.[26]

The next day, the reaction to the *Mail*'s headline was split: the *Daily Telegraph* effectively called for Dacre to be jailed and carried a cartoon of the *Mail* editor flicking ink upon the Old Bailey's scales of justice, and a former senior judge, Lord Donaldson, was horrified by the paper's actions and accused Dacre of contempt of court. Another judge, however, Lord Denning, congratulated the *Mail* for 'a marvellous piece of journalism', while Stephen Lawrence's mother, Doreen, said the front page was 'wonderful'. The Lawrence family's local MP also backed the paper, as did, a few days later, the Prime Minister, John Major.

The five young men, of course, never did sue. Just as in Sunny Harmsworth's day, whereas other newspapers covered and commented upon the Lawrence case, the *Mail* raged. And the *Mail*'s sense of outrage had been harnessed to supreme effect, said former Mailman Tim Miles, who covered many gruesome murders himself in his days as the paper's crime reporter. 'This was a black boy,' Miles told the author, 'and it stands there in black and white that Paul Dacre is no Nazi like some are so desperate for him, and his paper, to be. That was an extraordinary front page. You would never – never – have seen that on page one of the *Guardian*. Never.'[27]

Dacre didn't sleep too well until a week later, when a fax arrived at the office confirming he was not going to be charged with contempt of court.

The story has, to many, come to define his editorship, and it was the only front page that hung in a frame for years in his office.

Stephen's murder had also led to a public inquiry in 1998 that concluded that the Metropolitan Police was 'institutionally racist'. A change in the law of double jeopardy – in which an accused person could not be tried twice for the same crime – followed in 2003, applicable in murder cases for which new and compelling evidence emerged.

Then, almost fifteen years after that headline in January 2012, two of the men were finally found guilty of Stephen Lawrence's murder after a cold case review by forensics officers uncovered DNA evidence that put them firmly at the scene of the crime. It was a sweet day, a day to savour for Paul Dacre. The *Mail* editor has never given a TV interview in his twenty-five years in the job, but Dacre did finally appear on camera – in a video filmed for his own website. In this scripted monologue, Dacre sounded like the proud head teacher of a minor public school, a string of spittle on his lip that perhaps his school prefects off-camera were too afraid to alert him to.

> I always tell people who ask that the secret to editing is to be both bold and cautious. It's knowing when to be which that's the problem. That day in February 1997 I think we were bold in a way that the *Mail* can always be proud of. [28]

Here sat perched on the edge of a desk one of the most loathed, invisible men in Britain and – though he did seem something of a zealot with lips nipped tight for battle – he was all too human.

Only a month after the 'MURDERERS' headline, the *Daily Mail* was gearing up for the biggest political story of the year when John Major called the 1997 general election. Dacre now faced probably the most difficult political decision of any *Daily Mail* editor since its birth: could the paper turn its back on the Conservatives after 101 years of support?

Tony Blair's rise to power had caused consternation in Kensington High Street, with many Mailmen and Femails personally backing Blair. The *Daily Mail*, though, was born a Tory. Even so, on the other side of London, the once equally arch Thatcherite *Sun* did switch sides and backed Blair. The political tide had clearly turned in favour of 'New' Labour, yet Paul Dacre, unlike Rupert Murdoch, simply seemed incapable of turning with it; Murdoch had realized Blair couldn't lose, it was a campaign he knew his *Sun* would win. Dacre remained unconvinced.

For the man who paid Dacre's wages, though, it was a very different story; Lord Rothermere had personally warmed to the Labour leader, seeing Blair as 'a very capable, very charming, very astute man, full of enthusiasm and drive . . . He unquestionably comes from the British middle classes, as does his wife.'[29]

Tony Blair was, nevertheless, a conundrum for Rothermere and his editor-in-chief, Sir David English; a few years after Rothermere and English had reinvented the *Mail* as a tabloid, the proprietor had made the paper's politics very clear: it would always support the Conservatives.[30] But Blair was a far different type of Labour leader from what the paper's hierarchy had been used to dealing with, certainly since Thatcher had taken power.

The Labour chief even came to dinner at Room One, Northcliffe's big room for big ideas. Room One had been turned into a dining room where top politicians would come to dine and remark upon the quality of the cuisine. Harold Wilson, Labour leader from 1963 to 1976, was 'a frequent and popular visitor'[31] who was even capable of sharing a joke or two with these Tories. But the Labour Party leader of the 1980s, Neil Kinnock, always declined Sir David's polite invitations. Wilson, of course, won three general elections. Kinnock won none. When the *Daily Mail* left Fleet Street, Vere had Room One dismantled panel by panel and reassembled at the *Mail*'s new offices in Kensington, but Kinnock still declined these invites and discouraged other senior Labour Party members from fraternizing with the enemy.

'In the end, only one member of the Shadow Cabinet had the guts to defy the Whip and enter our lair,' wrote Sir David in the *Spectator* in 1995.

> That man was Tony Blair. It was a pretty refreshing start
> to a relationship with a Labour politician. But we all liked
> it and him. And so Tony became a regular visitor, at that
> time our only link to the paranoid and neurotic Labour
> Party of Neil Kinnock. It wasn't until Blair took over that
> lunches with a Labour leader became fun once again.
> Much more fun, incidentally, than when members of
> the current [John Major] Government came gloomily to
> dine. In contrast Blair – whether he was alone or with his
> minders – radiated frankness and honesty.[32]

Blair spoke the *Mail*'s language, and he had no desire to tear down all that Thatcher had built. For instance, English was a governor of his old grammar school in Bournemouth and liked Blair's attitude to education; the Labour man believed in choice and had no plans for a one-size-fits-all school system. Blair also said the days of the print unions would not return under a New Labour government. At one lunch, Dacre challenged Blair on the social and welfare costs of single mothers and the potential damage the breakdown of the traditional family was causing to society as a whole. To Dacre's surprise, wrote English in the *Spectator*, Blair

said he shared his concerns, adding that the situation was betraying
a generation of children.[33]

> That brought us to welfare as a major issue. The debate
> was intense but it was Blair who cut through everything
> with the remark: 'Well, we all agree the welfare state has
> got to be radically reformed. Who's going to do it? You
> may find I am the only one who has the will to do it.'
> A thoughtful silence followed. Of course, when the fresh-
> ness and the charm of our exchanges with the inventor
> of new Labour recedes after his departure, we are not
> left entirely without scepticism . . . equally, we are not
> without scepticism towards the present Government.[34]

It now seemed that the unthinkable could actually happen and
the *Mail* might back Labour in the general election, with Lord
Rothermere even telling the BBC he had 'a suspicion'[35] some of his
papers would back Blair. Vere's personal politics were never quite so
clear as the *Mail*'s. He was no politico and he never craved direct
influence over events in the way Northcliffe and his grandfather had;
this Harmsworth seemed perfectly content for his paper to follow its
readers, as interpreted by its editor. 'Now, when I appoint an editor,
I only appoint people who I believe to be of great talent,' he told the
BBC. 'And people of great talent have their own opinions. And they
like working for me because I let them have their own opinions.' His
editors would, of course, seek the proprietor's view. '. . . if you are the
person who decides on their salaries they will naturally want to ask
your opinion, I mean – even my dog does that.'[36]

Dacre's *Daily Mail* never did back Blair, but the paper's backing of
John Major was a limp affair. The *Mail*'s editor, like the broken cogs
that were grinding around inside the Tory Party machine, was far too
busy obsessing over Europe, as illustrated in a dull, ill-defined and
unwinnable campaign called 'the Battle for Britain'.[37] Then, the day
before the election, its front page was wrapped in the Union Jack,
across which was scrawled:

There is a terrible danger that the British people, drugged
by the seductive mantra 'It's time for a change', are
stumbling, eyes glazed, into an election that could undo
1,000 years of our nation's history.[38]

Tabloids tend not to publish long lists of names – because they're
boring. But, inside, the *Mail* printed a list of Tory candidates who
backed the campaign and would rule out joining the single currency
and ceding more power to Brussels. But once the pound had fallen
out of the ERM, arguing for Britain to ditch the pound for the euro
was pretty much a non-starter for both parties anyway. And Dacre's
leader page was beginning to feel as heavy as just about anything
Bunny Harmsworth ever composed:

It was the one issue that brought this drear election to
life. Two weeks ago the *Daily Mail* published a front-page
editorial, headlined The Battle for Britain, which started
with the words: 'There is a deafening silence at the heart
of this election and its name is Europe' . . . Our article
argued that this election could be the last opportunity for
the British people to decide on whether they wished to
remain an independent sovereign nation . . .[39] [Etc.]

English's paper had never sounded this dull; Sir David's words
were usually bright and naturally free-flowing, the words far less
fussed and agonized over – just like those of Sunny Harmsworth.
Some staff had begun to, quietly, call Dacre 'the Grim Tweaker',[40]
due to his fondness for angrily, endlessly, fiddling with every
word on every page. *Mail* readers were urged to stick with Major
partly because Blair had never served in government, which in itself
was absurd; he was only twenty-five when Labour was last in power
and didn't become an MP until 1983. On polling day, 1 May 1997,
the Tories, and maybe the *Mail*'s editor, were truly clutching at
straws.

Tony Blair leads New Labour into today's General
Election buoyed by a record-breaking lead in the polls.
The Tories were praying last night that another record
statistic – the army of an estimated four million 'don't
know' voters – could still sink his chances and provide the
biggest political upset this century.[41]

Most Mailmen and Femails, even the truest and bluest Tories
sitting there in the open-plan office, knew Tony Blair was heading
to Downing Street. Some even slipped out to vote Labour; Lynda
Lee-Potter certainly voted for Blair,[42] and maybe even Sir David
English – the boy brought up in Bournemouth and encouraged
towards a career in newspapers by his staunchly Socialist grandfather
– put an X in the box that would usher in the Blair years.

Election day was a bad day at the office for Paul Dacre. As the
results began to come in, and even Baroness Thatcher's once safe
Finchley seat fell to Labour, Dacre is said to have shouted across the
newsroom: 'What the fuck is going on? These are fucking *Daily Mail*
readers!'[43] It was the Tory Party's worst result since 1832, and Blair,
said the *Mail*, was 'Sweeping to power on a tidal wave'.[44] Tony
Blair was the youngest Prime Minister in almost two centuries, a few
days shy of his forty-fourth birthday. Paul Dacre, forty-eight, is said
to have picked up his red Cabinet minister style briefcase and gone
off on holiday.[45]

Some Mailmen thought Dacre had truly blown it after his proprietor had firmly and publicly backed Blair, and Vere's enthusiasm for
the new PM only increased. Viscount Rothermere – unlike grandfather Bunny – rarely wrote articles for his newspapers, yet a couple of
weeks after Blair was swept into Downing Street he picked up his pen
in favour of the new Prime Minister – not for his *Daily Mail* but for
his *Evening Standard*.

Max Hastings, the *Standard*'s editor, had been free – the same
as Paul Dacre – to do as he pleased, and he backed the winner.
Vere even announced in the *Standard* that he was about to shuffle
over from the cross benches in the House of Lords – those Lords

unaligned with the main political parties – to sit with the Labour lot. Though Rothermere rarely went to Westminster, as it was a little too far from his Paris home and, anyway, he thought hereditary peers such as himself were dinosaurs that should be made extinct, it was a symbolic gesture.

The Tories, he wrote, were 'like a magnificent salmon, that, overcoming all obstacles, spawns the next generation and drifts spent and ruined back to the sea'.[46] And Labour had caught 'the developing popular mood', exactly like popular newspapers are supposed to do. Blair 'understands absolutely the temper of the times and the spirit of the age'.[47] He offered Blair's administration his full support. 'Tony to me is like a breath of fresh air, a new spirit,' he later told the *Observer*, 'he's a modern man who understands the need for social caring and who understands also the need for prosperous business.'[48]

To some on the *Mail* editorial floor, Vere's words felt like their ship had hit a mine, and many feared – and plenty of others hoped – Dacre was doomed. But Dacre's position was pretty much blast-proof, having presided over a circulation increase of around 300,000 – almost 20 per cent – in the five years since he took over from English.

'I am quite clearly in favour of a common market but I am not in favour of a federal Europe. Nor is the *Daily Mail*,' Vere told the *Financial Times* three days before the election, yet added that perhaps his editor did go too far. 'Sometimes I think Paul would like to tow England out into the middle of the Atlantic. I am not sure that is what I want to do.'[49]

The *Daily Mail* is a business, and it's in the business of selling newspapers. And the post-election *Mail* may have seemed to be steaming furiously around in circles in the middle of a big blue ocean politically, but other newspaper owners would surely have given Dacre command of a newspaper had Lord Rothermere pushed his skipper overboard. After the 1997 election, Rothermere praised Dacre on BBC Radio, saying he was 'probably the most brilliant editor in Fleet Street' . . . and he was entitled to express the anti-European views his proprietor didn't share . . . but, he added ominously, 'if they start to affect circulation, that will be different'.[50]

14

Two Funerals
and a Promotion

It had been a busy, defining year, for Paul Dacre with his outra-
geous 'Murderers' headline and the beginning of the Blair years in
power. By the summer of 1997 he had truly established himself as
the most formidable editor in Fleet Street, but the *Daily Mail* had
yet to face probably the biggest story of the decade at the end of that
August . . . and 1997 was to turn out to be Sir David English and
Vere Harmsworth's last full year alive.

Just as with the J. F. K. cliché, most people seemed to be able
to recall where they were when they heard the news that Princess
Diana had been killed in a car crash; *Daily Mail* columnist Lynda
Lee-Potter, for instance, was shaken awake in the early hours of the
morning when a BBC producer rang her home, but they weren't
seeking a comment – they were actually trying to find her radio
presenter daughter Charlie to ask her to present a programme of
special coverage. She drove into the office listening to her daughter
host the show on her car radio. The *Daily Mail* building is just down
the road from the princess's Kensington Palace home, and Lee-Potter
arrived as men and women headed up to Kensington Palace from the
Tube station carrying bouquets of flowers.

'She spoke for everyone's need for hugs and contact,' Lee-Potter
eulogized. 'She forged passionate feelings in us all. I have both praised

and criticized her. Last week I wrote harsh things. Now that it's too late I am full of regret and shame and guilt. But I thought the rest of her life lay ahead and there would be time to redress the balance when the time was right. Now I will never have another chance.'[1]

Indeed. Britain's most vitriolic housewife (and all the tabloid press) had in recent weeks been hounding 'the people's princess', as Britain's youthful new Prime Minister Tony Blair would christen her in a speech after her death, over her relationship with Dodi Fayed – the man who would be killed alongside her in a Paris underpass. Lee-Potter had been one of the few to be broadly supportive, at first, of Princess Diana's affair with her new playboy lover in the summer of 1997,[2] and then, just four days before the crash that killed them both, she wrote: 'Princes need a modest mother.'

> Teenagers want their mother to be modest, ordinary and scandal free. They can't bear any hint of her having a sexual life. The sight of a paunchy playboy groping a scantily-dressed Diana must appal and humiliate Prince William. Unfortunately she appears determined to reveal to the world that she and Dodi are lovers and can't keep their hands off each other. I suggest they show a little self-control when they are on public view on the deck of the luxurious Fayed yacht.[3]

That was fairly mild compared to some of what the *Daily Mail*'s most important voice had written about the princess in the years before her death; some of her words were downright nasty. For instance, in the winter of 1995 she wrote: 'Praise – that's all Diana really wants . . . Princess Diana has an addictive nature and is clearly now addicted to the old, the poor, the dying and publicity.'[4] And only a month before the princess's death she warned: 'Don't be taken in by Diana . . . Diana is a fine actress. She can act being hurt, vulnerable or in despair. She can act being utterly natural and unspoilt. She can bewitch old and young, male and female. She can play poor little me to perfection. Unfortunately, she acts so much she's lost sight of the truth.'[5]

The princess was known to be utterly obsessed by her own press and read every word Lee-Potter wrote about her, indeed she once even phoned Paul Dacre when there was an international debate about whether or not Princess Diana had cellulite. 'I've just seen your Ms Lee-Potter in Marks & Spencer,' the Princess told the *Mail* editor. 'I bet *she's* got cellulite!'[6]

Lee-Potter had worried in the past in print about the future of Prince Charles and Princess Diana's marriage long before they split, writing that 'the corrosive spotlight continually on their marriage must at times be monstrous and at the moment, it seems to me, is on the verge of being wicked'.[7] The *Daily Mail* spotlight, of course, radiated no heat.

Yet the reputation of the Press as a whole was at an all-time low after the death of 'the people's princess'. To many it was the Press who killed her, hounded as she was in those last hours by paparazzi snappers in hot pursuit. It was the tabloid newspapers and celebrity magazines who paid the bounties to these lawless freelance photographers; *they* created the market and would regularly outbid each other for these pictures, generating ever higher fees.

Upstairs at Northcliffe House, Sir David English – as chairman of the newspaper industry's Code of Practice Committee – tried to limit the damage, moving quickly to draft a new Code to try and suppress the market in photographs. And Viscount Rothermere's 'own sense of outrage'[8] led him to lay down the editorial law in a way he'd never done before: no paparazzi photographs could be bought by his newspapers without his personal consent (which he was most unlikely to give). Sir David had actually been widely praised a couple of years earlier for measures that had allowed thirteen-year-old Prince William the right to 'walk, study and play' when he started school at Eton without press intrusion, measures that largely held throughout his childhood.

After the death of the princess, Sir David got the industry to agree to stamp out the taking of pictures in private places and banned the use of photographs generated by 'persistent pursuit'. 'Public opinion following the death of the Princess was telling us loud and clear that we needed to look to our laurels,' Sir David said in the *Daily Mail* in May 1998, 'and to make sure our own rules on privacy and harassment were as tough as they could be.'[9]

It would prove to be one of his final acts.

Sir David English loved a party.

The bashes he liked best of all were the ones where he could sit at the head of a very long dinner table and incite argument, direct debate and generally steer the flow of the conversation in the direction that amused him most. And in June of 1998, the still-supreme *Mail* being was about to be handed an invite to the tallest press table there has ever been for a press man; he'd have a seat alongside Northcliffe, Beaverbrook, Hartwell, Kemsley, Camrose, Thomson of Fleet and, of course, Rothermere himself: the Prime Minister was about to make English a Press Lord for his 'services to journalism'.

As well he might be. By the early summer of 1998 the *Daily Mail* he had rescued in 1971 was in rude health; Paul Dacre had adjusted the formula but he hadn't radically changed it – the paper looked exactly the same and people still bought it to read English's columnists Lynda Lee-Potter, Ian Wooldridge and Nigel Dempster. Dacre had put on something like 700,000 readers since he'd taken over from Sir David, a timeframe during which hundreds of thousands of readers had deserted weaker organs.

Yet, even if circulation had collapsed under David English, some who knew both men believe that Lord Rothermere's relationship was so tight with his editorial guru they would simply have gone down together with the Associated Newspapers ship as it sank into the abyss. They did have disputes now and again, but Harmsworth would never have sacked English and David English would never have quit in anger or left to edit *The Times*. Even five years after Dacre had taken the reins of his *Daily Mail* and had put on circulation and even won awards – the *Daily Mail* won National Newspaper of the Year at the British Press Awards in 1994, 1995 and 1997 – it was clear who was Viscount Rothermere's supreme editorial being. It wasn't Paul Dacre.

'I think he [English] is one of the greatest editors ever to walk in Fleet Street,' Rothermere told the *FT* in April 1997. 'I don't know any editor since Northcliffe who was such a total master of his art.'[10]

Lord Rothermere would simply never personally feel the same for Paul Dacre as he did for Sir David. The *Mail*'s compact double-act still ultimately ruled at Northcliffe House – they just existed on a higher plane than the editorial floor, where the *Mail*'s editor was given a free hand to ritually abuse his staff and tear up the paper as deadlines hurtled up to meet them.

Yet Viscount Rothermere, by now in his early seventies, spent most of his time in France and made it clear that he wanted to step away from his businesses and 'find some sort of gentle decline' so that he could hand over the family firm to his son, thirty-year-old Jonathan. 'I want to spend the rest of my life living on a mountain top,' he told the *Observer*, 'skiing down it every morning and being carried up it every evening.'

It was only Sir David English who kept him away from that mountain. 'We more or less agree that we will work on together for as long as we can,' Sir David told the same *Observer* interviewer, Lynn Barber. 'We've always worked as a team and we've decided to go on doing that.'[11] Only three things could force Sir David away from the *Mail* group, he added: Vere quitting, extreme ill-health and death . . . the grim reaper would, indeed, come calling a year later. For them both.

Some of Sir David's best friends had been worried about him for months, and the last time his old friend Tony Burton saw him was at a big dinner party in upstate New York thrown in English's honour shortly before he died.

'He was very, very quiet, perhaps sad because of Irene,' he told the author, 'or – if you want to be silly – he knew it was all coming to an end and . . . listen, a central fact people must understand about David English was that he adored Irene and was devastated by her illness – he even set up a trust fund for her care, suggesting that he feared he might die before she did. My feeling is that he was terribly sad in his last months, largely because of Irene.'[12]

So Tony Blair's new Labour Government smiled benignly upon Sir David – despite the way his paper had ripped into old Labour – and the English name was added to the Queen's Birthday Honours List, with his elevation to be announced on 13 June 1998. He needed to choose a name. Sunny Harmsworth had simply invented the name Northcliffe, and Bunny had followed his lead by creating the title Rothermere, but Sir David didn't get the chance to conjure up his own; he collapsed a few days before the official announcement.

'He'd had various ailments of a not particularly worrying nature, some form of internal upsets and he was having medication,' his oldest friend, Chris Rees, told the author, 'but he wasn't ill in the sense that he was having time off work or anything. And then he collapsed in the bathroom one morning getting ready to go to work and was found there by his driver still conscious, sort of, and he was carted off to St Thomas's. It was a stroke, a blood clot in the brain.'[13]

St Thomas's Hospital is just across the Thames from Westminster, where many a politician has battled for the approval of those millions of *Daily Mail* readers right there in the middle of England – the ground where they fear elections are won or lost. Sir David faced his own battle, as he lay dying in a hospital bed with his friend Vere gently stroking his hand – a battle he knew his friend was losing. Lord Rothermere had dashed from Paris with his wife Maiko when he received the news, and would now never get the chance to scoot along to make room for his friend on the padded red leather benches at the House of Lords. 'It was so very, very sad,' Maiko, the Dowager Lady Rothermere, told the author, 'we could even see the Houses of Parliament on the other side of the river from his bedroom. Vere was devastated. Heartbroken. He loved David so much, I always thought of them as like a cat and a dog. David was a cat, so feline and female, and Vere was a big cuddly doggy. They were so very, very lucky to find each other.'[14]

Chris Rees and his family were closer to the Englishes than pretty much anybody. They regularly went on holiday together, and Rees had even joined the *Mail* in the seventies, from where he rose to be managing editor of the *Daily Mail* and then deputy editor of the

Mail on Sunday. 'We were with him when he actually died in the hospital, David's three children were there and my wife and I were there,' Rees told the author. 'He gave a little gasp and he was gone.'[15]

A little while earlier, Tony Burton had taken a call at dawn in upstate New York from Sir David's eldest daughter, Nikki, to tell him her dad had collapsed with a stroke and was in a coma. 'I booked a seat on the next flight to London but before take-off learned that he was dead,' he told the author. 'I went anyway and spent some time with his family but declined an offer to see his body; I didn't want to see him lifeless – he was such an electrically energetic character. And I didn't wait for the bullshit of the funeral either, my sister-in-law offered to drive me to Heathrow and since Nikki lived on the way to the airport she invited us to stop off at her house.'

Burton is heading on towards his ninetieth year now, and the term 'grizzled old hack' could well have been coined in his honour, yet, nevertheless, he is human and the pain surfaces most when he recalls the impact of Sir David's death on the family of his friend. 'That was the only time I ever met David's grandchildren, still not in their teens. They were devastated, crying and bewildered. Nikki played a video of David having fun with the kids; he was prancing around in the garden with a German helmet on his head while the kids shrieked with laughter.

'David English was just about the most fascinating character I have ever met in my life . . . I loved the man.'[16]

The newspapers, of course, ran their obituaries and the tributes flowed in from everyone from Tony Blair to the Prince of Wales. English himself had once said of this moment: 'I wouldn't want any highfalutin things said about me but I would like journalists to say: "He was pretty good and, frankly, he ran a tough ship, but he wasn't as bad as they say he was. His bark was worse than his bite, and he actually did lead people rather than drive them."'[17]

Yet Sir David, who was a wily old hack at heart far more than an editor – possessed, as he was on occasion, with his own particular brand of 'truth' – did actually keep one line back for himself that was missed by all of Fleet Street's finest, including his own *Daily*

Mail; they all had him dying just a couple of weeks after his sixty-seventh birthday. Not true. He was, actually, sixty-eight;[18] English had knocked a year off his true age for his *Who's Who* entry sometime before.[19]

The newspaper presses stop for no man, whatever his age, and Paul Dacre soon took Sir David's place as editor-in-chief at Rothermere's right hand, overseeing the *Evening Standard* and the *Mail on Sunday* as well as the *Daily Mail*. But the short stretch of road they shared without Sir David was far rockier for Paul Dacre than the one travelled by English and the *Mail* proprietor. Rothermere had already stated pretty clearly – at least for the usually enigmatic Vere – before the election that Dacre was safe . . . *so long as circulation didn't suffer.*

Another warning was to follow very soon after Sir David's death: don't go downmarket. Vere didn't want the *Mail* to dumb down any more as the price of victory in a new circulation battle. By then, the *Daily Express* was far behind, selling over a million fewer copies than the *Mail*, but the *Daily Mirror*'s plump red buttocks were now within biting distance, selling only around 100,000 copies more than the *Mail*. Again, like the *Express*, the *Mirror*'s demise was largely because it had also fallen into the same kind of malignant, corporate management that managed to forget the readers along the way – the *Mirror* had miraculously managed to shed 500,000 readers in the same period Dacre had increased the *Mail*'s circulation by 700,000.[20]

Lord Rothermere actually cared, deeply and emotionally, about his family's *Daily Mail* and he had chosen his path three decades before and stuck with it; Vere Harmsworth had invested and kept investing while his enemies committed slow circulation suicide. In 1971, he had inherited a moribund *Daily Mail*, a dying *Daily Sketch* and a fading *Evening News*, but by 1998 his business was in bloom, vibrant, the leader in its field; he owned three successful and highly profitable newspapers: the *Daily Mail*, the *Mail on Sunday* and the *Evening Standard*. The cost-cutting waves whipped up by the bean-counters of other newspaper groups never swamped the *Mail*. The accountants surely must have tried, only for Vere to file their memos where they belonged: in the bin.

It could have all gone horribly wrong, like it did for the *Express* when Beaverbrook's playboy son took the wheel. It's worth noting, however, that the *Daily Mail* has never, in its entire existence, sold close to 4 million copies a day like the *Express* once did; the *Mail* didn't ruin the *Express*, the *Express* ruined itself. And Rothermere's father, of course, nearly sank the *Mail* by spinning the wheel this way and that, then repeatedly dropping anchor in unfamiliar waters, sacking editors and allowing his second wife Ann to act like the editor-in-chief. Northcliffe's *Mail* only ever had one editor – other than Sunny himself and, perhaps, Kennedy Jones (but neither held the title). Vere's *Mail* only had two . . . the first was never sacked and his second is still there, a quarter of a century after his appointment. None of the offspring of the other old-school Press Lords now owns a national newspaper in Britain. Only the Harmsworths remain. In 1997, Vere was, according to the *Sunday Times* Rich List, Britain's ninth richest man – worth £1.2 billion.[21] It was not quite third richest like grandfather Bunny, but it wasn't bad going, especially considering that for Vere, just like Northcliffe, it had never been about the money; the *Mail* could have generated far more raw cash for the Harmsworth coffers.

Nobody called Lord Rothermere 'mere Vere' any more, but Viscount Rothermere wasn't your average newspaper proprietor or even remotely close to your average *Mail* reader; he was a Buddhist billionaire who liked to refer to himself as a 'nobleman' yet thought the royal family were finished; he had little interest in buying a collection of huge homes, boats or private aircraft. 'Vere was an instinctive genius and hugely unconventional, I mean he was a Buddhist! Or, he thought he was a Buddhist anyway,' ex-Mailman and one-time monk Richard Addis, who was by then editor-in-chief of the *Express* group, told the author. 'Vere was often very mysterious and very perceptive.'[22]

The *Daily Mail* could have tumbled downmarket behind *The Sun* and the *Daily Mirror* in the 1970s chasing mass circulation, had Vere so desired. In an interview with the *Daily Telegraph* not long after Sir David's death, Rothermere worried that Dacre's *Daily Mail* was doing exactly that – dumbing down to meet the red-tops:

I don't agree with him [Dacre], and I've told him so.
We've gone too far down-market and I want it to
stop . . . What I say to Paul is: 'The market is moving
towards us. If we go down to meet it, we'll endanger our
own market position.' It's fine to be catching up with
the *Mirror*, but not at that price. At the moment Paul is
playing a very dangerous game of footsie. He has to be
very careful.[23]

Paul Dacre was also playing a very dangerous game with his
career, some at the time believed. 'I speak to Paul Dacre every day,
but I believe in leaving successful editors alone,' Rothermere had
told the *Telegraph*, 'and Paul is independent . . . *to the degree of his
success.*'[24] Peter Preston, the highly respected media pundit and
former editor of the *Guardian*, added those italics at the time in
a piece for the *Observer* pondering whether Vere Harmsworth was
'baiting a fiendish trap' for his new editor-in-chief; if Dacre's *Daily
Mail* pulled ahead of the *Daily Mirror*, the tabloid 'sensationalism
and slovenliness' Vere so reviled would be tacitly confirmed. But if
the *Mail* didn't pile on the readers, then the 'degree of his success'
could be questioned. 'Catch 22-as-catch-can,' wrote Preston.[25]
Then again, this may well just have been Viscount Rothermere's
own particular kind of joke.

Vere Harmsworth had been very fortunate to find the perfect
editor for his *Daily Mail* and David English had been very lucky to
find the perfect proprietor. Theirs was a symbiotic tale and it seems
one could not exist without the other, just like an oft-told story that
has appeared in many a local newspaper over the years; an old married
couple had met as youngsters and stayed together for half a century or
more of loving wedlock. Then one spouse dies . . . and the other dies
swiftly afterwards. The surviving partner cannot stand alone in the
world. And there is actually plenty of evidence in science for 'broken
heart syndrome'. So it was to be, in a way, with Vere Harmsworth,
the third Viscount Rothermere, and Sir David English, the editor
who had almost joined him in the Press Lord club.

A friend once said that Lord Rothermere loved newspapers, women and dogs 'in that order',[26] and it was dogs that had brought Vere Harmsworth and the second Lady Rothermere – a Korean hand model who was born in Japan called Maiko Lee – together. Maiko loved canines too, and had helped organize a dogs' charity fundraiser in New York in 1978 that was to be held the same day Vere arrived on Concorde from London. Vere was invited by a friend to the party at which he, at the age of fifty-three, struggled to cope with the disco tunes. 'The music was very loud,' Lady Rothermere, who was twenty-nine at the time, told the author, 'and Vere's friend said [in the squeezed, back-of-the-throat accent of the true English aristocracy], "This is Vere," and I thought he said "Bear"; and he looked just like a great big teddy bear! With a beautiful face and a big happy tummy, and I knew at that moment that God had sent this man into my life. And I was with him until the day he died.'[27]

Two decades later, as Vere prepared to leave his home in the French countryside on what was to prove to be his final business trip to London, that day was about to come – and it seems Rothermere's best friend knew it.

'Vere had a dog, an Akita called Ryu-ma,' said Lady Rothermere, 'and Vere was so much in love with this dog. And the dog adored his papa. But Ryu-ma was in such a mood, such a mood, he was just hiding under the table. I said: "Roo-mee boy, come here! Daddy's going today to England. You're not going to see him for a little while, you must come! Rhoo-mee, come on, boy!" But no. He wouldn't come. Normally Ryu-ma would jump in the car and enjoy the ride with Vere and the driver to the airport. But he was in such a mood, he just wouldn't go. Dogs sense these things; he knew his papa was going to die.

'So I went with Vere to the airport instead, so he could get on a small private plane that was waiting for him there. It was so strange, at the airport, I said, "Vere, thank you very much for the beautiful life you gave to me." And I don't know why I said it. And Vere, I'll never forget it, said: "My dear Maiko, you have given me the most beautiful life – I shall miss you so very much." And then he gave me a cuddle – we had a long, long, long cuddle together – and then he took the plane and he went.'[28]

When he arrived in London, being a good Englishman, the viscount went for a nice cup of tea at his daughter's house before heading to his son's place at Eaton Square for dinner; he began to complain of a severe pain in an arm at the dinner table and collapsed with a heart attack.

'His son Jonathan rang me at nine o'clock in the evening,' said Lady Rothermere, 'and he said, "Please sit." So I sat. And he said, "Daddy's dead."'[29]

The third Lord Rothermere, Vere Harmsworth, died in the same hospital as Sir David on 1 September 1998 – just twelve weeks after his partner.

15

At the Court of 'King Paul'

The two founders of the modern-day *Daily Mail* were no more; Dacre had been appointed editor-in-chief by Vere before he died but he had *not* been given English's more senior post as chairman of Associated Newspapers – Vere had resumed that himself. Anyway, the chairman of a newspaper company need not be an editor – and Paul Dacre is an editorial man to his socks; he has reigned supreme over content ever since. But he does not, of course, make the *Daily Mail* on his own. A multitude of Mailmen and Femails have helped Dacre define and remake it daily over the last quarter of a century – newspapers are not shapes tipped from a mould, they are hammered into shape every day by living men and women. The *Mail* has long been the best-staffed newspaper in 'Fleet Street', and some of those men and women offer a fascinating insight into how the post-David English-era *Daily Mail* actually functioned.

Dacre and his senior team, much as they must surely hate it, have themselves been observed by trained observers for years: men and women whose job it is to study people for a living and then write it down for the consumption of others. Inside the *Mail* there have been people who did – and still do – truly believe in the *Daily Mail* cause, whatever it happened to be that day. These hacks tend never to speak publicly about their trade, either on principle, which is fair enough, or because they're afraid of retribution. Paul Dacre himself explained this principle best in the *British Journalism Review*:

> Our biggest fault is our compulsion to shit on our own
> [kind]. The way British newspapers – and the so-called
> quality papers are the worst offenders – so venomously
> slag each other off never ceases to depress me. We have
> a dismal enough image with the public as it is without
> fouling our own nest.[1]

Then there are those for whom working on the *Daily Mail* was only their trade, not their religion, and they were neither afraid nor in awe of Paul Dacre nor anybody else at the *Daily Mail*; they were simply hard-working people who now feel strongly that the same incredulity and journalistic cynicism they'd apply to any story outside the office is also – absolutely – applicable indoors. The *Daily Mail* is only a product and Paul Dacre is not a cartoon monster – Dacre is just a man and he is also, actually, just an employee: Dacre might make it in his own image but he does not own the *Daily Mail*.

The *Daily Mail* is a pyramid at the top of which sits the fourth Viscount Rothermere. Jonathan Harmsworth, however, rules from a distance – many staffers have never met the man; he is not a physical presence in the *Daily Mail* newsroom like young Sunny Harmsworth was in his day. Bunny's great-grandson exists upstairs.

Some Mailmen and Femails are bolder than others, however, and every now and then one or two peel away from the pack to take an insane career risk by sneaking up to the sixth floor at Northcliffe House in Kensington . . . just to take a glimpse inside another world; up there is Harmsworth territory – it is from the sixth floor that his young Lordship Jonathan reigns.

One Femail, 'Elsa', was guided up the stairs behind the art-deco façade (newspaper owners adore art-deco façades) of the old Barkers department store building one evening by a colleague. They knew they were safe because all the chiefs were distracted down below by a leaving do. 'This guy was a mate of mine,' she told the author, 'and he whispered, "I've got to go up to the sixth floor, do you wanna have a peek?" And it was literally, literally, another world. It's unbeliev-able up there, like walking into an amazing hotel. They've got this astonishing boardroom with oak panel walls and oil paintings all around. If you were gonna shoot a Barbara Taylor Bradford novel of the, you know, "the office of the great retail magnate" – this is *the* place. I just couldn't believe my eyes; down below it's all grey Formica and this shit utilitarian carpet, and you go up there and it's absolutely striking. I felt like I was in a completely different century, never mind a different floor.'[2]

'Elsa' had a point; the Harmsworths *are* from a completely different century, and by the start of the new millennium, when she went exploring those upper floors, it had been 112 years since the middle-class boy Sunny Harmsworth had launched *Answers to Correspondents*, the organ upon which this family empire was constructed. Bunny's 'Rothermere' title was, of course, tooled in a different era too, and the name 'Viscount Rothermere' follows the hereditary principle and so is attached to Harold Harmsworth's heirs for the foreseeable future. It fell first to Esmond, then to Vere and then . . . it was a matter of confusion. Three decades before, in 1966, it wasn't exactly clear on whom it *could* next be bestowed.

Vere had two daughters he adored, but he had no son and there-fore – under the still-active rules of feudal England that hand every-thing to the eldest male child – no heir. Yet Vere's father, Esmond, the sixty-nine-year-old second viscount, had remarried and his young wife soon fell pregnant with Esmond Jr. This would mean, after Vere, Esmond Jr – the second viscount's second son – would have become the fourth Viscount Rothermere. Far more importantly – due to the complex system that Bunny Harmsworth had constructed – Esmond Jr would also have inherited the family firm (the company, effectively, follows the Rothermere title). Vere's first wife, Patricia – nicknamed 'Bubbles' by satirical magazine *Private Eye* for her effervescent, champagne personality and love of a party – however, wasn't about to let that happen. Bubbles had suffered severe complications and – most likely – undiagnosed postnatal depression after the birth of daughters Geraldine and Camilla, and her doctors had told her to have no more babies. However, she ignored them and read up on how some people claimed the sex of a child could be influenced and soon fell pregnant with Harold Jonathan Esmond Vere Harmsworth, who arrived in December 1967. This boy, Jonathan for short, would be the next to receive the Rothermere name and control of the company that held the *Mail*. Jonathan's parents' marriage, though, soon fell apart and by the end of the 1970s his father was with another woman.

'I fell in love with Maiko,' Vere told the *Observer*, 'but I did not cease to love Pat. Maiko's love is so calm and peaceful. Pat was tempestuous and exhausting, like a tropical storm that takes its energy from its surroundings.'[3]

The Harmsworths were firmly part of Britain's elite by the time Jonathan came along; Jonathan went to Prince Charles's old public school, Gordonstoun, up in Scotland, and then on to Duke University in the US – his mother advising him against impaling himself upon the spires of an olde-English university: 'If you go to Oxford, Jonathan, people will only come to your room and take drugs and get depressed,' she told him. 'Go to an American university with all that open air.'[4]

It didn't really much matter where or what he studied, as Jonathan was being groomed by his father to take over the family firm from birth. He worked briefly as a reporter and sub-editor in Glasgow before joining the Harmsworths' local paper interests in the Home Counties. When his father passed away in 1998, he had already risen to be managing director of the *Evening Standard*. Unlike his dad, this incarnation of Viscount Rothermere could hardly have inherited a healthier ship and, at thirty, Jonathan was exactly the same age as his great-grand-uncle[5] Alfred when he'd founded the *Daily Mail*.

This is not the only similarity between the two Harmsworths born 100 years apart . . . Jonathan also sired a son to a girl who was employed to help his mother, just like Sunny had with his mother's nurse Louisa Jane in 1882. Bubbles had an assistant, a girl from New Zealand who – according to the *Daily Express* – was not particularly impressed by the viscountess's lofty title. 'Bubbles was a big woman and always complained about having sore legs and sore calves,' another Rothermere employee told the paper. 'They made her life a pain and everyone would sympathize and make her feel like a patient but when she asked this girl what to do the response was: "Go on a diet."[6]

Lady Rothermere, who died in 1992 after an accidental overdose of sleeping pills, liked this no-nonsense approach from the Kiwi girl and so did her son. The pair are said to have fallen for each other during a road trip across the USA and then moved into an apartment together in North Carolina while Jonathan studied at Duke in the mid-1980s. Then, after two years as a couple, she fell pregnant and returned to New Zealand – apparently at her own insistence, and they split up. Harmsworth went on to marry Claudia Clemence, the daughter of a property developer, in 1993, and the couple have five children.

Unlike Sunny Harmsworth, however, whose lovechild was a secret to even his closest relatives, all this became public in 2001 shortly after the *Express* newspaper group was acquired by Richard Desmond. Desmond, again like Sunny Harmsworth, is another Hampstead boy who began with magazines . . . though not quite the same 'useless information' that got the Harmsworths started. Desmond's organs were of the type men held firmly in one hand, titles such as *Asian Babes*, *Big Ones International* and *Horny Housewives*. Celebrity pap, though, was where the real money was, and Desmond launched *OK!*, a rival to the 'aren't you wonderful' gushings on sale in Spanish-born *Hello!*

Paul Dacre is apt to use the 'P' word – pornographer – whenever Desmond's name pops up in conversation or, indeed, in his paper; in which another outraged former *Express* reporter and top Mailman, Geoffrey Levy, described Desmond as 'the People's Pornographer' when the *Express* sale to Desmond went through.[7] It was also, for Paul Dacre, another P word – personal: his dad spent most of his working life on the *Sunday Express* and Dacre himself, of course, got his first job straight from university on the *Daily Express*.

'I'm not going to mince my words,' Dacre told his old student newspaper. 'I thought it was a very sad day for Fleet Street when a pornographer was allowed to buy a once-great national newspaper.'[8] Adding in another interview: 'As long as I've got energy in my body, I'm going to devote everything to try to see him off.'[9]

Desmond, who happens to be Jewish, doesn't much like being referred to as a pornographer and he responded in kind in the pages of his *Express* by taunting the *Mail* over the first Rothermere's Fascism. His papers also began to expose the personal life of Jonathan Harmsworth, the fourth Rothermere, on the grounds that Dacre's moralizing *Mail* preached the kind of 'family values' that its proprietor had seemingly failed to live up to. This was Blair's Britain, though, not Victorian London, and there has never been any suggestion that Jonathan Harmsworth denied his son or behaved dishonourably in any way. It is simply a fact of life that children are sometimes born out of wedlock and parental relationships break down. Indeed, Harmsworth stated clearly with regard to the Desmond spat that he 'wasn't that offended by it'.

> He [Desmond] seemed to think the fact that I have
> an illegitimate son is of some concern. In fact, my
> son . . . I'm very proud of my son, he's a member of my
> family, we go on holiday together and my children are
> very proud to call him their brother, so I don't make a
> secret of it and frankly the idea that I'm offended by it is
> slightly offensive.[10]

It all got slightly ridiculous when the *Mail*'s chief executive at the time, Murdoch MacLennan, stepped in to try and negotiate a cease-fire that never held. 'I think the proof is in the pudding, so to speak,' Rothermere said at the Leveson inquiry. 'The *Express* continued to attack me.'[11] From the same stand, Desmond had also described the *Daily Mail*'s editor as the 'fat butcher', adding 'only two weeks ago Dacre vilified me in his horrible rag'.[12]

This was all great sport for the neutral observer and media commentators, though it's doubtful many *Mail* or *Express* readers cared much about all this out in Middle England. And Viscount Rothermere certainly doesn't reside in Middle England; Rothermere technically isn't – for tax purposes – even English. He's 'French', just like his father. Great-grandfather Bunny Harmsworth was the master of numbers and he set the tone for – quite legally – paying as little tax as possible by creating trusts and offshore companies to actually hold the firm. The *Daily Mail* now belongs, effectively, to a company in Bermuda called Rothermere Continuation Ltd, and Vere bequeathed to his son not just the title 'Viscount Rothermere' – he also passed down his non-domiciled 'tax genetics'.[13] Thankfully for all the world's Mailmen, unlike Great-grandpa Bunny and Grandfather Esmond, Jonathan Harmsworth *does* genuinely share Northcliffe's and his father's deep love for the *Daily Mail* newspaper. Though he's not in his office on the sixth floor of Northcliffe House every day.

Former Mailman 'Terry' has been invited up there by his Lordship on several occasions. 'He has this office with very, very thick carpet, it's like walking on jelly up there,' he told the author. 'It's just so incredibly anachronistic. This idea of the super powerful press baron at the top of the office with very thick carpets and old-fashioned furniture and "seven" secretaries and everything. It's . . . you almost wanna give him a smack like – "wake up and smell the mustard". This is not how the world is. My view is that Jonathan enjoys the pomp and circumstance. And that he's too weak a character to make any change to it. He's not a radical, he's a very conventional thinker. I mean, conventional to the point of, well – being a bit thick. That's what a lot of people think.'[14]

They used to say the same thing about his father, 'mere Vere', and, anyway, downstairs on the *Daily Mail* editorial floor there can be but one ruler, and editor-in-chief Paul Dacre is an intelligent man – and he is as loyal to young Jonathan as he and Sir David had been to Vere. Dacre is the man who makes the *Mail*, not Rothermere. And the Associated Newspapers editor-in-chief works damn hard for his Harmsworth masters – he certainly puts in the hours down below in *Daily Mail* HQ.

Associated Newspapers left Fleet Street at the end of the 1980s for a building that was purpose-built as a department store after the Second World War and, though it was never quite in the league of Harrods up the road, Barkers was Kensington's answer to Debenhams or C&A: a place where the middle classes went shopping for everything from a pair of socks to bedlinen or a nice new coat. In the late 1960s,[15] women would peruse the store's wares on the third-floor aisles, shuffling through rack after rack of nylon slips and wedding gowns, Scottish tweeds, and wool dresses, ladies' Burberrys and Aquascutum coats . . . and it all somehow seems rather apt that this is now the editorial engine room that propels the 'female-friendly' *Daily Mail* machine forward.

Every weekday morning Paul Dacre's chauffeur glides a large company car down into the basement car park under that old store – now called Northcliffe House and also home to a Whole Foods Market – and drops him off by the lift. The *Mail*'s editor-in-chief pushes the button and emerges upstairs on to the *Daily Mail* editorial floor carrying his red 'Cabinet minister' style briefcase, then strides on down the 'corridor of power' (or the 'boulevard of broken dreams' as it is also called by some older hands) and into his office while his senior staff fidget at their desks fixing their lists.

It is inside various meetings – or conferences, as they're called – that 'prudish and prickly' Paul Dacre forms the next day's *Daily Mail* around his, and his top team's, worldview (and it's entirely plausible that this was, in fact, the exact same spot by the window where 1960s women shuffled through racks of knickers, tights and sexy stockings).

Up until about 11.30 or so each morning the senior staff sit out on the editorial floor anxiously awaiting a secretary's voice over the Tannoy calling the first conference of the day. 'You could always tell what sort of a mood Dacre was in by how agitated and stressed Lesley, his PA, sounded,' said 'Mo', who spent many years shuffling into the editor's office in answer to that call. 'Dacre takes all conferences from behind his very large oak desk in his huge office. It's very plush and chintzy, a bit like a hotel room. Posh, thick beige carpet, curtains, flat screen telly, lots of sofas. A big bookcase. Pictures of country scenes on the walls. He guzzles cups of tea and pops various pills throughout but he doesn't even have a computer in there and he doesn't know how to work the system. Stories are printed out for him to read, on paper.'[16] After an initial meeting of senior editors, the news editor and picture editor join in and the meeting 'usually descends into Dacre having a go at the news editor for all the stories he thinks the paper missed or didn't cover well'.[17]

'Paul has very few ideas himself but surrounds himself with loads of people who do at pre-conference,' former senior MailMan 'Sean' told the author. 'And he always envies things in other papers which the *Mail* doesn't have so those might become ideas too. He listens to the [BBC Radio 4] *Today* programme and watches the BBC at 6 p.m. He has very few contacts. The Prime Minister Gordon Brown used to provide stories. Iain Duncan Smith still does. But he went through a spell of refusing to even take David Cameron's phone calls.

'Paul, and he got this from Sir David, they both saw themselves as being completely across the waterfront – and that was one of the challenges of any exec there – the paper had to have all the fun and the froth of *The Sun* and all the serious stuff that was in *The Times* and all the sex and smut and aristo stuff that was in the *Telegraph*. It was never enough to just say we out-Sunned *The Sun* today or [that] we've beaten the *Telegraph*. Paul and Sir David saw themselves as being in competition with the entire print network which meant that it was very hard to win every day because you can't beat everybody every day. It's quite unforgiving from that point of view. There was always something to bite an exec on the backside.'[18]

For those on the *Mail* staff not in love with life under artificial light, being shut away for hour after excruciating hour in Dacre's bunker can be torture: 'Half the day is taken up with endless conferences,' 'Mo' added, 'one after another from 11.30 until about 2 p.m. It's the bane of every section head's life and the reason why everything runs so late and the working hours there are so insane. He bangs the desk a lot and swears. Oddly though he rarely swears – directly – at women. He'll swear in their presence and while he'd call the features editor (male) a "cunt" he would never call the *Femail* or books editors – women – one. And he does get very angry. He does this weird thing where he throws himself back on his chair. One time he lost his balance and fell right over, landing on his back!'[19]

The representatives sent from some departments are more welcome than others, with showbiz being the lowest life form, explained 'Robin': 'You'd walk in there and be treated like some sort of bimbo who's got all this fluffy meaningless news. It's a weird one because it's massively important to the *Daily Mail* package but it gets no respect.'[20] Sport has long been a massive draw, with many men, in particular, buying the paper solely for its football coverage, which David English thought was massively important from when the paper first went tabloid. But in-depth debates about the political climate of the day or the big news story or some celebrity's cellulite would require little input from the sport department, despite the section head having to sit through it. Paul Dacre, although he's been known to take in the occasional international game of rugby, is not a massive sport fan. 'Sport always came last in conference,' former head of sport Bryan Cooney told the author. 'And it was a poor last because it was considered like the comics, you know – the games show. One day, I didn't have time for all this haranguing and questioning. So I took a double-page spread in with me and I utilized my time by not listening to what was going on – because I knew I was last – and I started drawing up the spread I had in mind. And every time I looked up, Dacre was watching me. I could see it. So, right at the end when he said "Sport!" and I began my spiel he said: "Oh, uh, would it help you if we moved sport forward to first on the agenda?" And I said: "Immeasurably." He said: "Right." So thereafter sport became the first thing on the agenda.' As soon as he'd gone through his list, Cooney would dash for freedom.[21]

Unfortunately for 'George', a conference regular, he always had to stay until the end. 'I have developed my own theory about Paul Dacre over the years, and that's that he is very much this shy and awkward, slightly scared chap who has built this weird fucking feudal court around himself to make himself feel more secure in the world, you know? And he really is the Absolute Ruler. I'd watch him sitting behind this huge desk in conference, harrumphing at the news list, with all these weird courtiers trying to win points, it seemed to me. Screeching away about "Alan Rubbisher" [Alan Rusbridger, then editor of the *Guardian*] and anything mildly liberal. Year after year, on and fucking on it went. They were utterly obsessed with the bloody *Guardian*, it defines exactly what they do *not* want their *Daily Mail* to be. Dacre would grumble away himself under his breath about "Polly fucking Toynbee" [the *Guardian* writer] as he marched to the lift. Everything Dacre learned about the world outside, it seemed to me, came from these courtiers. The more rabid loons in conference would just whisk Dacre up into a frenzy, and convince him there were hordes of Romanian refugees marching up High Street Ken – which Dacre could well believe, because he barely left his fucking office. The Stephen Lawrence story was one of those very rare exceptions where he actually met a member of the public – a plasterer working on his home!'[22]

Some *Daily Mail* staffers often joked that the Lawrence case came about because Dacre had had a 'near life experience', in the same way another campaign against plastic bags was launched after Dacre was infuriated after seeing one stuck in a tree in the countryside. The obsession with the *Guardian*, say some, is easily explained by the need to have something to rail against in the absence these days of any real mid-market competition, since the demise of the *Daily Express*.

Conference sets a far more fearful tone than it did in English's day, say insiders. 'Paul is not somebody who, for instance, takes public transport,' said former senior MailMan 'Sean'. 'He's not somebody who goes outside of his bubble. You know it's a paper that's sometimes very critical of people inside "media bubbles". But Paul was completely in a media bubble of his own.

'It always amused me that, you know, his shoe leather never wore out. Because every day he was on a carpet in the office; he strode out the door and was in a car which deposited him either at home or a restaurant. But it was not like he ever crunched gravel anywhere. He never did any shopping. He would be horrified at what modern Britain had become but he was never part of it. And [he] travelled most of the time in his car – with the doors locked! On one occasion, the conversation in conference turned to cash machines and Dacre didn't know what an ATM machine was. It occurred to me that this is somebody that is quite sheltered,'[23] he added.

One particular couple were discussed frequently in conference for years: Tony and Cherie Blair. Dacre didn't seem to like them at all; he never really trusted Blair. A Northcliffe House story, shared by many, was that Dacre had taken offence one day when Cherie had openly breastfed their new son Leo at a *Daily Mail* summit on the sixth floor as the country geared up for the general election in 2001, which the Prime Minister won. After the election, the *Daily Mail* front page simply declared: 'He's Back. Disaster for the Tories as Blair powers to historic second term but the real winner is . . . apathy.'[24]

Domestic politics, though, soon fell away when the global political landscape totally changed one Tuesday afternoon in 2001 – September the 11th. The day started off the same as any other day in the *Daily Mail* newsroom, the endless conferences were almost over and the machine was in motion for the construction of the next day's paper . . . until the first World Trade Center tower was struck at just before 2 p.m. London time. Any decisions taken about the next day's paper were ripped apart for a special edition with thirty-two pages of coverage of the 9/11 attacks.

'On September 11th 2001, I saw Dacre on the floor the most he ever had been' in the daytime, senior reporter 'Cyn' told the author. 'That same night I saw him quite stressed laying out the paper and he was annoyed at Jon Steafel [the paper's news chief, who later became deputy editor before falling out of favour] for some reason. I was nearby and I heard him say to Steafel: "Don't disobey me!" And I thought at the time "disobey" was a rather patriarchal word to use.'[25]

The *Mail*'s coverage began with a stark and hugely effective front-page photograph of a vast cloud of dust where the twin towers of the World Trade Center had once been. It was a front page reminiscent of the iconic *Daily Mail* edition during the Blitz that had captured St Paul's standing tall against the Nazi firestorm, except this time the iconic structures were no more. 'APOCALYPSE, New York, September 11, 2001.'[26]

'The nightmare is beyond exaggeration,' the paper said in its Comment column. 'Yesterday, September 11, 2001, is a date which will live in infamy as surely as the day Japan attacked Pearl Harbor . . . And nobody – not the Afghan Taliban, Saddam Hussein, Muammar Gaddafi or any other instigator of terrorism – can hope to escape retaliation, once culpability has been established. That said, this is a time for cool heads.'[27]

On page eight, the British Prime Minister's position was clear from the start: '"This is our battle too," pledges Blair.'[28] Military action against Osama bin Laden and Al Qaeda soon followed in Afghanistan, but then, less than eighteen months later, the focus had shifted to Iraq and Saddam Hussein's suspected cache of weapons of mass destruction.

Dacre's peers admired his paper during this period, and his *Daily Mail* won National Newspaper of the Year at the British Press Awards in 2000 and again in 2002. Dacre's tenth year in the top chair was also marked with a personal accolade when he was handed the Media Society Award for the individual or organization judged to have made 'the most outstanding contribution to the media'. The fifty-three-year-old supreme *Mail* being was, by then, already the longest-serving editor in 'Fleet Street'.

'It's been ten exhilarating years,' he told his paper, 'and I am honoured to receive this award, not only on my own behalf but also on behalf of all the brilliant and dedicated journalists who devote themselves to the *Mail*.'[29]

Unfortunately for those 'dedicated journalists', the accolades meant that they were in for a tougher time than ever. Dacre loathed any kind of complacency and the worst time for executives was often directly after the paper won an award. 'There was never a question of you walking in and being told that was a great story or that was a great paper,' former senior Mailman 'Sean' told the author. 'Any praise was very cursory. He didn't hand out praise at all, actually. Almost never. It wasn't a happy clappy place to work because, from the very top, he saw himself as the enemy of anything that indicated that you were resting on your laurels. It's fair to say that Paul took that on from Sir David who had been very much like that too.'[30]

By this point Tony Blair and the *Daily Mail* were not exactly friends, partly because Dacre thought Blair was unpicking some of Thatcher's reforms and also because his Government had waved through Richard Desmond's purchase of the *Express* newspapers. But mainly because Dacre simply didn't trust the man and loathed his PR advisers, led by chief 'spin-doctor' and former *Daily Mirror* journalist Alastair Campbell. As Dacre told the *British Journalism Review* that year in an interview marking his first decade in the job:

> I think he [Blair] is a chameleon who believes what he
> said to the last person he talked to . . . Now, I don't have a
> good relationship with him, although I get messages from
> senior ministers every other day with a view to seeing
> if there is any common ground we can discuss . . . I'm
> afraid I feel rather strongly that we have a Government
> that is manipulative, dictatorial and slightly corrupt. No.
> 10, in particular, cannot stand dissent. It has broken the
> second chamber, weakened the Civil Service and sidelined
> Parliament.[31]

The circulation figures for January 2003 were to be Paul Dacre's all-time high at over 2.5 million. By the spring of that year, the paper said, Britain was 'Stumbling along the road to war'.

> That America and Britain will win the shooting war
> against Iraq is beyond doubt. But just as certainly, they
> are losing the propaganda war. Indeed, the closer military
> action looms the less convincingly warranted it seems.
> And the more ethically dubious the case that Mr Blair
> puts for it appears.[32]

The bombs fell on Baghdad and only two years later Tony Blair won his third general election. The *Mail* had been urging its readers to give Blair 'a bloody nose' and had published a definitive guide to tactical voting the day before the polls opened.

Paul Dacre would surely insist that his *Daily Mail* is not a tabloid newspaper in the red-top sense of the word: it's not the *Daily Star, The Sun* or the *Daily Mirror*. Yet, on polling day itself, the only mention of the election on the front page was an election day sweepstake kit . . . Seven years after the deaths of Sir David English and Lord Rothermere, the paper looked as though it indeed was becoming the slovenly tabloid they had feared it would.

'Yes You Did Give Him A Bloody Nose! Blair had paid a heavy price for his lies over Iraq last night as a voter backlash devastated his Commons majority,' the paper said when the results came in.[33]

Blair's majority was slashed but he was back in Downing Street for a historic third term; yet the paper was already considering the Prime Minister's future on its front page by asking 'How Long Can He Go On?'[34] Which was exactly what many inside the *Daily Mail* were wondering too about their editor-in-chief. There seemed to be no stopping the man.

After his office emptied following his conferences, the absolute ruler had time to sit back in his big room for big ideas, but some Mailmen speculated that, on occasion, he might kick off his sensible shoes and have a cheeky little power nap on a sofa; he still had, after all, a very long day ahead of him. But some busy executives found themselves in a bit of a bind when they strolled down the 'corridor of power' to his office and had to work out whether or not to enter the boss's lair: busy people with lots to do, they didn't want to take a number and sit and read a magazine.

'It can be a dilemma,' said Mailman 'Mike', 'if the door is shut, you come back later. If it's open – knock, and in you go. But if it's ajar? One day it was ajar and I just thought "fuck it, I'm busy" and I knocked and sallied forth clutching some papers. Dacre used to park his briefcase behind his chair in the corner and he'd been brushing his hair with this huge fucking brush – he almost needed two hands to wield the fucking thing, it was like a bloody broadsword. And he just about fell off the chair in a scramble to get it back in his case before I saw it. He had rapidly receding hair and I remember thinking to myself, "Christ, Paul, you don't need that fucking thing to deal with what you've got there on top". . . and he wouldn't have liked that.'[35]

Most of Paul Dacre's life since 1992 has been spent in this office, fourteen to eighteen hours most weekdays. Though his holidays have got longer over the years, most of his waking hours have been dedicated to the *Daily Mail* cause. That's something like a dozen years solid if added together into one sleepless shift spent – up to the time of writing, he's still going strong – mostly in one room; though it be a comfortable room. Papillon didn't do that kind of time. Yet Dacre does expect others to work similar kinds of hours. 'He wanted people to work twenty-four hours a day,' said former feature writer Jane Kelly (who later fell out with Dacre). 'He'd grind people down. He's even worked at Christmas, he wanted people in on Christmas Day and Boxing Day, New Year, New Year's Day. One guy came in on Boxing Day and the editor was there and he said, "Why have you been out for lunch?" Even on Boxing Day! And they had a big argument and this chap left, in the end.'[36]

The intense work rate he holds himself to has, though, had an impact on his health. In 2003 Dacre spent several months off work due to a heart problem and was even too ill to go to his own father's funeral service at the journalists' church, St Bride's. Dacre senior's friend and former *Express* colleague David Eliades did, however, attend. 'Paul's wife Kathy was there and she said he couldn't go because he was in hospital with some sort of heart trouble, heart murmurs – some kind of heart disturbance. He was working eighteen-hour days in those days and I think he probably still is. I asked Kathy, "Are you gonna stop him working these hours?" And she said: "He won't do those hours again, I'll tell you!" But he does and he's been doing it for a long time now. I don't think he has an awful lot of anything else in his life really. Whereas David English did, for instance – David liked jazz, we had mutual friends who were jazz musicians.'[37]

It seems nothing much changed for Dacre when he returned from his stint on the sick. He just went back into his big office and sat at his big desk. 'He usually eats lunch there too,' said 'Mo', 'made

for him by an in-house butler service and served on silver platters . . .
He tries to eat more healthily since his heart surgery and eats these
fruit kebabs every lunch time.'[38]

For a while, Dacre did actually go outside and take in some fresh
air at a little square garden around the back of *Daily Mail* HQ.
'There was a regime,' said former senior *Mail* executive 'Gavin', 'that
we called the Lunch Walk which I think was as a result of doctor's
orders. But it was a very, very solitary walk. I saw it take place a few
times, it was more like a march with Dacre not engaging with anyone
or anything. But, of course, that all fits, doesn't it? You don't want
to go outside if the place where you have meaning is in the *Daily
Mail*; you really don't want to go out of that because you lose your
meaning. And it certainly indicates that there wasn't a great deal of
inner confidence there, you know; the ability to just be ordinary and
disappear in a crowd.

'It's funny though because it does become very addictive, working
at the *Daily Mail*. To feel that it all really – *really* – matters. I think
a lot of people get a sense of meaning from working at the *Mail*,
the importance [with] which everything is invested every day; you're
grappling with things, fighting with people. It's a kind of corporate
madness, I think. And people do sometimes find it quite hard when
they leave the *Mail* and enter a world which is much more boring,
and balanced and you realize that nothing matters that much . . . And
you don't actually matter that much either.'[39]

After conference the bosses of each department stride down the
'corridor of power' and out on to the editorial floor, and back to their
seats, where they begin forming a newspaper in the image sketched
out in the air over that rather large desk by their absolute ruler. These
top Mailmen are usually, but by no means always, the true believers
in the *Daily Mail* cause and they generally do similar hours to
Dacre in the ruthless pursuit of the paper's goals.

Mailmen and Femails may have had to be 'first on the story and
the last to leave',[40] but often stories that hacks were already working
on outdoors were swiftly killed or seriously wounded in conference

and fresh ideas had to be pursued. Some executives, especially anyone who had received a bit of a roasting over Dacre's desk, would arrive back in the newsroom 'totally wired, pale and manic'.[41]

'So, these editors would emerge blinking into the light post-conference,' added 'Penny', who'd generally be out on the road by this point, 'and you'd get this call with some story idea that has suddenly become *the* most important thing on planet earth. But it can be three o'clock before you actually receive it because they spend so much fucking time gassing in conference that the message doesn't actually get transmitted for ages.'

'As a junior, on the road, it could be very, very tough,' she added. 'But it then actually got to be very easy because the *Mail*'s angles are so narrow. It was a formula; we lived in a very clean and clear, black and white "1950s" idyllic world. You loved these people for your paper, or you loathed them. Just flick the switch. It was nothing personal. And once you grasped that kind of logic, life did get much easier in terms of the reaction to what you filed. But, of course, we all know the world is not really like that; we live in it too. Well, at least . . . some of us do!'[42]

Paul Dacre has always had a firm grasp on British politics but his abiding interest is not in the fleeting nitty-gritty 'news of the day', say many who have worked directly for him over many years; he remains a features man at heart. That said, he often whips his news desk the hardest. 'The news editor's job on the *Daily Mail* is probably the toughest job in Fleet Street,' former *Mail* executive 'Sean' told the author. 'This bloke has to go into conference with thirty or so stories on his news list but Dacre would ask very detailed questions about any one of them, and he had to know the answers and be able to explain those stories succinctly to someone with a very short attention span. Heaven forbid if he lacked knowledge or underplayed or overplayed a story. The editor would be very quick to spot that. He had to talk equally knowledgeably about everything from a health story in the *British Medical Journal* to what had come from the eleven o'clock Downing Street briefing to some human story involving a horse in the West Country. The only way to answer those questions was to brief himself thoroughly on absolutely everything. It's a damn tough job.'[43]

Perhaps the toughest news editor of Dacre's reign was Tony Gallagher (now editor-in-chief of *The Sun*), who'd worked for the paper in New York and was brought back initially as deputy news editor – just like Dacre. Gallagher ran the news department from the end of the 1990s through to the mid-2000s and shared his boss's phenomenal work rate as well as lots of US entry stamps in his passport. Unlike Dacre, however, Gallagher was highly rated as a writer and an on-the-road hack.

'Tony Gallagher looked like the fucking grim reaper to me,' said 'Robin'. 'I always thought of him as like this figure of death, he always looked so pale and so withered, you know, like a villain in a fantasy movie, a *Lord of the Rings* kind of villain. He seemed to aspire to that kind of B movie culture, you know, "the news editor who never sleeps".'[44]

Gallagher put the fear of the devil into his reporters and was the polar opposite of Tim Miles, who had been a news editor capable of quickly forgiving a reporter who had tried but failed. Gallagher, say his staff, was murderously tough on them. He would rise early and read the final editions of the newspapers at home before going for a run. He'd arrive well before 9 a.m., eat a packed lunch at his desk – allowing himself precisely fifteen minutes for a coffee in the mid-afternoon – and stay until after 10 p.m. when the first edition was done.

For news reporters, it could actually be tougher when in favour, as the best young operators were sent out on ever-more-important stories and all reporters, being human, eventually fail. 'At the time you are in that world of living to please this machine – a machine that only later you see couldn't actually care less about you,' former reporter 'Cyn' told the author. 'The pace was relentless and exhausting. Utterly. Yet for young, ambitious souls tasting exciting national paper success it was also utterly thrilling. Getting scoops and front-page bylines was such a buzz. But you felt you just had to act invincible and strong to stay at the top, to be admired by the desk. Working on the *Mail* could be a sort of lonely hell.'

Many, but not all, of Gallagher's reporters were utterly terrified of the man and his sackings became legendary. He had little time for some senior hands whom he felt were past their peak, but he was no less brutal with younger hacks – many of whom had quit a comfortable job on a local paper to seek a golden future on 'Fleet Street' yet often had only a tenuous freelance relationship with the *Mail*. Gallagher is said to have told one bright young thing he was 'a low flyer' and another that he 'wasn't bashing doors down for the *Daily Mail*'. 'Young reporters were taken into Gallagher's bunker and fired,' 'Cyn' told the author. 'But instead of letting them go gently with maybe a positive "look this a tough place and maybe it's just not for you, you just need more experience" or whatever, he would tear them to pieces. One guy, who was such a lovely gentle giant, was so upset by being roasted by Tony on his last day – next morning after being sacked – he was literally sick on the desk. I felt so sorry for him. And, okay, he clearly wasn't tough enough for the *Daily Mail* but he didn't deserve that.'[45]

'I was bollocked regularly by Gallagher,' sighed 'Ray'. 'And I always remember the time that a good friend wrote a really good scoop, and I said to him, "Wow, well done, mate! Did anybody say anything about that great story?" And his answer was [that the news desk had said] "You got anything decent for us today or are you a one-hit wonder? Oh, and tuck your shirt in." It was a weird fucking place to work, the *Daily Mail* – I'd worked on other national newspapers and there, if you did a good job or came up with a good story you'd be rewarded with a nice lunch or something. It could be friendly. You could get bollocked occasionally too, of course, but there was definitely a carrot and stick kind of culture. At the *Mail* there was no carrot. There was either stick or absence of stick. Any day where you got no stick was a good day. I remember two girls, news reporters – there was a corner where the big machines to print off all the bits of paper were, and they were sitting behind the printers just sobbing and sobbing after being publicly dressed down – one by Gallagher and the other by his deputy Chris Evans.'[46]

In Gallagher's defence though, most of the youngsters that were let go were actually coming to the end of a short-term contract that was not being renewed rather than being ritually dismissed, and he didn't shirk from delivering the bad news himself. Other *Mail* department heads, over the years, have simply left this unpleasant task to the managing editor's office.

Even a brief stint as a *Mail* hack looks good on a CV; many who failed to make it at the *Daily Mail* have gone on to have very successful careers elsewhere. 'The *Daily Mail* remains the best newsroom in Britain and reporters who can work there can work anywhere,' former senior hand 'Sean' added. 'But it is true that it is a tough, tough place to work. It is. Only the best thrive there and if a reporter was not good enough they'd get found out very quickly. It's a hard place to work and not everybody makes it. Fleet Street is littered with people who didn't quite make it on the *Daily Mail* but went on and prospered elsewhere.'[47]

The trouble with news is that most of it cannot be controlled; a handle can be developed upon political news for which there are fixed points of reference, such as Prime Minister's Questions, policy announcements, scheduled debates and elections every four or five years. Some preparation can be done for events, anniversaries and big court cases and the like, for which background studies can be meticulously constructed and published when the case begins or ends. Aside from stunts and campaigns, news is generally reactive not proactive. Shit, as they say, happens.

Features and comment, on the other hand, *can* be controlled; a tone can be set and the editor's voice can most certainly ring through – the overlord can colour in the paper's heroes and 'punish' in print the paper's villains.

Space is at a premium on any newspaper, as there are only so many stories that can fit upon a page – so the competition between departments on the *Daily Mail* for that precious space is fierce. And of all the departments under Paul Dacre's ultimate command, *Femail* – and the paper's features aimed at females – is perhaps that which is most woven into the paper's very DNA. But that doesn't mean it gets any respect from other departments.

'There was total and utter disdain for the people who work on *Femail*, and did all the featurey stuff,' 'Ray', a former Mailman on the news desk, told the author. 'It was one of those weird battles. Yet the fact is that *Femail* is often responsible for people actually buying the paper and when those "water cooler" pieces were given prominent space in the paper, then you could guarantee – you could absolutely guarantee – that the people who ran the news desk would be in a foul, foul mood and all their staff would be in for a rough time.'[48]

The *Femail* department was physically removed in an annexe from the main newsroom, beyond a set of double doors – Femails seemed to enjoy just a little more light and air, away from the heat and smoke of the main *Mail* machinery. Other editorial staffers would watch those Femails go – male and female – as they strolled on through those rose-petalled doors, grumbling that what went on down there was just a load of old pap.

'We were sheltered from some of the bigger thunderstorms but we felt the kind of trickle down,' said long-term Femail 'Penny'. 'But *Femail* is where a lot of the main pressure of the paper is because, in a way, *Femail* kind of *is* the *Daily Mail*; those features are the paper's beating heart.'[49]

Another long-term Femail, who was respected by Dacre, was celebrated (behind her back) for the 'coffee and croissants' chats she would have with prospective *Femail* employees. Ahead of joining team *Femail* from outside, many a young reporter over the years – if they didn't already know someone who actually worked there – was persuaded by an image of a jolly workplace where staff all lounged around chatting and coming up with ideas in a healthy working environment in which one's opinions and ideas were always listened to, valued and discussed with respect. The executive would trill like a chatty hairdresser in a West London salon, telling these youngsters: 'Oh, you know in the morning, it's really nice. We sit around the desk with coffee and croissants chatting about the stories of the day.'[50]

'Elsa' worked for several hacks at *Femail*, but this woman is the only one who still gives her cold sweats. 'I used to see it, over the years – time and time again – people would arrive into this silent, stressful zone of the commissioning desk,' she giggled. 'Total silence and stress. And you could see them thinking, "Err, where? Where's? Where's the coffee and croissants?" They'd arrive into this kind of fucking Mordor-type place . . . and "coffee and croissants" became this shorthand for the space between life on the outside, and life on the inside.'[51]

Staff in other departments may well have thought those Femails were having an easy ride writing their fluffy features but it was, possibly, the toughest place of all to work.

'All these stories must appear as if by magic for the editor,' added 'Penny'. 'But he's not a stupid man, and he even ran these departments himself back in the day. The *Femail* chief was great at saying,"That's fine, I'll make it happen" – but of course, she didn't. It was us plebs that made it happen. She was ferociously hard. She was quite a nice person personally, but she was fucking ruthless. She had to be though. It's incredibly masculine at the top of the *Mail*.'[52]

That male control over the *Daily Mail* – a newspaper aimed specifically at women – took an interesting twist over marital breakdown with a piece written by a female lawyer at the start of the brand-new millennium: 'Divorce: Why we women are to blame – Britain's leading female divorce lawyer argues it is the aggression of her own sex that's responsible for soaring rates of marital failure.'

> Twenty years as a divorce lawyer have finally led me to the disturbing conclusion that in most cases it is women and women alone who are responsible for the dissatisfaction in so many relationships.[53]

'Women and *women alone*' is certainly an interesting take, and any husband caught in bed with his secretary would surely get an interesting reaction if he reached under the pillow and handed it to his furious wife.

'As for the women thing,' former senior Femail 'Elsa' groaned, 'they have such a complex attitude – I think Dacre must have mother issues or something; there is nothing but nothing they like more than a woman turning on other women. Basically their dream headline would be "Why I, as a career woman, am ashamed of my choices and envy my stay-at-home-mum sister because my career has given me cancer" – they have sort of done that, already: a hardy perennial is pitting two sisters against each other – one a stay-at-home-mum, the other a "career woman" with the headline: "Who do YOU think is happiest?" Guess what the outcome always is!'[54]

That 'divorce is caused by women' story made it into the paper, but the vast majority of *Femail* ideas don't survive conference. Long lists of commissioned stories for *Femail* – and other features in the paper aimed at female readers – would be laid before the editor but only about one in eight ever made it into the paper (and many would already have been commissioned and paid for from freelancers); the bar for a *Femail* kind of story has always been especially high, whether or not it is actually written by a writer working for *Femail* or one working for features – some staffers say there is no real difference between the two departments, though features like to consider themselves somehow 'more profound'.

Celebrities are sifted and selected by his Femails to have their personal lives examined by 'Dr' Dacre right there on his office desk like some kind of outraged gynaecologist, examining Middle England's moral malaise – analysing their late-night partying, their love lives and their cellulite: there tends, say some who were there, to be a core handful of famous names that get shuffled on and off Dacre's operating table every few months – or years – as their careers rise and fade. It is, in a way, a compliment if their name survives long enough on that list to actually be turned into a story in the paper. If they were deemed of little interest, Middle Englanders would never read about these people – not in the *Daily Mail* newspaper (the *MailOnline* bar for what constitutes 'a celebrity', on the other hand, is millimetres high – space, of course, is not at such a premium on the web). Dacre gave his diagnoses, and the *Femail* and features editors would scurry back to their desks elbowing each other on the way as they clutched the remains of what made it through conference.

The names would change but the knife strokes would remain pretty much the same. 'You have to understand,' said former Femail 'Jo', 'it can be very subtle. You didn't actually have to be told anything but then it'd be "The *Daily Mail* Hatchet Job". Basically, and I'm not joking, you'd actually just get a piece of paper sometimes. A writer would go to the toilet and come back and there'd be a cutting about Patsy Kensit or somebody . . . there was a certain group that they were obsessed with for a while, Patsy Kensit was one of them, Zoe Ball too, after she had her affair – and there'd just be a cutting on your desk and you would know you had to pull together something for Saturday, and it was always laced with a degree of misogyny. And you just had to – you didn't need instruction, that's the thing – you just knew what they wanted, this slight pulling apart of someone's life.'[55]

Patsy Kensit's life was a fascination for *Femail* for many years, especially after she married Oasis frontman Liam Gallagher. Her tabloid life can literally be laid out in *Daily Mail* headlines: from 'Life with the Oasis stars: Cocaine binges, all-night parties, porn and infidelity',[56] and 'The egos, drugs and drink that killed Patsy's marriage',[57] to 'Maneater Patsy meets her match, as TV football pundit Ally McCoist turns his back on their affair, how the predatory Miss Kensit gambled and lost',[58] and on to 'From Man-Eater To Matron . . . No longer pursued by men, no more the toast of the town, even TV roles are drying up for Patsy, single mum and very much alone.'[59] These Patsy headlines may read like vindictive character assassination but it was rarely ever anything personal for the Femails who actually wrote these pieces.

It did, though, eventually get to be too much for Femail 'Jo', after several years spent running a scalpel up and down the lives of the rich and famous. She quit altogether. 'In the end, I just couldn't do it any more,' she told the author. 'But there was always a degree of distance for me. I like to think I never wrote anything that I felt was horrifically unfair, I guess you can argue that it's all a question of degrees. I think the only way I could do it was to retain a degree of neutrality – actually, you could argue this is worse – but it was very much "press button A". It was a formula. You just needed a couple of pieces of new information, a couple of fresh quotes and the rest was a bit of a cuts job [old stories kept in a file in the paper's library] laced through with this sort of *Daily Mail* style. I didn't whip myself up, I would remain completely neutral – you just knew what was expected – and it was like assembling the pieces on a production line. And then sort of knit it all together, and sprinkle a bit of *Daily Mail* magic dust over the whole thing.

'So, it was never a visceral "let's get them!" thing – not for me. But that's what's utterly fascinating about it. If you were a success at it – you didn't really need to be briefed or told anything. You just knew, as I say, just from a cutting being dropped on your desk and you'd be "right then, that's my project for the week, is it?"'[60]

Sometimes a Mailman or Femail would be in the dangerous position of actually meeting the famous target and finding they really liked them and, being human, that fact could filter into the words filed into the machine – a dangerous career move at the *Daily Mail*. One time 'Elsa' was told to interview a celebrity who had been paid to speak to the paper – these payments would give a writer permission, some staffers say, to have 'a more intimate go'.

'The trouble is, when you're the person actually writing this stuff up, once you have spent any amount of time with most human beings – unless they are, literally, a psychopath – most people are really quite nice. There are very, very few complete wankers – out in the real world, there's not that many utterly dreadful people. So, I came back from interviewing this lovely person and I injected the correct notes of cynicism into the piece but I hadn't wielded the axe, you know. I was very fair and warm to them. And I remember my editor coming over and saying, "This just isn't working, it isn't strong enough." And I found myself defending them, and the boss just said, "If you like these people, you're working in the wrong fucking place," and walked away.'[61]

Another *Femail* 'favourite' whose life has been splayed out in headlines on his big desk for almost as long as Paul Dacre has been the *Mail*'s editor is Victoria Beckham, Spice Girl and spouse to former England football captain David Beckham. Posh had craved attention after watching the American TV series *Fame* as a seven-year-old, but that little girl could not have realized that the price would be headlines such as 'Last night Victoria Beckham looked painfully thin in another tiny dress. Today, *Femail* asks . . . What IS wrong with Posh?'[62] The piece goes on to quote an anorexia expert, two mothers, a doctor and even includes 'the man's view', by chubby and bespectacled future parliamentary sketch writer Quentin Letts, who thought Posh looked like a 'scrawny chicken'.[63]

Victoria Beckham didn't kill, maim or even call anyone a 'cunt' in order to attain her fame, yet one attack, in the spring of 2004 after her husband's alleged affair with a PA came to light, would have been more befitting of a serial killer – it wasn't even Posh who was cheating. It was simply an old-fashioned beating in the playground by a school bully from Australia called Amanda Platell, the *Mail*'s columnist and former Tory Party 'spin doctor', who offered her own 'provocative view of why the Sisterhood had no sympathy for Mrs Beckham' under the headline 'Why We Women Hate Posh':

> My first reaction on hearing that David Beckham may have been playing away with his former PA Rebecca Loos was, who could blame the poor soul? And I was not alone . . . When she [Victoria] started dating the brilliant yet shy David Beckham, she was like a spider devouring her mate after sex. She consumed him and then fed off his talent and his fame. She's still doing it, and that gets to the crux of why women hate her . . . As a female role model, she is past parody; as a model of physical beauty, she is past plastic. Victoria is greedy, grafting and grace-less. Everything about her is fake – the tan, the breasts, the lips, the nails, the hair. The only real thing about Victoria Beckham is her ambition. And that's why women can't stand her, and why we are all siding with David. That girl had it coming. She's as brittle as her acrylic nails and about as Posh, too.[64]

Platell's pasting of Posh was too much even for the most fearsome Femail of all, Lynda Lee-Potter, who reached down into a cloud of pulled hair and broken fingernails to offer poor Posh a hand up off the ground. Lee-Potter was a housewife, not a pugilist, and would, fairly often, even regret what she had written and apologize publicly on her page – she seemed to know, mostly, where the line was. As well she should of course – she had helped draw it in the first place.

> Victoria Beckham has had a humiliating and devastating time, but in public she's never faltered. She's put on an outwardly proud and glossy face, and it's been said that all women hate her, but I certainly don't.[65]

Lynda Lee-Potter was adored by Paul Dacre perhaps even more so than by the man who had created them both, David English.[66] But some outside the *Daily Mail* fence couldn't understand how the nation's deadliest housewife could possibly 'know' all the things that appeared on her page, and disagreed with her flexible opinions on just about everything.

'She drives me barmy,' said journalist and future Foreign Secretary Boris Johnson in 2003, as he sent Lynda tumbling down into *Room 101*, the BBC programme into which interviewees get to banish their pet hates.

> I suppose it's really professional jealousy – she just seems to have fantastic natural insight into her subjects. And I don't understand how she knows quite so much about human relationships – particularly the details of marital relationships.

Her 'brilliant interpolations about peoples' natures' reminded Boris of a massively detailed Victorian-era model of a dinosaur – constructed upon the flimsiest of evidence. 'She has not much to go on, just a fragment of bone or whatever, but she produces this great beast and I don't know how she does it . . . How can she know this stuff about people's private lives? How can she? The answer is that she doesn't,' he bumbled, 'she can't possibly. She doesn't. It's inconceivable that she does. It's bluff, it's bluff.'[67]

The world's first ever Femail herself still bears the scars from Lee-Potter's pen. Shirley Conran had left the *Mail* shortly before it turned tabloid and went on to find fame with a book on how to minimize housework called *Superwoman*, plus a raunchy bestselling novel called *Lace*. Lynda and Shirley had both worked for the *Mail* at the end of the 1960s, and there was bad blood between these women.

'Lynda Lee-Potter was a sort of showbiz writer, an interviewer, when I was on the *Mail*. But she was on features, she wasn't anything to do with me,' Conran told the author. 'Then she trashed me about ten times in her column and kept my ribs in her bottom drawer. She wrote something like "I would rather scrub London airport at dawn than ever work for Shirley Conran again." Well, she never *had* worked for me – she worked for the features editor. I was quite sore about Lynda Lee-Potter for a while.'

Some of Conran's former *Mail* staff, the first ever Femails, wrote to the *Mail* to defend Conran, which the paper published on the Letters page. 'And from then on she had her knife in for me. She said I was too fat to be wearing trousers when I was about to go on a book-signing tour . . . I was just on her blacklist. She was very good in her way, perfect for the *Mail* – just as in Western films you hired a gun; Lynda was a first-class, hired bitch.'[68]

It was, however, all coming to an end for Lynda Lee-Potter, and Dacre-era Femails such as Amanda Platell, who'd given Posh that 'relentless savaging', would step in to try and fill the void.

Every Tuesday at 10 a.m., the *Mail*'s single most important voice would sit with Dacre in his office and they would gently discuss what she was going to put in her column the next day. The last piece of copy she'd handed her editor was in exactly the same vein as she'd started when she was a junior feature writer on the old broadsheet *Mail* – it was a warm interview[69] with TV presenter Gloria Hunniford about the death from cancer of her daughter, the TV presenter Caron Keating. Lee-Potter had left Dacre's office complaining of a headache: she never returned. The pain turned out to be caused by a brain tumour. Six weeks after her defence of Mrs Beckham, the message 'Lynda Lee-Potter is away' began to appear where her words had once been.

Lynda Lee-Potter died in October 2004, aged sixty-nine, on a Wednesday – the day of the week on which her column had appeared for three decades.

16

The British Invasion

The *Daily Mail* at birth was itself an innovation: Sunny Harmsworth combined elements from his magazines and the 'new' journalism of his day to create something new in a fusty newspaper environment. And it took off. Later, he was the first to spot that broadsheets were physically just too big for the train and created the tabloid size. Every innovative step the *Mail* has ever taken seems to have somehow been heralded in some way by Sunny Harmsworth. And he spotted one more thing over a distant horizon that would be the future shape of his *Daily Mail*: the online newspaper.

Sunny often talked of a thing called the 'simultaneous newspaper'[1] – the same paper, essentially, published across the whole of the USA and Great Britain. Why not the world? 'Given the man, the capital, the organization and the occasion, there seems to be no reason why one or two newspapers may not presently dominate,' he wrote in 1901. 'Is it not obvious that the power of such a paper might become such as we have not yet seen in the history of the Press? I am convinced that the press has its best days to come.'[2]

By 2016 his paper was indeed a global phenomenon called *MailOnline*, the most visited English-language newspaper website in the world.

Yet the *Daily Mail* was awfully late to the digital party – perhaps not surprisingly, seeing as its editor-in-chief doesn't even have a computer on his desk. Everything is printed out for him to read on paper – even, reportedly, his emails. 'He actually does have a computer in a corner but he never uses it ever,' said *Mail* insider 'Sean'. 'It's three yards from his actual desk. He does, however, have a big computer screen off to his left which constantly scrolls through *MailOnline* all day and the poor old news editor is then summoned in if he's missing something that Paul sees four feet down the home page. He doesn't do email at all but relies on his PA Lesley to send emails on his behalf.'[3]

Dacre didn't think much of the Web threat in 1999 in his monotone speech at the *Mail*'s annual staff frolic at Hampton Court the year after David English and Vere Harmsworth died. These were the days when the *Mail*'s circulation was still rising towards its ultimate high. 'A lot of people say that the internet is the future for newspapers,' he told his staff. 'Well, I say to that: bullshit.com.'[4]

Five years later and the *Mail*'s digital offering was generated by a massive staff of six:[5] *Mail* boys and girls who essentially reproduced a few of the paper's stories online. But by 2006 it was perfectly clear that the World Wide Web was now very much an existential threat to the future of the *Daily Mail* and all newspapers; something had to be done. And it turned out that those half-dozen or so young-sters in the corner cutting and pasting those pages were seeds for the future, perhaps even more so than *Femail* had been almost forty years before. The *Daily Mail*'s limp digital offering needed to be retooled and refuelled; the tiny little editorial backwater required a period of sustained investment if the *Daily Mail* name was to live on. And young Viscount Rothermere began spending big in the mid-2000s.

Jonathan Harmsworth had already proven himself willing to take bold risks with the family firm, not long after his dad died in 1998; it was clear to the brand-new Press Lord that free newspapers being pushed into people's hands were about to become a fact of city life in London and beyond. Harmsworth decided that if his company didn't launch a free sheet, his competitors would. So he asked Dacre and his team to create *Metro*. It took a huge bite out of the company's *Evening Standard* but it's much better, surely, to have these clumps of flesh digested in-house than by some Swedish player that was in the market at the time or by Rupert Murdoch, who had also spotted the opening. *Metro* became hugely profitable but it also, probably, restricted the *Mail*'s growth potential. The fourth viscount was clearly following in his father's footsteps – Vere had risked all by going tabloid. And Jonathan sacrificed his *Evening Standard* to fight off the freesheets (the first Associated newspaper Dacre ever edited was sold off to a Russian businessman, former KGB agent Alexander Lebedev, in 2009 for one English pound – and itself soon became a freesheet).

'I think Jonathan and Vere are quite similar,' Vyvyan Harmsworth – who also works with the current Lord Rothermere on the family's charitable foundation – told the author. 'Jonathan is very astute and he's got his finger firmly on the pulse. And being a younger man, from a totally different generation, he probably understands how the media works better than you could have expected his father to have understood it. He took over very young, in a very difficult time and it's a very difficult job. He realized that the world was moving forward and he's kept in step with it.'[6]

Maybe the ultimate sacrifice will eventually be the *Daily Mail* newspaper itself, in favour of the vast global market online. 'For Associated, the whole is very much larger than the sum of its parts,' said Dacre. 'Similarly with *MailOnline*. Yes, the *Mail* was late to the internet revolution – though through our tardiness, we avoided losing the millions that others expended on the web in those early days . . . But there's money in those *MailOnline* figures and, again, hopefully the whole will be bigger than the sum of the parts.'[7]

Rothermere accepted that it would take years for *MailOnline* to generate enough cash to pay its own way – never mind turn a profit – and this brand-new twenty-first-century *Daily Mail* vessel clearly had to have a skipper who wasn't phobic about computers.

Mailman Martin Peter Clarke took the helm in 2006; he was given his own budget and his own staff. *MailOnline* was to be an entirely separate operation from the newspaper from the start – mostly to protect the mothership *Daily Mail* newspaper, the *Mail* chiefs fearing that the energy of the paper's staff would be dissipated in the infinite space online (a fundamental mistake made by bean-counter managers on other British newspapers).

Clarke was born in Dartford,[8] a town to the south-east of London, in August 1964 – just as local boys Mick Jagger and Keith Richards were giving blues music back to white America with their Rolling Stones. Dacre's digital shadow comes from much lower down the social pecking order than the comfortable middle classes of his master; his dad, Robert, was an accounting machine mechanic when he married mail order firm worker Doris. Their boy went to Gravesend Grammar before heading west to the University of Bristol, where he was editor of the fiercely left-wing student paper *Bacus*.

Bacus soon got in trouble, however, over a story about a secret strip show at a university building 'where the performer allegedly "undressed one unfortunate, and very drunk, member of the 25-strong gathering intent on showing him what audience participation was all about"'. The story was retold in the university's current magazine *nonesuch* in the winter issue of 2008:

> The front-page report was variously described as 'totally untrue', 'grossly inaccurate' and 'fictitious'. Bacus was now regularly getting out of hand and the Union began to question its £3,500 funding of the mischievous paper . . . Thus in 1985, Martin Clarke (now BA 1985) quit from his position as editor after only one month in the job, when the Union refused to guarantee funding for the paper beyond Christmas.[9]

Clarke graduated from Bristol University the same year as that other Mailman Tony Gallagher – the brutal former news editor who went on to become deputy editor of the *Mail*, editor of the *Daily Telegraph* and editor-in-chief of *The Sun*. Clarke went on to work for a press agency in Bristol before joining the *Mail* in 1987 at the age of twenty-three. Clarke, and later Gallagher, were among the raft of *Mail* boys who arrived in the dying days of Fleet Street when Sir David English was still editor but actually matured into

Mailmen under Paul Dacre. Unlike Stewart Payne and others from the previous generation, who viewed Dacre as far more comical than he ever intended to be, to this new intake Dacre was the boss.

For years Clarke was a 'picture taster', the junior Mailman who'd trawl through thousands of wire and staffer photographs and select a dozen or so for the picture editor to present to the editor in conference. Few hacks rise to be senior editors from the picture desk but Martin Clarke was keener – and more explosive – than most. Former *Daily Mail* photographer Clive Limpkin recalled how this young junior desk hand briefed him to get a shot of Susan Hampshire outside her Chelsea home – the actress knew the *Mail* were after her and did not want her picture taken.

'Martin told me to get there "at the crack of dawn" and when I arrived around 6 a.m. her car had already gone so, realizing I'd missed her, I went for a coffee and read the papers. When I told the picture editor that Hampshire must have driven off in the middle of the night, Martin overheard and said it wasn't in the middle of the night . . . as he'd checked the mews on his way into work at 5 a.m., when her car was still outside her home. It was the first – and only – time I've ever experienced a picture desk man show such dedication. And it was not lost on the management – who soon moved him upwards to higher things.'[10]

After the picture desk, Clarke spent time inside Dacre's features department and the news desk before leaving the *Mail* fold in 1995 to further his career as news editor on the *Daily Mirror*. 'I always got on well with him,' one of his former *Mirror* reporters told the author, 'but he did drive the newsroom very hard when he came here.'[11] Clarke didn't drive the *Mirror* reporters hard for very long, though; he earned the tag 'Mickey Rourke' after his stint at the *Mirror* – as he was only the paper's news editor for '9½ Weeks'.[12]

He returned to the *Mail* – up in Glasgow, as editor of a new Scottish edition at the age of thirty; Paul Dacre spotted, rightly, the potential for circulation growth outside the *Mail*'s traditional heartlands in the south of England and also an opportunity to nurture this young talent. Scotland was a tough, cut-throat newspaper game with too many papers chasing too few readers when Clarke first crossed the border. He cut the *Mail*'s price and quickly trebled its north-of-the-border sales (from a very low base). He also nailed the *Mail*'s core market in Scotland by toning down its Middle England bias and making it more palatable to a certain kind of Scot: middle-aged, middle-class women.

Sir David English's former features editor Sue Douglas was watching the growth of this new *Mail* incarnation from fifty miles away in Edinburgh, where, in 1997, she worked as a senior executive for hotel billionaire twins Frederick and David Barclay – who had recently acquired the *Scotsman*, Scotland's fusty old 'newspaper of record' (the Barclays now own the *Telegraph*). Douglas, with the Barclay brothers' top media man Andrew Neil, appointed Clarke its editor.

'He "*Mail*-ized" it and made it accessible,' Douglas told the author. 'He attacked that terribly posh Scottish "Edinburrrrr" attitude on the *Scotsman*, which was just not gonna wash with us.'[13]

Clarke began to earn a reputation on the *Scotsman* as a truly brutal old-school 'Fleet Street' editor after senior writers and sub-editors found themselves 'being showered with expletives'. The *Scotsman*'s picture editor quit after being ordered to get better pictures from his 'fuckin' monkeys'; Clarke thought its investigation unit was a 'crock of shit' and disbanded it, so its boss quit. Associate editor Lesley Riddoch – whose articles kept getting spiked – brought a claim for constructive dismissal.[14] She was awarded £11,000 in an out-of-court settlement. She later told the author: 'I met him after a Press Fund lunch a few years later and went up to thank him for the £11k. He said, "You always were a ballsy bastard – do you want a drink?"

'I hadn't quite counted on that but couldn't refuse. We spoke for about two minutes – or rather I listened while he told me what a "total fuck-up" the *Scotsman* had been, then he abruptly left. I turned round and saw the entire Scottish press corps watching. Apparently they fully expected one of us to deck the other.'[15]

'He was a total bastard,' one hack told the *Guardian* in 1998, 'a maniac who seemed to enjoy making our lives hell.'[16] 'The stories were always "mince" or "shit" and a typical conference might end,

"You are all fucking cretins and this is all crap,"' another hack added. 'He once said to me: "You've got to go and shout at the bastards or they won't respect you."'[17]

Clarke's staff may have felt like a monster had been let loose in their newsroom but his boss Sue Douglas thought he was marvellous. 'Look, at least Martin's a character,' she told the author. 'Most editors these days are not. They're just bland, boring corporate types. Martin is a character, and I liked that. And I liked the fact that he had a real reputation and a bit of madness, and people loved him or hated him. Martin Clarke is utterly driven, and ambitious beyond belief . . . He really cared about getting there and so, yeah, he would trample on people all the way. And I suppose the most difficult thing about him is he's got a real temper and people didn't like that. But it wasn't the nasty bullying of David English. Martin would just fly completely off the handle.'[18]

Myths began to merge with the man, the best of which being one yarn in which a rock-hard former soldier-turned-journalist didn't exactly cower at the shoes of this red-faced *Mail*-trained bully. According to a profile of Clarke in the *Independent on Sunday* in 2006, the tough Scot simply asked for a wee word in private. 'The man took him outside,' an insider told the paper, 'and we understand he threatened to kill him. Whatever happened, Martin never spoke to him like that again.'

One day when staffers went to investigate hammering against the wall of the editor's office, they found Clarke bashing the phone against the walnut panelling – apparently in conversation with 'Donald fucking Dewar', the Secretary of State for Scotland. 'He can be an energizing, dynamic force, but he's not a stickler for accuracy and he's not at all rigorous about detail,' another *Scotsman* hack added. 'He shook up a moribund newspaper,' added another. 'But in the course of it, he spent too much, drank too much, smoked sixty Silk Cut a day, went clubbing so much he was badly hung over in the morning, and alienated staff in the most dramatic way.'[19]

Clarke also met and, in 1998, married Veronica – a local woman six years his senior who had three children to a previous husband she'd married when she was nineteen. The couple would later have a son of their own.[20]

After a year or so at the *Scotsman*, the *Mirror* group hired Clarke back to become editor-in-chief of their Scottish *Daily Record* and *Sunday Mail*. The *Mail* monster roamed this newsroom with much the same impact as at the *Scotsman*. 'I don't run democracies,' Clarke himself was quoted as saying in a profile in the *Guardian*, 'I run newspapers.'[21]

This is precisely the attitude that can get one a full Fleet Street editorship, and some hacks began to talk of Clarke fast becoming a national newspaper editor south of the border; he was soon called down to London by the *Mirror*'s bosses. However, instead of being given the editor's chair at their *Daily Mirror*, *Sunday Mirror* or *Sunday People*, his employment with the group abruptly ended.[22]

So he again returned home to Associated, relaunching and editing the newly acquired *Ireland on Sunday* in the same inimitable Mailman style and causing uproar among the staff. Clarke, apparently, would stub his cigarettes out on the carpet floor and ritually humiliate colleagues – howling out across the newsroom: 'Are there any journalists out there or did they all win their jobs on the back of a Rice Krispies packet?'

By the time he returned to London to be executive editor of the *Mail on Sunday*, he had done it again – circulation had trebled. Martin Clarke was the best, most battle-proven Mailman in Dacre's stable of junior talent, and the fact that Clarke was appointed by Lord Rothermere to run the digital operation in 2006 was the surest sign of just how important the threat from the Web was now being taken.

'He is a much more sophisticated human being than he appears,' said a workmate from his days in Scotland. 'I didn't understand, until I met Paul Dacre, that everything Clarke did was modelled on the behaviour of his hero [Dacre]. He believed that was the way you did it.'[23]

Clarke's new office was kitted out with a lot more computers than Dacre's, and he used them to begin to fashion a website he'd like to read, not entirely unlike a digitally enhanced version of David English turning the old broadsheet *Daily Mail* into a 'compact'. His picture desk credentials came to the fore from the start – his photograph-heavy approach was to reap the rewards for Viscount Rothermere when his revamped, replenished and reinvigorated *MailOnline* was relaunched.

The shop window of Clarke's digital *Daily Mail* is a single 'tabloid' front page. A very, *very* long tabloid front page. Story after story after story, photo after photo, just keeps rolling on by. It's a scroll not a newspaper. If a snapshot of a moment's digital *Daily Mail's* stories were printed out on tabloid-sized newsprint and rolled out down the street, it'd be well over sixty feet long. If Clarke climbed on to the roof above the sixth floor of Northcliffe House and dropped it – it would still curl up several times on the street below. And that's before a reader has even clicked through to read a single story or look at a picture or perused the sport or *Femail* sections or even read their horoscope. It's an approach that devours a massive amount of content; the digital *Daily Mail* publishes around 1,000 stories a day, and *10,000* pictures.[24] 'We come from a print background,' Clarke told an ad:tech conference, 'and we weren't, to be frank, that sophisticated in digital terms when we started out. So we just kept it simple.'[25]

It would be missing the point to view Clarke's creation as just an old-school newspaper on the Web, a mistake those with a dead-tree kind of mind who run other newspaper groups are prone to make. As Clarke himself explained in a live video 'hangout' with Australian marketing website Mumbrella:

> The reason *MailOnline* has become a success is because
> we cover the waterfront. It's all the news you need to
> know, all the news you wanna know. The big stories. The
> lighter stories. The completely amazing stories. You're
> just competing for people's time. So, I'm competing with
> people spending time on their Facebook page looking at
> pictures of their new niece when they could be looking at

pictures of Kim Kardashian. What you have to decide is what you want your site to be, and make it as compelling and as sticky and engaging and interesting and fascinating – and as fun – as possible.[26]

It is a far more direct and immediate relationship than that between a newspaper editor and his readers – Clarke has even referred to himself as being 'like a DJ' when he is editing the site's homepage. Indeed, *MailOnline* fans can see the DJ updating the tunes in real-time; hang around for a few minutes and it's sure to change. Again, unlike a newspaper, Clarke's team know exactly how many people are reading each story; they know if a headline or a photo is working or not by checking how many people are actually reading it. They have the data, and the numbers are there to be read immediately. Journalistic instinct is what gets the story on the homepage in the first place but the clicks are what keep it there.

'The thing about a digital product is, you're not entirely in control of it,' added Clarke.

> The readers are in control – the readers will very much get to decide what kind of a website it evolves into. But that's a big leap that you have to make as an old print journalist into understanding digital. You have to kinda let go a bit and empower the readers and let them define your product rather than you saying 'Right, this is what I – as an editor – think that the product needs to be and these are the stories I'm gonna print' and, you know, you can kinda like it or lump it. In digital it's a far more two-way interaction that goes on in real-time 24/7. We let the readers decide what they're interested in, that's why *MailOnline* is so sticky and why it's so addictive and why people love it so much. It's because we make sure that when you land on that page, the stories that you see first are the ones that we think you're gonna read – and we know you're gonna read them because we're looking at what everyone in the last five

minutes has read. And it's a good bet that if everyone else has read stories one, two and three – then you're probably gonna read stories one, two and three.[27]

Just like Sunny Harmsworth almost 120 years before, Clarke grasped a central fact missed by the heavy newspapers of Harmsworth's day: people don't live in niches, it is actually possible to be interested in the political climate in Iran at the same time as looking at pictures of some celebrity's cellulite.

'We don't think "we're the professional journalists, that story is important – we're gonna put it at the top" even if no one is reading it,' Clarke said at ad:tech.

> That doesn't mean you're guided slavishly by the clicks and stuff floats to the top purely on whether it's being used. Obviously, if there's a big important story there that you think people should be reading and they're not reading – then I always tell my people then, that's our fault. If they're not reading that story that they should be reading, it's because you've sold it wrong – you've got the wrong headline, you've got the wrong picture. Or whatever. And we play around until, hopefully, we hit pay-dirt and we get a reaction from people.[28]

These chats with his staff about hitting 'pay-dirt' are very much true to the *Daily Mail* management formula, as digital Mailman 'Marlon' told the author. 'One day I was working on a story at a computer and Clarke sat down at the machine next to me. He just started growling and barking – calling everyone a cunt this, and a fucking cunt that. Then he settled down. So I finished the story I was working on but just kept typing at a screen because I really didn't want to make eye contact with the man, in case it set him off again. But he knows what he wants for his site, and – you have to understand – it very much is *his* site. I was not aware of any editorial control whatsoever from above him. When I first joined I was told that so long as I got the photograph right, I'd do fine. And not to worry so much about the words – that Clarke didn't care about the words.'[29]

Martin Clarke is a Mailman with, wrote the *Guardian*'s media diarist Roy Greenslade, all 'the man-management skills of a galley-master on a Greek trireme'[30] – a trireme being a large warship with many oars that dominated the Mediterranean 2,500 years ago. It would prove to be an apt metaphor, as Clarke and his oarsmen would quickly come to dominate the clear blue digital waters between Britain, the USA, and Australia.

A rainy little island off the west coast of Europe, though, was always going to be too small to contain the digital *Daily Mail*. There simply aren't enough clicks in Britain to make a – free – newspaper website work, and, though the World Wide Web might have been invented by a Brit, it speaks American English. From the beginning of Martin Clarke's operation, traffic grew in the States like a weed. Of *MailOnline*'s 5 million daily users in 2010, more than half were outside the UK, mostly in the US.[31]

'When we first started *MailOnline*,' explained Viscount Rothermere to the Newsworks' Shift conference in 2013,

> we started seeing a lot of traffic from the US and we didn't
> know how to monetise it so, it was a bit irritating to be
> honest with you in the beginning. We didn't really want
> it. And, being unashamedly opportunistic . . . I remember
> reading an interview with [*Guardian* editor] Rusbridger
> and he was talking about making the *Guardian* 'a global
> newspaper' and I thought 'actually, that's a pretty cool
> idea'. So I started talking to Paul [Dacre] and Co. and
> said 'Why don't we follow the traffic? Why don't we put
> some people into California – into LA?' And that worked.
> Then they said we really want to be in New York, that's
> the centre, that's the place to be for news journalism. So
> we started building a team in New York. And it's just
> continued to grow, we just followed our success if you
> like. It's really that simple.[32]

By the autumn of 2014, Rothermere had spent something like £35 million on the relaunched *MailOnline* and boosted traffic to 11 million users per day.[33] Around two-thirds are now outside the UK, again mostly in the USA. Yet the States has, historically, been a tough market for any British press baron to enter; it's a city-based newspaper culture rather than national – due to the sheer distances involved – and the start-up costs of launching a newspaper from scratch could put a spaceship into orbit. It's a different tale with the Web because newspaper websites don't need a big bang launch – they can work their way under American skin insidiously. And now British hacks – broadsheet as well as tabloid – are finding what they'd long suspected: they're simply better at the journalism game than some of their heavier cousins on the other side of the Atlantic . . . and American readers, it would seem, agree. Paul Dacre spent six years working in the US in the 1970s and has firm opinions on the US newspaper industry.

> Is it a coincidence that America's printed press – for years protected by its monopoly status, so pompously up itself, eschewing anything so tawdry as personality journalism that might actually sell papers – is now dying?[34]

British journalists are great at connecting with real people inside their real homes about their real cares and their real concerns; the similarities far outweigh the differences, be they British homes, American or Australian. Physical distance means nothing online, the English-speaking world has become one market for news – though each territory does receive its own content created with essentially the same *Mail* formula.

'People getting up in the morning in Sydney are already coming to *MailOnline*,' said Clarke when the site started hiring Down Under:

> because people don't really care where they get their news from so long as it's the news that they want. Whereas in the past you had to buy the papers that were

in your shop, and there was a limited number of papers in your shop, so you had to buy an Australian paper if you were an Australian person and a British paper if you were a British person. Online – you can go and get your news from anyone in the world.[35]

The *New York Times* was once the world's biggest English-language online newspaper but *MailOnline* overtook the grey old lady in December 2011, with the *Times'* management sniffily insisting that the *Mail's* mass market appeal, and taste in celebrity tittle-tattle, was not quite the same proposition.[36] The *Guardian's* online presence, however, *is* a direct competitor – and the *Guardian* also overtook the *NY Times* in 2014.[37] The *New York Times*, though, did erect a paywall, which was always going to limit access as all walls are built to do.

Media commentators on both sides of the pond have started calling this 'the British invasion of news', much like the Beatles and the Rolling Stones' musical invasion of the early sixties, though not nearly as sexy. American digital firms, of course, have swamped the entire planet, and MSN, Google and Yahoo! are also now in the news game; these are the real competitors for free sites like *MailOnline*, not just other newspapers.

A huge global draw for *MailOnline* is the infamous 'sidebar of shame' – a column of celebrity froth that runs down the right-hand side of that endless scroll. The sidebar of shame is basically content about 'celebrities' wearing clothes, performing the tricky task of walking through an airport or possibly news of one low-grade celebrity copulating with another. The first thing that hits a casual *MailOnline* reader is just how low the bar is to gain space. Unless a reader consumes this material regularly, it is populated by folk that they've probably never heard of.

Martin Clarke doesn't like the term 'sidebar of shame', preferring 'right rail of fame'. As he explained to Mumbrella:

Remember, the *Daily Mail* is not a red-top tabloid.
We're a middle market newspaper. Our copy is not

sensationalist or the kind of stuff you'd see in *The Sun* or the *Mirror*.[38]

Thirty seconds or so spent perusing the site itself would suggest otherwise. Vere Harmsworth, the third Lord Rothermere and the joint father of the modern *Daily Mail*, had resisted tearing down this path. It was not befitting of the Harmsworth family name. Even Paul Dacre himself has expressed contempt for these hollow, empty stars in a galaxy so full there's barely any space left to shine out from. Inside the pages of his 'journalistic primer' the *Sunday Express* in his father's day, famous faces always featured on page three.

> The lead article under the title 'Meeting People' was an
> interview – not with the kind of half-baked trollop who
> passes as a celebrity these days but with, say, the mother
> of a newly chosen British Nobel Prize winner.[39]

It's fair to say Kim Kardashian is unlikely to ever win a Nobel Prize, yet Kim is – at the moment – *MailOnline*'s number-one celebrity obsession; no Kim Kardashian picture story is too small for that scroll, and she often features several times a day, often using shots she takes herself and posts on social media. She might be kissing her husband Kanye West, landing at an airport . . . going shopping, adjusting her top, basically anything. Yet the Kardashian clan from which she sprang are not Dacre's *Mail* types at all; they're stars of a reality TV show mostly focused upon sisters Kim, Kourtney, and Khloé.

The very concept of the Kardashians is enough to pop a billion blood vessels across Middle England; if the world is going to hell, as many British *Daily Mail* newspaper readers surely believe, then the Kardashians are whipping the rump of the digital dog that's pulling the cart. Old-school *Daily Mail* readers aren't, though, necessarily, *MailOnline* consumers, and there are very few clicks in the English shires. *MailOnline* does not express quite the same level of moral outrage as her 120-year-old sister, unless it is a story actually taken from the paper itself. Similarly, it does not resist the Kardashians and their ilk's crunching of the family values that Dacre's *Daily Mail* holds so dear. It is the readers of *MailOnline* – and countless purely gossip sites – that make folk like Kim Kardashian famous. The public put her there; it's a simple fact that the daily life of a Nobel Prize winner will never be as interesting as Kim Kardashian's.

Digital *Daily Mail* readers are a different crowd to those who traditionally buy the newspaper. The core audience is young, slightly more female than male, well educated and well off. They dip in around twice a day and stay for about thirteen minutes a stop – on the phone on the way to work, then at their office desktop when they should be working – it has even been banned by one London trading room after the boss got fed up seeing his staff looking at *MailOnline* on their screens.[40] Readers then stop by in the evening. It's a day-long conversation between the reader and Clarke's staff who are pulling hard on that scroll in real-time. It'd be a pretty dull conversation if *MailOnline* said the same thing all day. Many arrive via a Google search, aggregator or from a link sent via email to a friend which they clicked without knowing – or caring – where they were being led.

'We're quite good at converting those people who come via Facebook or whatever,' said Clarke, 'who then see some content down the right rail and get sucked in, and sucked in, and sucked in – and next thing you know, you're bookmarked and they're coming to you despite themselves.'[41]

MailOnline can even track their moods in a way that is impossible for a newspaper. There's a big difference in what people read 'leaning forward' in the day and what they read 'leaning back' in the evening; they are more playful and relaxed at night, preferring the lighter material, the features and gossip. *This* is where the big money is, as it provides the kind of information that is gold to editorial – and to advertisers. They can push different content to suit the mood, and readers may be relaxed enough to get out the credit card. As ever more people register their personal information, and as the site evolves, they will be able to target these people individually with content and products they know, for a fact, they like.

Yet *MailOnline* consumers are not all gullible teenage girls who want to grow up to be Kim Kardashian. Meagan Hatcher-Mays, for example, is a registered lawyer in New York State and a legislative assistant in the House of Representatives . . . one never knows, she could be President one day. She's also a contributor to *Jezebel* blog, where she wrote:

> I need to make an announcement regarding my credi-
> bility as a potential future professional woman and as a
> human being capable of empathy. I read the *Daily Mail*.
> Every single day. That feels good to say. I once admitted
> that I read the *Daily Mail* (or 'DM' as us regular readers
> call it) to a lawyer friend of mine, and she scoffed so hard
> I thought she broke her jaw. 'Why don't you just read
> *The Independent*?' she scoffy scoff scoffed. Why don't I
> read *The Independent*?! Who am I, some fancy prince? A
> wise little lord parading around in my tailcoat and cravat,
> filling my elegant mind with news of the day? No. No,
> ma'am. I AM A MONSTER. I'm admitting this to you
> now because I know I'm not the only one who suffers
> from this particular affliction. I want you fellow DM
> beasts to know you're not alone. But guys, that website is
> awful and we should probably stop reading it. We have
> to stop reading it! I can't stop reading it. Why can't I stop
> reading it? I know I should be ashamed of my *Daily Mail*
> addiction, because that whole site is a shrine to everything
> that our dumb culture needs to deconstruct. But I'm not
> ashamed! Every decent freedom fighter worth their salt
> needs a break every now and again.[42]

Louise Mensch is a former Tory MP who has attacked the paper for sexism and for trivializing prominent women, to which Dacre's *Daily Mail* responded by saying her voice was 'dental-drill shrill, shrieky enough to curdle a mobile blood bank'. She is, nevertheless, hooked on the paper's website. 'One of the reasons it's so egregious is because it's so readable,' she told the *New Yorker*. 'We're clicking on "Oh my God, one of the WAGs couldn't put her hair up because she'd freshly painted her nails" . . . and then you're thinking, Why am I reading this? I'm an adult.'[43]

The legion of *MailOnline* readers are right there on the page, leaving comments beneath every story; *MailOnline* receives over 120,000 comments every week. 'They're a surprisingly different group of people' from the paper's readers, says Lord Rothermere. '*MailOnline* is a much younger audience and, of course, it's a much more international audience. And their choice of stories is slightly different as well – and they expect things to be very immediate.'[44]

Readers can't, however, comment on Rothermere himself; it's one of several words that's automatically blocked. But most Americans don't know, and don't care, who Rothermere is. The *Daily Mail* has no legacy in the United States, as Stephen Colvin, a former CEO at *Newsweek* explained: 'In the US, 95 per cent of the people who visit the website have no idea there is a newspaper associated with it.' And Clarke sees that as a good thing. 'Without a print product, you've got no legacy, no baggage. You can just be who you want to be.'[45]

To help increase market recognition among the ad men of Madison Avenue, the *Mail* bought the dailymail.com domain name off the Charleston *Daily Mail* for a reported million dollars.[46]

MailOnline's future may be being driven by US consumers but it's fair to say at least one stellar American isn't a fan: George Clooney branded it 'the worst kind of tabloid'[47] in 2014 after extracting – and rejecting – an apology over 'a completely fabricated story' that he felt put his now wife Amal Alamuddin in real danger. As Clooney told *USA Today*:

> I'm, of course, used to the *Daily Mail* making up stories –
> they do it several times a week, and I don't care . . .
> I accept the idea that freedom of speech can be an
> inconvenience to my private life from time to time.[48]

Clooney was furious, though, when he read that his soon-to-be mother-in-law had told 'half of Beirut' that she opposed her daughter's wedding on religious grounds because she is a member of Lebanon's Druze community and 'it says they joke about traditions in the Druze religion that end up with the death of the bride'.

'Let me repeat that: the death of the bride,' wrote Clooney.

> First of all, none of the story is factually true. Amal's mother is not Druze. She has not been to Beirut since Amal and I have been dating, and she is in no way against the marriage – but none of that is the issue . . . The irresponsibility, in this day and age, to exploit religious differences where none exist, is at the very least negligent and more appropriately dangerous . . . The *Daily Mail*, more than any other organization that calls itself news, has proved time and time again that facts make no difference in the articles they make up. And when they put my family and my friends in harm's way, they cross far beyond just a laughable tabloid and into the arena of inciting violence. They must be so very proud . . . they've exposed themselves as the worst kind of tabloid. One that makes up its facts to the detriment of its readers and to all the publications that blindly reprint them.[49]

Clooney, alongside a handful of truly global A-list stars, has transcended any real need for the tabloid or gossip press and can somehow get in and out of an airport without being photographed. There are also still plenty of actors, musicians and other artists who just happen to be famous because they are really rather good at what they do – and have never courted this kind of low-grade fame. For the true A-listers the rules of the game change. A Clooney is a very different creation from a Kardashian.

'We made a big error,' Martin Clarke told the *FT*, adding, 'Our best readers are celebrities. They love the pictures of themselves. I'm not hobnobbing with celebrities every day, but when I do run into people like the Kardashians, they adore what we do.'[50]

Another criticism of *MailOnline* comes from within the trade itself: other journalists are often highly critical about where the website finds those 1,000 stories a day and 10,000 photos. *MailOnline*, Rupert Murdoch told the Leveson inquiry into the Press, 'just steals . . . they steal gossip from everybody. It's a great sort of gossip site – or bad, whichever way you look at it – and comes right up to the barrier of what is fair use of other people's material.'[51]

MailOnline resisted these accusations and even launched legal proceedings in 2015 against former employee James King and the – now defunct – *Gawker* website for claiming its 'editorial model depends on little more than dishonesty, theft of copyrighted material and sensationalism so absurd that it crosses into fabrication' and that the *Mail* takes a 'buccaneering approach to accuracy and intellectual property'.[52]

In the end, the case settled with no money changing hands and with the article remaining on the website untouched, followed by a lengthy *Daily Mail* rebuttal below it. The rebuttal begins with a similar stipulation to the above that 'We utterly refute James King's claim that DailyMail.com depends on "dishonesty, theft of copyright material", and the publication of material we "know to be inaccurate".'[53]

Internal rules have been tightened in recent years, yet one freelance, Martin Fletcher, complained as recently as April 2016 to the *Guardian* media commentator Roy Greenslade after his *Times* story about the desecration of British war graves in Iraq was 'repackaged' by *MailOnline*. Fletcher had even funded the expensive trip to Iraq himself. The *Mail* later paid him for his work 'with no admission of liability'.

> I've had a huge response from numerous fellow journalists whose work has been likewise abused by *MailOnline* . . .
> I am incensed by *MailOnline*'s dishonesty and its debasement of honest journalism.[54]

Yet the *Daily Mail* newspaper once had probably the best reputation in Fleet Street for the fees it paid and the speed with which it paid them. Even the kill fees – cash for a commissioned story that never made it into print – were often better than the fees paid by other papers for stories they used. Even old hands such as David English's first hire for the reborn *Daily Mail*, photographer Mickey Brennan, have had issues with *MailOnline*. 'They used a picture of mine I'd taken when I'd first got to New York of P. G. Wodehouse when he was knighted by the Queen and the website used it huge without any accreditation,' he told the author. 'And I came across it and went fucking mad. Actually I contacted Dacre and eventually I got a couple of hundred quid out of it but I was fucking furious about it – they're a bunch of thieves.'[55]

Inside *MailOnline* newsrooms in London, New York, Los Angeles and Sydney there are battalions of *MailOnline* staff whose entire job it is to collate such stories, any dreams from their student days of a journalist of the year award or a Pulitzer prize surely fading with every pull on the oar that propels Martin Clarke's digital trireme.

The *Daily Mail*'s digital whelps are part scavenger, part sub-editor and headline writer, part reporter and picture taster, part adman, and they're often a whizz with Photoshop and video too. They're also part celebrity-magazine gossip writer; it's a vital skill to be able to spot a Kardashian in a crowd. At a team briefing in 2010, when *MailOnline* had risen to become the most popular newspaper website in the UK with almost 18 million readers a month – a 446 per cent audience growth in three years – Clarke told his staff: 'This shows that, firstly, I am a fucking genius, and secondly, that you are all doing really well.'[56]

As of summer 2016, *MailOnline* employs over 800 people – around half of them journalists (and around half the total staff work overseas, mostly in the US).[57] Just like the readers, it's a different breed to those employed by the paper. 'They're younger,' a then forty-eight-year-old Martin Clarke told the ad:tech conference in November 2012.

And have different attitudes and outlooks, which is healthy. But we have some old people, I'm not the oldest person who works in our outfit: nearly, but not quite. But obviously it's younger and I don't think it's a bad thing for that . . . The opportunities for young journalists are digital. Any young journalist who doesn't want to master this medium is nuts.[58]

This new breed is generally better educated than hacks have ever been, yet they often forget a verb or the definite article and sometimes seem to apply grammar taken from a language where everybody converses in 'txt msgs'. Raw copy, though, has always been full of typos and mangled grammar; that's partly why sub-editors exist. But things move too fast now for ponderous ranks of subs to clean up that snowstorm of words and pictures. Routine checks and attempting to get a response from the subject of a story – the very basics of journalism to which Dacre's *Daily Mail* newspaper most certainly subscribes – are also lacking at *MailOnline*, said Dominic Ponsford, editor of *Press Gazette*. 'I don't think it's particularly in the culture of the people there to be making phone calls and doing extra checks,' he told the *Guardian*. 'Most people's job is to repackage stuff.'[59]

Working for *MailOnline*, a former staffer told the (Murdoch-owned, therefore a competitor) *Wall Street Journal*, was like 'Hoovering up the Internet and vomiting it back out'.[60] Clarke's former boss, and former top Femail, Sue Douglas, doesn't think much of the site's content either. 'There is no real journalism in there [within *MailOnline*], is there? It's just *Hello!* magazine writ large. Digitally. It's about celebrity culture. It's about fame . . . and that's about it. You go into a newsroom these days and all you can hear is the sound of keys clicking on a keyboard. It's all just so deadly quiet, it's like working in a bloody bank. You don't become a hack to work in a fucking bank, do you? In the old days you'd be writing and somehow you'd have to close off what was going on around you

without sticking your fingers in your ears. People would be talking
and shouting, and on the phone. Now, all these kids are doing is
looking things up on the Internet. In total silence.'[61]

Irrespective of any criticisms, Clarke's formula for the newest
incarnation of the *Daily Mail* is working and, like English, he likes to
throw a party to celebrate the site's successes. He even hired a yacht
in the early summer of 2015 (and again in 2016) on the French
Riviera, the holiday destination of choice for the Victorian-era
Harmsworths, for celebrities and admen. George Clooney, presumably, wasn't invited to the *Mail*'s Cannes Lions Festival bash: that's
the festival for the admen, not the invitation-only A-lister Cannes
Film Festival the previous month (George and Amal Clooney did
actually attend that one).

The party predictably got a mention on the *MailOnline* scroll
with twenty-four pictures, and a couple of videos. Pregnant Kim
Kardashian was there, of course, number one on the guest list.

> The stunning star wowed . . . in a sheer black outfit
> that left little to the imagination . . . the beauty made
> sure all eyes were on her as she arrived fashionably
> late . . . showing off her shapely figure in her daring
> attire . . . figure-hugging and almost dangerously
> sheer . . . she looked amazing . . . curvy Kim . . . revealed
> her undergarments worn to protect her ample cleavage
> and shapely bottom half . . . her perfectly applied
> make-up accentuated her eyes, lined in black to give
> her the advantage of a striking gaze . . . her long dark
> brunette locks were worn down for the occasion, a long
> and glossy waterfall down her back and over her shoulders
> . . . Kim finished off her eye-catching attire with a pair of
> classic black strappy sandal heels . . . The fashion-loving
> businesswoman and TV favourite . . .[62]

A reader would need a toffee hammer to break off all the sugar-
coating and actually find a living woman inside. This Kim 'scoop'

was written by Lucy Mapstone, *MailOnline*'s assistant showbusiness editor at the time, a 'showbiz and fashion enthusiast, online editor and journalist with a passion for excellent copy, speedy coverage, glossy images and the permanent scroll of on-going news'.[63] Although unaccompanied by flowery description, *MailOnline* even published snaps of a rather grumpy-looking Englishman outdoors struggling in the sunlight called 'Martin Clarke',[64] without wearing his – once obligatory for all the world's Mailmen – tie.

Desired. Demanded. Devoured. Declared the *MailOnline* branding at the same yacht party; the future of news, says Clarke, is all about brands: big brands such as CNN, MSN and Facebook. As of July 2016, *MailOnline*'s daily number of readers is around 15 million.[65] The *Mail* has a long way to go yet to catch the biggest British player; the BBC has a weekly global audience of 348 million[66] (and, of course, is underwritten by a tax on TVs so has no existential requirement to turn a profit[67]): 'There are going to end up being four or five big global news brands,' Clarke told the *Financial Times*. 'We need to be one of them, we're going to be one of them.'[68]

The digital *Daily Mail* isn't just competing with newspapers; its competition is the internet itself. It's free to the user, so it needs enough eyeballs to make it pay – or, more precisely, to make *advertisers* pay; nothing new there, independent television has done this from the start and plenty of free sheets (including Associated's own *Metro*) make a tidy profit with no cover price. *MailOnline* is Associated Newspapers' future, as is, it seems – internally – Martin Clarke.

'As a journalist, it's much more fun to be part of a company that's growing than one that is constantly re-trenching and shrinking. Much more fun,'[69] he added. 'What I'm proudest of about *MailOnline* is that it insures us as a newspaper against the future.'[70]

17

People Like Us

The future of the *Daily Mail* brand may well have been all but secured by its flourishing digital sister, but *MailOnline* is a scroll that exists only on screens, and the newspaper remains very much king at Associated Newspapers. Editor-in-chief Paul Dacre still constructs an actual physical newspaper every weekday night, a task he has often referred to as being similar to that of 'a conductor'. So most evenings this conductor, this tyrant, strides out of his office trailing deputy and assistant editors in his wake, arrives at his back bench and taps his baton upon his lectern, then warms up the show with a 'cunt' or two.

'I have a very considerable orchestra of talents and the *Daily Mail* is the representation of the broad views of some very, very clever journalists and executives and their consensus, and their views,' he told the BBC, adding, 'Yes, [there is] lots of shouting because shouting creates energy, energy creates great headlines – great headlines married with great pictures, great pictures sublimate great words . . . imagine the joy of putting together 96 pages from nothing.'[1]

Dacre's *Daily Mail* has all the latest technology money can buy, yet it is built by hand the old-fashioned way just like in Sunny Harmsworth's day, with everything printed out for Dacre and his senior team to edit on paper. It's a tactile, visceral thing to make a *Daily Mail*, with the tyrant Paul Dacre tearing into every page with his pencil. 'He does get so, so angry sometimes,' said former

Mailman 'Marc', who was often on the edges of the back bench. 'I was always slightly disappointed I didn't receive one of his famous "double cuntings" – where he'd manage to call you a "cunt" twice in one sentence as he's putting the paper together.'[2]

As edition time approaches fast, the editorial floor is abuzz with senior Mailmen dashing about clutching scratched and torn bits of paper, articles that Dacre and his top aides have demanded be changed as they force life into the *Mail* monster through words and pictures.

'Stories are given back to you with all sorts of marks and comments on them – it's like having your bloody homework marked,' sighed 'Mo'. 'They write things like: "what a load of old waffle" and "for fuck's sake I have lost the will to live" . . . and the stupid thing is that the editors all contradict each other. One will tell you to take a section out while another tells you to move it higher up the copy and make more of it. Trying to decipher it all is a nightmare. Dacre oversees and approves every headline and deck on every feature and *Femail* story. He cares less about news. The agonizing that goes into the *Daily Mail*'s poncy headlines you would not believe.'[3]

Dacre spends most of the day in his office and strides out on to the floor at 7 p.m. or so, deciding on what is going to make it into his paper and what is going to be binned; rewriting copy, mainly the intros, and writing and approving headlines; making the pieces of the jigsaw fit together. It can be a hot and noisy, stressful place to be for all those concerned.

'He can be very shouty and abusive but other times he can be quite jovial,' said 'Ian'. 'He can be very funny and dry when the mood takes him. One of the subs is a lesbian which he is fascinated by and he's always trying to engage her in conversation about her life – she and her partner have children.'[4]

Most of the poor plebs out on the floor, however – the toiling sub-editors and the reporters and the junior desk men – have very little contact with the supreme *Mail* being when he is out on the floor conducting his orchestra; which is very different to the early days of David English, when the boyish editor seemed to know everybody. Dacre's *Daily Mail* is all about hierarchy and structures, say staff – it's simply not the done thing for more junior staff to talk to their editor.

'Dacre was hardly ever on the editorial floor during the day and in all my years there I never saw him once talking to a [junior] reporter,' said 'Cyn'. 'He never spoke to me directly once, and I was there for years. *His* behaviour causes *so* much insecurity at the *Mail*. I used to describe it to my friends as a "hideous den of whispers". Everyone would just whisper to each other, *all* so terribly insecure. The atmosphere was *so* tense on the floor. It was thick with fear.'[5]

There was some good news for Dacre one evening in June 2007 when he could finally lay out a newspaper declaring the departure of Tony and Cherie Blair. His Comment page summed up the *Mail*'s position on the Blair years in a few killer paragraphs: 'Snapshot of Britain on Blair's last day'.

> History will remember Tony Blair as the most accom-
> plished actor-politician of modern times – the man who
> made Labour electable after 18 years and went on to win
> three victories in a row. Nothing can take that (or the
> Northern Ireland settlement) away from him. But he will
> also be remembered as the Prime Minister who squan-
> dered all his opportunities and brought the governance of
> Britain – through breathtaking incompetence, spin and
> deceit – into disarray and disrepute. Abroad, in vast areas
> of the globe, our reputation lies in tatters.[6]

A day later, and Gordon Brown was moving into No. 10, with a full-page photo on the *Mail*'s front page and Dacre no doubt enjoyed signing off a headline that read: 'Bye, Tony. Missing you already.'[7] Dacre had long admired the new PM, telling the *British Journalism Review* in 2002:

> I disagree with a lot of what he says, but I think he is
> a genuinely good man; he's a compassionate man with

strong socialist principles and I think he's an original
thinker and a man of enormous willpower and courage.[8]

Peter Mandelson, the former Labour Cabinet minister, also
witnessed the surprisingly close relationship between the *Mail* editor
and Brown when they all had dinner together early in the Blair years:
'Dacre was Gordon's favourite journalist and newspaper editor –
quite how they were able to conjure up such warmth – hahaha –
I don't know, but they did.'[9] Dacre, it seems, felt Gordon Brown was
'one of us' – possibly the single most important compliment from
the *Daily Mail*.

Not everyone who has appeared in the *Mail* during Dacre's tenure
turned out to be 'one of us' in a *Daily Mail* sense, though, often
much to Dacre's chagrin. Sometimes a member of the public – a
civilian not party to the press game and not insulated by PR people –
stumbles blindly into those carefully constructed pages. Each evening,
Dacre and his top team shuffle through a heap of photographs on the
back bench and choose which is best to illustrate the tale in that
evening's template . . . around the space taken up by the adverts.
These civilians have to look the part that the *Mail* has assigned for
them . . . which can lead to an uncomfortable conversation when
a Femail has to inform them that their clothes are, well, not quite
middle class enough for the newspaper. Orders are dispatched for a
new set from *Daily Mail* central casting.

'It's all about "people like us",' former Femail 'Penny' told the
author. 'And they have to look good in a wrap dress and be a certain
size. Every story – with the very occasional exception – has to adhere
to a template. So that, no matter how good the story is, if the person
doesn't look like they might be a *Daily Mail* reader – it's never gonna
work. So you either have to be able to make them *look* like one or
forget it.'[10]

'Christ almighty,' added 'Jo', 'have you ever tried to wrestle a
size 22 woman into a wrap dress and kitten heels? I had to do it all
the time! They might have an incredibly vivid story but it doesn't
matter if they don't *look* right. The make-up artist and hair – they're

enormous budgets – and they're being sent every day, several times a day, to several stories. That's happening every day of the week; there'll be at least two or three out there right now, on jobs for *Femail* and features. You know, "ju-jing" people up. And that ethos, for sure, stems from Paul Dacre; this story will only be meaningful if he thinks it's "someone like us".'[11]

Sometimes reality bites back, of course, such as the time when the paper paid a lot of money for the people inside one big story of the day – the central character of which, unfortunately, happened to be splattered in tattoos. The paper's make-up girls did an amazing job in turning this man into somebody suitable for the pages of the *Daily Mail*, and the editor didn't notice that he wasn't his kind of man as he selected the best photographs that night for the paper. 'They'd put him in the blue shirt and the chinos – which is the default setting for the kind of "let's make this man look middle class" – and some kind of chino-style blazer,' chuckled 'Penny'. 'And then Dacre saw him on *Daybreak* [a morning TV show] two days after we'd run our piece, in all his tattooed glory and went crazy because he hadn't realized quite how much he simply wasn't really "one of us"!'[12]

Columnists too can cause a bit of a conundrum when Dacre makes up his paper; they are paid a lot of money, of course, and are guaranteed precious space. But placing those opinions on a page can be akin to laying a ticking stink bomb on a page that is sure to go off in the morning – if not on the breakfast table of *Mail* readers (very few *Mail* readers, actually, ever complain about their paper), then certainly in the newsrooms of the *Guardian* and the BBC, and these days lead to a cacophony of agitated tweets on Twitter. Probably the most famous in recent years, however, was not even placed in the paper by Dacre's own hand in October 2009 – he had taken a rare few hours' leave from the paper, as he'd promised to treat his wife to a night at the opera. Somebody else signed off columnist Jan Moir's comments about the death of Boyzone singer Stephen Gately that evening. Gately, who'd been 'outed' as a gay man by *The Sun* in 1999, was found dead on the sofa of his house in Majorca by his boyfriend and a man the couple had met the previous evening in a nightclub. The singer had, it seems, smoked a joint that night – the supposed threat from cannabis is an ongoing *Mail* obsession; its health risks are debatable but one spliff does not knock a man dead. Likewise, two men – even three, four, fifty-five – having *protected* sex doesn't tend to kill the participants; though the thought of such abominable acts could give an old *Mail* reader in the shires a heart attack. Gately was only thirty-three but died from an undetected heart condition. But this didn't stop 'Fleet Street' – not just the *Mail* – commenting on his 'lifestyle' before his family even had the chance to bury their boy.

'All the official reports point to a natural death, with no suspicious circumstances,' wrote Moir, who is not a coroner nor a qualified physician.

> The Gately family are – perhaps understandably – keen to register their boy's demise on the national consciousness as nothing more than a tragic accident . . . But, hang on a minute. Something is terribly wrong with the way this incident has been shaped and spun into nothing more than an unfortunate mishap on a holiday weekend, like a broken teacup in the rented cottage. Consider the way it has been largely reported, as if Gately had gently keeled over at the age of 90 in the grounds of the Bide-a-Wee rest home while hoeing the sweet pea patch. The sugar coating on this fatality is so saccharine-thick that it obscures whatever bitter truth lies beneath. Healthy and fit 33-year-old men do not just climb into their pyjamas and go to sleep on the sofa, never to wake up again. Whatever the cause of death is, it is not, by any yardstick, a natural one.[13]

The Press Complaints Commission – the press monitor of which Dacre chaired the Code Committee – received a record 25,000 complaints, its website buckling under the weight. And Stephen Fry wrote on Twitter: 'I gather a repulsive nobody writing in a paper no one of any decency would be seen dead with has written something loathesome and inhumane.'[14] *Guardian* writer and broad-caster Charlie Brooker added: 'Jan Moir's rant about the Boyzone star Stephen Gately is a gratuitous piece of gay-bashing . . . I'm still struggling to absorb the sheer scope of its hateful idiocy. It's like gazing through a horrid little window into an awesome universe of pure blockheaded spite.'[15]

Dacre admitted that the piece could have used a bit of 'judicious sub-editing' but insisted the column was fair comment. 'I would die in a ditch to defend any of my columnists' rights to say what they wish, and my right to suggest that occasional sentences or words could be adjusted . . . Ms Moir, who used to work for the *Guardian* by the way, hasn't a homophobic bone in her body.' Dacre's paper later published an attack on Moir's words by another columnist, Janet Street-Porter, who 'profoundly disagreed' with Moir's piece.[16]

Newspaper columnists are ten a penny but great columnists – the ones that are utterly in tune with the readers of their paper (though they'd often be completely out of place on other organs) – are incredibly hard to find. The three pillars of English's new *Daily Mail* were gone – Wooldridge and Dempster had followed Lee-Potter into the great newsroom in the sky in 2007 (a later English signing, Keith Waterhouse, also joined them in 2009).

Dacre hasn't shown quite the same talent-spotting gifts as his predecessor. Richard Littlejohn is the current columnist said by insiders to best reflect Dacre's own views but Littlejohn is a *Sun* creation really – it was on Rupert's red-top that the policeman's son from Essex first made his name as a columnist in the early 1990s (and he actually went back to *The Sun*, only to return again). 'Paul would be the first to admit, I'm sure,' said one insider, 'that you have to make best use of the talent you have at hand. Ian Wooldridges and Lynda Lee-Potters don't grow on trees.'[17]

Lynda Lee-Potter has been the hardest to replace – Alison Pearson did it for a while but she left and went to the *Telegraph*. Dacre gave the paper's literary editor, Sandra Parsons, a bash, against the advice of senior colleagues, and she didn't last. 'She didn't have that "voice",' an insider told the author. 'She didn't have the warmth. A columnist is a kind of weird alchemy, isn't it? You have to be consistent yet surprising. That's incredibly hard to pull off.'[18]

Mum-of-two Sarah Vine is the current choice as Lynda Lee-Potter's replacement. 'It makes me chuckle now that Sarah Vine has been brought in,' said 'Jo'. 'What'll be fascinating to watch is how long that great love affair between Vine and the powers-that-be lasts. As with almost all love affairs, it will almost certainly sour.'[19] Indeed. Lynda Lee-Potter was a housewife with a doctor husband who was the son of an air marshal – but Jeremy Lee-Potter was never a prospective Prime Minister. Vine's future as the *Mail*'s 'Wednesday witch', media pundits thought, was on rocky ground in July 2016 when Prime Minister David Cameron stood down over Britain's exit vote from the EU. Vine's Tory MP husband, Justice Minister Michael Gove, betrayed Brexit frontman Boris Johnson and put his own name forward instead to become Prime Minister. Gove, once the news editor of *The Times* – who admitted during his bid for PM that 'whatever charisma is I don't have it' – didn't make the final round of voting and was promptly sacked by incoming Prime Minister Theresa May, while the man he'd 'stabbed in the back', Boris Johnson, was made Foreign Secretary.

Gove had been egged on by his wife, it seems, who misfired an embarrassing email to him and his advisers into the inbox of a member of the public in which she'd claimed her boss would support his bid to get a top job in any government led by Boris.

> Crucially, the membership will not have the necessary
> reassurance to back Boris, neither will Dacre/Murdoch,
> who instinctively dislike Boris but trust your ability
> enough to support a Boris Gove ticket. Do not concede
> any ground. Be your stubborn best.

Several newspapers published the email and Dacre backed Theresa May – not Boris Johnson nor Michael Gove. Whether Vine lasts as long as Lee-Potter is yet to be seen, but she most certainly is 'one of us' in the internal *Daily Mail* sense, as pretty much all staff have to be – or at least pretend to be – if they want to keep working on *his* newspaper.

One female features journalist, for example, was poached after one of Dacre's most senior Mailmen was impressed with the words under her byline on a broadsheet newspaper. But she didn't fit in, insiders claim, with the *Mail*'s own idea of what a female looked like. 'She's a brilliant writer,' said 'Jo', 'but she was very much not a *Daily Mail* "poppet", if you know what I mean; there's a certain look to most *Daily Mail* female writers, they're all very well groomed and usually quite attractive – of a certain "type", I think you can fill in the rest – and this girl was quite loud and bolshy. And it wasn't very long before she was gone. Your face has to fit there, no question. Everything has to fit the template . . . even the people!'[20]

'I think that sense of you're either with us or against us runs incredibly strong on the *Mail*,' former lead Femail 'Penny' told the author. 'This sense of loyalty is ferocious. You're either one of them or you're not. And if you're one of them you're expected to conform to a largely unwritten set of rules, and that's why it's got that slightly Mafia-style feel . . .! Well, nobody writes the rules down for the Mafia either, do they? They're just understood in a very basic way and, like the Mafia, they are subtly reinforced, albeit not by violence. It's interesting, they're clearly very aware of who they want to be on the inside of the fortress.'[21]

Another *Femail* executive was put under so much strain that she put on a lot of weight.

'You can't show weakness there – once they sniff it, you're fucked,' said 'Elsa'. 'It's a kind of collective effort. I think if Dacre undermines you in conference, the others sense weakness and it's kind of "nature red in tooth and claw". And she was just too nice for the Mail. I remember thinking from the very beginning when she first commissioned me, "you're too nice" – she was just so eminently reasonable – and I thought . . . "You're never gonna last." And she left very abruptly. She went for lunch one day, and just never came back.'[22]

A granite-hard *Femail* editor called Lisa Collins, who was thought by some to have what it took to actually be the *Daily Mail*'s first female editor, fell out of favour with the supreme *Mail* being in the end. 'I saw Lisa Collins in tears in the toilet a couple of times,' said 'Jo'. 'And she was tough, she took no prisoners. I would just see her under enormous stress, you know. Barking orders. And it was all a legacy of the conflicts in the conferences, where it all stems from. The demands that were made in conference would filter out and filter down. I never attended conference but you didn't need to because you felt it all around you. All the time.'[23]

Collins left the paper despite Dacre giving her the relatively cushy job of editor of Weekend, the Saturday magazine Dacre had founded.

Of an evening, the *Mail*'s editorial cycle rises to a crescendo in the newsroom as the conductor waves his baton pencil manically in the air and stabs at copy – stories are killed, pictures are chosen, headlines have been written and approved – and most of the pages begin to be battered into place. But it is 'seat of the pants' stuff most evenings as edition time rapidly approaches – it can only be left so late until it becomes a real panic; if the paper runs late, the presses run late, the trucks leave late . . .

'Dacre often won't even ask what the front-page splash is until about 8 p.m.,' said 'Mo'. 'And whenever any of the senior execs complain about the hours or threaten to leave he always says that he doesn't want people to work late, to be exhausted etc. . . . but it's not true. If you try and leave at, say, 8 p.m. and he sees you he'll make a big point of shouting it out across the newsroom, "Oh look, Mo is going home! Nice of you to pop in." You know, that sort of thing. Dacre often doesn't decide what he wants to go on the features pages until 8 p.m. too, then at 9 p.m. he is screaming at the production editor for being late off stone.'[24]

'The paper that eventually emerged . . . would be viewed as a disaster until [Dacre] got involved in it,' said senior *Mail* hand 'Sean'. 'I think he really saw himself as coming to the rescue: it was shit in everybody else's hands until he got involved himself at nine o'clock at night.'[25]

Dacre stays until the first edition has been sent after 10 p.m., when he strolls down the 'corridor of power' for his briefcase and jacket and heads to the lift, presses the button and goes down into the car park and off into the dark night by chauffeur-driven car . . . only to phone his back bench when he gets home, complaining bitterly about stories in the first editions of other papers that have been couriered hot-off-the-press straight to his house. The *Mail* is clearly what he – not him alone, sure, but certainly more than any other human being – *feels*. Editing the *Daily Mail* is a visceral, emotional experience for Paul Dacre. And he is in total command of his product after a quarter of a century as editor. He loves what he does, he loves his *Daily Mail*.

> I'm blessed to have some of the most talented journalists
> in Fleet Street around me . . . I think they'd say he's a hard
> bastard but he leads from the front. And that he works as
> hard as them and possibly harder. And that's fair. I'd hope
> they'd say that anyway.[26]

Well, some would and some wouldn't. Some former Mailmen and Femails still carry the scars from their *Mail* days. It got way, way too much in the end for long-term reporter 'Cyn', and, whether Dacre worked harder than her or not, *he* is the man she blames.

'They were dubbed the "crying steps" by the young writers,' she told the author, 'a depressing, grey fire escape through a set of double doors leading off the *Femail* department in the Kensington offices of the *Daily Mail*. At some point nearly every day when I was there one of the journalists – female usually – would quietly push open the doors, sit on the steps and sob. At the very least they would walk down the three floors to the fresh air and freedom of Derry Street just to try and shake off their sadness for a brief moment before walking slowly back up to their desks. Perhaps they still do, for there is no doubt the same, insipid nasty bullying culture remains on the paper. The reason? Editor-in-chief Paul Dacre. He is still setting a culture of bullying and hate in the building. Yes, "hate". An atmosphere of insecurity, bitchi-ness and fear permeates the entire paper. It's a hideous, joyless place to work. His distaste for large parts of the world – working women, gays, immigrants to name just a few – will come back to bite him.'[27]

'Cyn' quit and senior Femail 'Penny' did too, though she feels less emotional about the impact the *Daily Mail* and its editor had on her life personally. There is no bitterness, just a slightly stunned curiosity at her experience of working with the man.

'What I find fascinating about him is the disconnect between the world and the value system he espouses and the way he appears to relate to people day to day. There is an enormous disconnect, isn't there? I mean, calling people cunts to their faces and instilling terror and yet, in your paper, you are constantly rolling out spreads of "here's a street in the 1950s when Britain was a better place where everyone respected each other". For a clearly enormously intelligent man, I find it fascinating that he . . . the kind of recognition of the slightly schizophrenic nature of his approach to life. He must see it.'[28]

There are signs, however, that Dacre isn't always as overbearingly confident as he seems. One legend about him relates how he emerged from his lair as the edition went to press one evening unhappy about the main op-ed feature. The assistant editor in charge of features (in most versions this is Richard Addis) sat through the normal thirty minutes of blistering insults and broken pencils as Dacre scratched holes in the proofs and etched his own words through the paper and on to the shaking desktop beneath. As the emotional storm subsided and the page was sent to press, the battered underling is supposed to have stopped Dacre and said quietly but firmly, 'You are *mad*, you know, Paul.' Dacre said nothing.

The next morning at 8 a.m., so the story goes, the telephone rang on the assistant editor's desk. 'Come and see the editor please.' All signs indicated a summary firing for incompetence the night before for the features chief. Insubordination . . . and a direct, public insult to the editor. The normal pre-dismissal words followed when he arrived at Dacre's room: 'Sit down and shut the door.'

Then came a surprising twist. Dacre's brow was said to have wrinkled up; his entire face shrouded with pain and doubt, he said: 'Look. You know what you said last night? I've been thinking about it . . .

'I'm not really mad, am I?'

18

The Death of the Newspaper

It's rude to publish an obituary before there is actually even a corpse to bury or burn but still: the end appears truly nigh for ink on newsprint – the numbers say it all. In May 2016, the *Daily Mail* newspaper sold 1,551,430[1] copies a day – a full million less than at its peak at the end of 2003. Its circulation graph is pointing inexorably to the grave, shedding at least 4 per cent of its readers every year: over 60,000 fewer copies a day – that's an annual loss of more than the whole daily sale of the *Independent* of 55,000 when it ceased printing in March 2016. Sunny Harmsworth's first ever *Daily Mail* 120 years earlier on 4 May 1896 sold 397,215 copies. Crudely – and, indeed, conservatively – if the numbers behave the same, the *Daily Mail* will have fallen below this level by its 150th birthday in May 2046.[2]

'Every Wednesday at about 6 p.m., I, in concert with other editors, receive a chart of Fleet Street's circulation performance for the previous week, on a year by year comparison,' Dacre said in a speech.

> Let me tell you, it's not a happy experience. I exaggerate
> not when I say ALL the figures, even those for papers
> cutting their prices, are worryingly in the red. We are,
> to use that exhausted cliché, in the middle of a perfect
> storm of horrifically rising newsprint prices, disappearing

classified revenues, diminishing display advertising,
the rise of cannibalistic and parasitic internet sites,
the ubiquity of the frees and, now, most worryingly
of all, readerships – their living standards reduced by
the economic crisis – who have less and less disposable
income to spend on newspapers.[3]

The *Daily Mail*'s circulation was at 2.3 million when Dacre delivered that Society of Editors speech in 2008, but it has been on the slide ever since. For an editor who was once used to selling newspapers in ever-increasing numbers, Dacre has had to content himself with the fact that the decline of his paper's sales was not as great as that of some of its rivals. It is easy to blame the internet, but papers were already in trouble before the Web appeared.

'The biggest conundrum for me, ten years ago [in 2003],' said the current Lord Rothermere,

was that we were seeing a decline in young people reading
newspapers. It wasn't anything to do with the internet,
it was just a general apathy. They felt that newspapers
didn't speak to them or they were getting their news from
the television, and so forth. And I think the internet,
actually – and the proliferation of news as 'content' on the
internet – has meant that young people are more likely
to engage with our newspapers. So, it's actually given us
access to an entirely new generation.[4]

MailOnline is the most visited English-language newspaper website in the world, with around 15 million or so unique visitors a day. And it is starting to generate cash to cover the decline in profits from the company's newspapers. *Daily Mail* content is now read by more people – more *young* people – than ever before. And it's always hiring: the old newspaper has a shrinking editorial staff of around 330, fewer than half *MailOnline*'s ever-expanding total staff of over 800.

There has long been gossip in 'Fleet Street' about who will one day take over from Paul Dacre as editor of the *Daily Mail*. Whoever actually edits the newspaper day to day, few insiders would bet against Martin Clarke being the next supreme *Mail* being as editor-in-chief (or a more modern title for the same role). The chief digital Mailman already communicates directly with the proprietor, Viscount Rothermere. Clarke may have shed the *Daily Mail* tie in favour of washed-out jeans and refer to himself as a DJ instead of a conductor, but there is no denying he is Paul Dacre in digital form.

Clarke's brand of what he calls 'journalism crack'[5] has a long road ahead, and Clarke, as a personality, is far more David English than Paul Dacre. And his digital *Daily Mail* is, perhaps, exactly what a British tabloid newspaper would always have been had it not been kept in a straitjacket made from ink and paper. 'Sometimes I think there are still things we do just because we used to be a newspaper and because that's the way everyone's always done it,' said Clarke, 'that we don't need to do any more.'[6]

Sunny Harmsworth spent big to make his *Daily Mail* what it was, and his heir, the fourth Viscount Rothermere, is spending big on *MailOnline*. The digital *Daily Mail* has many areas in which it can still grow – English is a dominant language in India and there are, of course, other languages; Spanish is vital not just in Spain and Latin America but in parts of the USA. *MailOnline* recently advertised for a Mandarin speaker to join the team[7] – the capitalist British newspaper company even has a digital 'content swap' deal with the *People's Daily* newspaper in China, the Communist Party's official organ (*MailOnline* gets forty stories a week from the *People's Daily* and vice versa).[8] *MailOnline* already carries lots of video content to dress up stories – used in much the same way as photographs – and live blogs are regularly launched for breaking news and sporting events. Television too is migrating to the internet and Martin Clarke has plans for bespoke TV content.

Jonathan Harmsworth, the fourth Viscount Rothermere, was asked by advertising journal *Campaign* where he thought his company's 'future power' lay: '*MailOnline*,' he replied. 'I feel very optimistic about that. If we make the right calls and invest more in content and grow our traffic, it can be a bigger business than the *Daily Mail* – financially, in terms of reach, and everything else.'[9]

A note of caution, though, would be wise around now – things can and do go wrong, horribly wrong; the *Daily Express* had a daily sale of 4,328,000 in 1961, and it now sells around 408,000.[10] It took the *Express* half a century to shrink to a tenth of its size. The loyalty newspapers historically enjoyed from their readers is a lot harder to achieve these days online. Indeed, many people reading a story on a screen don't know, and don't care, what brand name is sitting there at the top – especially as they didn't pay for it. Failure can come a lot faster in the digital world; social networking pioneer MySpace, for example, was way out in front of Facebook around a decade ago – at a time when the *Daily Mail* barely had a website at all. *Myspace* was sold to Rupert Murdoch and fell away. Even Google was once a digital minnow to the mighty Yahoo! (which was bought by Verizon in 2016).

DMGT, the parent company, issued a profit warning to investors in May 2016 after a 29 per cent fall in profits in the six months to the end of March that year for DMG Media – the arm that holds the *Daily Mail, Mail on Sunday, Metro* and *MailOnline*. Advertising revenues for its print titles fell by 13 per cent (and this decline actually increased to 15 per cent for the first quarter of 2016) – total revenues for the *Daily Mail* and *Mail on Sunday* fell 7 per cent, from £260 million to £242 million. In the same period, though, digital advertising grew 23 per cent on an underlying basis, with total *MailOnline* revenues climbing to £44 million.[11] Those numbers tell it all, really; the newspapers are still in command . . . but the future is digital.

'*MailOnline* could be an incredibly dominant business for a long time to come,' former Mailman Richard Addis, who was editor-in-chief at the *Express* group, told the author. 'That number-one position is so powerful in the media. It can last you for fifty years. It's fascinating to watch that transition, how a title can change from being very rooted and very politically engaged with British national life. The *Daily Mail* and British life, they're just synonymous, aren't they?

In the future, it could be completely detached from Britain – nothing to do with Britain at all.'[12]

Dacre is editor-in-chief at Associated Newspapers and, therefore, ultimately in charge editorially of *MailOnline* – Clarke, technically, answers to him. 'Nominally Martin still reports to him but Martin really takes no notice of Paul,' said insider 'Sean'. 'And they have quite a tricky relationship in the sense that Paul never wants to contradict him and doesn't want to overrule Martin. So, if there's an argument over staff then Paul nearly always gives way. Partly I think that's because Rothermere wants *MailOnline* to be his baby and he's underwritten a very substantial investment in *MailOnline* which he hopes one day will pay off (it keeps losing money, by the way – it's lost a ton of money). That's partly why I think Paul is nervous of Martin. So they have a slightly tricksy relationship because Martin is a hard character.

'They all think that Martin's a barbarian and uncouth and un-house-trained and there's truth in all of that actually. He's quite an unpleasant person. He's really, really talented but he's not a likeable chap in any way, shape or form.'[13]

That loss of power surely stings. But Dacre is an ink and newsprint man to his sensible shoes. The idea of him viscerally forcing together a webpage and counting its real-time clicks is absurd; the supreme *Mail* being has no real abiding love for the World Wide Web. It is a fact, though, that his *Daily Mail* newspaper is in decline – he has now presided over eight years or so of steadily falling sales of the newspaper that has been his life's work.

His pay packet, though, must help alleviate the pain.

Dacre is the best-paid editor in British newspaper history; he had an especially good year in 2014, when he earned £2.4 million, up a quarter on the previous year. Though that did fall by a million in 2015 – largely because his annual bonus was redirected to the company's long-term incentive plan.[14] He has invested wisely too; the Dacre family own a 17,000-acre Scottish estate – where people pay to shoot grouse and stalk deer – which, incidentally, has received hundreds of thousands of euros in EU subsidies for the editor of a newspaper that campaigned so vociferously for Brexit.[15] Both his sons went to Eton.

'His farm in Scotland has probably broadened his range of interests – he does go shooting,' added an insider. 'But that was something he took up quite belatedly, about 15 years ago because young Lord Rothermere is a keen shot . . . The relationship between Rothermere and Dacre has kept very close, but it's clear that Paul's power is not what it was when Jonathan was a much younger man. Rothermere and the board will decide who the next editor will be, not Paul. Once Paul leaves that job, what's he going to do? There's no other job he wants to go on to. That's part of the reason there's a bit of paralysis there . . . It's not like he wants to go and be a peer or run a think tank or a charitable foundation. All he wants to do is edit the *Daily Mail*. I don't even think he wants to go up to the boardroom. I don't think he'd be a great success up there. And Paul is quite an insecure man. His knowledge is newspapers and that's where his power base is. He's got no interest in moving off that job. I think he will keep making the case to Jonathan that he should stay in that job until he's seventy-five!'[16]

The editor-in-chief's weekday abode is a pretty £4.5 million[17] mews cottage with hanging baskets full of plants down a little cobbled lane behind the Portuguese Embassy in Belgravia, from where his chauffeur picks him up and takes him on the eight-minute drive to work and, on occasional evenings, to the Garrick Club, where Dacre can mix with its male-only membership: Cabinet ministers, senior bureaucrats, decrepit judges, and actors Damian Lewis, Hugh Bonneville and his biggest fan, Stephen Fry. The Garrick has been described as 'more daycare centre than a club',[18] due to the age of its members.

Some would argue that Paul Dacre left the middle classes far behind long ago and has almost made the leap of the Harmsworths, though they don't hand out peerages to men of the Press like they used to (Sunny Harmsworth, though, was already hugely wealthy when he founded the paper and he remained effectively editor-in-chief until the day he died).

Dacre may still be doing rather well, but his staff have been feeling the pinch in recent years. Section heads were told in 2014 to take at least one story off their long lists – the paper lifeboats that get them safely across Dacre's carpet in conference. 'There's still an embarrassment of riches, in terms of what's presented to the, you know, the fucking "Emperor",' snorted 'Jo', 'the tray of features from which he can choose.'[19] But freelancers haven't had a raise in years, and 'kill fees' – the money paid for a story that didn't make it into print (that were once more than other papers paid for a story they ran) – have also been frozen or cut.

'I think the more they trim back, the less the *Mail* can ask because the *Mail* expect so much more. There's no feature for the *Mail* that doesn't have a trail of drama behind it in terms of checks, queries,' a regular freelancer told the author. 'And yeah, the *Mail* pay twice what the *Express* does but you can knock out a story for the *Express* in a couple of hours.'[20]

The smartly attired middle-class folk who populate the paper are also slowly losing their dress sense. 'The hair and make-up budget is being slashed to ribbons,' said 'Penny', 'and it'll be interesting to see what impact that has on the people in the paper! I'm no management consultant but I could go in there tomorrow and in about two hours save them two million quid. Just the picture budget alone is huge, the hair and make-up. The re-shoots. The vast amount spent on polishing "the *Daily Mail* myth" is just nuts.'[21]

Sir David English loved a good foreign tale in his paper, it helped differentiate his *Daily Mail* from the filthy red-tops, but the foreign desk is not what it once was, as one retired foreign correspondent told the author: 'Dacre was – is – much, much more "little England" than David English. The last proper foreign editor quit about five years ago: since then the foreign desk has been downgraded to a few "phone answerers". His view on a foreign tale is, unless it can be reflected through the prism of Brexit/Middle England, he seems really not interested at all. For all his money, experience and foreign homes, he is a true little Englander.'

Sub-editors too, the folk who toil away long into the evening far from natural light constructing the paper – the last set of eyes to peruse those words before the reader – have also been hit. Margaret

Ashworth joined English's *Mail* in the mid-1970s and worked her way up to become the sub in charge of the front page until she retired in 2012. Whereas David English was proud to have 'the finest table in Fleet Street' and would reward a sub who wrote a great headline with a case of champagne, his successor Dacre 'has never really grasped what subs do, apart from, as he sees it, holding up production', she told the *Press Gazette*. 'I think he fears subs rather as people in the Middle Ages feared monks, because they were the only ones who could do the magic reading and writing.'[22]

Fear, that word again, always seems to follow Dacre around. At least he can escape his troubles at the family holiday home in the British Virgin Islands, from where he returns a month or so later with a nice deep tan and a tank refilled with rage. There are plenty of things that still make him very, very angry indeed: the BBC and its imposing of 'a liberal, leftish mono-culture'[23] upon society; he doesn't much like newspapers that are propped up by a trust (the *Guardian*) or wealthy owners (*The Times*) either; he truly loathes some senior judges who seem to be creating a privacy law by stealth; and, of course, the *Express*'s proprietor, the 'pornographer' Richard Desmond, has a special place in his heart.

Though the *Daily Mail* may well be on its way to selling half as many copies a day as it did during Dacre's peak years, its power – or more correctly, its *perceived* power – remains as high as it has ever been in the modern era. It is the first newspaper that many desk editors at the BBC and the *Guardian* reach for in the morning. Indeed, perhaps the most interesting thing of all about the *Daily Mail* is not even the *Daily Mail* itself but the reaction to it: it is truly despised by many people, people who are not – and were never intended to be – its core readership. And yet it seems those who hate it the most are those that believe most in its power.

Paul Dacre has managed to keep himself tucked safely away in the shadows for most of his reign. But he was forced out into the light, a little, in a row over former Labour leader Ed Miliband's father, the Marxist academic and writer Ralph Miliband.

Geoffrey Levy, a Mailman in his seventies who is firmly part of the Dacre 'old guard', wrote a piece eighteen months before the general election – which Ed always seemed destined to lose – in May 2015. 'The Man Who Hated Britain. Red Ed's pledge to bring back socialism is a homage to his Marxist father . . .'[24] The story got far more coverage after Miliband reacted angrily to it and demanded – and received – a right of reply (alongside which the *Mail* cheekily reprinted the offending piece). But the best part of the row was a live debate on the BBC's *Newsnight* programme between Blair's former media chief Alastair Campbell and *Mail* deputy editor at the time Jon Steafel, who turned out to be a polite and portly middle-aged Mailman with an almost perfectly spherical head. Campbell wanted to make this fight personal, wondering out loud – very loud – why Dacre himself was absent. 'What you've got to understand about the *Daily Mail*,' growled Campbell, is that 'it is the worst of British values posing as the best. If you do not conform to Paul Dacre's narrow, twisted view of the world – as all of his employees like Steafel have to do – you get done in. All I say, to all the politicians in Britain, once you accept you are dealing with a bully and a coward you have absolutely nothing to fear from them.' Campbell suggested Dacre was 'losing the plot' and Steafel and Rothermere knew it. 'The real poison comes from people like Dacre. He's a coward. He's a bully. He doesn't have the guts to come and defend himself against anybody and the sooner he's gone from British public life the better.'[25] Steafel left the paper in the summer of 2016 shortly after having being shunted aside to make way for Dacre's new deputy and potential successor, Gerard Greaves, from the *Mail on Sunday*.[26]

Dacre doesn't do telly but he did respond later, writing a piece for the *Guardian* headlined 'Why is the left obsessed by the *Daily Mail*?' and seemed slightly paranoid, suggesting it may even have been a dark bid by Miliband and the BBC to 'neutralize' Associated Newspapers.

'The screech of axe-grinding was deafening as the paper's enemies gleefully leapt to settle scores,' Dacre wrote; 'any newspaper which dares to take on the left in the interests of its readers risks being howled down by the Twitter mob who the BBC absurdly thinks represent the views of real Britain . . . Not to put too fine a point on things, we were right royally turned over. Fair enough, if you dish it out, you take it.'[27]

Ever more people now know the name 'Paul Dacre', including 50,000 people who signed a petition in June 2016 calling for him to be sacked over his paper's support for Britain leaving the EU and for spreading 'misinformation and fear' over migration.[28] Another 'fan' is Stephen Fry . . . they may both be members of the Garrick Club but it's a fair bet they don't lounge together upon a leather sofa.

> Dacre is, all those who have had the misfortune to work
> for him assure me, just about as loathsome, self-regarding,
> morally putrid, vengeful and disgusting a man as it is
> possible to be . . . He absolutely despises me and thinks
> I stand for everything that is wrong about Britain and I
> think exactly the same of him.[29]

Dacre does have his fans, though, and it is worth reiterating: 1.5 million people still put their hand in their pocket and pay (as of autumn 2016) 65p – 90p on Saturdays – for his newspaper in a fast-declining market. The actual number of readers – more than one person tends to read each copy of a newspaper – is estimated to be around 3.35 million.[30] Most of those people don't know – and don't care – who its editor is. Stephen Lawrence's mother praised Dacre for raising the profile of their son's murder case, and the mother of computer hacker Gary McKinnon is sure the paper's campaign on his behalf helped force the Government to withdraw his extradition to face charges in the US in 2012.

An interesting, slightly sideways take on the man was actually offered by the paper's astrologer, Jonathan Cainer, who died in 2016. Dacre signed Cainer from *Today* in his first year as *Mail* editor, but Cainer later saw it in his stars to join the *Express* and then the *Mirror* before returning home to what he once described as 'a newspaper dedicated to the subtle propagation of bigotry'. Cainer was a spiritual, liberal, peace-loving – and hugely wealthy, thanks to his tailored forecasts and phone lines – man who often disappeared for weeks to India. Yet he did find common ground with the editor of the *Daily Mail*. 'Working with Paul Dacre is very interesting,' he told the *Observer*. 'He's a living legend and a very shy man. He's also incredibly passionate: of all the mystics and intuitives and clairvoyants I've come into contact with, Dacre has a vibe about him of a magician.'[31]

Dozens of senior Mailmen and Femails spent years watching this 'magician' at close quarters as he expended almost his entire existence upon the *Daily Mail*. 'It *must* be psychological – we'd need Freud in the room,' said 'Terry', 'but very crudely it must be something to do with having lots of brothers and not feeling very important. And then feeling that you're a bit of a clutz as an adult. Then a desperation to "be someone" and then find yourself in a system which was extremely clear and simple. That's the great thing about a newspaper; it's just like a ship. There is *one* captain. You go up the hierarchy until you become the captain: *the* editor. Then you have total power. It's a total dictatorship.

'Yet his passions and the latent violence in his language and behaviour must be based on panic, fear – upon really, really deep emotions. I've always thought his rage was bluster to disguise a frailty – whatever the frailty is. And his political positions are so visceral, that's the only way to describe them; they're not logical or scientific or analytical at all, it's just "I'm feeling this." Again, it must be closely related to real fears . . . all those things to me are signs of insecurity. But I was never afraid of him at all. I'm still not. I just think he's a "complicated" human being. In many ways I'm very, very fond of him.'[32]

Sir John Junor, editor of the *Sunday Express* for three decades, was, it seems, the primary source for what young Paul Dacre thought an editor should be. But J. J. was a monster who bullied his two children and belittled and cheated on his wife, as his daughter Penny wrote in her biography of her father, *Home Truths*.

The father I knew as a child was a much more likeable
character than the volatile, didactic man he grew into.
The intolerance of age obviously contributed to that, but I
think the power he wielded as editor of the *Sunday Express*
for all those years changed him.

The *Mail* editor actually agreed to one of his very few interviews
to help Penny Junor with her book, and she wrote: 'Paul Dacre,
as a powerful editor himself, agrees it's a danger that goes with the
territory.'

'He had huge political power,' Dacre told her,

and huge respect and reverence by his own company and
by politicians. That's a dangerous, heady mix. You have
a job to which you devote a hundred hours a week, and
you're used to everyone dropping everything for you,
doing everything at your beck and call, never questioning
your judgement – and people didn't question JJ's judgement, he didn't like it if they did. Going home after that
can be very difficult.[33]

Yet go home he must. And though Paul Dacre is not remotely the
same kind of animal as John Junor – who died of gangrene of the gut
after a lifetime of hard liquor and womanizing – Dacre was forced to
stay off work in the early summer of 2015 as he convalesced after 'a
routine operation'. When he's not working, he is generally at the Dacre
family's main home in the countryside, near the village of Ticehurst in
East Sussex. As he told BBC Radio Four in the only proper broadcast
interview he has ever granted, 'I'm a very ordinary man.'

I am so boring. I go home. I wander around my garden
which I love. I read. I listen to music. I go to the pub and
have a drink with friends. And I retire to the bosom of
my family. From which I draw great strength.[34]

Most weekends, if the weather's fine, Paul Dacre is a picture of the typical, ageing middle-class Englishman sitting beside the lawn in a sunhat holding a nice cup of tea, rising gently to snip a rose for his drama teacher wife, Kathy, the girl from Liverpool whom he met at Leeds University. She is, says an insider, 'very much the power behind the throne'.[35] Most weekdays she is in their country pile and he stays at his mews house in London but they speak frequently on the phone. It's an interesting union and Dacre is clearly besotted by her, as he told the BBC's Sue Lawley.

> I do firmly believe that you cannot become a strong
> editor unless you have a strong family behind you and
> you understand the problems of a family. And no man
> can become a success unless he has a wife to pick him up
> when he's down, to put up with his shouting when he's
> tired and to encourage him in the dark moments. And my
> wife has. I've been very blessed in having that wife.[36]

Kathy Dacre is a drama teacher, not a screaming, foul-mouthed editor of a tabloid newspaper; the arts tend to be populated by people of a liberal bent, folk far more likely to take the *Guardian* than the *Daily Mail*, and their son James, who is a successful theatre director, clearly has his mother's genes. 'I have no idea if Kathy is left wing,' insider 'Sean' told the author, 'but you'd have thought she'd be a "luvvie" knowing her circle . . . But the love of the theatre is not something that she's transmitted to Paul. He has very little interest in the arts or theatre other than a bit of opera; he goes to the Glyndebourne opera festival in Sussex every year. But the theatre just didn't seem to move him at all.'[37]

The editor likes big weighty biographies and works of history, which are collected in for him by the *Mail*'s books department and which he reads on holiday. And he is, say insiders, a keen box set watcher – *Breaking Bad*, *The Sopranos* – and will often arrive on a Monday morning and discuss Sunday night's television at length.

At the end of that interview on *Desert Island Discs* – as per the format – the one book he chose to take to this mythical island was the Royal Horticultural Society's *A–Z Encyclopaedia of Garden Plants* and his luxury item was a year's subscription to the *Guardian*.

> It's a brilliant paper in so many ways but its patronizing, 'right on' sanctimonious political correctness gets me so angry. It would give me the energy and the willpower to get off that island and come back to England and I could sell my story – my Robinson Crusoe lifestyle story – to the *Daily Mail* for a fortune. And retire to my garden.[38]

Paul Dacre celebrated his twenty-fifth year as editor in 2017, a year before his seventieth birthday, yet it seems highly unlikely that he will voluntarily swap his mark-up pencil permanently for his garden snips any time soon – if he has the ability to push his lawnmower or get on his knees to weed, he would surely rather spend that energy on his *Daily Mail*.

'Paul is like all editors,' Vyvyan Harmsworth, whose great uncles founded the paper, told the author. 'They don't like giving up at all. David English went on right to the end (as editor-in-chief) too – with a very sick wife whom he adored. So I wouldn't speculate at all on Paul Dacre giving up any time in the near future. And this is the secret, probably, of the family business. This is, what, now the fourth generation? The skill of being a proprietor is to appoint your editor and let him get on with it and not to interfere.' And even if the word 'newspaper' does become just a metonym like 'Fleet Street', Vyvyan believes his family will be involved until the very end. 'The Harmsworths will be there as long as newspapers are there, in one form or another. We're moving with the times, as it were, with *MailOnline* – which has a tremendous and astonishing readership. As long as that progresses, we will go on publishing. I'd be very surprised if "newspapers" ever ended and the *Daily Mail* and our group wasn't the very last to stop publishing.'[39]

As his current editorial heir tends his English country garden, another Mailman's grassy plot hasn't seen a fresh flower in decades. Alfred C. Harmsworth's grave in a north London cemetery is looking pretty sorry for itself these days, and the two words 'Viscount Northcliffe' have all but faded from his headstone.

Sunny Harmsworth was the boy who liked to press ink on to paper and created a very simple formula for his *Daily Mail* while trying always to speak directly to *his* readers – without caring a damn about its critics. Bunny & Son may have been Harmsworths but they lacked Northcliffe's editorial gene, and Beaverbrook's *Express* stole his formula . . . then David English and Vere Harmsworth stole it back again. And despite Paul Dacre's quarter of a century in the top chair, the modern *Daily Mail* remains, say some who worked for both men, David English's darling. It is still *his* 'compact' template that Dacre colours in each day.

The paper's founding father may well have been dead for almost 100 years but Northcliffe's voice, retuned to speak to the class in the middle of the modern era, still rings through in the paper and online. Sunny Harmsworth's *Daily Mail* – love it or loathe it – seems sure to live on for a long time to come.

KEY
BIBLIOGRAPHY

BOOKS

Conrad Black, *A Matter of Principle*, McClelland & Stewart, 2011.

Richard Brooks, *The Great Tax Robbery: How Britain Became a Tax Haven for Fat Cats and Big Business*, Oneworld Publications, 2013.

William E. Carson, *Northcliffe, Britain's Man of Power*, Dodge Publishing Co., 1918.

Tom Clarke, *My Northcliffe Diary*, Victor Gollancz, 1931.

Paul Ferris, *The House of Northcliffe: The Harmsworths of Fleet Street*, Weidenfeld & Nicolson, 1971.

Richard Griffiths, *Fellow Travellers of the Right: British Enthusiasts for Nazi Germany 1933–39*, Oxford University Press, 1983.

History of the Times: The 150th Anniversary and Beyond, 1921–1948, published by The Times, 1952.

Kennedy Jones, *Fleet Street and Downing Street*, Hutchinson, 1920.

Penny Junor, *Home Truths: Life Around My Father*, HarperCollins, 2002.

Cecil H. King, *Strictly Personal: Some Memoirs*, Weidenfeld & Nicolson, 1969.

Lynda Lee-Potter, *Class Act: How to Beat the British Class System*, Metro Books, 2000.

F. A. McKenzie, *Mystery of the Daily Mail*, Associated Newspapers, 1921.

Louise Owen, *The Real Lord Northcliffe: Some Personal Recollections of a Private Secretary 1902–1922*, Cassell & Co., 1922.

Max Pemberton, *Lord Northcliffe: A Memoir*, Hodder & Stoughton,1922.

Reginald Pound and Geoffrey Harmsworth, *Northcliffe*, Cassell & Co., 1959.

Jean Rook, *The Cowardly Lioness*, Sidgwick & Jackson, 1989.

Roger Thomas Stearn, *War Images and Image Makers in the Victorian Era: Aspects of the British Visual and Written Portrayal of War And Defence c. 1866–1906*, PhD thesis, King's College University of London, 1987.

S. J. Taylor, *The Great Outsiders: Northcliffe, Rothermere and the Daily Mail*, Weidenfeld & Nicolson, 1996.

S. J. Taylor, *The Reluctant Press Lord: Esmond Rothermere and the Daily Mail*, Weidenfeld & Nicolson, 1998.

S. J. Taylor, *An Unlikely Hero: Vere Rothermere and how the Daily Mail was Saved*, Weidenfeld & Nicolson, 2002.

J. Lee Thompson, *Northcliffe: Press Baron in Politics 1865–1922*, John Murray, 2000.

Keith Waterhouse, *Streets Ahead: Life After City Lights*, Hodder & Stoughton (Sceptre paperback), 1995.

H. G. Wells, *Experiment in Autobiography*, 1934, Project Gutenberg Canada ebook no. 539.

R. McNair Wilson, *Lord Northcliffe: A Study*, Philadelphia, J. B. Lippincott, 1927.

NOTE ON SOURCES:

A number of background checks (births, etc.) were carried out by Gregor Murbach of Murbach Research – an independent researcher recommended by the National Archives who has worked for several media organizations including the BBC (http://www.nationalarchives.gov.uk/irlist/default.asp?action=1&slctcatagoryid=5). Gregor Murbach's website: http://murbachresearch.com.

NOTES

Introduction

1 John Cleese and Eric Idle at *Live Talks Los Angeles* on 18 November 2014. 'So, Anyway...' https://www.youtube.com/watch?v=AsEeBNonbZQ.

2 *Monty Python Live (mostly)*, O2 Arena, July 2014. https://www.youtube.com/watch?v=psmcz2vYKjs.

3 Gary Lineker's Twitter feed, 1 October 2013: https://twitter.com/garylineker/status/385167178586005505

4 'More than 50,000 sign petition calling for Daily Mail editor to be sacked', *Guardian*, 22 June 2016.

5 Paul Dacre, 'The Debt We Journalists Owe Sir David', *Daily Mail*, 11 June 1998.

6 'The Minx' media diary, *Daily Telegraph*, 4 October 2002.

7 Author interview with 'Terry', former senior Mailman, London, 6 October 2014.

8 *Newsnight*, BBC Two, 1 October 2013. https://www.youtube.com/watch?v=w-GMTxycAXY.

9 Paul Dacre, *Desert Island Discs*, BBC Radio Four, 25 January 2004.

10 Paul Dacre, 'Why is the left obsessed by the Daily Mail?', *Guardian*, 12 October 2013. http://www.theguardian.com/commentisfree/2013/oct/12/left-daily-mail-paul-dacre.

11 'National press ABCs: Daily Star and Times boost sales while Trinity Mirror's Sunday tabloids take a tumble', *Press Gazette*, 18 August 2016.

12 The average yearly rate of decline between January 2010 to January 2016 in ABC circulation figures was 4.69%. At this rate, the circulation would drop below the million mark in July 2025.

13 'Independent prints souvenir pullout as it moves to online only', *Guardian*, 25 March 2016.

14 'National press print ABCs for January: Mirror losing ground against cut-price Star ahead of new launch', *Press Gazette*, 18 February 2016.

15 Author interview with Vyvyan Harmsworth, senior member of the Harmsworth clan (he is descended from Vyvyan Harmsworth, brother of Alfred and Harold Harmsworth, the founders of the *Daily Mail*) and former Head of Corporate Affairs at Daily Mail and General Trust, 2 December 2016.

Chapter 1

1 Reginald Pound and Geoffrey Harmsworth, *Northcliffe*, Cassell, 1959.

2 H. G. Wells, *Experiment in Autobiography*, 1934, Project Gutenberg Canada ebook no 539.

3 Pound and Harmsworth, *Northcliffe*.

4 ibid.

5 Paul Ferris, *The House of Northcliffe: The Harmsworths of Fleet Street*, Weidenfeld & Nicolson, 1971.

6 Max Pemberton, *Lord Northcliffe, A Memoir*, Hodder & Stoughton, 1922.

7 ibid.

8 Ferris, *The House of Northcliffe*.

9 Pound and Harmsworth, *Northcliffe*.

10 *Answers to Correspondents*, 16 June 1888, bound back issues at the British Library, London.

11 Pound and Harmsworth, *Northcliffe*.

12 *Answers to Correspondents*, 30 June 1888, bound back issues at the British Library, London.

13 Pound and Harmsworth, *Northcliffe*.

14 S. J. Taylor, *The Great Outsiders: Northcliffe, Rothermere and the Daily Mail*, Weidenfeld & Nicolson, 1996.

15 Pound and Harmsworth, *Northcliffe*.

16 Cecil H. King, *Strictly Personal: Some Memoirs*, Weidenfeld & Nicolson, 1969.

17 Pound and Harmsworth, *Northcliffe*.

18 ibid.

19 Back issues of *Answers to Correspondents*, the British Library, London.

20 Pound and Harmsworth, *Northcliffe*.

21 Ferris, *The House of Northcliffe*.

22 Pound and Harmsworth, *Northcliffe*.

23 Back issues of *Answers to Correspondents*, British Library, London.

24 Ferris, *The House of Northcliffe*.

25 Kennedy Jones, *Fleet Street and Downing Street*, Hutchinson, 1920.

26 'Through Failure to Fortune', *Daily Mail*, 25 November 1898.

27 Pound and Harmsworth, *Northcliffe*.

Chapter 2

1 *Daily Mail*, 4 May 1896.

2 Ferris, *The House of Northcliffe*.

3 Lord Northcliffe, 'The Rise of the Daily Mail', *Daily Mail*, 4 May 1916.

4 Pound and Harmsworth, *Northcliffe*.

5 Jones, *Fleet Street and Downing Street*.

6 Pound and Harmsworth, *Northcliffe*.

7 G. W. Steevens, 'Bank Holiday – The Migration of London', *Daily Mail*, 4 August 1896.

8 Lord Northcliffe, 'The Rise of the Daily Mail', *Daily Mail*, 4 May 1916.

9 G. W. Steevens, 'What War Feels Like. No Emotions and No Moral', *Daily Mail*, 10 June 1897.

10 Pound and Harmsworth, *Northcliffe*.

11 'Lord Northcliffe – His Views, Plans and Career', *New York Times*, 11 October 1908.

12 Pound and Harmsworth, *Northcliffe*.

13 Arthur Keppel-Jones, *Rhodes and Rhodesia*, McGill-Queen's University Press, 1983.

14 *Daily Mail* Archive, British Library.

15 *Journal of Historical Review*, Volume 18, Number 3, Institute of Historical Review, 1999.

16 Ferris, *The House of Northcliffe*.

17 'Pandering to Sentiment', *Daily Mail*, 23 July 1901.

18 'Pro-Boer Methods', *Daily Mail* leader page, 24 January 1902.

19 'The Need for More Men', *Daily Mail*, 23 February 1900.

20 'Woman's Suffrage Meeting', *Daily Mail*, 27 June 1896.

21 J. Lee Thompson, *Northcliffe – Press Baron in Politics 1865–1922*, John Murray, 2000.

22 'Suffragettes in Parliament', *Daily Mail*, 24 October 1906.

23 Lady Charlotte, 'When Women Vote – What Will Happen?', *Daily Mail*, 19 February 1907.

24 Thompson, *Northcliffe – Press Baron in Politics*.

25 Pound and Harmsworth, *Northcliffe*.

26 ibid.

27 Ferris, *The House of Northcliffe*.

Chapter 3

1 Harmsworth's net worth was £886,000, say several biographies of Northcliffe. The thisismoney.co.uk (owned by the same company as the *Daily Mail*) historic inflation calculator gives a figure of £97,360,853.94 for 1901 to 2015 (the Bank of England site gives a higher figure of £98.2 million).

2 Ferris, *The House of Northcliffe*.

3 ibid.

4 ibid.

5 ibid.

6 Multiple articles, *Daily Mail* Archive, British Library, London, plus Ferris, *The House of Northcliffe*.

7 Taylor, *The Great Outsiders*.

8 The 'Under the Iron Heel' series ran for a fortnight in the *Daily Mail* from 24 September 1897.

9 'Death of Mr Lovat Fraser', *Daily Mail*, 21 April 1926.

10 Lovat Fraser, 'Why Should Britain Fight?', *Daily Mail*, 27 November 1912.

11 Lovat Fraser, 'A Dream of War in the Air', *Daily Mail*, 18 June 1914.

12 Tom Clarke, *My Northcliffe Diary*, Victor Gollancz, 1931. Note: the *Daily Mail* in its anniversary edition of 2014 stated that the 1914 paper had made a great deal of the assassination but I could find no record of this in the archives at the British Library.

13 *Daily Mail*, 5 August 1914.

14 'The Tragedy of the Shells – Lord Kitchener's Grave Error', *Daily Mail*, 21 May 1915.

15 Letter from Northcliffe to Keith Murdoch, 30 September 1915.

16 Pound and Harmsworth, *Northcliffe*.

17 *History of The Times, The 150th Anniversary and Beyond, 1921–1948*, published by *The Times*, 1952.

18 Lord Northcliffe, 'Lord Northcliffe On the Battlefield of Verdun', *Daily Mail*, 6 March 1916.

19 Pound and Harmsworth, *Northcliffe*.

20 ibid.

21 Clarke, *My Northcliffe Diary*.

22 ibid.

23 King, *Strictly Personal*.

24 Lord Northcliffe, 'Fashioning The New England', Weekly Dispatch, 10 December 1916.

25 'By the Man Who Dined with the Kaiser – Secret Service Work', *Daily Mail*, 28 January 1916.

26 *Daily Mail*, October 1916.

27 *The Somme 1916 – From Both Sides of the Wire, End Game (Part 3)*, Peter Barton and BBC TV, 2016.

28 Pound and Harmsworth, *Northcliffe*. Daily communique to the *Times* staff, 27 February 1917.

29 King, *Strictly Personal*.

30 H. G. Wells, 'Mr Wells and the Monster', *Daily Mail*, 24 August 1917.

31 Lovat Fraser, 'Why Prussia Must Pay', *Daily Mail*, 23 September 1918.

32 Lovat Fraser, 'The Island of Dreams', *Daily Mail*, 1 July 1913.

33 'A Glorious End', *Daily Mail*, 12 November 1918.

34 Thompson, *Northcliffe Press Baron in Politics*.

35 ibid.

36 Taylor, *The Great Outsiders*.

37 'Mr. Lloyd George Overdoes It', *Daily Mail*, 17 April 1919.

38 Ferris, *The House of Northcliffe*.

39 ibid.

40 Clarke, *My Northcliffe Diary*.

41 Ferris, *The House of Northcliffe*.

42 ibid.

43 'The Scandal of Ronald True', *Daily Mail*, 12 June 1922.

44 Lord Northcliffe, 'Incognito in Germany – Why Brussels Should Be Avoided by Tourists Crossing the Frontier', *Daily Mail*, 10 June 1922.

45 *History of the Times, The 150th Anniversary and Beyond, 1921–1948*, published by *The Times*, 1952.

46 King, *Strictly Personal*.

47 *History of the Times: The 150th Anniversary and Beyond, 1921–1948*.

48 ibid.

49 Pemberton, *Lord Northcliffe*.

50 Ferris, *The House of Northcliffe*.

51 ibid.

52 ibid.

53 Clarke, *My Northcliffe Diary*.

54 Ferris, *The House of Northcliffe*.

55 ibid.

Chapter 4

1 Ferris, *The House of Northcliffe*, and King, *Strictly Personal*.
2 'Rothermere's Son Slain', *New York Times*, 20 November 1916.
3 'Death of Lord Rothermere's Eldest Son', *Observer*, 17 February 1918.
4 King, *Strictly Personal*.
5 Taylor, *The Great Outsiders*, and S. J. Taylor, *The Reluctant Press Lord: Esmond Rothermere and the Daily Mail*, Weidenfeld & Nicolson, 1998.
6 King, *Strictly Personal*.
7 Ferris, *The House of Northcliffe*.
8 King, *Strictly Personal*.
9 Pound and Harmsworth, *Northcliffe*.
10 'Daily Mail Shares Kept from Editor,' *New York Times*, 1 December 1926.
11 King, *Strictly Personal*, p. 73. Conversion: £1,411,262,580, thisismoney.co.uk (*Mail*-owned) inflation calculator for 1926.
12 King, *Strictly Personal*.
13 'More Light on the Red Letter, How the Daily Mail Got It, Full Statement By Mr. Marlowe', *Observer*, 4 March 1928.
14 'Moscow's Orders', *Daily Mail*, 25 October 1924.
15 'More Light on the Red Letter, How the Daily Mail Got It, Full Statement By Mr. Marlowe', *Observer*, 4 March 1928.
16 Richard Norton-Taylor, 'Zinoviev letter was dirty trick by MI6', *Guardian*, 4 February 1999.
17 'For King and Country', *Daily Mail* editorial, 3 May 1926.
18 'Trade Unions and the Daily Mail', *Daily Mail*, 4 May 1926, and 'Focus on Fact – The General Strike', *Daily Mail*, 4 May 1976.
19 Sarah Bradford, *Elizabeth: A Biography of Her Majesty the Queen*, Penguin, 2002.
20 'Surrender of the Revolution – TUC Strike Called Off Unconditionally – Victory for the People', *Daily Mail*, 13 May 1926.
21 'Editor's Son Killed', *New York Times*, 22 April 1913.
22 'Uncle Shylock', *Daily Mail*, 20 July 1926.
23 Viscount Rothermere, 'Britain and the US, An Anglo-American Accord, Essential to World Peace', *Daily Mail*, 9 August 1926.
24 'Viscount Rothermere and Mr. Baldwin, Reply to Violent Speech', *Daily Mail*, 18 March 1931.
25 Viscount Rothermere, 'Will Wall-St. Swallow Europe?', *Daily Mail*, 26 July 1929.
26 Audited Bureau of Circulations: circulations, however, are unreliable in this period and mostly rely on 'T. B. Browne's Advertiser's ABC'.
27 Peter Lewis, 'Farewell to this Fleet Street giant', *Daily Mail*, 13 July 1978.
28 King, *Strictly Personal*.
29 Taylor, *The Great Outsiders*.
30 'The Late Mr. Thomas Marlowe, 27 Years Editor of Daily Mail', *Daily Mail*, 7 December 1935.

Chapter 5

1 Taylor, *The Great Outsiders*.
2 ibid.
3 King, *Strictly Personal*.
4 Taylor, *The Great Outsiders*.
5 ibid.
6 ibid.
7 Ferris, *The House of Northcliffe*.
8 ibid.
9 ibid.
10 'The Saviours of Italy', *Daily Mail* editorial, 19 December 1922.
11 Viscount Rothermere, 'What Europe Owes to Mussolini', *Daily Mail*, 17 September 1923.

12 'Mussolini Today, Special Interview By Viscount Rothermere', *Daily Mail*, 28 March 1928.

13 Viscount Rothermere, 'Will the Republic Endure?', *Daily Mail*, 8 October 1929.

14 'Germany and Inevitability – A Nation Reborn', by Viscount Rothermere, Munich, *Daily Mail*, 24 September 1930.

15 'Hitler's Special Talk to the Daily Mail', from Our Special Correspondent Rothay Reynolds, Leipzig, *Daily Mail*, 27 September 1930.

16 Viscount Rothermere, 'My Hitler Article and Its Critics', *Daily Mail*, 2 October 1930.

17 Neil Tweedie and Peter Day, 'When Rothermere urged Hitler to invade Romania', *Daily Telegraph*, 1 March 2005.

18 'Youth Triumphant', by Viscount Rothermere, Somewhere in Naziland, *Daily Mail*, 10 July 1933.

19 ibid.

20 Ferris, *The House of Northcliffe*.

21 Richard Griffiths, *Fellow Travellers of the Right*, Oxford University Press, 1983.

22 ibid.

23 ibid.

24 ibid.

25 ibid.

26 Viscount Rothermere, 'The Perils of Pinhead Pacifism', *Daily Mail*, 17 November 1933.

27 Taylor, *The Great Outsiders*.

28 ibid.

29 ibid.

30 Viscount Rothermere, 'Hurrah for the Blackshirts!', *Daily Mail*, 15 January 1934.

31 Griffiths, *Fellow Travellers of the Right*.

32 Viscount Rothermere, 'Give the Blackshirts a Helping Hand', *Daily Mail*, 22 January 1934.

33 Ferris, *The House of Northcliffe*.

34 'Germany on Her Feet Again', by Viscount Rothermere, Munich, Christmas Eve, *Daily Mail*, 28 December 1934.

35 Viscount Rothermere, 'Adolf Hitler at Close Range', *Daily Mail*, 4 June 1935.

36 Viscount Rothermere, 'Get Together With Germany', *Daily Mail*, 13 July 1936.

37 Viscount Rothermere, 'An Anglo-German Pact Means Peace', *Daily Mail*, 25 May 1937.

38 Viscount Rothermere, 'Some More Postscripts', *Daily Mail*, 20 May 1938.

39 Viscount Rothermere, 'Germany and Inevitability – A Nation Reborn', *Daily Mail*, 24 September 1930.

40 Viscount Rothermere, 'The Prisoners of Czecho-Slovakia', *Daily Mail*, 12 February 1937.

41 ibid.

42 ibid.

43 Viscount Rothermere, telegram to Adolf Hitler, 1 October 1938; Chris Horrie, *Tabloid Nation: The Birth of the Daily Mirror to the Death of the Tabloid*, Andre Deutsch, 2003.

44 Spartacus Educational website, Stephanie von Hohenlohe, accessed 12 July 2016. http://spartacus-educational.com/Stephanie_von_Hohenlohe.htm.

45 Griffiths, *Fellow Travellers of the Right*.

46 Neil Tweedie and Peter Day, 'When Rothermere urged Hitler to invade Romania', *Daily Telegraph*, 1 March 2005.

47 Viscount Rothermere, 'Further Postscripts', *Daily Mail*, 13 May 1939.

48 Viscount Rothermere, 'Further Postscript', *Daily Mail*, 17 June 1939.

Chapter 6

1 Taylor, *The Reluctant Press Lord*.

2 ibid.

3 Dennis Griffiths, *Fleet Street: Five Hundred Years of the Press*, British Library Publishing Division, 2006.

4 'War's Greatest Picture: St Paul's Stands Unharmed in the Midst of the Burning City', *Daily Mail*, 13 December 1940.

5 'Chronology of Key Events in the History of the Daily Mail', Gale Archive.

6 Taylor, *The Reluctant Press Lord*.

7 ibid.

8 ibid.

9 David Adams Richards, *Lord Beaverbrook*, Penguin Canada, 2008, and A. J. P. Taylor, *Beaverbrook*, Hamish Hamilton, 1972.

10 ibid.

11 1947: *Express* 3,855,000, *Mail* 2,076,000. 1939: *Express* 2,546,000, *Mail* 1,533,000. 1930: *Express* 1,693,000, *Mail* 1,845,000. 1921: *Express* 579,000, *Mail* 1,533,000. 1910: *Express* 400,000, *Mail* 900,000. Source: ABC.

12 S. J. Taylor, *An Unlikely Hero: Vere Rothermere and How the Daily Mail Was Saved*, Weidenfeld & Nicolson, 2002.

13 Andrew Lycett, *Ian Fleming*, Weidenfeld & Nicolson, 1995.

14 ibid.

15 Taylor, *The Reluctant Press Lord*.

16 ibid.

17 *Time* magazine, 5 June 1950.

18 *The Best of Vincent Mulchrone*, a Daily Mail Publication, 1978.

19 ibid.

20 Vincent Mulchrone, 'How I got mixed up with these cow kickers', *Daily Mail*, 30 July 1966.

21 ibid.

22 Taylor, *The Reluctant Press Lord*.

23 ibid.

24 *The Best of Vincent Mulchrone* by Vincent Mulchrone, Revel Barker, 2008.

25 Vincent Mulchrone, 'This Beatlemania', *Daily Mail*, 21 October 1963.

26 *Daily Mail*, 7 January 1967.

27 'Holes in the Road', *Daily Mail*, 7 January 1967.

28 'LSD: "I had the feeling of experiencing the birth of the universe", by Hugh McLeave, Daily Mail Science Correspondent, *Daily Mail*, 22 April 1966.

29 'Pushers, pills and penalties', *Daily Mail*, 3 July 1967.

30 Jon Henley, Rupert Murdoch and the battle of Wapping: 25 years on', *Guardian*, 27 July 2011.

31 Taylor, *The Great Outsiders*.

32 Taylor, *The Reluctant Press Lord*.

33 ibid.

Chapter 7

1 Viscount Rothermere, Vere Harmsworth, *Desert Island Discs*, BBC Radio 4, 14 April 1996.

2 Lynn Barber, 'A Lord unto himself', *Observer*, 29 June 1997.

3 Viscount Rothermere, Vere Harmsworth, *Desert Island Discs*, BBC Radio 4, 14 April 1996.

4 Geoffrey Levy, 'The Making of a Newspaper Legend', *Daily Mail*, 11 June 1998.

5 Author interview with Tony Burton, close friend of David English and *Daily Mail* reporter, 15 November 2014.

6 Taylor, *The Reluctant Press Lord*.

7 ibid.

8 Author interview with Cyril 'Chris' Rees, close friend of David English and *Daily Mail* managing editor, 17 November 2014.

9 King, *Strictly Personal*.

10 Author interview with Tony Burton, 15 November 2014.

11 ibid.

12 ibid.

13 ibid.

14 ibid.

15 Taylor, *The Reluctant Press Lord*.

16 Terence Lancaster, 'Obituary: Sir David English', *Independent*, 12 June 1998.

17 'Silly Stunt – Newsmen Off Easy in Mail Theft', Reuters News Agency, 19 September 1952.

18 Author interview with Barry Norman, former *Daily Mail* showbiz writer and *Daily Sketch* reporter, 13 November 2014.

19 Geoffrey Levy, 'The Making of a Newspaper Legend', *Daily Mail*, 11 June 1998.

20 Taylor, *The Reluctant Press Lord*.

21 Waxey Gordon, says Wikipedia, 'was sentenced to 25 years' imprisonment in Alcatraz, where he died of a heart attack on June 24, 1952 . . . In *The Waxey Gordon Story*, a 1960 episode of *The Untouchables*, Gordon was played by Nehemiah Persoff.'

22 Terence Lancaster, 'Obituary: Sir David English', *Independent*, 12 June 1998.

23 Author interview with Tony Burton, 15 November 2014.

24 ibid.

25 ibid.

26 'My Mentor: Ann Leslie on Sir David English', *Independent*, 8 May 2006.

27 Jean Rook, *The Cowardly Lioness*, Sidgwick & Jackson, 1989.

28 Author interview with Shirley Conran, creator of *Femail* and senior *Daily Mail* executive, 21 November 2014.

29 ibid.

30 ibid.

31 *Femail*, edited by Shirley Conran, *Daily Mail*, 29 October 1968.

Chapter 8

1 Taylor, *The Reluctant Press Lord*.

2 Dacre, 'The Debt We Journalists Owe Sir David', *Daily Mail*, 11 June 1998.

3 Taylor, *The Reluctant Press Lord*.

4 Noel Barber, 'Here's our new man at the top', *Daily Mail*, 10 March 1971.

5 *The New York World*, 1 January 1901.

6 Author interview with Brian Freemantle, former *Daily Mail* foreign editor, London, 25 March 2014.

7 Taylor, *The Reluctant Press Lord*, and *An Unlikely Hero*.

8 Taylor, *An Unlikely Hero*.

9 Author interview with Brian Freemantle, 25 March 2014.

10 Author interview with Barry Norman, 13 November 2014.

11 ibid.

12 'What We Believe', *Daily Mail*, Comment, 3 May 1971.

13 Author interview with Brian Freemantle, 25 March 2014.

14 ibid.

15 Michael Leapman, 'Obituary: Viscount Rothermere', *Independent*, 3 September 1998.

16 'Every Woman Needs Her Daily Mail', *Daily Mail*, 31 March 1973.

17 Author interview with Charlie Whebell, former messenger boy on the *Daily Mail*, 14 November 2014.

18 Author interview with Anthea Disney, former *Daily Mail* editorial executive and New York bureau chief, 10 January 2014.

19 Author interview with Brian Freemantle, 25 March 2014.

20 Author interview with Anthea Disney, 10 January 2014.

20 Author interview with Brian Freemantle, 25 March 2014.

22 Author interview with Anthea Disney, 10 January 2014.

23 Terence Lancaster, 'Obituary: Sir David English', *Independent*, 12 June 1998.

24 Author interview with Michael Brennan, former *Daily Mail* and freelance photographer based in Manchester, London and New York City, 15 January 2014.

25 Author interview with Charlie Whebell, 14 November 2014.

26 'Thalidomide: The Fifty Year Fight,' BBC Documentary, 2014.

27 Taylor, *An Unlikely Hero*.
28 Author interview with Charlie Whebell, 14 November 2014.

Chapter 9

1   'Ancient British Dishes: No1 . . . Rook Pie', *Daily Mail*, 12 May 1972.
2   Jean Rook, 'Introducing a very important lady in your life . . .' *Daily Mail*, 5 May 1971.
3   Jean Rook, 'It's all bang, smash, grab, isn't it?', *Daily Mail*, 12 May 1971.
4   Jean Rook, 'Talking about nuisances, what secretary can't tell when her boss has had a row with his wife?', *Daily Mail*, 9 June 1971.
5   Jean Rook, 'Philip's pearls of wisdom often drop with a clang', *Daily Mail*, 23 June 1971.
6   Rook, *The Cowardly Lioness*.
7   Taylor, *An Unlikely Hero*.
8   Lynda Lee-Potter obituary, *Daily Telegraph*, 21 October 2004.
9   'Tributes to Sir David, a Giant of Journalism', *Daily Mail*, 11 June 1998.
10 Lynda Lee-Potter, *Class Act – How to Beat the British Class System*, Metro Books, 2000.
11 Lynda Lee-Potter obituary, *Independent*, 21 October 2004.
12 Rod Gilchrist, 'Obituary letter: How the "she cat" got her claws', *Guardian*, 21 October 2004.
13 'Come off it Mrs Thatcher . . . Let's see you hit back with a bit of the snooty, steel-blue-eyed bitch!', *Daily Mail*, 15 December 1971.
14 'Margaret Thatcher talking to Lynda Lee-Potter – The criticism has been vicious. But you build an armour . . . you know it's untrue', *Daily Mail*, 8 February 1972.
15 David English, 'Tony at our table', *Guardian* (reprinted from the *Spectator*), 6 October 1995.
16 'Profile: Hard news man switches channels: Sir David English: The former Daily Mail editor reveals to Jason Nisse that he has lost none of his competitiveness', *Independent on Sunday*, 7 November 1993.
17 Author interview with Brian Freemantle, former *Daily Mail* foreign editor, London, 25 March 2014.
18 Author interview with Anthea Disney, 10 January 2014.
19 'Tributes to Sir David, a Giant of Journalism', *Daily Mail*, 11 June 1998.
20 Author interview with Brian Freemantle, 25 March 2014.
21 Vincent Mulchrone and Angus MacPherson, 'Sleeping peacefully and flying to a new life – the waifs of Vietnam', *Daily Mail*, 7 April 1975.
22 Author interview with Brian Freemantle, 25 March 2014.
23 ibid.
24 ibid.

Chapter 10

1   Ian Mather, 'The big scoop flop', *Observer*, 22 May 1977.
2   Taylor, *An Unlikely Hero*.
3   David English, 'A message from the Editor to you the reader', *Daily Mail*, 25 May 1977.
4   Taylor, *The Reluctant Press Lord*.
5   Taylor, *An Unlikely Hero*.
6   ibid.
7   David English, 'The Editor of the Daily Mail talks to the Tory leader in her only major interview of the campaign', *Daily Mail*, 17 April 1979.
8   'It's history – a woman takes over No 10. Prime Minister Maggie!', *Daily Mail*, 4 May 1979.
9   David English, 'We Fought Them, We Beat Them and We Shall Keep On Fighting Them', *Daily Mail*, 1 April 1981.
10 Author interview with Brian Freemantle, former *Daily Mail* foreign editor, 25 March 2014.
11 Daniel J. Wakin, 'Rev. Sun Myung

Moon, Self-Proclaimed Messiah Who Built Religious Movement, Dies at 92', *New York Times*, 2 September 2012.

12 James Gibbins, 'Beggars in bowlers', *Daily Mail*, 22 May 1978.

13 James Gibbins, 'On Which the Sun Never Sets', *Village Voice*, 17 July 1978.

14 James Gibbins, 'Now Jim Plays the Iron Man', *Daily Mail*, 31 May 1978.

15 James Gibbins, 'Abraham Carter . . . ! The latest bizarre scheme to save his face', *Daily Mail*, 27 June 1978.

16 James Gibbins, 'On Which the Sun Never Sets', *Village Voice*, 17 July 1978.

17 James Gibbins, 'I Was Mugged by the Washington Post', *Washington Post*, 23 July 1978.

18 James Gibbins, 'The Press', *Spectator*, 29 September 1978.

19 'The Press: "Scoop" by Patrick Marnham', *Spectator*, 29 September 1978 (via the *Spectator* archive – http://archive.spectator.co.uk/article/30th-september-1978/15/the-press)

20 Author interview with Simon Winchester, former *Daily Mail* bureau chief in New York City, 12 January 2014.

21 ibid.

22 Author interview with senior Mailman 'Terry', 6 October 2014.

23 '"Bullets that shattered a myth", David English goes back to Dallas where 25 years ago as a White House Correspondent he reported on the murder of President Kennedy', *Daily Mail*, 22 November 1988.

24 Author interview with Brian Freemantle, 25 March 2014.

25 '"Bullets that shattered a myth", David English goes back to Dallas where 25 years ago as a White House Correspondent he reported on the murder of President Kennedy', *Daily Mail*, 22 November 1988.

26 Author interview with David Eliades, former *Daily Express* reporter and friend of David English, Peter Dacre and Paul Dacre, 13 November 2014.

27 ibid.

28 Author interview with Brian Freemantle, 25 March 2014.

29 Author interview with David Eliades, 13 November 2014.

30 Alun John, 'Birth of a National', *Gentlemen Ranters – the last pub in Fleet Street*, 13 July 2007. www.gentlemenranters.com/19.html.

31 ibid.

32 Author interview with Susan Douglas, former senior *Daily Mail* and *Mail on Sunday* editorial executive, 26 March 2014.

33 Alun John, 'Birth of a National', *Gentlemen Ranters – the last pub in Fleet Street*, 13 July 2007. www.gentlemenranters.com/19.html.

34 'Tributes to Sir David, a Giant of Journalism', *Daily Mail*, 11 June 1998.

35 Author interview with Richard Addis, former senior *Daily Mail* editorial executive, 6 October 2014.

36 Dacre, 'The Debt We Journalists Owe Sir David', *Daily Mail*, 11 June 1998.

37 S. J. Taylor, *An Unlikely Hero*.

Chapter 11

1 Evidence: London Electoral Register for the Southgate Constituency 1955 and 1965, plus the passenger manifest for the Cunard ocean liner RMS *Queen Elizabeth* from New York, landing in Southampton on 6 March 1958 with Peter and Joan Dacre and their five sons: Paul, Clive, Martin, Nigel and Myles.

2 Lauren Collins, 'The Wayward Press: Mail Supremacy – the newspaper that rules Britain', *New Yorker*, 2 April 2012.

3 Peter Dacre obituary, *Daily Telegraph*, 25 March 2003.

4 ibid.

5   Paul Dacre, quoted in Penny Junor, *Home Truths: Life Around My Father*, HarperCollins, 2002.
6   Author interview with Barry Norman, 13 November 2014.
7   Author interview with David Eliades, 13 November 2014.
8   Paul Dacre, *Desert Island Discs*, BBC Radio 4, 25 January 2004.
9   Paul Dacre, Society of Editors speech in full, *Press Gazette*, 9 November 2008.
10 'Profile: That's enough fawning on the Tories – Ed: Paul Dacre, a fresh stamp on the "Daily Mail"', *Independent*, 3 October 1992.
11 Author interview (via email) with Michael Sadgrove, school contemporary of Paul Dacre and now the Very Reverend Dean of Durham, 17 December 2014.
12 Author interview with 'Sean', former senior *Daily Mail* executive, 24 November 2016.
13 Pearson Phillips, 'This POISON spread in the name of peace', *Daily Mail*, 19 March 1968.
14 Paul Dacre, *Desert Island Discs*, BBC Radio 4, 25 January 2004.
15 'The man who hates liberal Britain', by Peter Wilby, *New Statesman*, 20 December 2013.
16 Paul Dacre delivers the Cudlipp Lecture, London College of Communication, 22 January 2007.
17 'Dacre's press gang, the real Brian Clough and my time with the Foxes', Jon Holmes diary, *New Statesman*, 13 January 2013.
18 'Union News Wins Student Paper of the Year', *Union News*, 2 May 1969.
19 'Paul Dacre', Profile with Mark Coles, BBC Radio Four, 6 October 2013.
20 Author interview with Michael Brennan, 15 January 2014.
21 Paul Dacre, *Desert Island Discs*, BBC Radio 4, 25 January 2004.
22 Author interview with Michael Brennan, 15 January 2014.
23 *Gentlemen Ranters – the last pub in Fleet Street*, 5 October 2007, www.gentlemenranters.com.
24 ibid.
25 Author interview with Anthea Disney, 10 January 2014.
26 Author interview with Tony Burton, 15 November 2014.
27 Author interview with Anthea Disney, 10 January 2014.
28 Marriage certificate, 24 September 1979, Peter Dacre and Ann Elizabeth Jarvis. Sheffield Registry Office.
29 Author interview with Phil Finn Jr (now deceased), former *Daily Express* staff reporter and *Daily Mail* freelance in New York City, and his wife Anne-Marie, 11 November 2014.
30 *Gentlemen Ranters – the last pub in Fleet Street*, 5 October 2007, www.gentlemenranters.com.
31 Author interview with David Eliades, 13 November 2014.
32 Author interview with Phil Finn Jr and his wife Anne-Marie, 11 November 2014.
33 As told to the author by George Gordon and Michael Brennan, January 2014.
34 Author interview with Michael Brennan, 15 January 2014.
35 ibid.
36 ibid.
37 Author interview with David Eliades, 13 November 2014.
38 Author interview with Simon Winchester, 12 January 2014.
39 'One step away from public execution', from Paul Dacre in New York, *Daily Mail*, 26 October 1979.
40 'It's a bedroom farce', from Paul Dacre in New York, *Daily Mail*, 20 October 1979.
41 Author interview with David Eliades, 13 November 2014.
42 Paul Dacre, *Desert Island Discs*, BBC Radio 4, 25 January 2004.

43 Author interview with George Gordon, former *Daily Mail* bureau chief in New York and long term *Mail* reporter, 13 January 2014.

44 ibid.

45 'America column by Paul Dacre, signing off, Goodbye to all this', *Daily Mail*, 10 October 1980.

46 Author interview with George Gordon, former *Daily Mail* bureau chief in New York and long term *Mail* reporter, 13 January 2014.

47 Paul Dacre, Society of Editors speech in full, *Press Gazette*, 9 November 2008.

48 Paul Dacre, *Desert Island Discs*, BBC Radio 4, 25 January 2004.

49 Author interview with Tim Miles, former *Daily Mail* reporter, crime reporter, chief reporter and news editor, 8 December 2014.

50 ibid.

51 ibid.

52 ibid.

53 Author interview with Stewart Payne, former *Daily Mail* reporter, 19 January 2015.

54 ibid.

55 Author interview with Gill Swain, former *Daily Mail* reporter, 20 January 2015.

56 Author interview with Stewart Payne, 19 January 2015.

57 Author interview with 'Barry', former senior Mailman, 4 July 2015.

58 Author interview with Stewart Payne, 19 January 2015.

59 ibid.

60 ibid.

61 ibid.

62 Author interview with Tony Burton, 15 November 2014.

63 Author interview with Stewart Payne, 19 January 2015.

64 Author interview with Gill Swain, 20 January 2015.

65 Author interview with former Mailman 'Glen', 29 August 2016.

66 Author interview with Tim Miles, 8 December 2014.

67 ibid.

68 ibid.

69 Author interview with Stewart Payne, 19 January 2015.

70 Paul Dacre, Society of Editors speech in full, *Press Gazette*, 9 November 2008.

71 Author interview with Susan Douglas, former senior *Daily Mail* and *Mail on Sunday* editorial executive, 26 March 2014.

72 'Profile: That's enough fawning on the Tories - Ed: Paul Dacre, a fresh stamp on the Daily Mail', *Independent*, 3 October 1992.

73 Author interview with Susan Douglas, 26 March 2014.

74 ibid.

75 ibid.

76 Author interview with 'Terry', 6 October 2014.

77 Author interview with Susan Douglas, 26 March 2014.

Chapter 12

1 'Edited Highlights', *Spectator*, 6 February 1988.

2 Ian Wooldridge, 'Zola Deserves Warm Welcome After All We Put Her Through', *Daily Mail*, 9 April 2003.

3 Author interview with Stewart Payne, 19 January 2015.

4 Author interview with Vyvyan Harmsworth, senior member of the Harmsworth clan (he is descended from Vyvyan Harmsworth, brother of Alfred and Harold Harmsworth, the founders of the *Daily Mail*) and former Head of Corporate Affairs at Daily Mail and General Trust, 2 December 2016.

5 Author interview with Susan Douglas, 26 March 2014.

6 ibid.

7 ibid.

8   Author interview with Tony Burton, 15 November 2014.

9   Andrew Alderson, 'At the court of King David – David English', *Sunday Times*, 12 July 1992.

10 Author interview with Tony Burton, 15 November 2014.

11 Author interview with Stewart Payne, 19 January 2015.

12 Author interview with 'Barry', 4 July 2015.

13 Author interview with 'Terry', 6 October 2014.

14 Author interview with Gill Swain, 20 January 2015.

15 'Profile: That's enough fawning on the Tories - Ed: Paul Dacre, a fresh stamp on the Daily Mail', *Independent*, 3 October 1992.

16 Dave Hill, 'Major's Knight Editor', *Guardian*, 9 March 1992.

17 David English, 'This is my New Crusade', *Daily Mail*, 29 April 1988.

18 'Profile: Hard news man switches channels: Sir David English: The Former Daily Mail editor reveals to Jason Nisse that he has lost none of his competativeness', *Independent on Sunday*, 7 Novemeber 1993.

19 'Sir Geoffrey the Assassin', *Daily Mail*, 14 November 1990.

20 'Majestic Maggie', Lynda Lee-Potter column, *Daily Mail*, 14 November 1990.

21 'Too Damn Good for the Lot of Them', *Daily Mail*, 23 November 1990.

22 Author interview with Cyril 'Chris' Rees, 17 November 2014.

23 Author interview with Tony Burton, 15 November 2014.

24 Author interview with Anthea Disney, 10 January 2014.

25 Author interview with Tony Burton, 15 November 2014.

26 'John Leese, brilliant editor who achieved success with the highest of standards', *Daily Mail*, 1 March 1991.

27 Paul Dacre, *Desert Island Discs*, BBC Radio 4, 25 January 2004.

28 ibid.

29 Graham Lord, 'John Junor: "A bigot and blatant hypocrite who lost 2.5m sales over 32 years"', *Press Gazette*, 10 April 2013.

30 Penny Junor, *Home Truths: Life Around My Father*, HarperCollins, 2002.

31 Graham Lord, 'John Junor: "A bigot and blatant hypocrite who lost 2.5m sales over 32 years"', *Press Gazette*, 10 April 2013.

32 Paul Dacre, Society of Editors speech in full, *Press Gazette*, 9 November 2008.

33 Author interview with Anne de Courcy, former *Daily Mail* and *Evening Standard* writer, 10 January 2014.

34 Taylor, *An Unlikely Hero*.

35 Author interview with 'Kevin', *Standard* and *Mail* writer, 9 October 2014.

36 Author interview with 'Kerry', *Standard* staffer, 30 October 2013.

37 Author interview with Andrew Knight, former executive chairman of News International (owner of *The Times*), via email, 27, 28 and 29 February 2016.

38 ibid.

39 Rupert Murdoch at the Leveson Inquiry, 26 April 2012, sourced from the National Archive's web archive.

40 Andrew Alderson, 'At the court of King David – David English', *Sunday Times*, 12 July 1992.

41 ibid.

42 Author interview with Andrew Knight, 27 February 2016.

43 'New Chairman for Associated Newspapers and a New Editor for the Daily Mail After 21 Years', *Daily Mail*, 11 July 1992.

44 Andrew Alderson, 'At the court of King David – David English', *Sunday Times*, 12 July 1992.

45 ibid.

46 Author interview with 'Terry', 6 October 2014.

Chapter 13

1 Bill Hagerty, 'Paul Dacre: the zeal thing', *British Journalism Review*, Vol. 13, No. 3, 2002.

2 Paul Dacre, *Desert Island Discs*, BBC Radio 4, 25 January 2004.

3 Author interview with 'Duncan', 6 October 2014.

4 Author interview with 'Terry', 6 October 2014.

5 'Profile: Hard news man switches channels: Sir David English: The Former Daily Mail editor reveals to Jason Nisse that he has lost none of his competativeness', *Independent on Sunday*, 7 Novemeber 1993.

6 Author interview with 'Duncan', former senior Mailman, 9 October 2014.

7 Author interview with 'Terry', 6 October 2014.

8 Bill Hagerty, 'Paul Dacre: the zeal thing', *British Journalism Review*, Vol. 13, No. 3, 2002.

9 Author interview with George Gordon, 13 January 2014.

10 Jason Lewis, 'Abortion hope after "gay genes" findings', *Daily Mail*, 16 July 1993.

11 'Gay gene anger', Andy Seale and Miss M. M. Rees, *Daily Mail*, letters page, 22 July 1993.

12 Author interview with 'Terry', 6 October 2014.

13 Author interview with Jane Kelly, former *Daily Mail* feature writer, 9 December 2013.

14 Author interview with 'Duncan', 9 October 2014.

15 Author interview with 'Roy', former *Daily Mail* feature writer, 11 November 2013.

16 Author interview with 'Terry', 6 October 2014.

17 Bill Hagerty, 'Paul Dacre: the zeal thing', *British Journalism Review*, Vol. 13, No. 3, 2002.

18 'Coming tomorrow, the Daily Mail's fabulous new WEEKEND magazine', Friday, 15 October 1993.

19 'Awards hat-trick for the brilliant Mail', *Daily Mail*, 17 February 1996.

20 Conrad Black, *A Matter of Principle*, McClelland & Stewart, 2011.

21 Satish Sekar and Paul Peachey, 'Spate of racist stabbings in Eltham had gone unpunished', *Independent*, 4 January 2012.

22 'Daily Mail editor Paul Dacre "met Stephen Lawrence"', BBC London, 27 January 2012.

23 Bill Hagerty, 'Paul Dacre: the zeal thing', *British Journalism Review*, Vol. 13, No. 3, 2002.

24 'MURDERERS', *Daily Mail*, 14 February 1997.

25 Author interview with long-term Mail man, 12 January 2015.

26 'Video: Paul Dacre, Daily Mail Editor, on the risks he and the Mail ran to secure justice for Stephen Lawrence', *MailOnline*, 4 January 2012.

27 Author interview with Tim Miles, 8 December 2014.

28 Paul Dacre, 'A glorious day for justice: How the Mail's monumental risk could have put editor Paul Dacre in court . . . but instead did "a huge amount of good and made a little bit of history"', *Daily Mail*, 4 January 2012.

29 'Triumph of the middle classes: The Daily Mail's proprietor shares his thoughts on the election with Philip Stephens', *Financial Times*, 28 April 1997.

30 Lynn Barber, 'A Lord unto himself', *Observer*, 29 June 1997.

31 David English, 'Tony at Our Table', *Spectator*, October 1995.

32 ibid.

33 ibid.

34 ibid.

35 Viscount Rothermere, Vere Harmsworth, newspaper proprietor, 'castaway' on *Desert Island Discs*, BBC Radio Four, 14 April 1996.

36 ibid.

37 'The Battle for Britain', *Daily Mail*, Comment, 15 April 1997.

38 *Daily Mail*, 30 April 1997.

39 ibid.

40 Roy Greenslade, '18 years of certainty, 16 days of doubt', *Guardian*, 17 May 1997.

41 David Hughes, 'The Great Don't Know Factor', *Daily Mail*, 1 May 1997.

42 'I'd like to vote for the Tories, but . . .' 'After voting Labour in 1997, I want to vote Tory in the next General Election . . .' Lynda Lee-Potter column, 8 October 2003.

43 Roy Greenslade, '18 years of certainty, 16 days of doubt', *Guardian*, 17 May 1997.

44 *Daily Mail*, Comment, 2 May 1997.

45 Roy Greenslade, '18 years of certainty, 16 days of doubt', *Guardian*, 17 May 1997.

46 Lord Rothermere, 'Why I have joined Labour', *Evening Standard*, 23 May 1997.

47 Peter Hillmore, 'Rothermere's switch to Labour pains the Mail', *Observer*, 25 May 1997.

48 Lynn Barber, 'A Lord unto himself', *Observer*, 29 June 1997.

49 'Triumph of the middle classes: The Daily Mail's proprietor shares his thoughts on the election with Philip Stephens', *Financial Times*, 28 April 1997.

50 Stephen Glover column in the *Spectator*, 30 May 1997.

Chapter 14

1 Lynda Lee-Potter, 'She spoke for everyone's need for hugs and contact', *Daily Mail*, 1 September 1997.

2 Lynda Lee-Potter, 'Go on Di, Dodi's the best catch around', *Daily Mail*, 13 August 1997.

3 Lynda Lee-Potter, 'Princes need a modest mother', *Daily Mail*, 27 August 1997.

4 Lynda Lee-Potter, 'Praise – that's all Diana really wants', *Daily Mail*, 6 December 1995.

5 Lynda Lee-Potter, 'Don't be taken in by Diana', *Daily Mail*, 16 July 1997.

6 Michael Leapman, 'The NS profile: Lynda Lee-Potter', *New Statesman*, 25 September 2000.

7 Lynda Lee-Potter, 'She's a winner of a wife, so why do they keep on trying to wound her?', *Daily Mail*, 29 April 1987.

8 'Editors in pledge on privacy', *Daily Mail*, 18 September 1997.

9 'Press shows way in self regulation', *Daily Mail*, 7 May 1998.

10 'Triumph of the middle classes: The Daily Mail's proprietor shares his thoughts on the election with Philip Stephens', *Financial Times*, 28 April 1997.

11 Lynn Barber, 'A Lord unto himself', *Observer*, 29 June 1997.

12 Author interview with Tony Burton, 15 November 2014.

13 Author interview with Cyril 'Chris' Rees, 17 November 2014.

14 Author interview with the Dowager Lady Rothermere, 17 July 2014.

15 Author interview with Cyril 'Chris' Rees, 17 November 2014.

16 Author interview with Tony Burton, 15 November 2014.

17 Geoffrey Levy, 'The Making of a Newspaper Legend', *Daily Mail*, 11 June 1998.

18 Evidence: 1. Civil registration index (births): David English, born Bef. June 1930, Woodstock, Oxfordshire (mother's maiden name: Brazenor). 2. Civil registration index (deaths): Sir David English, died in 1998, DOB: 26 May 1930. 3. *Oxford Dictionary of National Biography* – DOB: 26 May 1930 in Combe, near Woodstock. 4. Alaska, passenger manifest (possibly in English's handwriting), 16 December 1962 – DOB: 26 May 1930. 5. Passenger

manifest from Hamilton, Bermuda, 27 October 1961: 5/26/30 (again, probably in English's handwriting).

19 *Who Was Who 1996–2000*, British Library, London.

20 Audit Bureau of Circulations figures (for January each year): *Daily Mail*: 1997=2,344,183, 1992=1,675,453. *Daily Mirror*: 1997=2,442,078, 1992=2,900,000. *Daily Express*: 1997=1,241,336, 1992=1,524,786.

21 Lynn Barber, 'A Lord unto himself', *Observer*, 29 June 1997.

22 Author interview with Richard Addis, 6 October 2014. And Christopher Silvester, 'Young Turks in command', *Guardian*, 27 November 1995.

23 Graham Turner, 'Bah to humbug and hypocrisy', *Daily Telegraph*, 5 August 1998, and Peter Preston, 'Elusive, enigmatic and almost extinct. Long live Lord R', *Observer*, 16 August 1998.

24 Preston, 'Elusive, enigmatic and almost extinct. Long live Lord R', *Observer*, 16 August 1998.

25 ibid.

26 Geoffrey Levy, 'A giant with a love of mischief', *Daily Mail*, 3 September 1988.

27 Author interview with the Dowager Lady Rothermere, 17 July 2014.

28 ibid.

29 ibid.

Chapter 15

1 Bill Hagerty, 'Paul Dacre: the zeal thing', *British Journalism Review*, Vol. 13, No. 3, 2002.

2 Author interview with 'Elsa', former *Daily Mail* writer, 24 March 2014.

3 Lynn Barber, 'A Lord unto himself', *Observer*, 29 June 1997.

4 Alison Boshoff, 'Young heir who was groomed to be press baron', *Daily Telegraph*, 3 September 1998.

5 I used the form commonly used these days by genealogists when constructing family trees to try to maintain a clearer connection between siblings of a previous era than when following the usual 'great-great' form.

6 'He preaches about single parents, so why does his own illegitimate son have to live with his mother on the other side of the world?', *Express*, 22 February 2001.

7 Geoffrey Levy, 'From Asian Babes to Crusader . . . the rise of the "People's Pornographer"', *Daily Mail*, 23 November 2000.

8 'Dacre speaks out on Murdoch and Desmond', *Press Gazette*, 25 October 2006.

9 Bill Hagerty, 'Paul Dacre: the zeal thing', *British Journalism Review*, Vol. 13, No. 3, 2002.

10 Viscount Rothermere, Jonathan Harmsworth, Leveson Inquiry, 10 May 2012.

11 ibid.

12 'Hilarity at Leveson Inquiry as Counsel refers to Richard Desmond as Paul Dacre', Leveson Inquiry on YouTube, 12 January 2012.

13 Richard Brooks, *The Great Tax Robbery: How Britain Became a Tax Haven for Fat Cats and Big Business*, Oneworld Publications, 2013.

14 Author interview with 'Terry', former senior Mailman, 6 October 2014.

15 'Kensington High Street Winter Sale', display ad, *Daily Mail*, 24 December 1966.

16 Author interview with 'Mo', former *Daily Mail* executive, 5 November 2013.

17 ibid.

18 Author interview with 'Sean', former senior *Daily Mail* executive, 24 November 2016.

19 Author interview with 'Mo', former *Daily Mail* executive, 5 November 2013.

20 Author interview with 'Robin', former *Daily Mail* showbiz writer, 9 December 2013.

21 Author interview with Bryan Cooney, former head of sport at the *Daily Mail*, 11 December 2013.

22 Author interview with 'George', former *Daily Mail* staffer, 28 October 2013.

23 Author interview with 'Sean', former senior *Daily Mail* executive, 24 November 2016

24 David Hughes, 'He's Back', *Daily Mail*, 8 June 2001.

25 Author interview with 'Cyn', former senior *Daily Mail* reporter, 30 November 2013.

26 'Apocalypse', *Daily Mail*, 12 September 2001.

27 'A date which will live in infamy', *Daily Mail*, 12 September 2001.

28 '"This is our battle too," pledges Blair', *Daily Mail*, 12 September 2001.

29 'Ten years of success at the Mail', *Daily Mail*, 29 October 2002.

30 Author interview with 'Sean', former senior *Daily Mail* executive, 24 November 2016.

31 Bill Hagerty, 'Paul Dacre: the zeal thing', *British Journalism Review*, Vol. 13, No. 3, 2002.

32 'Stumbling along the road to war', *Daily Mail*, 3 March 2003.

33 'Yes You Did Give Him A Bloody Nose', *Daily Mail*, 6 May 2005.

34 David Hughes, 'How Long Can He Go On?', *Daily Mail*, 7 May 2005.

35 Author interview with 'Mike', senior *Daily Mail* executive, 5 December 2014.

36 Author interview with Jane Kelly, 9 December 2013.

37 Author interview with David Eliades, 13 November 2014.

38 Author interview with 'Mo', 5 November 2013.

39 Author interview with 'Gavin', former senior *Daily Mail* executive, 7 October 2014.

40 Dacre, 'The Debt We Journalists Owe Sir David', *Daily Mail*, 11 June 1998.

41 Author interview with 'Robin', 9 December 2013.

42 Author interview with 'Penny', former reporter, 23 March 2015.

43 Author interview with 'Sean', former senior *Daily Mail* executive, 24 November 2016.

44 Author interview with 'Robin', 9 December 2013.

45 Author interview with 'Cyn', 30 November 2013.

46 Author interview with 'Ray', former *Daily Mail* writer, 8 December 2014.

47 Author interview with 'Sean', former senior *Daily Mail* executive, 24 November 2016

48 Author interview with 'Ray', 8 December 2014.

49 Author interview with 'Penny', 23 March 2015.

50 Author interview with 'Elsa', former *Daily Mail* writer, 24 March 2014.

51 ibid.

52 Author interview with 'Penny', 23 March 2015.

53 Vanessa Lloyd Platt, 'DIVORCE: Why we women are to blame . . .', *Daily Mail*, 9 February 2000.

54 Author interview with 'Elsa', 9 March 2016.

55 Author interview with 'Jo', former *Daily Mail* writer, 22 March 2015.

56 Alison Boshoff, 'Life with the Oasis stars: Cocaine binges, all-night parties, porn and infidelity', *Daily Mail*, 6 January 2000.

57 Richard Pendlebury and Alison Boshoff, 'The egos, drugs and drink that killed Patsy's marriage', *Daily Mail*, 26 May 2000.

58 Alison Boshoff, 'Maneater Patsy meets her match', *Daily Mail*, 28 September 2001.

59 Alison Boshoff, 'From Man-Eater to Matron . . .' *Daily Mail*, 17 December 2002.

60 Author interview with 'Jo', 22 March 2015.
61 Author interview with 'Elsa', 24 March 2014.
62 'What IS wrong with Posh?', *Daily Mail*, 2 December 1999.
63 Quentin Letts, 'The Man's View', *Daily Mail*, 2 December 1999.
64 Amanda Platell, 'Why We Women Hate Posh', *Daily Mail*, 8 April 2004.
65 Lynda Lee-Potter, 'No, I for one don't hate Posh', *Daily Mail*, 14 April 2004.
66 Lynn Barber, 'A Lord unto himself', *Observer*, 29 June 1997.
67 Boris Johnson, *Room 101*, BBC TV, 10 November 2003. https://youtu.be/x8WF0ey27Y0.
68 Author interview with Shirley Conran, 21 November 2014.
69 Lynda Lee-Potter, 'My Darling Caron', *Daily Mail*, 15 May 2004.

Chapter 16

1 Ferris, *The House of Northcliffe*.
2 ibid.
3 Author interview with 'Sean', former senior *Daily Mail* executive, 24 November 2016.
4 Media Diary, *Guardian*, 26 July 1999.
5 Dugald Baird, 'Mail Online's 10th birthday: from the sidelines to the sidebar', *Guardian*, 15 May 2014.
6 Author interview with Vyvyan Harmsworth, senior member of the Harmsworth clan (he is descended from Vyvyan Harmsworth, brother of Alfred and Harold Harmsworth, the founders of the *Daily Mail*) and former Head of Corporate Affairs at *Daily Mail* and General Trust, 2 December 2016.
7 Paul Dacre, Society of Editors speech in full, *Press Gazette*, 9 November 2008.
8 Evidence: Birth certificate, 26 August 1964, and several other checks by Murbach Research.
9 'The not so bacchanalian Bacus (1972–1992)', *nonesuch*, Winter 2008, centenary issue 1.
10 Author interview with Clive Limpkin, former *Daily Mail* photographer, 2 July 2015.
11 Author interview with 'Gary', *Daily Mirror* reporter, 15 July 2015.
12 Lauren Collins, 'The Wayward Press: Mail Supremacy – The newspaper that rules Britain', *New Yorker*, 2 April 2012.
13 Author interview with Susan Douglas, 26 March 2014.
14 Rob Brown, 'Horror! Mail man let loose', *Independent*, 16 June 1997; and Stuart Millar, 'At 33, with successful editorships of the Scottish Daily Mail, the Scotsman and now the Record under his belt, Martin Clarke has attracted more praise, criticism, loyalty and disgust than most', *Guardian*, 10 August 1998.
15 Author interview with Lesley Riddoch, 18 November 2016.
16 Stuart Millar, 'At 33, with successful editorships. . .', *Guardian*, 10 August 1998.
17 Jane Thynne, 'You've got to go and shout at the bastards or they won't respect you', *Independent on Sunday*, 3 September 2006.
18 Author interview with Susan Douglas, 26 March 2014.
19 Jane Thynne, 'You've got to go and shout at the bastards or they won't respect you', *Independent on Sunday*, 3 September 2006.
20 Background checks by Murbach Research.
21 Stuart Millar, 'At 33, with successful editorships . . .', *Guardian*, 10 August 1998.
22 Roy Greenslade, 'Off the Record', *Guardian*, 4 September 2000.
23 Jane Thynne, 'You've got to go and shout at the bastards or they won't

respect you', *Independent on Sunday*, 3 September 2006.

24 'Gorkana meets . . . MailOnline's Martin Clarke', Gorkana website, 20 March 2015.

25 'A New British Invasion? MailOnline's Staggering Growth', ad:tech conference, New York, 7–8 November 2012. http://library.fora.tv/2012/11/08/A_New_British_Invasion_MailOnlines_Staggering_Growth#GdomXSDVgC7MiZ8m.99

26 'In a video hangout with Mail Online's Martin Clarke, Mi9 CEO Mark Britt and Mumbrella editor Alex Hayes talking about the new joint venture between the companies, Clarke declared the Mail Online would have little trouble fitting in with Australian journalistic culture.' Streamed live on 27 November 2013. https://www.youtube.com/watch?v=zzuMVYDNCh8

27 ibid.

28 ad:tech conference, 7–8 November 2012.

29 Author interview with 'Marlon', former *MailOnline* journalist, 26 March 2014.

30 Roy Greenslade, 'Off the Record', *Guardian*, 4 September 2000.

31 Gina Lovett, 'Daily Mail looks to make it big in the US', *New Media Age*, 8 July 2010.

32 'DMGT chairman Lord Rothermere talks to Rufus Olins', Newsworks' Shift 2013 conference on 16 April 2013. Published 23 April 2013. https://www.youtube.com/watch?v=zp_3DrlxUPs.

33 Henry Mance, 'MailOnline and the next page for the "sidebar of shame"', *Financial Times*, 24 September 2014.

34 'Paul Dacre's (Society of Editors) speech in full', *MailOnline*, 10 November 2008.

35 Mumbrella video hangout, 27 November 2013.

36 'Mail Online overtakes NY Times as top online newspaper', BBC News, 26 January 2012. Spokesperson Eileen Murphy: 'In any case, a quick review of our site versus the Daily Mail should indicate quite clearly that they are not in our competitive set.'

37 Mark Sweney, 'The Guardian overtakes New York Times in comScore traffic figures', *Guardian*, 21 October 2014.

38 Mumbrella video hangout, 27 November 2013.

39 'Paul Dacre's (Society of Editors) speech in full', *MailOnline*, 10 November 2008.

40 MediaPost conference, 20 February 2013.

41 ad:tech conference, 7–8 November 2012.

42 Meagan Hatcher-Mays, 'I Read the Daily Mail Every Single Day Because I'm a Monster', *Jezebel*, 14 June 2013. http://jezebel.com/i-read-the-daily-mail-every-single-day-because-im-a-mo-513278977.

43 Lauren Collins, 'The Wayward Press: Mail Supremacy – The newspaper that rules Britain', *New Yorker*, 2 April 2012.

44 'DMGT chairman Lord Rothermere talks to Rufus Olins', Newsworks' Shift 2013 conference on 16 April 2013.

45 Kara Bloomgarden-Smoke, 'British Invasion: How "Journalism Crack" Conquered the Internet: Mail Online publisher Martin Clarke wants to get even bigger', *New York Observer*, 19 March 2014.

46 Henry Mance, 'MailOnline and the next page for the "sidebar of shame"', *Financial Times*, 24 September 2014.

47 'Exclusive: George Clooney rejects "Mail" apology', George Clooney, Special for *USA Today*, 11 July 2014.

48 'Exclusive: Clooney responds to "Daily Mail" report', George Clooney, Special for *USA Today*, 9 July 2014.

49 ibid.

50 Henry Mance, 'MailOnline and the

next page for the "sidebar of shame"',
Financial Times, 24 September 2014.

51 Lisa O'Carroll, 'The Thoughts of
Chairman Murdoch', *Guardian*,
26 April 2012.

52 Court documents filed to the New York
County Clerk 09/03/2015. NYSCEF
DOC. NO.2 Supreme Court of the
State of New York.

53 Eriq Gardner, 'Gawker Agrees to
Supplement Story About DailyMail.
com in Settlement With Mail Online',
The Hollywood Reporter, 30 November
2016. http://www.hollywoodreporter.
com/thr-esq/gawker-agrees-alter-
story-dailymailcom-settlement-mail-
online-951352.

54 Roy Greenslade, 'Mail Online rips
off freelance journalist . . . yet again',
Guardian, 28 April 2016. http://
www.theguardian.com/media/
greenslade/2016/apr/28/mail-online-
rips-off-freelance-journalist-yet-again.

55 Author interview with Michael Brennan,
15 January 2014.

56 James Robinson, 'MailOnline: what
is the secret of its success?', *Guardian*,
15 November 2010.

57 Stephen Lepitak, 'MailOnline publisher
Martin Clarke talks international
expansion, paywalls, Snapchat, Facebook
& programmatic advertising', *Drum*,
4 July 2016.

58 ad:tech conference, 7–8 November
2012.

59 Peter Walker, 'George Clooney row with
Daily Mail boils over as actor shuns
apology', *Guardian*, 11 July 2014.

60 Lukas I. Alpert, 'MailOnline Wins
Readers, Will Target Profit', *Wall Street
Journal*, 20 November 2014.

61 Author interview with Susan Douglas,
26 March 2014.

62 'Pregnant Kim Kardashian shows off her
ample curves in transparent black dress
as she arrives at MailOnline yacht party
during the Cannes Lions festival', by

Lucy Mapstone for *MailOnline*, 24 June
2015.

63 Lucy Mapstone LinkedIn profile.

64 'DailyMail.com unveils plans for new
daily US television series with number
one daytime talk show host Dr. Phil Mc-
Graw', by Carol Driver for *MailOnline*,
25 June 2015.

65 Jasper Jackson, 'Newspaper websites
break traffic records with Brexit
coverage', *Guardian*, 21 July 2016.

66 Dominic Ponsford, 'BBC says audience
for international services has grown to
348 million per week', *Press Gazette*,
29 April 2016. http://www.pressgazette.
co.uk/content/bbc-says-audience-
international-services-has-grown-348m-
week.

67 William Turvill, 'Website ABCs: Mail
Online attracts new record 14.8m unique
daily browsers and 238m over month',
Press Gazette, 18 February 2016.

68 Mance, 'MailOnline and the next page
for the "sidebar of shame"', *Financial
Times*, 24 September 2014.

69 Mumbrella video hangout,
27 November 2013. https://
www.youtube.com/
watch?v=zzuMVYDNCh8.

70 Lauren Collins, 'The Wayward Press:
Mail Supremacy – The newspaper that
rules Britain', *New Yorker*, 2 April
2012.

Chapter 17

1 Paul Dacre, *Desert Island Discs*, BBC
Radio 4, 25 January 2004.

2 Author interview with 'Marc', former
senior *Daily Mail* reporter and desk
editor, 26 October 2013.

3 Author interview with former *Daily
Mail* executive 'Mo', 5 November 2013.

4 Author interview with 'Ian', former
Daily Mail executive, 25 November
2013.

5 Author interview with 'Cyn',
30 November 2013.

6   'Snapshot of Britain on Blair's last day', *Daily Mail*, Comment, 27 June 2007.

7   'Bye, Tony. Missing you already', *Daily Mail*, 28 June 2007.

8   Bill Hagerty, 'Paul Dacre: the zeal thing', *British Journalism Review*, Vol. 13, No. 3, 2002.

9   Ginny Dougary, '"I was being tripped up by Gordon and his people. That wasn't fair" – Peter Mandelson's explosive memoirs are the most eagerly anticipated publishing event of the year', *The Times*, 10 July 2010.

10   Author interview with 'Penny', 23 March 2015.

11   Author interview with 'Jo', 22 March 2015.

12   Author interview with 'Penny', 23 March 2015.

13   Jan Moir, 'A strange, lonely and troubling death . . .', *Daily Mail*, 16 October 2009.

14   Jack Bremer, 'Mail columnist throws a shadow over Gately funeral', *The Week*, 19 October 2009.

15   Charlie Brooker, 'Why there was nothing "human" about Jan Moir's column on the death of Stephen Gately', *Guardian*, 16 October 2009.

16   Paul Dacre at the Leveson Inquiry, 6 February 2012.

17   Lunch with insider, 12 January 2015.

18   Author interview with 'Elsa', 24 March 2014.

19   Author interview with 'Jo', 22 March 2015.

20   ibid.

21   Author interview with 'Penny', 23 March 2015.

22   Author interview with 'Elsa', 24 March 2014.

23   Author interview with 'Jo', 22 March 2015.

24   Author interview with 'Mo', 5 November 2013.

25   Author interview with 'Sean', former senior *Daily Mail* executive,
24 November 2016.

26   Paul Dacre, *Desert Island Discs*, BBC Radio 4, 25 January 2004.

27   'Cyn' via email. Author interview with 'Cyn', former senior *Daily Mail* reporter, 4 December 2013.

28   Author interview with 'Penny', 23 March 2015.

Chapter 18

1   'National press ABCs: Daily Star and Times boost sales while Trinity Mirror's Sunday tabloids take a tumble', *Press Gazette*, 18 August 2016.

2   The average yearly rate of decline between January 2010 to January 2016 in ABC circulation figures was 4.69%. At this rate, the circulation would drop below the *Mail*'s first edition sales in August 2044.

3   'Paul Dacre's (Society of Editors) speech in full', *MailOnline*, 10 November 2008.

4   'DMGT chairman Lord Rothermere talks to Rufus Olins', Newsworks' Shift 2013 conference on 16 April 2013.

5   'British Invasion: How "Journalism Crack" Conquered the Internet: Mail Online publisher Martin Clarke wants to get even bigger', by Kara Bloomgarden-Smoke, *New York Observer*, 19 March 2014.

6   A Keynote Conversation with Mail Online's Martin Clarke, Interviewer: Steve Smith, Columnist. MediaPost, 20 February 2013. https://www.youtube.com/watch?v=VW6FPX8_gpk

7   'MailOnline, Journalist – Mandarin Speaker', Gorkana jobs, posted 11 April 2016.

8   Roy Greenslade, 'What is Mail Online doing in partnership with the People's Daily of China?', *Guardian*, 12 August 2016.

9   Arif Durrani, 'Media: Rothermere plots global domination for Mail Online',

Campaign, 17 May 2013.

10 Source: ABC circulation figures.

11 Mark Sweney, 'DMGT issues profit warning after double-digit fall in print ads', *Guardian*, 26 May 2016.

12 Author interview with Richard Addis, 6 October 2014.

13 Author interview with 'Sean', former senior *Daily Mail* executive, 24 November 2016.

14 Mark Sweney, 'Daily Mail's Paul Dacre sees pay fall by almost 40%', *Guardian*, 18 December 2015.

15 Kevin Rawlinson and Jasper Jackson, '*Daily Mail* editor received £88,000 in EU subsidies in 2014', *Guardian*, 30 March 2016.

16 Author interview with 'Sean', former senior *Daily Mail* executive, 24 November 2016.

17 House price estimate from the *Mail*-owned website Zoopla.

18 Simon Jenkins, 'The Garrick Club's vote to keep women out is sad rather than sexist', *Guardian*, 7 July 2015.

19 Author interview with 'Jo', 22 March 2015.

20 Author interview, 22 May 2015.

21 Author interview with 'Penny', 23 March 2015.

22 William Turvill, 'After 39 years of fighting "boffins, toffs and cads", Daily Mail style guide writer reveals all (including Dacre's sub-editor "fears")', *Press Gazette*, 16 April 2015.

23 Paul Dacre, Society of Editors speech in full, *Press Gazette*, 9 November 2008.

24 Geoffrey Levy, 'The man who hated Britain', *Daily Mail*, 27 September 2013.

25 'Alastair Campbell: "The Daily Mail is run by a bully and a coward"', BBC *Newsnight*, 1 October 2013.

26 'Jon Steafel Out At The Mail', Media Guido, 16 August 2016. http://order-order.com/2016/08/16/jon-steafel-mail/

27 Paul Dacre, 'Why is the left obsessed by the Daily Mail?', *Guardian*, 12 October 2013.

28 Jasper Jackson, 'More than 50,000 sign petition calling for Daily Mail editor to be sacked', *Guardian*, 22 June 2016.

29 Timur Moon, 'Stephen Fry Brands Daily Mail Editor Paul Dacre "a Frothing Autocrat" as Olympics Spat Escalates', *International Business Times*, 10 August 2013.

30 National Readership Survey trends data, December 2016 (http://www.nrs.co.uk/nrs-print/readership-and-circulation-trends/trend-charts/).

31 David Smith, 'A liberal and one-time anarchist who opposes the war in Iraq, the country's favourite astrologer has the tabloids falling over each other ready to pay him millions', *Observer*, 20 June 2004.

32 Author interview with 'Terry', 6 October 2014.

33 Penny Junor, *Home Truths: Life Around My Father*, HarperCollins, 2002.

34 Paul Dacre, *Desert Island Discs*, BBC Radio 4, 25 January 2004.

35 Author interview with 'Sean', former senior *Daily Mail* executive, 24 November 2016.

36 Paul Dacre, *Desert Island Discs*, BBC Radio 4, 25 January 2004.

37 Author interview with 'Sean', former senior *Daily Mail* executive, 24 November 2016.

38 Paul Dacre, *Desert Island Discs*, BBC Radio 4, 25 January 2004.

39 Author interview with Vyvyan Harmsworth, senior member of the Harmsworth clan (he is descended from Vyvyan Harmsworth, brother of Alfred and Harold Harmsworth, the founders of the *Daily Mail*) and former Head of Corporate Affairs at Daily Mail and General Trust, 2 December 2016.

INDEX